EUROPEAN UNION AND THE DECONSTRUCTION OF THE RHINELAND FRONTIER

MICHAEL LORIAUX

CAMBRIDGE
UNIVERSITY PRESS

CAMBRIDGE UNIVERSITY PRESS
Cambridge, New York, Melbourne, Madrid, Cape Town, Singapore, São Paulo, Delhi

Cambridge University Press
The Edinburgh Building, Cambridge CB2 8RU, UK

Published in the United States of America by Cambridge University Press, New York

www.cambridge.org
Information on this title: www.cambridge.org/9780521707077

First published 2008

Printed in the United Kingdom at the University Press, Cambridge

A catalogue record for this publication is available from the British Library

Library of Congress Cataloguing in Publication data

Loriaux, Michael Maurice.
European Union and the deconstruction of the Rhineland frontier / Michael Loriaux.
p.   cm.
Includes bibliographical references and index.
ISBN 978-0-521-88084-8 (hardback) – ISBN 978-0-521-70707-7 (pbk.)
1. European Union–Boundaries.   2. European Union countries – Economic integration.
3. European Union countries – Relations.   4. Social integration – European Union
countries.   5. Geopolitics – European Union countries.   6. European Economic
Community countries.   I. Title.
D1065.E85L67   2008
943'.4088–dc22
2008017481

ISBN 978-0-521-88084-8 hardback
ISBN 978-0-521-70707-7 paperback

EUROPEAN UNION AND THE DECONSTRUCTION OF THE RHINELAND FRONTIER

The Rhineland region includes the core regional economy of western Europe, encompassing Belgium, Luxemburg and parts of the Netherlands, France, Switzerland, and Germany. Throughout history there have been tensions between this region's roles as a frontier and as western Europe's economic core. Michael Loriaux argues that the European Union arose from efforts to deconstruct this frontier. He traces Rhineland geopolitics back to its first emergence, restoring frontier deconstruction to the forefront of discussion about the EU. He recounts how place names were manipulated to legitimate political power and shows how this manipulation generated the geopolitics that the EU now tries to undo. Loriaux also argues that the importance of this issue has significantly affected the nature of the EU's development and helps condition a festering legitimation crisis.

MICHAEL LORIAUX is Professor of Political Science at Northwestern University.

For P.E.

CONTENTS

PLATES

FIGURES

ACKNOWLEDGMENTS

I gratefully acknowledge the ideas, the reactions, and the time so generously given to me by students, colleagues, and friends, especially Karen Alter, Hendrik Spruyt, Bonnie Honig, Chris Swarat, Diego Rossello, Sara Watson, Zirwat Chowdhury, Marion Gutwein, Peter Hayes, Alex Jaunait, Marc Crépon, Ariane Chebel-d'Appollonia, Barbara Cassin, Friedrich Kratochwil, Beate Jahn, R. B. J. Walker, Samuel Weber, and Meredith Jung-en Woo. Brigitte Schroeder made the very kind and welcome gift of books on Rhineland history and politics from the library of her father, historian Friedrich Gudehus, carefully annotated in his hand. I have received useful, suggestive readings from several "generations" of students of our Paris Program in Critical Theory, and the usual thorough wringing out that takes place in "North–South" meetings with our colleagues from the University of Chicago. Charles Lipson, Alex Wendt, and John Mearsheimer, in particular, were generous with their time and comments. I am particularly grateful to Mary Barker, from whose questions and curiosity the idea of this project first emerged. I am also most grateful to Melinda Kleehamer, who gave generously of her time to read, react, and make suggestions. Jake the Dog urged key revisions and helped with the typing. I have dedicated this book to my wife Peggy: "Nothing is greater or better than this, than when a man and a woman keep house together sharing one heart and mind" (*Odyssey*, 6.182–4).

1

Myth and geopolitics of the Rhineland frontier

What is European Union about?[1] Referenda in France, the Netherlands, Ireland, and Denmark have spawned doubts about the EU's future. The union's champions had been wagering for decades that once Europeans experienced its benefits they would gratefully ratify the project at the polls. In the words of former EU trade commissioner Pascal Lamy, "the people weren't ready to agree to integration, so you had to get on without telling them too much about what was happening."[2] But as it turns out, the "people," not having heard too much about what was happening, are now demanding greater clarity about what they are being asked to ratify. The question "what is European Union about?" has become, for the first time in a half century, a topic of public debate. Although the EU's success is undisputed – peace in Europe is secure, the economy sound and in spots dynamic, and the EU a force to reckon with in international economic affairs – sympathy and support for the European Union have been eroded by uncertainty and frustration regarding its aims and purpose. Debate is often oppressively technical. The European federalist ideal no longer stirs the imagination with its vision of a more humane instance of political life. But the specter haunting the European Union is one not so much of failure as of loss of moral horizon. It is the specter of tedium, of ossification as the EU becomes merely the local manifestation – *cum* welfare – of global capitalism. "In more than thirty years of polling," a public opinion analyst remarked, "indifference [toward the EU] has never been as apparent as in the early years of this century."[3] For another observer, there are grave

---

[1] The European Union has known several "aliases." Unless the context requires a historically more appropriate denomination, I will use the terms "European Union" or "European project" throughout.

[2] Quoted in Cris Shore, *Building Europe: The Cultural Politics of European Integration* (London: Routledge, 2000), p. 18.

[3] Nicolas Weill, "En trente ans, l'euroscepticisme n'a cessé de croître sur tout le continent," *Le Monde*, April 8, 2005. Of those surveyed, 31% were "decidedly uninterested," 13% "critical," and 9% "opposed"; 47% were either sympathetic or strongly in favor.

questions regarding the EU's legitimacy, which are, "by far," the greatest obstacle to the union's success.[4]

In this book I try to recover the political and civilizational possibilities inherent in European Union by evoking its original purpose: the deconstruction of the Rhineland frontier. By deconstruction I mean something more than "dismantling" barriers to travel and commerce. I mean interrogating myths of self and other, and, through that interrogation, the discovery of new possibilities that are more powerfully mobilizing and legitimating. But that interrogation does not come readily. EU debate, from the beginning, has occurred within a linguistic framework of named spaces, named peoples, and the "naturalness" of the frontiers that separate them. This discursive frame has had the effect of hiding, or of distracting deliberation from, European Union's original purpose. Commonsense discourse, habits of speech and thought, cramp and confine reflection and leave undiscovered representations of European space that could prove more powerfully mobilizing. To recover the worlds of political possibility that European Union opens up, one must therefore free discourse from the constraints of habit. To do so, I propose to trace the principal representational elements of EU discourse to their first emergence, when what today is common sense was still radically innovative, even whimsical. Awareness that the terms we use so casually are rooted not in "nature," but in the poetic imagination, has the effect of freeing deliberation and debate from a vocabulary of obfuscation, and reveals in the narrative of Rhineland geopolitics – the geopolitics that engendered European Union – the contours of a Europe that is not simply about using markets to tame frontiers, but about deconstructing frontiers so as to bring to light a civilizational space that is, like daily life in today's Europe, intensely urban, cosmopolitan, multilingual, and less hierarchical than in the past.

Deconstructing the Rhineland frontier

A mere hundred kilometers from its source in the Alps the Rhine is drafted into the task of demarcating political space. It separates Switzerland from Austria and Germany. Past Basle, it divides Germany from France. Downstream from Karlsruhe it traces the edge of the historically contested left bank, "fanning out," delta-like, to include, as "frontier," the buffer states – Belgium, Netherlands, and Luxemburg – which emerged from the 1815 Treaty of Vienna. From 1870 to 1945, this Rhineland frontier was

---

[4] Shore, *Building Europe*, p. 19.

a geopolitical tinder box. The Franco-German War, in 1870, occasioned the collapse of the second French empire and the creation, in Versailles' Hall of Mirrors, of the second German empire. It engendered two of Paris' most politically charged monuments: the Mur des Fédérés in the Père Lachaise cemetery – place of execution of the Paris insurrectionists and pilgrim shrine of the French Left – and the Basilique du Sacré-Cœur, expiatory offering for France's political sins and, for many years, pilgrim shrine of France's anti-republican and Catholic Right. Unlike the monuments, the war's political progeny, the Second Reich and the Third Republic, were short-lived. The Second Reich met with destruction in 1919 at the hands of the French, and the Third Republic in 1940 at the hands of the Germans. The Great War (1914–18) killed 10 percent of the two countries' working population, left 10 percent disabled and unemployable and 30 percent handicapped. Peace was marred by economic and political decline, which fueled right- and left-wing extremism. Civil conflict hastened the outbreak of a second "world" war that caused the collapse of both the Third Republic and the Third Reich and the death of another 200,000 French and 3 million German combatants. European Union was formed in the wake of this war to pacify this unstable Rhineland frontier.

This frontier region has no name, so I refer to it simply as the "Greater Rhineland." The Greater Rhineland, topographically, is the area drained by the Rhine and its tributaries, the Neckar, Main, Ruhr, Moselle, and Meuse (see figure 1.1). It covers two countries (Belgium and Luxemburg)

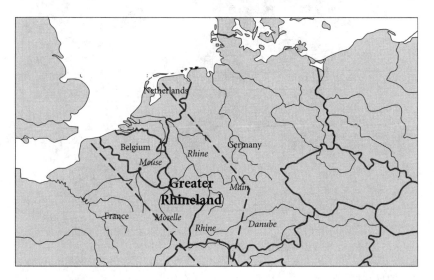

Figure 1.1 The Greater Rhineland

and important parts of four others (Netherlands, France, Germany, and Switzerland). Despite the fact that the Greater Rhineland is criss-crossed by international frontiers, it is the site of the European Union's core regional economy. EU literature portrays it as a "golden triangle," defined by vertices at London, Milan, and Frankfurt (see figure 1.2). Roger Brunet describes the Greater Rhineland as a "megalopolis," an area of high urban

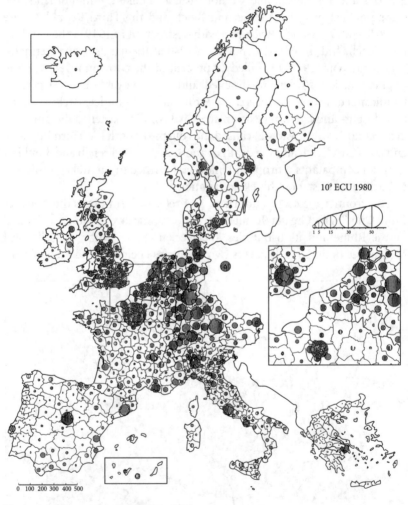

Figure 1.2 Industrial value added, 1980

Source: Priscilla de Roo and Jean-Paul Laborie, *Atlas de l'aménagement du territoire* (Paris: La Documentation Française, 1988), p. 191.

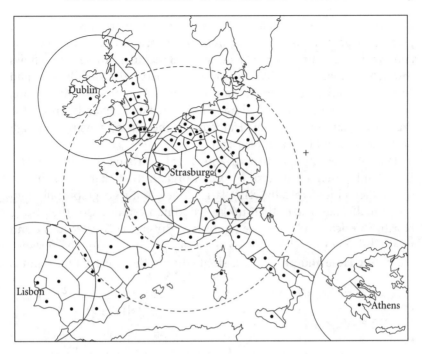

Figure 1.3 Population density, 1990

Source: John Cole and Francis Cole, *The Geography of the European Community* (London: Routledge, 1993), p.56. The distribution of population in the EC shown by 100 dots, each dot representing 1 percent of the population of the EC in 1990.

and population density that extends east from London, follows the Rhine south, then jumps the Alps into northern Italy, straddling what was historically and remains today the principal commercial axis between the Mediterranean and the North Sea. Jacques Lévy ascribed the region's economic importance to its placement at the heart of an urban network that includes many of Europe's greatest cities (see figure 1.3).[5] From ports at Rotterdam, Amsterdam, and Antwerp, the Rhine reaches out to the North Sea, the Baltic, and the Atlantic. In the south, through Alpine passes – the Simplon and St. Gothard – it draws Milan, Turin, and the Po Valley into its economic vortex. The Greater Rhineland, reaching out to southern England and northern Italy, boasts a world-class concentration of economic power: finance in Frankfurt, Zurich, and London; industry in Milan, Essen, and Stuttgart; ports in Rotterdam

---

[5] Roger Brunet, *Territoires de France et d'Europe* (Paris: Belin, 1997); Jacques Lévy, *Europe: une géographie* (Paris: Hachette, 1997).

(the world's busiest), London, and Duisburg (the world's busiest inland port). Navigable by ocean-going freighter from Rotterdam to Duisburg and by barge train from Duisburg to Basle, the Rhine itself flows through the megalopolis like an artery and a nerve, drawing Brussels and Antwerp, Stuttgart and Amsterdam into its web of activity. At its core, western Europe's aging coal-and-steel heartland extends from the Franco-Belgian province of Hainaut to the Ruhr, passing through Lorraine, Luxemburg, and Saarland.

Though densely populated and highly urbanized, the Greater Rhineland exhibits a pattern of urban organization that is peculiar to it. Smaller cities typically relay larger ones, both geographically and functionally, along axes that link metropolitan centers, as is the case in North America and Japan (see figure 1.4). But in the Greater Rhineland small and medium cities are eccentric to any such axis. The distance separating large and/or medium-sized cities in the Greater Rhineland is

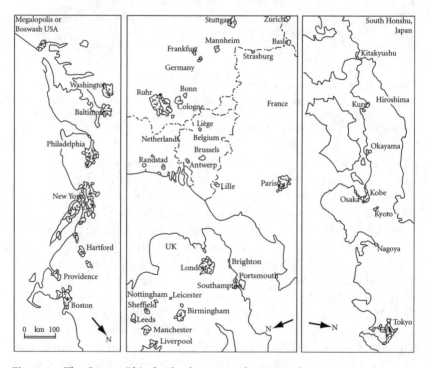

Figure 1.4 The Greater Rhineland urban network compared

Source: John Cole and Francis Cole, The Geography of the European Community (London: Routledge, 1993), p.60. A comparison of major urban centers in the USA, the EC, and Japan. All three maps are on the same scale.

small, and the functions they fill are similar and competitive rather than complementary and hierarchical.[6] This peculiar pattern of urbanization reflects the historical development and political specificity of an urban network that arose independently of, and indeed prior to, the emergence of London, Paris, and Berlin as metropolitan centers by virtue of their status as nation-state capitals. From Roman times to the present, the principal activities of the Rhineland cities have been those of a commercial and industrial core economy, which the rise of the nation-state only subsequently relegated to the "frontier."

Physical geography enabled this peculiar pattern of Greater Rhineland urbanization. The Rhine flows longitudinally across a continent deployed latitudinally. The Northern European Plain extends from St. Petersburg to Dunkirk at the foot of low (3,000–4,000 feet) hunchbacked mountains and plateaus: the Ardennes and the Eifel, the Hunsrück and the Taunus, the Vosges, the Black Forest and the Swabian Plateau. These highlands trap moisture drifting inland from the Atlantic and turn it into fluvial battering rams that force their passage to the sea. The Elbe, Moldau, Weser, and Oder, the Meuse and the Moselle, the Seine, the Loire, and the Danube all have their source in these highlands and flow into the Baltic, the North Sea, or the Black Sea. Where the rivers meet the sea rise northern Europe's port cities: Nantes, Le Havre, Bremen, Hamburg, and Danzig. To the south, however, the high Alps bar access to the Mediterranean and its ports. Rivers rising in the Alps, such as the Po, the Rhône, and the Inn, flow south to the Mediterranean or north to the Danube and the Black Sea. Access to the west and north by these Alpine rivers is obstructed by the middle band of low mountains and plateaus. The Rhine is unique in that it rises in the Alps but empties into the North Sea. In a geological past it followed a more compliant course through the valley of the Doubs to the Rhône and the Mediterranean, but at some point in its history it turned its currents north, breached the highlands, cut the picturesque Rhine gorge, and provided the North Sea coastlands with direct access to the Alpine passes. Its geographic peculiarity enriched both the Swiss cities – Berne, Zurich, and Lucerne – that guarded the passes, and the lowland ("netherland") cities – Bruges, Antwerp, Cologne – where Rhine River merchandise was transferred to sea-faring vessels (see figure 1.5).

---

[6] Coal and steel engendered a similar network in northern England. The Rhineland network goes back to the Roman conquest.

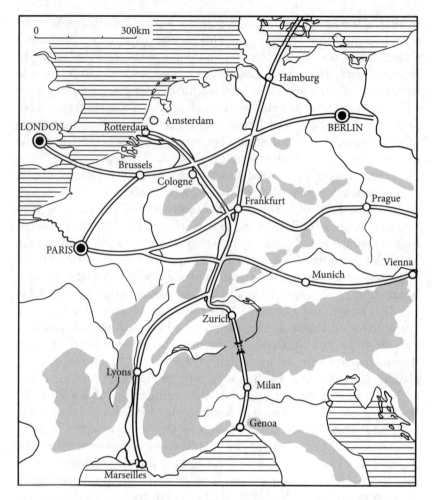

Figure 1.5 The Greater Rhineland crossroads
Source: Etienne Juillard, *L'Europe rhénane: géographie d'un grand espace* (Paris: A. Colin, 1968), p.15.

This is not to say the Rhine cannot serve as a "frontier." Like half a dozen rivers flowing into the North Sea and the Baltic, it is eminently capable of slowing armies advancing along the east–west contours of the northern plain. But the power to obstruct east–west circulation distinguishes the Rhine from its neighbors less than does its capacity to move traffic north and south, from sea to sea. Superb strategists, the Romans erected a system of fortifications to secure the crossroads of this north–south highway. Those fortifications have become today's cities: Cologne, where the Rhine meets the northern plain and land routes west to the ports of Flanders; Koblenz, where the Moselle joins the Rhine and gives access to the Burgundian plateau and its rivers flowing west and south; Mainz, opposite the plain formed by the Rhine's confluence with the Main, giving access to the Elbe, the Hessian plateau, and the Baltic; Strasburg, with its passage to the Swabian plateau and the headwaters of the Neckar and the Danube; Basle, where one leaves the Rhine for the Alpine passes via the Aar and the Neuss or, alternatively, the headwaters of the Saône via the Doubs.[7] Albert Demangeon and Lucien Febvre depict the Rhine as "a street along which, leisurely or hurriedly, worried or carefree, merchants and militaries, travelers and students pass by in an endless parade."[8]

Rhineland geopolitics has been marked by the anxious coexistence between the Rhine-as-frontier and the Rhine-as-conduit to the Mediterranean. Rome's Rhine frontier flourished commercially, but met with destruction in the third and fifth centuries as its economic dynamism attracted barbarian armies. In the eighth and ninth centuries, the Greater Rhineland flourished again, not as frontier but as the heartland of a new "Roman" empire restored by the victorious barbarians. When Carolingian commerce collapsed and deprived Baltic Sea populations of revenues, a new wave of invasions swept the Greater Rhineland. But its towns and cities rose again from their ruins, and, by the thirteenth century, rivaled those of Italy in prosperity and cultural achievement. In the sixteenth century, however, religious strife weakened the towns while the expansion of agrarian monarchies on the periphery of this urbanized, economic core revived "ancient" claims on the Rhine as a customary, even "natural," frontier. The Treaty of Vienna, in 1815, conscripted the Greater Rhineland into the emerging nation-state system by ratifying France's border on the Rhine and by establishing the Netherlands (which included present-day Belgium and Luxemburg) as a buffer between France and Prussia (which the peace settlement installed on the Rhine to oppose French expansionism). But the settlement did not prove durable. The industrial era had dawned, and with it the exploitation of coal and iron, riches that had hitherto played a secondary, though not insignificant role in the Rhineland's prosperity. By the end of the century, the mineral wealth and industrial development of the Ruhr

[7] Etienne Juillard, *L'Europe rhénane* (Paris: Armand Colin, 1968), pp. 13–18. Cf. Albert Demangeon and Lucien Febvre, *Le Rhin* (Paris: Armand Colin, 1935), pp. 33–5.
[8] Demangeon and Febvre, *Le Rhin*, p. 75.

and other Rhineland provinces had catapulted Germany, unified in 1871, ahead of Great Britain as Europe's premier industrial power. And in an age when wars were fought with steel and chemicals, Rhineland industry helped turn Germany into one of the most formidable military powers in the world.

Thus we arrive politically and economically at the power competition of two powerful nation-states, Germany and France, separated by a system of frontiers that shunted Rhineland resources into the production of national military might. To rid itself of this threat to its *national* security, the nation-state called France sought to move the frontier east, to "undo" German unification and create a client state in the Rhineland. The nation-state called Germany, by the same logic, sought to move the frontier west, to enclose the Rhine and its resources within the boundaries of a unified empire. Neither state prevailed. The only solution found to defuse the contest was to dismantle the frontier and place the nation in question. The Greater Rhineland states (with Italy) launched the "European" project to "deconstruct" this frontier.

The EU has pursued this project of frontier deconstruction not merely by sweeping away the barriers to movement that it erected – commonplace liberalization – but by sweeping away the barriers separating legal and policy spheres by unifying policy space. Contrary to much theory about the EU, policy unification targeted the most exemplary competences of the sovereign state: coal and steel as defense industries, money, and today (with some hesitation) military security. More than half a century has passed since French and German soldiers fought one another. Today, they train side by side in an integrated military division. People, goods, and money cross the Rhine as freely as they cross the Mississippi. France and Germany collaborate in high-technology research projects, many of which have military applications. French and German currencies have been replaced by a common European currency. The government of each is formally represented in all the various ministries of the other. And it is estimated that about 80 percent of French and German law is of EU origin, and thus commonly held.

Of course one might concede that the EU was once about deconstructing the Rhineland frontier, but object that the EU of twenty-seven member states is about something else, and something more. In response to this objection I document, in chapter 8, the enduring centrality of Rhineland geopolitics to EU construction up through the adoption of the common currency. But the argument I advance here is not primarily a causal one.

Rather, it is one of critical conceptualization. Without abandoning the historical claim that EU is about deconstructing the Rhineland frontier, the more important claim is that attention to European Union's original geopolitical purpose makes available to us a more legitimating and mobilizing representation of the European project.

Myth and anonymity

The EU's geopolitical purpose is obfuscated by a discursive framework that either hides it or distracts from it. EU debate is framed by myths of place and separation that either reject the Greater Rhineland to the margins – the periphery – of legitimate national space, or ignore it altogether by gesturing toward a teleological Europe. European Union, in commonsense discourse, is about pacifying or erasing the "unruly edge" of the nation-state. It is not, in commonsense discourse, about placing this unruly "edge" at the center of our representation of the European project. The deconstruction of the frontier therefore requires something both Commission and states have eluded, the deconstruction of the myths that engender and marginalize the Greater Rhineland as frontierland.

The term myth, as used here, means several things. To begin, myth is *mythos*, a narrative of origin as opposed to an account (*logos*) of historical fact. The myth of origin explains identity, place, and culture. The Rhineland as frontier is fashioned by a myth of origin that emerges and reemerges in history to legitimate "France" and "Germany" as political entities, and to justify or contest their claims to territory. A second understanding of the term corresponds to more common usage – to call something a myth is to challenge its truth. To call the Rhineland frontier a myth is to contest its representation of the differences between the peoples it is supposed to separate. It is arguably true, for example, that the Greater Rhineland is home to several nations as defined by culture and language. But, as shown in chapters 6 and 7, cultural memory and national language itself were, to a large extent, nineteenth-century constructs. The frontier – so says the myth – was erected by states to defend "national" cultures as conveyed by "national" languages. But historical examination exposes the frontier as an arbitrary container of populations that states forged into nations *after* the frontier was drawn.

"Myth" is used in a third way to designate something more than a contested or "mis"-representation. It is used to designate a "commonly accepted," or "commonsense," misrepresentation that informs and even structures deliberation about what to do and how to act. Just as myth nourishes ritual in religious life, it nourishes routine in secular life. Routine can become so ingrained in social relations that people lose the urge to question it. To understand the importance of this observation, it is helpful to recall philosophy's long-lived tradition of doubt regarding the referential power of language, that is, the common sense that "words" have meaning because they designate "things." Skeptics, from Sextus Empiricus to the present, have questioned whether the thing the word designates exists independently of the word. There is no way to know this with any assurance because we are "prisoners" of the language in which the question is asked. Though we use language to represent the world we cannot free ourselves from our dependence on language to set up an "independent, objective test" of language's "referential performance." It is as if we were locked in a room with a television as our only source of information about the world outside. Language, like the television, confronts us with all sorts of flickering images that we suspect represent the world, but there is no way to be sure without going out to look. Locked in the room, we can only speculate whether we are watching a documentary or a cartoon. In like manner, we are "locked in language" and can only speculate whether our linguistic construction of the world is truth or art.[9] In the words of the nineteenth-century philologist Wilhelm von Humboldt: "By the same process whereby [man] spins language out of his own being, he ensnares himself in it."[10] Ernesto Laclau and Chantal Mouffe explain:

[9]   See Barry Stroud, *The Significance of Philosophical Scepticism* (Oxford: Clarendon Press, 1984), ch. 6. See also Jacques Derrida, *Of Grammatology* (Baltimore: Johns Hopkins University Press, 1997) on the "presence" of the thing being designated. Skepticism has exercised modern philosophers of science since the publication of Thomas Kuhn, *The Structure of Scientific Revolutions* (2nd edn, Chicago: University of Chicago Press, 1970). The problem of reference can be credibly dealt with by adopting a pragmatic criterion of truth. See Richard Rorty, "Is Natural Science a Natural Kind," in Ernan McMullin, ed., *Construction and Constraint* (Notre Dame: University of Notre Dame Press, 1988) and Arthur Fine, "Science Made Up," in Peter Galison and David J. Stump, eds., *The Disunity of Science: Boundaries, Contexts, and Power* (Stanford: Stanford University Press, 1996). Social science, however, does not fare particularly well when measured by this criterion, given normative disagreement over the goals being pursued. See Mary Hesse, "Theory and Value in the Social Sciences," in Christopher Hookway and Philip Pettit, eds., *Action and Interpretation: Studies in the Philosophy of the Social Sciences* (Cambridge: Cambridge University Press, 1978). In this view, which I make my own, social science becomes a site of moral debate. My goal is not so much to "explain" – explanation is always contestable – but to "argue a case" for a certain vision of the possibilities European Union opens up.

[10]   Quoted in Ernst Cassirer, *Language and Myth* (New York: Dover, 1953), p. 9.

the fact that every object is constituted as an object of discourse has *nothing to do* with whether there is a world external to thought ... What is denied is not that ... objects exist externally to thought, but the rather different assertion that they could constitute themselves as objects outside of any discursive condition of emergence.[11]

Such skepticism suggests, or authorizes suspicion, that our construction of the world is mythical. For the neo-Kantian Ernst Cassirer, writing in the early twentieth century, myth is an ineradicable, indeed ineluctable, part of our conceptual apparatus, a kind of nonempirical, symbolic "form," *eidos*, that we use to impose mental order on the world. It is a pre-logical conceptual tool, an "*organ* of reality, since it is solely by its agency that anything real becomes an object for intellectual apprehension."[12] Skepticism warrants suspicion that our construction of the world is grounded not "in preoccupation with the objective view of things and their classification according to certain attributes, but in the primitive power of subjective feeling."[13] Social thought today commonly treats as mythical constructs the concepts of social life – states, classes, markets, nations – that we habitually treat as "external objects." Such concepts "explain" the world to us and inform our action in it. They generate and justify routines – secular rituals – that embed themselves in discursive and institutional habit. As they guide our action in the world, they mold, through the medium of our actions, the world they claim to describe. Their foundational logic and warrant, however, tax our powers of rational demonstration.

EU discourse, by this understanding, is "mythical." Myth engenders, grounds, legitimates, brings to light an "ontopology," or conceptual organization, or mental map, of European space. The term "ontopology," proposed by philosopher Jacques Derrida, ascribes ontology – being – to a thing's *topos*, its place, its "*situation*, to the stable and presentable determination of a locality, the *topos* of territory, native soil, city, body in general."[14] But when speaking of Europe, the myths that comprise our commonsense representations of European space, our European ontopology, coexist in tension, in dissonance. It is this dissonance that

---

[11] Ernesto Laclau and Chantal Mouffe, *Hegemony and Socialist Strategy: Towards a Radical Democratic Politics* (London: Verso, 1985), p. 108. Quoted in David Campbell, *National Deconstruction: Violence, Identity, and Justice in Bosnia* (Minneapolis: University of Minnesota Press, 1998), p. 25.

[12] Cassirer, *Language and Myth*, p. 8.   [13] Cassirer, *Language and Myth*, p. 35.

[14] Campbell, *National Deconstruction*, p. 80. See also Craig Calhoun, *Nationalism* (Buckingham: Open University Press, 1997).

makes it difficult to grasp what European Union "is about." The Rhineland frontier, as ontopology, is a site of division, encounter, and rivalry. It is the place where nations meet and face off, the tense edge of national space. The nations – France and Germany – that the frontier separates, that the edge delineates, are, as ontopology, places that enable the cultivation of a language, a culture, and a narrative that attaches language to place. In the modern era they have organized themselves as states – nation-states – to defend that territory as the nurturer of nationhood, as the condition of national existence. The nation-states touch along their edge, the infinitely tenuous line of separation, the international frontier, or border. Crossing the frontier means more than entering a land ordered by an alien legal and administrative authority; it means entering a land occupied by people of idiosyncratic language and culture. By contrast, "Europe" as ontopology is, as Anthony Pagden points out, a "highly unstable" concept. Its spatial frontiers and peripheries have forever been indeterminate.[15] The ontopology "Europe," as will be shown in subsequent chapters, emerges not from culture, language, or physical geography, but from the commitment to a transcendent purpose, a *telos*. In the ninth century, that purpose was Christian evangelization; in the twentieth it was the promotion of a kind of human flourishing, the definition of which was much influenced by Christian social thought. The shared purpose – the commitment to moral and political improvement – makes Europe "real," gives it ontopological standing. By this representation, Europe's teleological progress was disrupted by the retrograde experiment with nationhood. But that experiment's tragic end rekindled Europe's unity of purpose. Europe is becoming "real" again. According to this ontopology Europe is foundational; the nation-state is accidental. European cultural unity, defined as project, is real; national cultural unity is derivative and artificial.

These ontopologies, as mythical constructions of political space, frame, constrain, and confuse debate about European Union. Either they consign the Rhineland regional economy to the *margins*, or edge of nation-states depicted as "elemental atoms" (atom: privative *a-*, and *temnein*: cut, divide) of international organization, separated by "natural" frontiers, which is to say that there is something fundamentally "natural" about the frontier (whether or not the legal line of demarcation respects that naturalness),

---

[15] Anthony Pagden, "Europe: Conceptualizing a Continent," in Pagden, ed., *The Idea of Europe* (Cambridge and New York: Cambridge University Press and Woodrow Wilson Center, 2002), p. 45.

or, inversely, they deflect attention by dissolving the *site* of the frontier into a more abstract place, "Europe," and by directing our gaze toward a more distant future. The images of Europe that frame deliberation, in other words, either marginalize, or conceal, the place whose necessary political reorganization gave birth to European Union. By subjecting the myths, the commonsense representations, the ontopologies, to critical examination we authorize ourselves to reframe debate, to rearticulate it around a *re-presentation* of the Greater Rhineland as *place*, as site of a conceptually clearer and more compelling project.

The inaugural moments of EU discourse

Although we are "prisoners" of myth, we need not be prisoners of *just any* myth. We can contest myth by interrogating the referential power of the language that conveys it. We can, therefore, "free ourselves" from the discursive dissonance of EU discourse by interrogating the referential power of its mythical components. We can achieve that freedom by tracing the elements of EU discourse back to their point of emergence, to the point in time at which habit and common sense "disappear" in the whimsy of artistic creation, in the performative speech acts that beget ontopological language. We can, in other words, "free ourselves" from commonsense ontopology by going back in history to the time when speech, rather than "designate," in fact "invented." Speech acts, *coups de force*, acts of verbal violence "gave birth" to the ontopology that we use so casually today, though it erects a screen between us and a more mobilizing understanding of what the EU is about. Discursive *coups de force* closed horizons, opened others, and forced the discursive representation of space in radically new directions. For Derrida,

> It is probable ... that such a *coup de force* always marks the founding of a nation, state, or nation-state. In the event of such a founding or institution, the properly *performative* act must produce (proclaim) what ... it merely claims, declares, assures it is describing. The simulacrum or fiction then consists in bringing to daylight, in *giving birth to*, that which one claims to reflect so as to take note of it, as though it were a matter of recording what *will have been there*, the unity of a nation, the founding of a state, while one is in the act of producing that event.[16]

---

[16] Jacques Derrida, "The Laws of Reflection: Nelson Mandela, in Admiration," in Derrida and Mustapha Tlili, *For Nelson Mandela* (New York: Seaver Books, 1987), p. 18. Quoted in Campbell, *National Deconstruction*, p. 26.

The *coups de force* reveal themselves when we locate the horizon of our habitual representations of space in the imagination and poetic license of an author. That horizon is inscribed in texts infused with such fantasy that they mark the limit, the terminal point, beyond which it is no longer possible to reconstruct a rational history of the concepts they convey. Because they mark the limit of rational investigation, we must consider the texts, *faute de mieux*, as constitutive of our commonsense ontopologies.

The first text is Julius Caesar's *The Gallic Wars*. The conjunctive clause – "proximique sunt Germanis qui trans Rhenum incolunt" – despite its brevity, gave birth to three discursive, mythical offspring: Germania, Gallia, and the Rhine frontier that separates them.[17] The distinction between "Gaul" and "German" is questionable, for reasons detailed in chapter 2, and the claim that the Rhine separated them is simply false. And yet the clause was prelude to, and justification for, enormous investments in manpower, both military and industrial, to "bring to light" the human geography it claimed "merely" to describe. If this book begins with Rome – admittedly an eccentricity in a book about the EU – it is because the long historical view allows us to witness, assess, and contemplate critically this constitutive act. The text that preserves that act is a living text, the foundation on which geopolitical discourse was based in the nineteenth century and the source yet today of habits of thought about Rhineland political space.

The second text is a forgery. Penned by an unknown eighth-century monk, it is a false deed according to which the Roman emperor Constantine bequeathed the government of the west to the bishop of Rome. The document brought the Roman papacy into alliance with the Frankish kingdom of the Greater Rhineland to "restore" the Roman, Christian empire. This *renovatio imperii* occurred within, and brought into being, a mythical place called "Europe," which, coterminous with Latin Christendom, excluded not only the lands beyond the Mediterranean that, once Roman, were now Muslim, but also the territories ruled by Christian Byzantium, Rome's legitimate successor. The "Donation of Constantine," like *The Gallic Wars*, was prelude to expenditures of capital and creative energy on an extraordinary scale to make the ontopology "true." The trace

---

[17] "Who are close to the Germans who live across the Rhine." Caesar is referring to the Belgae, inhabitants of one of the three parts – *Gallia est omnis divisa in partis tris* – of Gaul. Caius Julius Caesar, *Commentariorum de Bello Gallico* (Oxford: Oxford University Press, 1900), p. 1.

of that investment is preserved today in the crypts, porches, and arches of scores of European churches and monasteries.

The third text dates from 1761. An aspiring Edinburgh poet, James Macpherson, published a "translation" of an epic poem about a Gaelic hero, Fingal, which, he claimed, had been composed by a third-century bard named Ossian. The text was controversial. Detractors dismissed it as counterfeit. Supporters proclaimed its authenticity. As debate raged, Ossian's cultural impact spread like fire through the literary salons of Europe. The epic was rapidly translated into Italian and German. Goethe, Herder, and Klopstock fell under the bard's spell. Turgot, who would become Louis XVI's "anti-establishment" finance minister, introduced Ossian to France. Napoleon revered the bard. The epic, for Ossian's supporters, was evidence of an ancient, northern culture that, however "barbarian," had achieved a high level of literary sophistication as well as moral and political wisdom. The epic posited the existence of a rich, territorially rooted, cultural legacy that the hegemonic "classicism" of the French court and its princeling lackeys had marginalized and all but suppressed. The text invited scholars to shun the court, flee to the countryside, and listen to the "people" to retrieve the legacy. Philosophers and philologists, above all Herder and the brothers Grimm, dedicated their life's work to a kind of excavation of the cultural roots of Europe's authentic, autochthonous peoples, or "nations." That effort made routine the conceptualization of Europe as a patchwork of indigenous cultures, deeply rooted in place and time, and kept alive by "peoples" who worked the land and who spoke the language of the land. Discursive habit invited belief that linguistically and culturally monotonous nations "owned" territories, despite the fact that Europeans, *locally*, were generally polyglot and, in the trading towns, arguably "multicultural."

The Rhineland made a signal contribution to this intellectual event when poets and scholars like Joseph Johann von Görres, Achim von Arnim, and Clemens Brentano, working in the shadow of Heidelberg castle, gutted by the armies of Louis XIV little more than a century earlier, collected and published "ancient" tales and songs of the Rhine. The Rhine became foundational in the construction of German nationhood. The romantic gorge, home to the Lorelei – one of modernity's "ancient legends" – became emblematic of post-Enlightenment, romantic Europe and the destination of choice for thousands upon thousands of foreign tourists seeking exoticism and "authenticity."

The fourth text is not a literary work, but a constitutional decree that, in 1790, gave birth to the modern French *département*. French revolutionaries sought not only to rationalize France's legal and administrative structures, but to empower the citizen by making democratic participation accessible. Provinces – duchies, counties, and *généralités* – were abolished, and the *départements* made to replace them. The proposal brought originally before the constituent assembly conceived the *département* as a geometrically perfect square in a nine-by-nine cellular grid that covered all of France. It was one of a series of proposals that sought to bring Enlightenment reason to everything from territorial administration to weights and measures (kilograms and kilometers) and the months of the year (*vendémaire, brumaire*, etc.). Because the lines of the proposed grid bisected not only villages but churches, cottages, and vegetable gardens, the proposal was amended to respect customary boundaries. But the interruption of tradition into this whimsical proposal did not stop the reform from revolutionizing the discursive representation of French political space. The *départements* were named for features of physical geography, generally rivers and mountains: *département de la Meuse, département de Maine et Loire*. Customary definitions of place inherited from the *ancien régime* were denied relevance and meaning. France became a geometrical figure, a "hexagon," whose constituent components were "natural" components, facts of physical geography, and its frontiers "natural" frontiers.

In the nineteenth century, philological romanticism and revolutionary rationalism, acting in anxious alliance, refashioned the routine representation of political space. Whole territories were assigned to "nations," defined as culturally and linguistically homogeneous, authentic peoples. The territories were ideally, "naturally" defined, like the people who inhabited or possessed them. The "discovery" of this natural order again mobilized energies on an unprecedented scale. Museums were built. Schools were established or modernized. Children were instructed in the language and the culture of the nation to which they were now taught they belonged. In 1850, about half of all Frenchmen did not speak fluent French. About a fifth of the population did not speak it at all. By 1900, following a vast and costly effort to establish a republican and national system of education, French fluency had become all but universal – as well as definitional of what it meant to be "French." In 1850, the geographic referent for most Frenchmen was the province, the *pays*, the village. By 1900 all Frenchmen had been taught not only to identify with the mathematical figure of the "hexagon" but to value – unmathematically – their racial descent from "nos ancêtres, les Gaulois" as taught in school textbooks. The discourse of space partitioned among historically rooted, culturally homogeneous nations, divided by the Rhine, congealed as an "ontopology," as an ontology of place. Ossian and the *département* lent new authority to the myth of the Rhineland as natural frontierland, interposed between supposedly "ancient" and historically antagonistic nations. But they also fed conflict regarding how the term "natural" should be interpreted: nature as geophysical, as understood by the French, or nature as linguistic/cultural, as understood by the Germans. Was the natural frontier the river itself, or the linguistic frontier between Germanic and Romance dialects? The two texts, by inaugurating the ontopology of national authenticity, gave new form and intensity to the borderland antagonism that European integration today seeks to pacify.

Derrida's term *coup de force* connotes a "forceful blow," a violent and radical discontinuity in the historical narrative. We might try to tame the *coup de force* through a back-projected, historical reconstruction that "makes sense" of it, as the "effect" of some cause, for example. But our ability to do so is constrained by the fact that the *coup de force* is grounded as much in its author's creative imagination as in the determinant logic of some historical plot. Consider, by analogy, the history of Christianity. One can identify historical conditions that help us understand the emergence and spread of Christianity in the first and second centuries. But one cannot derive the person of Jesus and the theological construction of Jesus as Christ from those conditions. They emerge, not from some historical determinism, but from the imagery of Scripture. Yet the construction of Jesus as Christ per se exerted an autonomous, even hegemonic influence over the course of European cultural and political history. Nothing, for example, in the background historical conditions demanded that Christianity posit the Incarnation and the resurrection of the body (as opposed, say, to some spiritual, "disembodied" construction of the afterlife). And yet that assertion, as myth, motivated and legitimated belief in bodily resurrection and the cult of holy relics, which Frankish warlords used in the seventh century to wrest legitimacy and power from Roman bishops. Nor should we treat the texts as "cause" of historical effects, despite the fact that subsequent history reflects their substance. The cult of holy relics did not "cause" warlords to legitimate rule by demonstrating their power to import them, thought it enabled and perhaps invited them to do so. Myth creates a universe of discourse that frames deliberation about ambitions, interests, and ways to achieve them.

The texts discussed above were not chosen arbitrarily. They mark the points at which our commonplace conceptualizations of European space emerge. They demarcate the place where the conceptualization, as we follow it back in time, vanishes. Nor are the texts antiquities. They are living texts. They inaugurate the discursive myths that enable and constrain EU debate in our day. They "bring to light" the Rhineland frontier. They give birth to an "Ossianic" representation of Europe as a patchwork of ancient nations, defined by language and culture. They give birth to a "Carolingian" representation of Europe as site of a project of moral improvement. As we debate European Union in the present, whether in theoretical discussion or political negotiation, we activate these spatial representations as routine. Yet they emerged unforeseen, undetermined, creatively, from the human – the poetical – imagination.

New worlds of possibility

As we interrogate the vocabulary on which we depend to debate European Union, we can begin to discern pathologies that lodge within it. We discern "abnormality," characterized by Richard Rorty as the coexistence within a common universe of discourse of rival, incompatible meanings, conventions, and beliefs. Within the same signifier "Europe" coexist a representation of a Carolingian space that "explains" and *legitimates* frontier deconstruction, and a representation of Ossianic space with its attachment to *terroir*, its sense of obligation to the past, of indelibility of identity as cultural and linguistic fact, that *delegitimates* frontier deconstruction. The same word "Europe" connotes a space that is home and nursery to nations, and that is site to a progressive project to transcend nationhood. "When arguing for or against European integration," writes Neil Brenner, Europeans "call upon specific and contrasting narratives about its meaning and expected consequences."[18]

EU discourse is complicated by a second infirmity, an "autoimmunity," characterized by the named body's tendency to "protect itself and to sustain itself (*s'entretenir*) by imperiling itself (*en se menaçant elle-même*)."[19] Carolingian discourse subverts the task of frontier deconstruction by siting the EU experiment in the named place "Europe,"

---

[18] Neil Brenner, "Rescaling State Space in Western Europe: Urban Governance and the Rise of Glocalizing Competition State Regimes," in Mabel Berezin and Martin Schain, eds., *Europe without Borders: Remapping Territory, Citizenship, and Identity in a Transnational Age* (Baltimore: Johns Hopkins University Press, 2003), p. 171.

[19] Jacques Derrida, *Voyous* (Paris: Galilée, 2003), pp. 60–1. See Derrida, *Foi et savoir* (Paris: Seuil, 2000), p. 79.

thereby extending an invitation to all of "Europe" to participate in the deconstruction of frontiers, even though that project loses meaning and urgency as one moves away from Europe's Greater Rhineland core. Whereas integration's most committed champions have generally come from the Greater Rhineland core, where integration was embraced as a way out of the region's ruinous geopolitics, its most vociferous critics have generally emerged from the "periphery," among governments and populations that joined the EU for fear of being denied access to the Greater Rhineland regional economy. The representation of Europe as the site of a radical political experiment subverts that same experiment by inviting participation by populations who are indifferent to it.

Awareness of EU discourse's origins in poetic fancy or fraud, and awareness of its abnormalities and autoimmunities, authorize the imagination to *re-present* European space in ways that better explain and legitimate the "deconstructive" project. The term *deconstruction*, like "myth," has several meanings. It denotes, first, in a commonsense way, the act of dismantling the administrative, monetary, fiscal, and physical barriers to movement and exchange erected by the frontier. European Union has, by this understanding, been about deconstructing those barriers. But the deconstruction of the frontier as economic and political institution has left intact the myth of the frontier as separator of peoples. The deconstructive project has stopped half-way. The task that remains is a cultural, discursive, even literary project the realization of which requires the "tools" of cultural, discursive, literary deconstruction, such as the apprehension of the *coups de force* that are responsible for the language in which the project is discussed. Deconstructing the *myth* of the Rhineland frontier destabilizes the common sense that is the discursive site of that frontier. It is the natural extension, the unacknowledged next step, of the frontier's institutional deconstruction. Because the EU "is about" deconstructing the frontier, it should be about deconstructing the *myth* of representation that imposes frontiers on a space that, from time immemorial, has favored economic transaction and cultural encounter, about deconstructing a myth that consigns Europe's economic core to the margins of commonsense political space, about deconstructing the discourse that obscures that core in namelessness, that condemns it to its status as "place between," a place partitioned by named places delimited by the river that runs through it.

By assuming critical distance from the histories of named places in order to engage the narrative of this "place between," one discerns in that narrative a representation of European space that dissociates language and culture from territory, articulated by a network of polyglot and multicultural cities and towns. The deconstruction of the Rhineland frontier and the attendant rediscovery of the Greater Rhineland's centrality opens the imagination to a different style of political organization, plurilingual, less hierarchical, legitimated by cultural inventiveness rather than by the obligation to preserve identity as legacy, characterized by the networks of influence and expertise around which it is articulated. A space something like this once extended from northern Italy to the Netherlands and beyond. It existed independently of the territorial monarchies that arose along the economically more primitive periphery, and prior to the reorganization of those monarchies as nation-states. The towns that articulated this Greater Rhineland space rivaled the monarchies in power. By deconstructing, not merely the frontier, but the *myth* of the frontier, one brings to light a kind of legacy, experienced not as obligation but as possibility. By conceptualizing the "deconstructive" enterprise as one of recovering that legacy, one can reconceptualize political space, not as a culturally and linguistically totalizing space, protected and administered by a monopoly power, but as a cosmopolitan, transactional space, characterized by its plurilingualism.

Though the chapters are ordered chronologically, the argument of the book, it must be emphasized, does not proceed chronologically, from "cause" to "effect." Rather, it works "backwards," from commonsense representation of space in the present to the point in the past at which that representation first emerged in imagination and whim. It seeks to relativize foundational representations in the present by revealing the caprice of their invention in the past. One can weave a story around the person of Julius Caesar in a way that helps make sense of his text. One can show or speculate about the "political necessity" of the text. Of greater interest to the argument developed here, however, is the poetic license that attaches to his claim that the Rhine separates Gauls from Germans. However fanciful, it is that performative clause that survives in speech and thought, not the empire it sought to legitimate. One can also "make sense" of the forgery of the Donation of Constantine. One can place it against the backdrop of Byzantium's decline and the rise of the Pippinid court, and show or speculate about the historical forces that presided over its redaction. But more important to the present book is the boldness, the daring, the falsehood of the claim that imperial rule in the west was handed to the Church of Rome. The place called "Europe" was born of that lie. A forgery "forged" our commonsense representation of European space. Again, the representation survived, whereas the empire it sought to justify dissolved. Indeed, it fell victim to the myth that gave birth to it by inviting emperors to rule from Rome while turning their back on their power base in the Greater Rhineland. Similarly, one can "make sense" of the epics of "Ossian" by placing them in the context of growing contempt for French political and cultural hegemony and for the absolutist pretensions of princelings who nested within that hegemony's protective ecology. There is a compelling historical logic to the democratic, national revolution that sets Europe aflame in the late eighteenth century. Ossian's text makes sense when placed in that logic. But, as we contemplate Europe's possibilities in the present, it is more important to marvel at the brazenness of the claim to "translate" a text while refusing to produce the text that is being translated. One cannot derive, as conclusion from premises, the obsession for "ancient" (authentic or invented) literatures, traditions, and languages in the nineteenth century from cultural and political frustration in the eighteenth. It was the meat of the text, not the frustration in and of itself, that spurred enthusiasm for folklore and museums and the myth of nationhood that they nourished. It is that myth that European Union seeks, *nolens volens*, to deconstruct, and it is that deconstructive project that demands clarification.

The argument works from present to past rather than from past to present, but the exposition of the material proceeds chronologically, from past to present, in order to facilitate our appreciation of the disruption that the *coups de force* provoke in the historical narrative, and to relativize our commonsense representations of Greater Rhineland space in the present by replacing European Union in the "longue durée" of efforts to organize regional space. The *coups de force* are discussed in chapters 2, 3, and 6. Chapters 4 and 5 present the apogee of the medieval Rhineland's urban civilization and the collapse of that civilization following the Reformation, which set the stage for the Ossianic *coup de force* and the new inscription of Rhineland frontiers. Chapter 7 looks at the realization in fact, through state coercion, of the poetic imagery of nationhood. Chapter 8 recounts the efforts to deconstruct that realization after World Wars I and II. In chapter 9 I speculate how a new *re-presentation* might be "brought to light" in discourse and in practice.

2

Trans Rhenum incolunt: the inauguration of the Rhineland frontier

Trier's Porta Nigra, its amphitheater, the austere basilica, the prodigious Imperial and Barbara Baths, "two of the largest sets of baths in the Empire outside Rome,"[1] attest not only to the prosperity of this Roman outpost on the banks of the Moselle, but to the preeminence of the Roman Rhineland (see plate 2.1). It may be eccentric to begin a book on European Union with a chapter on Rome. But if, as I maintain, European Union is about deconstructing a discursively constructed frontier that bisects the heart of Europe's most vital regional economy, then it is not unreasonable to begin by asking how that frontier got there in the first place. By revisiting Caesar's campaign we witness the first mention of the Rhine frontier in text, and discover the political interests that motivated its enunciation. We can conduct an initial test of the referential power of the signifier "frontier" by exploring the nature of social relations that obtained there. From this exercise come three observations. First, the Rhine did not separate Gauls from Germans either before or after Caesar's proclamation. Second, Rome's systematic exploitation of the region's geographical endowments turned the Greater Rhineland into one of the most dynamic regional economies of the western empire. Third, the Greater Rhineland regional economy absorbed peoples beyond the *limes* and thus conditioned the atypical "invasion" by the Franks, who, unlike other "Germanic" tribes that migrated deep into Italy, Gaul, Spain, and north Africa, did not advance much beyond their Rhine basin home. If the European Union is about deconstructing a mythical frontier, the history of Roman Gaul reveals both the construction of that myth and its tense coexistence with the Rhine's vocation to facilitate movement and encounter, not exclusion and separation.

---

[1] Edith Mary Wightman, *Gallia Belgica* (Berkeley and Los Angeles: University of California Press, 1985), p. 235.

Plate 2.1 Trier: the Porta Nigra

The Rhineland and Rome before Caesar

There is no evidence that the Rhine served as a frontier before Caesar turned it into one. For the historian J. J. Hatt, the Rhine was the "Celtic river *par excellence*," the site of an advanced civilization that interacted intensely with the Mediterranean world, primarily through the Rhine–Rhône corridor and the Greek port of Massalia (Marseilles), the merchant center for goods imported from as far away as Corinth, Athens, Sparta, Rhodes, Chios, and the cities of Etruria.[2] Trade, controlled after 450 BC from tribal centers on the Marne and Moselle, involved sending tin from Britain, other ores, resin, pitch, honey, wax, amber from the Baltic, salt, hides, and the woolen products and salted pork described by Strabo, south to Massalia to exchange for wine and ceramics.[3] The Celtic populations grew powerful and let loose on the Mediterranean world one of its first recorded waves of barbarian expansion. Gallic armies sacked Rome in

[2] Quoted in Etienne Juillard, *L'Europe rhénane* (Paris: Armand Colin, 1968), p. 19. See Barry Cunliffe, *Greeks, Romans and Barbarians: Spheres of Interaction* (London: B. T. Batsford, 1988), p. 22; see also C. Goudineau, "La Gaule transalpine," in Claude Nicolet, ed., *Rome et la conquête du monde méditerranéen*, vol. II, *Genèse d'un empire* (Paris: Presses Universitaires de France, 1978), pp. 683–5, 693.

[3] Cunliffe, *Greeks, Romans and Barbarians*, p. 28.

387 BC and ravaged Greece in 279 BC.[4] In the west they crossed the Pyrenees to take possession of "Galicia." In the east they occupied Anatolia to become St. Paul's "Galatians" (who, according to St. Jerome, a Trier native, were speaking a Celtic dialect recognizable to him in the fourth century AD). The myth of the Gallic terror – *Gallorum autem nomen quod semper Romanos terruit* – became a fixture of Roman political culture.[5]

Nothing indicated in 450 BC that Rome would one day become master of Gaul, or even of a city like Massalia. Massalia and other Greek and Phoenician cities excluded Rome from Mediterranean trade. But Rome responded to exclusion by developing the premier military machine of the Mediterranean basin. By the third century, "about 13 percent of citizens were under arms at any one time, and about half served for at least one period of seven years."[6] Its armies halted the southward migration of the Celts, conquered central Italy, challenged the Greek cities for supremacy in the central Mediterranean, and engaged in war with Carthage for control of the western Mediterranean. Rome's military success in these campaigns came at a price. It kept the Roman citizen-soldier away from his fields. Farms went bankrupt. Default on a massive scale concentrated property in the hands of the senatorial class. The dispossessed crowded Rome's streets. The slaves that the farmer-soldier captured in foreign campaigns replaced him in the fields. Rome's political economy became a slave economy. The agricultural estate became a capital investment.[7] By the first century BC, more than a million slaves were brought to market each year – 10,000 might be sold on the market of Delos in a single day. Of Italy's 6 million inhabitants, perhaps a third were slaves. Replacement of this number "required the generation of 140,000 slaves a year," of which it is reasonable to think that "well in excess of 100,000 new slaves had to be acquired ... from war, trade, or piracy."[8] Rome began resettling the

---

[4] Cunliffe, *Greeks, Romans and Barbarians*, p. 195.

[5] "But it is the name of the Gauls that always terrified the Romans." Just. *Epit.* 38.4.9. Quoted in Stephen L. Dyson, *The Creation of the Roman Frontier* (Princeton: Princeton University Press, 1985), p. 7.

[6] Michael Mann, *The Sources of Social Power* (Cambridge: Cambridge University Press, 1986), vol. I, p. 253, citing K. Hopkins, *Conquerors and Slaves: Sociological Studies in Roman History* (Cambridge: Cambridge University Press, 1978), pp. 30–3.

[7] Paul Petit, *La paix romaine* (Paris: Presses Universitaires de France, 1971), pp. 162–6; Claude Nicolet, ed., *Rome et la conquête du monde méditerranéen*, vol. I, *Les structures de l'Italie romaine* (Paris: Presses Universitaires de France, 1977), pp. 103–16.

[8] Cunliffe, *Greeks, Romans and Barbarians*, p. 77; on slavery, see Nicolet, ed., *Rome et la conquête du monde méditerranéen*, vol. I, pp. 207–27.

soldier-farmers whom the slaves displaced in colonies, first in Italy, then in the provinces.[9]

> Between 80 and 8 BC, it is estimated that about half the free adult males in Italy were resettled in Italian towns or on new farms in Italy or the provinces, and between 45 and 8 BC about one hundred colonies were established overseas. Thus, in a single generation a quarter of a million adult males from Italy – one fifth of the population – were shipped off abroad.[10]

The need for slaves and land for displaced Italians generated a kind of "welfare-state imperialism."[11] Rome's militarized political economy placed a premium on expansion to feed the empire's hunger for slave labor, to create commercial opportunities for Italy's capitalist agriculture and industry, to provide opportunities for colonization, and to allay social tensions. Those pressures conditioned the rise of a professional army, part infantry and part corps of engineers, which laid roads and spanned rivers with stone bridges that left barbarians awe-struck, in order to control their conquests. They also conditioned the rise to power of ambitious warlords, who sought in war and conquest the opportunity to win a reputation, a clientele, and a war chest. Julius Caesar, the inventor of the Rhineland frontier, was such a warlord..

Rome's encounter with Gaul

Despite customary reference to rivers and mountains as the ancient ramparts of the empire – *vetera imperii munimenta* – neither Rome nor the northern barbarians envisaged the frontier as a simple line that followed a mountain crest or a river bed.[12] Though one encounters reports of frontiers among the northern barbarians, more typical is the case of the Nervii and the Remi, for whom – however much influenced by Mediterranean civilization – the forest of Thiérache demarcated

---

[9] See André Piganiol, *La conquête romaine* (Paris: Presses Universitaires de France, 1974), Book III, ch. 7 and Book IV, ch. 1. See also Nicolet, ed., *Rome et la conquête du monde méditerranéen*, vol. I, pp. 129–42; Jean Rougé, *Les institutions romaines* (Paris: Armand Colin, 1969), ch. 4.

[10] Cunliffe, *Greeks, Romans and Barbarians*, p. 62; see also Dyson, *The Creation of the Roman Frontier*, pp. 165–9.

[11] Mann, *The Sources of Social Power*, p. 257; for critical discussion, see Claude Nicolet, "L''impérialisme' romain," in Nicolet, ed., *Rome et la conquête du monde méditerranéen*, vol. II, pp. 899–903.

[12] "The ancient defenses of our empire," Tacitus, *Histories* IV.26. Ironically, rivers, as defenses, posed a greater obstacle to heavily armed Romans than to light-armed barbarians. See *Histories* V.14.

territorial claims as attested by the still-extant place name Fins, from *fines*. In contrast, the Pyrenees bifurcated linguistic and cultural entities like the Basques, and Ubii inhabited both banks of the Rhine at present-day Cologne. Rome, like other Mediterranean states, used geophysical features – mountains and rivers – to demarcate legal claims to space. But the politics of the frontier was more complicated than scratching a line on the ground. "Walls and forts were only part of a larger diplomatic, military, political, social, and economic system that embraced both sides of the frontier and created a *gradual* transition from Roman to non-Roman society."[13] Rome's frontier politics involved peoples who were migratory, whose social stratification was weak, and whose aristocratic class could not be seduced into friendship by the lure of Rome's urbanized, commercial, slave-labor political economy. Rome therefore enrolled peoples who lived beyond the legal perimeter as part of their defense against invasion – the Veneti and the Massiliots, for example, who, under the influence of the Greeks and Etruscans, had developed an urban and commercial civilization that induced them to share Rome's mistrust of migratory barbarians.[14] Rome also established alliances with Gallic and Germanic chieftains who had the power to discourage the formation of raiding parties and migrating war bands among the peoples they ruled.[15] "Inside" the frontier, Romans dwelt among a vast non-Roman majority. Rome's imperial genius lay in its capacity to coopt foreign elites, to admit them to the highest circles of honor and power.[16] Rome granted citizenship to barbarian elites and sometimes barbarian cities (e.g., Paul of Tarsus) as a reward for loyalty. To others it gave a subsidiary Italian citizenship. Others, still, were tribute-paying allies. Patrician families often mediated relations with barbarian leaders, lending Rome's frontier politics a highly personalized character.[17] Ambitious barbarian warlords mounted military operations to amass wealth, military prestige, and a retinue to show Rome how indispensable

---

[13] Dyson, *The Creation of the Roman Frontier*, p. 3. Emphasis is mine.

[14] Dyson, *The Creation of the Roman Frontier*, p. 51.

[15] Dyson, *The Creation of the Roman Frontier*, p. 65.

[16] From the first century BC to the third century AD, provincial elites were recognized as *socii*, admitted to the *ius italicus* and finally to the *ius romanus*. Not until 212 did the *constitutio Antoniniana* extend Roman citizenship to all residents of the empire. Monique Clavel and Pierre Lévêque, *Villes et structures urbaines dans l'occident romain* (Paris: Armand Colin, 1971), pp. 200–4. See Tacitus, *Annals* XI.24: "What else proved fatal to Lacedaemon and Athens, in spite of their power in arms, but their policy of holding the conquered aloof as alien-born?"

[17] Dyson, *The Creation of the Roman Frontier*, p. 85.

they were to its welfare. The frontier, in other words, did not assert a clear opposition between Roman and non-Roman. It was a complex site of assimilation and piracy, a site of development of "new societies within the frontier zone."[18] Caesar would radically disrupt this pattern.

Rome remained true to this conceptualization of frontier politics following the Punic Wars when it became master of the entire western Mediterranean basin. The acquisition of Massalia, with its trade relations with the barbarians of the Rhône–Rhine corridor, brought Rome into contact with the Saluvii and the Averni of Gaul, powerful Gallic communities that had long been in political and commercial relations with the Mediterranean.[19] Rome addressed the challenge with the tools it had honed in its long coexistence with Gallic tribes in Italy. It established a military fortress, *castellum*, at Aquae Sextae (Aix-en-Provence), north of Massalia, and entered into formal relations of friendship with the Aedui, who lived to the north of the Averni and controlled the strategic passage through the Burgundian watershed linking the Saône to the Seine, Loire, Meuse, Moselle, and Rhine. It defeated the Averni and their allies the Allobroges in battle so as to control the Rhône up to its confluence with the Saône. It constructed the Via Domitia between Italy and Spain to speed troop movements, and established an important citizen colony at Narbo (Narbonne), from which it policed both the mouth of the Rhône and the route through Tolosa (Toulouse) to the tin mines of Cornwall.

The Hellenized coast adapted readily to Roman rule. Rome's contacts with the Gauls in the hinterland were mediated through *emporia* such as Tolosa, Vienne, or Chalon-sur-Saône. Numerous amphorae found at Chalon-sur-Saône (Cabillonum) reveal the existence of a major marketplace in the heart of Aeduan territory. Caesar attests to the presence of numerous Roman merchants there at the time of his campaigns. Morcover, in his first encounter with the "Germanic" Ubii, on the Rhine, he wrote of a "large and flourishing city," and described the people there as "more civilized" (*humaniores*) than other "Germanic" peoples because of their commercial activities.[20]

---

[18] Dyson, *The Creation of the Roman Frontier*, p. 4.

[19] Goudineau, "La Gaule transalpine," p. 687. See Dyson, *The Creation of the Roman Frontier*, pp. 146–54. For chronology of Rome's penetration of southern Gaul, see Goudineau, "La Gaule transalpine," pp. 689–91.

[20] *propterea quod Rhenum attingunt multumque ad eos mercatores ventitant. De Bello Gallico* IV.3.3. The Ubii, alone among the peoples of the right bank, rallied to Caesar's cause.

Rome's efforts to pacify and exploit the barbarian periphery, moreover, were provoking profound change in the political economy. In the first century, the Aedui adopted a constitution modeled on that of republican Rome.[21] The shift to more formalized political institutions and a commercial economy accompanied the development of large, defensive *oppida*, fortified settlements on elevated terrain: Bibracte among the Aedui, Cenabum (Orleans) among the Carnutes (which boasted a permanent settlement of Roman merchants by the middle of the first century), and Avaricum among the Bituriges. Gallic urbanization often applied Mediterranean models. Only the northern fringes remained impervious to Roman blandishments.[22]

> The documentary, numismatic and archaeological evidence, taken together, shows that the tribes of central Gaul underwent a profound change in the period c. 120–60 BC, during which time the old order – the classical Celtic system – was replaced with a new centralized system of government, involving changes in the minting of coins and the development of *oppida*. To a large extent these changes can be ascribed directly to the proximity of the rapidly developing Roman [Mediterranean] province of Transalpina. The tribes of central Gaul were now becoming a contact zone with the Roman world. Through them much of the trade was articulated, and those tribes who, like the Aedui, were prepared to accept the situation grew rich. Stability and centralization, institutionalized in a new system of government, enabled the benefits of the proximity of Rome to accrue.[23]

Coup de force

Caesar's *coup de force*, the performative speech act that "gave birth" to the Rhine frontier, occurred in this context, not as fulfillment but as disruption. The invention of the Rhine frontier did not reflect customary practices but intervened as justification for the boundless

---

[21] Cunliffe, *Greeks, Romans and Barbarians*, p. 94. J. Harmand places this evolution in a longer process of political development tied to economic and social development first apparent among the Mediterranean peoples and only gradually manifesting itself among the barbarians of northern Europe. J. Harmand, "La Gaule indépendante et la conquête," in Nicolet, ed., *Rome et la conquête du monde méditerranéen*, vol. II, p. 710.

[22] Cunliffe, *Greeks, Romans and Barbarians*, p. 105.

[23] Cunliffe, *Greeks, Romans and Barbarians*, p. 97; see also Dyson, *The Creation of the Roman Frontier*, p. 154.

aspirations of a Roman warlord. Born into the senatorial class, Gaius Julius Caesar, like many ambitious aristocrats, exploited class tensions at Rome to promote his political career. His adversaries in the Senate saw him as a dangerously competent radical and denied him the customary triumphant welcome following a successful military campaign in Spain. Only his association with Pompey, in whose hands the Senate had placed the fate of the Republic, won him election to the consulate, in 59 BC. As Consul, he secured for himself an irregular military command in Cisalpine Gaul and Illyrica in 58, and, with it, the opportunity to prove his mettle, amass treasure, and return victorious to Rome.

Caesar's opportunity arose when the Aedui and the Sequani, powerful tribes with close ties to the Mediterranean world, entered into competition for control of the Rhône–Saône commercial corridor (see figure 2.1). The Sequani sought help against the Aedui from the Gallo-Germanic war band of Ariovistus. The Helvetii, on the eastern slopes of the Jura, also joined the fray against the Aedui. Roman diplomacy pacified the Helvetii and made peace with Ariovistus, honoring the latter in 59 BC with the title *amicus populi romani*, and enrolling him, along with the Aedui and the Sequani, in the defense of

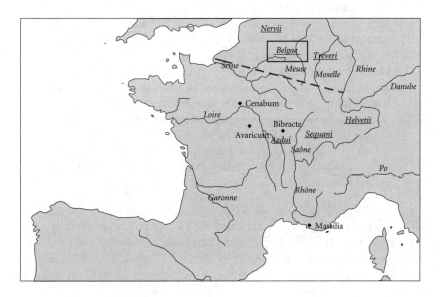

_ _ _ _ _ approximate limit of Belgae

Figure 2.1 Gaul before the Roman Conquest

the barbarian periphery.[24] Roman honors may have whetted Ariovistus' ambitions, causing him to advance claims that provoked the Helvetii to migrate west. This was Caesar's chance. He waged war on the Helvetii for disturbing the peace by migrating and then on Ariovistus for disturbing the Helvetii. The terror caused in Rome by the report of new Gallic migrations stirred sympathy and even enthusiasm for Caesar's campaign among the people, the *plebs*, but it caused only suspicion among the patricians. Caesar justified the intitiative by claiming to restore the natural order of things by confirming the Rhine as a natural barrier between "Gauls" like the Helvetii and "Germans" like Ariovistus. This was the *coup de force* that "gave birth" to the Rhineland frontier, which would be referenced in subsequent centuries to justify territorial claims in the Greater Rhineland.

> Gaul (*Gallia*) is a whole divided into three parts (*est omnis divisa in partes tres*), one of which is inhabited by the Belgae, another by the Aquitani, and a third by a people called in their own tongue Celtae (*Celtae*), in the Latin Galli (*Galli*). All these are different one from another in language, institutions, and laws. The Galli (Gauls) are separated from the Aquitani by the river Garonne, from the Belgae by the Marne and the Seine. Of all these peoples the Belgae are the most courageous, because they are farthest removed from the culture and civilization of [Roman *Provincia*], and least often visited by merchants introducing the commodities that make for effeminacy; and also because they are nearest to the Germans dwelling beyond the Rhine (*proximique Germanis, qui trans Rhenum incolunt*), with whom they are continually at war ... The separate part of the country which, as has been said, is occupied by the Gauls (*quam Gallos obtinere*) starts from the river Rhone, and is bounded by the river Garonne, the Ocean, and the territory of the Belgae; moreover, on the side of the Sequani and the Helvetii, it touches the river Rhine (*attingit ... Rhenum*); and its general trend is northward. The Belgae, beginning from the edge of the Gallic territory, reach to the lower part of the river Rhine, bearing towards the north and east.[25]

The text is confusing. By declaring, as a matter of fact, that the Rhine intervenes between Gallia and the Germans, Caesar conjured into existence two entities, Gallia and Germania, that one assumes were uniform within and distinct without. But the peoples of Gallia, only one of which is referred to as Galli, differ from one another by both language

[24] Dyson, *The Creation of the Roman Frontier*, pp. 169–70. On Caesar's campaigns, see Piganiol, *La conquête romaine*, pp. 501–6.
[25] Julius Caesar, *De Bello Gallico* I.1.

and custom, whereas the Belgae of Gallia resemble the Germani that live *trans Rhenum*. The definition of Gaul, its ontopology, is grounded solely in its geographic placement west of the Rhine. No unifying feature emerges from the text other than its location. No cultural or linguistic fact warrants the definition by location. Caesar might as easily have dropped all reference to Gaul and focused on the frontiers – the Seine, the Marne, and the Rhine – that separate the Galli from the warlike Belgae and Germani. The ontopology would be further complicated by the fact that "Gaul" thus defined, bounded by the Rhine, would eventually include, within the frontiers of Gaul, two administrative units called Germania Inferior, bounded on the north by the lower Rhine, and Germania *Superior*, bounded on the east by the upper Rhine.[26]

Caesar's *coup de force* is usefully compared with other contemporary constructions of Greater Rhineland geography. Germans were first distinguished from their Celtic neighbors in the *Histories* of the Greek-Syrian philosopher Posidonius of Apamea, who, writing in the mid-second century BC, may have provided Caesar with his initial grasp of transalpine geography.[27] But for Posidonius, the Germans were merely a branch of the Celts that lived on the right bank of the Rhine.[28] Again, the distinctive feature is physical geography, not human geography, not ethnicity, language, or culture. Dio Cassius, writing in the early third century AD, also characterized the Germans as a subgroup of the Gauls. And unlike Caesar, he applied the word *Keltoi* to the Germans and reserved the term *Galatoi* – Galatians – to the Gauls. The distinction in Greek endured into Byzantine times. The German-speaking peoples themselves did not use the word "German" nor did they display any awareness of belonging to a common "nation."[29] At the time Caesar

---

[26] Twentieth-century German nationalism would use the existence of a left-bank Germania to oppose French claims to the Rhine frontier. See, for example, Georg Künzel, "Deutschland und Frankreich im Spiegel der Jahrhunderte," in Rudolf Kautzsch, Walter Platzhoff, Fedor Schneider, Franz Schulz, and Georg Wolfram, *Frankreich und der Rhein: Beiträge zur Geschichte und geistigen Kultur des Rheinlandes* (Frankfurt: Englert und Schloffer, 1925), p. 76.

[27] Harald von Petrikovits, *Altertum*, pp. 58–9, vol. I of Franz Petri and Georg Droege, *Rheinische Geschichte* (Düsseldorf: Schwann, 1978). We have lost Posidonius' work and know it only by fragments. Though Rome's first direct encounter with Germanic tribes, Cimbri and Teutones, occurred in the period 113–101 BC, Julius Caesar is the first Latin writer known to have dealt with the Germans at any length. Dyson, *The Creation of the Roman Frontier*, pp. 75–6, 161–4.

[28] Wightman, *Gallia Belgica*, p. 13.

[29] Charles-Marie Ternes, *Römisches Deutschland: Aspekte seiner Geschichte und Kultur* (Stuttgart: Reclam, 1986), pp. 67–9; Petrikovits, *Altertum*, pp. 41–4.

wrote, the only people who referred to themselves as "German" were the Nervii and the Treveri, whom Caesar includes among the Belgae of Gaul.

This is not to say the category "German" was a fiction. Like *Gallus* it gestured toward perceived identity, or similarity, of geographic origin and, to a lesser extent, of language (recall Caesar's Gauls). Texts mention the invasion of the Germanic Bastarnae, who followed the Vistula from the Baltic to the Black Sea and threatened the cities of Greece in the third century BC. It is probable that "Germans" from beyond the Weser crossed the lower Rhine in the late second century BC. Historian Jacques Harmand attributes the construction of Gallic *oppida* not to the adoption of Mediterranean institutions of governance, but to the appearance of Germanic (or "Belgian?") war parties in the early years of the first century.[30] By the time of Caesar's campaigns, Germanic peoples, as defined by modernist scholarship, had occupied most of the land between the Weser and the Rhine. The Suebi, whence stemmed Ariovistus, descended from the Elbe to the banks of the upper Rhine. But it would be an anachronism to suppose that peoples identified as "Germanic" shared any "national" awareness or even common characteristics other than the geographical emergence from somewhere to the northeast. Even the claim to a common language or a common linguistic root is the work of eighteenth- and nineteenth-century philologists. The influence of Celtic culture on these peoples was so great "that any distinctive or 'original' Germanic culture must be seen as, at best, a back-projected myth."[31]

> The Germanic tribe, more than any other Germanic institution, has been the victim of an uncritical acceptance of Greco-Roman ideas concerning tribes inherited from both the Romans' own early traditions of tribal origins and from Greek ethnography. The tribe was a constantly changing grouping of people bound together by shared perceptions, traditions, and institutions. As these commonalities changed, tribes changed; they expanded to absorb other groups, they split apart to form new tribes, they disappeared into more powerful tribes.[32]

---

[30] Harmand, "La Gaule indépendante et la conquête," p. 709.
[31] Malcolm Todd, *The Northern Barbarians 100 BC–AD 300* (New York: Blackwell, 1987), p. 13.
[32] Patrick J. Geary, *Before France and Germany: The Creation and Transformation of the Merovingian World* (New York: Oxford University Press, 1988), p. 53.

Tacitus, writing at the end of the first century AD, found the Germans and the Belgae virtually indistinguishable.[33] Harmand disputes the Belgae's customary assignment to Celtic Gaul and suggests that they were the "extreme avant-garde of the world of the Germans."[34] Recent studies discover much intermixing among "Gauls" and "Germans" in Gallia Belgica and along the lower course of the Rhine, which explains why the Treveri and the Nervii may have claimed "German" ancestry.[35] Archeological remains – coins, *fibulae*, pottery, and burial practices – "show a cultural continuum across the Rhine" prior to Caesar's incursion.[36] Treveri politics was emblematic of this ethnic ambiguity. The Treveri cultivated relations with tribes of the right bank, were well disposed to Caesar, and were insensitive to Vercingetorix's call to Gallic resistance (though they would rebel against Rome a century later).[37] As for Ariovistus, he was related through marriage to the Celtic Norican leader Voccio, himself an *amicus populi romani*. Prior to Caesar's campaign, as noted above, the Senate had rewarded him with the title of *rex et amicus*, and dismissed the petition of Diviciacus, *vergobret* of the Aedui – also *amici populi romani* – for assistance against him. And though Caesar distinguishes the Belgians, the most warlike of the Gauls, from the Germans who lived "across the Rhine," with whom the Belgians were continuously at war, many of the warriors who followed Ariovistus, *Rex Germanorum*,[38] were Gauls or members of other non-Germanic groups. The name Ariovistus itself is Celtic.

Charles-Marie Ternes suspects that Caesar's decision to wage war on Ariovistus was motivated, not by the need to wage war on a "hostile nation" in today's understanding of that term, but by his desire to strike a *grand coup*, to reach "the mythological boundary (*mythische Schranke*) of the Rhine, to push forward to the end of the world, to drive human

---

[33] See Tacitus, *Histories* IV.70: the pathless wilds of Belgium; *avia Belgarum*. Tacitus' description of the Germans reads as though it was plagiarized from the second-century BC Greek historian Polybius' description of the Celts, found at II.17. It is true that in general "barbarians could, in Roman ethnography, be described with almost monotonous similarity." Geary, *Before France and Germany*, p. 41; and see pp. 39–43.

[34] Harmand, "La Gaule indépendante et la conquête," p. 702. Petrikovits, *Altertum*, p. 58.

[35] Todd, *The Northern Barbarians*, p. 10. See in this regard the analysis of Tacitus, *Germania* XXVIII. Though Harmand, "La Gaule indépendante et la conquête," pp. 703–4, places the Treviri among the remains of the Gallic peoples of La Tène III.

[36] Wightman, *Gallia Belgica*, p. 31.   [37] Ternes, *Römisches Deutschland*, pp. 102–7.

[38] Caesar, *De Bello Gallico* I.31.10.

capacities manifestly to their utmost limits and then, as it were, in full enjoyment of the god-like aura conferred by this extraordinary achievement (and with a full war-chest), to jump back into Italy's politics."[39] Caesar defeated Ariovistus, subdued the restless Belgae, and then took aim at the right bank of the lower Rhine and the southern coast of England. The forays across the Rhine and the Channel had little strategic significance – the invasion of Britain ended in near disaster – but they had a profound impact on the popular imagination in Rome. Caesar had carried the triumph of Roman arms beyond the limits of the known world. He not only tamed but humiliated the Gallic terror. "His exploits must have electrified his public in a way not unlike the American moon landing."[40] Only having tamed these wild fringes did he turn his attention to the tribes of the south, whose elites were generally well disposed to Rome, and where he could count on "the pro-Roman attitudes" of such tribes as the Aedui and the Remi.[41]

In pursuing his ambition, however, Caesar jettisoned Rome's customary frontier policy and aroused much opposition among the more conservative elements of the senatorial class.[42] Rather than support senatorial efforts to entice assimilated warlords to intervene between the empire and the "unformed" territories of the barbarian, Caesar advanced legal claims to territory in an exposed, forward position in direct contact with migratory barbarian raiding bands. "The Roman political world reacted to [Caesar's] enterprise only with incomprehension or fear ... There reigned at Rome a rather profound ignorance of the realities of independent Gaul, and Caesar would not have known more, before 58 BC, than his contemporaries."[43] By projecting the empire's territorial pretensions deep into the barbarian hinterland, Caesar expanded the empire to include peoples who had not yet demonstrated a desire for either cooptation or acculturation. Moreover, he demonized the one barbarian leader, Ariovistus, who might have stabilized the hinterland without the intervention of Rome's legions.

---

[39] Ternes, *Römisches Deutschland*, p. 46. But see Petrikovits, *Altertum*, p. 46: "Caesar bemühte sich ... um eine militärische vernünftige Grenze, als die er den Rhein ansah." Wightman, *Gallia Belgica*, p. 34.

[40] Cunliffe, *Greeks, Romans and Barbarians*, p. 111.

[41] Cunliffe, *Greeks, Romans and Barbarians*, p. 109.

[42] Cato proposed to give Caesar up to the Germans. See Nicolet, "L'impérialisme' romain," p. 889.

[43] Harmand, "La Gaule indépendante et la conquête," p. 719.

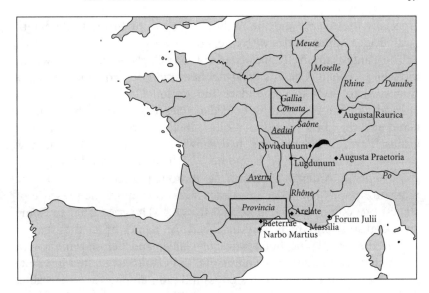

Figure 2.2 Roman colonization of Gaul before Augustus

The realization of the Rhine frontier

Following Caesar's assassination, Rome returned to its customary practice of prudently, patiently consolidating a territorial buffer between its citizens and *socii* and the unassimilable barbarians of the periphery (see figure 2.2). Most of Caesar's colonial foundations were in assimilated Roman Transalpina: Narbo, Arelate (Arles), Forum Julii (Fréjus), and Baeterrae (Béziers).[44] Only one colony was founded in conquered Gallia Comata: Noviodunum (Nyon) in the territory of the Helvetii – well situated with regard to the headwaters of the Rhine, the Rhône, and the Alpine passes leading to Italy. Following campaigns against Alpine tribes in 44–43 BC, Rome established two more colonies: Augusta Raurica on the Rhine (Augst, near Basle) and Lugdunum (Lyons) at the confluence of the Saône and the Rhône. In 25 BC, Rome established a military colony at Augusta Praetoria (Aosta) to control access to the Little St. Bernard Pass and the Rhône valley. Otherwise, Rome's pacification of Gaul was achieved, as in the past, by coopting the elites of the principal tribes of the Rhône–Saône–Rhine corridor,

[44] See Dyson, *The Creation of the Roman Frontier*, p. 159. Caesar granted Roman citizenship to the municipal elites of Provincia, furthering its assimilation to the point that the elder Pliny, in the first century AD, called it *Italia verius quam provincia*, "More truly Italy than a province." J. F. Drinkwater, *Roman Gaul* (Ithaca: Cornell University Press, 1983), p. 7.

especially the Averni and the Aedui, as well as by luring Gallic youth away from raiding parties with offers of a career in the Roman cavalry.

The contest among Rome's warlords for Caesar's mantle, however, induced Octavian, Caesar's great-nephew and adopted son, the future Augustus, to want to consolidate and exploit Gaul as a power base. "Already the huge amount of gold that Caesar brought with him from Gaul, and the good quality of Gallic auxiliary troops in the civil war against Pompei and his sons, had shown clearly how highly the new province should be valued by Rome."[45] During his second visit, in 27 BC, Augustus ordered a census, "a thorough piece of bureaucratic reorganization,"[46] in order to extract taxes to support the presence of 40,000–50,000 unproductive Roman troops.[47] The great Altar to Rome and Augustus, on which were inscribed the names of all the *civitates* within the geographic boundaries of Gallia, and before which were conducted ceremonies in the name of all of Gaul, was erected in 12 BC near Lugdunum (Lyons) to foster assimilation among the urban elite. A similar altar was erected in Cologne at an unknown date.[48] Northern Gaul, however, had not yet been subdued. To pacify the northern, "Belgian" periphery, Rome inaugurated a policy to which it would adhere off and on for the next four centuries. It resettled client peoples – "German" barbarians – from the right bank. In 39 or 38 BC, Tiberius, overlord of Gaul and future emperor, transferred the Germanic Sugambri west of the Rhine. Agrippa transferred the Ubii from their right bank home to their placement on the site of the future colony of Cologne. The Vangioni were also transferred west of the Rhine in the time of Augustus, as were quite possibly the Batavii. During this time, the Cananifatii may also have immigrated into imperial territory.[49]

Resettlement helped secure the Rhine frontier and bring Gaul "to light" as ontopology, peaceful and prosperous. But it problematized the Rhine's discursive representation as separator of Gaul and German. The Rhine's ontopological, mythical status was further ratified, not by the putative repulsion of invading barbarian hordes who were in fact actively being resettled on the left bank, but by the failure of Roman

---

[45] Petrikovits, *Altertum*, p. 53. *Oppida* were renamed to reflect the patronage of the imperial house: Augustodunum Aeduorum (Autun), Augusta Treverorum (Trier), Juliomagus Andecavorum (Angers).

[46] Cunliffe, *Greeks, Romans and Barbarians*, p. 127.

[47] See Clavel and Lévêque, *Villes et structures urbaines*, pp. 34–9.

[48] Drinkwater, *Roman Gaul*, pp. 24–5. See Petrikovits, *Altertum*, p. 54.

[49] Petrikovits, *Altertum*, p. 59.

armies to extend their rule to include the right bank – by their failure to colonize the "moon." That failure was caused not by "Germanic" resistance, but by geographic poverty. It is probable that the total population of Germania was less than 2 million. By the fourth century AD it still did not surpass 3 million. The population of Roman Gaul, by contrast, has been estimated at about 12 million.[50] Even by ancient standards, Germania was sparsely populated.[51] Evidence of efforts to clear forests is sparse prior to the first century AD. The subsistence economy of the barbarians was such "that large areas of arable land were not maintained."[52] Agricultural productivity was therefore not sufficient to support an army of occupation. When Rome tried to "pacify" the right bank in 12–7 BC and again in AD 4–5, the surplus required to supply Roman troops beyond the Rhine had to be levied in Gaul and transported. Moreover, the primitive state of agriculture beyond the Rhine meant fewer open fields through which to move and in which to maneuver Rome's sophisticated military machine.[53] Roman legions had to advance over terrain that their engineers had not yet tamed, in forests and marshes far from the well-paved highways of Italy and Gaul. In 9 AD the German leader Arminius defeated three Roman legions and eliminated virtually every Roman garrison on the right bank.[54] That achievement would be celebrated in bronze and verse in the nineteenth century. Though clad by German nationalist mythology in horned helmet and barbarian getup, Arminius, like many young warriors, Gallic or German, had served as an officer in the Roman cavalry. Rome subsequently concluded alliances with the Germanic Frisii and Batavii, stationed eight legions on the left bank in permanent encampments, and built fortresses on the right bank to secure a bridgehead in the lower valley of the Main.[55] Caesar's *coup de force* assumed some semblance of reality.

The Greater Rhineland political economy

Although circumstances, ambitions, and policies informed by the new ontopology turned the Rhine into a frontier, the fortification of the Rhine was not designed simply, perhaps even primarily, to keep

---

[50] Drinkwater, *Roman Gaul*, pp. 169–70.   [51] Todd, *The Northern Barbarians*, p. 5.
[52] Cunliffe, *Greeks, Romans and Barbarians*, p. 174.
[53] Harmand, "La Gaule indépendante et la conquête," pp. 703, 713.
[54] See Ternes, *Römisches Deutschland*, p. 62. On Arminius, see pp. 61–4.
[55] Drinkwater, *Roman Gaul*, p. 55.

barbarians "out." The threat of invasion from the "outside" was neither more nor less consequential than the threat of disorder and rebellion "inside." The choice of the Rhine as the site of permanent military encampments was based on two factors, proximity to the disorder in northern Gaul, whether from within or without, and the Rhine valley's natural geographical endowments, which facilitated the supply of a large military force. The occupation army of 44,000 consumed about 70 tons of wheat per day.[56] Since local production did not meet demand, the legions had to import supplies, primarily by the Moselle and the Rhine, and by roads that the Roman army constructed along or between the waterways. The conquest of Britain in 43 AD enhanced the strategic importance of the North Sea coast and spurred construction of more fortresses, highways, and ports along the lower Rhine and in Belgian Gaul. Rome also raised embankments to prevent flooding, and dug a canal between the Saône and the Moselle, which, by connecting the Rhine to the Rhône, made transportation by waterway possible from the North Sea to Lugdunum and the Mediterranean.[57] The middle Rhine valley attracted cultivators by its climate and soil. The Vosges, the Haardt, the Hunsrück, and the Taunus cast rain shadows over the Rhine and lower Moselle valleys, making summers warmer and less humid than in the surrounding areas, while the valley's proximity to the Atlantic made for mild winters. Accumulations of loess at the foot of the highlands, notably in Alsace, provided fertility.[58]

Agricultural endowments, ease of access to the Mediterranean, and military occupation fed economic growth. The military paid for its supplies in coin, the source of which was a monetary tax imposed on most of Gaul by the early first century AD. Tax levies in turn stimulated trade by forcing local populations to sell their surplus for coin. Michael Mann describes the arrangement as a sort of "military Keynesianism."[59] As a result, the Greater Rhineland by AD 50 was "well advanced on the road to becoming the power-house of Romanisation in the north-western provinces."[60] The emperor Claudius promoted the towns of

---

[56] Drinkwater, *Roman Gaul*, p. 129; Petit, *La paix romaine*, pp. 107–8, 113–18.

[57] Tacitus, *Annals* XIII.53, translated by John Jackson (Cambridge, MA: Harvard University Press, 1937), p. 93. Rivalries doomed this particular project, but Rome did not fail in subsequent efforts.

[58] Juillard, *L'Europe rhénane*, pp. 12–13.

[59] Mann, *The Sources of Social Power*, vol. I, p. 278. See Petit, *La paix romaine*, pp. 287–97; Geary, *Before France and Germany*, pp. 15–16.

[60] Drinkwater, *Roman Gaul*, p. 56.

both the Ubii and the Treveri to full colonial status.[61] Restlessness and resistance diminished. In AD 69, violence provoked by the fall of the Julian dynasty, the Rhineland's patron, was rapidly quelled. The new emperor, Trajan, rebuilt the garrison town at Vetera and admitted it to full colonial status with the name Colonia Ulpia Traiana. The transition to a Mediterranean-style urban structure was complete by the time of the Flavians (69–96).[62]

In AD 83 Roman armies consolidated the Rhine and Danube frontiers by conquering the Agri Decumates (approximately modern-day Baden-Württemberg), which they opened to Gallic settlers.[63] Rome secured the territory a century later by erecting a long palisade fronted by a deep trench that extended from the Rhine, north of Koblenz, to the Danube valley near Regensburg (see figure 2.3). Garrisons were placed at regular intervals along this palisade, behind which ran a military patrol road.[64] The word *limes* that referred to this patrol road was used, by the second century AD, to designate the imperial frontier in general.[65] The term captures beautifully the growing political, economic, and cultural ambiguities of the Greater Rhineland as "road" and "limit." Limit and highway, separator and vector of peoples, the Rhineland *limes* – and the river that defined it – spurred commercial, industrial, and urban growth. By the end of that century a systematic network of military roads had been laid on both banks of the Rhine and a canal cut between the Meuse and the Rhine that allowed ships to navigate between the two rivers without hazarding the North Sea.[66]

---

[61] See Tacitus, *Annals* XII.27; Clavel and Lévêque, *Villes et structures urbaines*, pp. 44–7. Prior to the *constitutio antoniniana*, urbanization occurred within a complex and highly hierarchical legal framework. See Petit, *La paix romaine*, pp. 280–7; Clavel and Lévêque, *Villes et structures urbaines*, pp. 170–6 and ch. 8; Petrikovits, *Altertum*, pp. 114–25. On Roman urbanism, see Clavel and Lévêque, *Villes et structures urbaines*, ch. 4. Note that only Cologne, under its new name of Colonia Claudia Ara Agrippinensium – so named in honor of Claudius' spouse-assassin, Agrippina, a native of the town – received a settlement of Roman veterans.

[62] Petrikovits, *Altertum*, pp. 77, 80.   [63] Drinkwater, *Roman Gaul*, p. 57.

[64] Ternes, *Römisches Deutschland*, pp. 127–9; Petrikovits, *Altertum*, pp. 97–112.

[65] The term eventually displaced the more traditional *finis*, as in "in finibus Ubiorum" (Tacitus, *Annals* I.31). *Finis* itself designates a frontier in terms both of a boundary and of a frontier in the American sense as a place where things start "thinning out." Tacitus also writes of the *imperium mari aut amnibus saeptum* (wall or fence: *Annals* I.9); and of *termini imperii* (*Annals* I.11).

[66] Ternes, *Römisches Deutschland*, pp. 30–1; Tacitus, *Annals* XI.20; Cunliffe, *Greeks, Romans and Barbarians*, pp. 131–2.

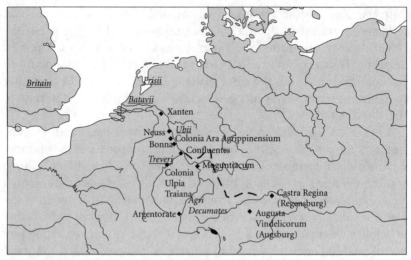

The discontinuous line designates the Rhine-Danube *limes*.

Figure 2.3 The Roman *limes*

The importance of the Greater Rhineland to the economic development of the entire Rhône–Saône corridor, and indeed the economy of Gaul, can scarcely be overstated. For Drinkwater, the military occupation of the Rhine frontier "created 'Gaul'."[67]

> The presence of the Rhine army acted, as it were, like a wind blowing across the top of a chimney-flue: the stronger it was the more draught it created to fan the fire of the Gallic economy. Indeed, to press the simile to its limit, the "flue" itself can be specifically located on the map, as the great north–south route of the Rhône–Saône corridor.[68]

By the third century, economic activity no longer depended on the military presence, which was reduced from eight to four legions, in comparison with the eleven needed to hold the line along the more volatile lower Danube frontier. The military occupation of the Danube did not have the economic impact that it had along the Rhine, where military demand had already caused the ceramic industry to migrate north to the Moselle, especially Trier.[69] Cologne was manufacturing glassware

---

[67] Drinkwater, *Roman Gaul*, p. 24.   [68] Drinkwater, *Roman Gaul*, p. 129.
[69] Cunliffe, *Greeks, Romans and Barbarians*, pp. 123–4; Drinkwater, *Roman Gaul*, p. 187; Petit, *La paix romaine*, pp. 338–9; Petrikovits, *Altertum*, pp. 61–3; Wightman, *Gallia Belgica*, pp. 145–7, 156–7.

and exporting it throughout the empire and indeed deep into barbarian territory.[70] Its port was second only to Lyons'. The Treveri, marginalized by the Julian dynasty, took advantage of the fall of that dynasty to exploit their favorable position between Cologne and the headwaters of the Saône to become Gaul's long-distance merchants *par excellence*. An ample Treveran diaspora assured the city's commercial dominance throughout the northwest and much of Gaul.[71] By the middle of the third century, Trier, Cologne, and Mainz were a showcase for the *pax romana*. The greatest densities of Roman monuments outside Mediterranean Provincia were in the Rhineland.[72] The proportions of Mainz's theater surpassed those of Orange, Arles, and even Lyons.[73]

> [We must envisage the Rhineland] as a highly developed region, the intense Romanisation of which was only later destroyed by its dangerously close proximity to Germanic invaders (but which still surfaces in modern times, for example in the odd occurrence of Mediterranean-style roof-tiles in an isolated area of Lorraine and eastern Champagne).[74]

The third-century Greater Rhineland political economy was strong enough to serve political ambition. In 259, following the capture of the emperor Valerian by Sassanids, Postumus, a military commander in Gaul, laid claim to the imperial throne. Because of barbarian pressures he was unable to make a Caesar-like run on the capital, so he named himself "Emperor of Gaul," established his capital in Cologne, repelled barbarian armies, restored peace, and ruled the Gauls "with their full consent."[75]

> The Gauls, heirs to a tradition of essentially Gallic activity and of Roman aloofness ... who even under a very strong and capable Roman emperor [Septimus Severus] had managed to replace Roman *miles* with Celtic leagues, responded well to the new Rhine-based Empire [of Postumus], and helped to make of it something more than just a disconnected limb

---

[70] Petrikovits, *Altertum*, p. 143. Belgium remained a major glass-producing area for the next twenty centuries.

[71] Ternes, *Römisches Deutschland*, pp. 87–91. On "Galliarum civitates non eodem honore habitae" see Tacitus, *Histories* I.8, 51. On the Treviri, see a revealing passage in the *Annals* at I.41. On the development of Belgica from Claudius forward, see Wightman, *Gallia Belgica*, pp. 80–8. See Ternes, *Römisches Deutschland*, Part III, ch. 2, "Bürger an Rhein und Main."

[72] Wightman, *Gallia Belgica*, p. 163.

[73] On the development of the cities of the Rhineland, see Ternes, *Römisches Deutschland*, Part IV, ch. 1, "Die Stadt."

[74] Drinkwater, *Roman Gaul*, p. 207.

[75] Petrikovits, *Altertum*, pp. 174–6; Wightman, *Gallia Belgica*, pp. 193–8; quote from p. 193; see also pp. 200–1, on usurpation of Carausius the Menapian.

of the Roman Empire ... The Gallic Empire was in fact founded on and supported by the essentially prosperous society and economy of High Roman Gaul ... [not just that] of the great aristocrats but also of the smaller farmers, the *nautae* and the *negotiatores*, and the urban traders and craftsmen. It was solidly based, and it worked.[76]

Roman armies eventually defeated Postumus. That defeat created a power vacuum on the Rhine that precipitated massive incursions by barbarians in the 270s. Northern and western Gaul suffered greater material damage from this wave of invasions than from those, better known, of the fifth century that ended Roman power in the west.[77] Civil war and invasion accompanied or perhaps caused a prolonged economic and demographic crisis in the west. The population of the city of Rome itself may have fallen from a million at the time of Augustus to less than half that by the middle of the fifth century. In southern Gaul over the next decades, Roman-style flatland towns were abandoned in favor of hilltop fortress-settlements.[78] In northern Gaul, cultivated fields reverted to forest. A resurgence of slavery suggests labor scarcity, and hence depopulation.[79] Industry throughout much of Gaul abandoned the city for the countryside where it atrophied to "a domestic or village level of production."[80] But economic activity in the Greater Rhineland recovered, even as the Gallic interior lapsed into

---

[76] Drinkwater, *Roman Gaul*, p. 225.

[77] Todd, *The Northern Barbarians*, p. 19. Though there are signs of decline in economic activity in the Rhineland in the late third century, they suggest military disruptions rather than endogenous stagnation. The artisan quarter at Xanten was in full activity at the time of its destruction by a Frankish raid. The Agri Decumates also abounds with evidence of lively activity prior to invasion by the Alamanni. See also Wightman, *Gallia Belgica*, p. 237.

[78] Richard Hodges and David Whitehouse, *Mohammed, Charlemagne, and the Origins of Europe: Archeology and the Pirenne Thesis* (Ithaca: Cornell University Press, 1983), p. 46.

[79] Wightman, *Gallia Belgica*, p. 243. Renée Doehaerd, *Le haut moyen âge occidental* (Paris: Presses Universitaires de France, 1971), p. 92.

[80] Hodges and Whitehouse, *Mohammed, Charlemagne, and the Origins of Europe*, p. 83. The impression of economic and demographic collapse prompts comparison with the Americas of the Conquista. *Ibid.*, p. 53. Scholars suspect plague, which we know decimated the minions of Atilla before his defeat on the Catalaunian Fields in 451. Norman Davies, *Europe: A History* (Oxford: Oxford University Press, 1996), p. 233. The vulnerability of pre-modern populations to plague was great. The Black Death carried off a third of the population of Europe in the fourteenth century. The displacement of Roman elites by barbarians may have also diminished the need to cultivate cash crops for taxes, depriving the cities of marketable goods, and/or market collapse may have forced the peasant population to abandon cash crops to assure subsistence. Hodges and Whitehouse, *Mohammed, Charlemagne, and the Origins of Europe*, p. 46.

prolonged economic crisis.[81] Merchants developed new markets to replace those destroyed by the invasions and depression. A triangular, North Atlantic trade pattern arose between the Rhine and Moselle rivers, Britain, and Aquitania. Exports from the Meuse and the lower Rhine increased.[82] The Rhineland and the Belgian hinterland, which had stimulated the Gallic economy in the first century with its import demand for military goods, became a net exporter of finished goods and raw materials to the rest of northwestern Europe.[83] The Belgian wool industry expanded when the Gallic hooded tunic, the *caracallus*, became fashionable throughout the empire.[84] Glassware, Cologne's specialty, replaced pottery on the tables of wealthy families throughout northern Gaul and Britain. Trier, despite the heavy damage inflicted by the invasions, evinced exceptional prosperity throughout the period of crisis.

Dissidence, invasion, collapse

The peoples beyond the *limes*, Alamanni and Franks, were generally excluded from the privileges of membership in the empire. And yet they participated intensely in the regional political economy, as clients, *amici*, pirates, mercenaries, invited settlers, vanquished, displaced settlers, and admiring imitators. As a consequence of their participation, the Alamanni and Franks did not "invade" the declining empire of the fifth century in the same sense as did other barbarian armies, but rather "took possession" of lands with which they had been in relation for generations. The Greater Rhineland is thus the site of a perplexing ambiguity. Economic integration coexisted with social and political separation. The term "dissidence," which suggests, etymologically, a "sitting together apart," a separation in settledness, may best convey

---

[81] See Petit, *La paix romaine*, Conclusion; Clavel and Lévêque, *Villes et structures urbaines*, ch. 3; Wightman, *Gallia Belgica*, pp. 191, 244–6. The causes of the crisis are complex and still debated. Growing pressure of population movements beyond the *limes* may explain the walls and the destructions; tax levies may have risen to meet the barbarian threat; imperial coin may have been debased to facilitate military payments, which probably disrupted and depressed long-distance and regional trade. An important cause of decline lay in the selective geographic pattern of economic growth. As industrial activity migrated to the barbarian marches, following the military, Gallia Belgica and the Germanies prospered at the expense of the Gallic interior. Even within Gallia Belgica, prosperity was limited to the eastern half of the province, which profited from greater proximity to the military markets of the two Germaniae.

[82] Wightman, *Gallia Belgica*, p. 276.   [83] Drinkwater, *Roman Gaul*, pp. 220, 224.

[84] The murderous emperor nicknamed Caracalla helped make it fashionable.

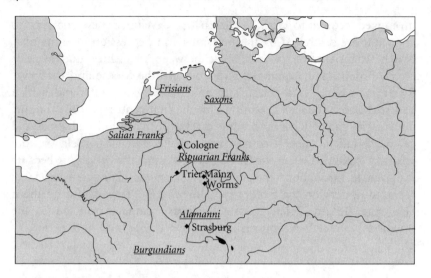

Figure 2.4 Frankish and Alamannic settlement of the Rhine "frontier"

this ambiguity by signifying the tension between people(s) interacting with one another across categories of "inside" and "outside," of belonging and exclusion.

Latin texts first refer to the Alamanni in 213. The German term, "all peoples," suggests some form of federation, which by the middle of the third century had wrested the Agri Decumates (Baden-Württemberg) from Roman control. But the term makes no reference to origin or tribe or language (see figure 2.4). Mention of the more northerly Franks, the *Francorum gentes*, by contrast, was rarer and later, despite (or perhaps because of) the fact that their economic and political connections with the empire were richer. The first textual reference dates from about 360.[85] The Franks were, again, a loose confederacy of tribes of the middle and lower Rhine.[86] Their appellation foregrounds their resistance to Roman rule and, again, makes no reference to place of

---

[85] Ternes, *Römisches Deutschland*, p. 134. See Petrikovits, *Altertum*, pp. 230–4.

[86] Chamavi, Chatti, Bructerii, Ampsivarii, and Salii. Other tribes, the Usipeti, Tubanti, and Chasuarii, also probably adhered to this federation, though – an indication of how loose it was – they retained their tribal appellations. "The 'West Germanic Revolution' was so thorough that, unlike the Goths, Burgundians, and other eastern barbarians who transmitted an ancient name and thus a sense of identity across successive social formations, most of the West Germanic tribes appear not to have even had a clearly defined myth or origin." Geary, *Before France and Germany*, p. 75; see also p. 78. Petrikovits, *Altertum*, pp. 234–5.

origin, tribal composition, or language. Unlike other tribal groups – Goths, Burgundians, Lombards – the Franks did not seek to preserve ancient traditions, nor congeal into stable kingdoms or *regna*. They were more focused on gaining recognition by, and perhaps entry to, the imposing and alluring empire across the river, with reference to which their name itself took on meaning.

Archeology does not support the view that the Germanic people as a whole were nomadic or semi-nomadic. Despite the piracy and the violence of roaming bands of young warriors, numerous remains of isolated farmsteads, hamlets, and some larger village-like agglomerations have been discovered which attest to the existence of stable communities, some occupying the same sites for decades or even centuries.[87] In some instances, the sophistication of planning evinced by Germanic villages is comparable to that of Roman Gaul. The first four centuries AD witnessed rapid technological and social change among the peoples of Germania, particularly those who lived within about 60 miles of the *limes*. One finds an abundance of Roman goods in this "frontier" zone.[88] The impact of Roman politics, commerce, and culture on Germanic society was clearly profound. Contact with the empire brought radical restructuring to Germanic society, just as it had to Gallic society centuries earlier. Traditional ties eroded; new groupings arose. Opportunist warlords and traditional leaders vied for the financial and political support of Rome: Roman titles to legitimize their position, and often Roman grain and iron to supply their armies.

Dissidence and the growing prosperity of the Germanic peoples became a threat to the empire when the interior of Gaul, and Rome itself, lapsed into durable economic and demographic crisis. Following the third-century invasions, the emperor Diocletian (284–305) implemented far-reaching reforms to restore Roman authority in the region. He separated the military from the civilian administration, split the empire into a western and an eastern half, and placed the government of each under a co-emperor, or *Augustus*.[89] He established the capital of the eastern empire at Byzantium and moved that of the western empire to Milan. He created the rank of *Caesar* to assist the *Augustus* regionally and to succeed him to the imperial throne. The Caesar of the

---

[87] Todd, *The Northern Barbarians*, pp. 99–100.

[88] The archeological remains of a Frankish settlement at Essen-Hinsel, for example, reveal that no less than one third of the remains of ceramic plate ware was of Roman origin. Petrikovits, *Altertum*, p. 230.

[89] See Rougé, *Les institutions romaines*, ch. 7.

west installed his capital at Trier, prompting much of the building activity mentioned at the beginning of this chapter.

Diocletian and his successors introduced a number of important military reforms designed to create a frontier defense in depth. That defense relied on soldier-peasants, *laeti*, drawn from barbarian populations and resettled in imperial territory.[90] The *laeti* were used to back up the core forces of infantry and cavalry, in which the number of barbarian mercenaries – always important in the cavalry – was great and growing greater.[91] To implement this policy, Maximian, Diocletian's co-emperor in the west, resettled large numbers of Franks on the left bank of the lower Rhine as well as in Belgian Gaul.[92] Thus the Alamanni and Franks, whom the Rhine frontier was designed to exclude from imperial space, assumed a central role in the military defense of the frontier. Rome also pursued its customary strategy of establishing patron–client relations with barbarian peoples living beyond the frontier, rewarding barbarian chieftains for their loyalty by recognizing their authority and providing them with subsidies and gifts. Meanwhile Roman merchants exploited the markets that emerged beyond the Rhine.[93] Some northern tribes grew dependent on Roman exports, especially food, in return for which they supplied the empire with amber and slaves (whose importance was again on the rise in the context of demographic crisis).

In addition to the servile *laeti*, Rome resettled many tribes as *foederati*, allies of Rome, on the left bank.[94] Franks and other barbarians enlisted voluntarily in the ranks of the Roman army. Marcus Aurelius, Diocletian, and Constantine created entire Frankish units: *cohors VII Francorum, ala I Francorum, ala VIII Francorum, laeti Franci, numerus Ampsivariorum, numerus Bructerorum, cohors XI Chamavorum*, etc. Some Frankish leaders climbed to the highest spheres of imperial

---

[90] See Wightman, *Gallia Belgica*, p. 253.

[91] These administrative and military reforms – a virtual militarization of the empire – obviously had profound social consequences, which need not be related here. See Petrikovits, *Altertum*, pp. 183–6. See also Wightman, *Gallia Belgica*, pp. 206–8. The term *laeti* itself (in this context) is not Latin, but appears to be of German origin. Petrikovits, *Altertum*, p. 181. The *laeti* turned occasionally on their Roman hosts. See Petrikovits, *Altertum*, p. 192.

[92] Todd, *The Northern Barbarians*, p. 20; Ternes, *Römisches Deutschland*, p. 141.

[93] Todd, *The Northern Barbarians*, p. 22.

[94] See Rougé, *Les institutions romaines*, p. 57. The term *foederatus* defined a kind of privileged bilateral relationship from the earliest days of the Republic. Its utilization in the context of the late empire is intriguing, since the *foederati* were resettled within the boundaries of the empire. But residence within those boundaries had conferred citizenship since the third century AD.

politics.[95] Valentinian I, in recognition of his growing reliance on Frankish warriors, adopted the title *francicus maximus*.[96] "Together, barbarian warlords and Roman emperors cooperated in the creation of the new barbarian world."[97]

Closer integration between Roman and northern barbarian, Wightman observes, was causing "the whole balance of the Empire, to judge by its most important officials, [to shift] further north."[98] Close contact between German and Roman militaries brought improvements to German military technology and strategy. New tools and weapons appeared, often copied on Roman models.[99] The bronze-tipped spear, which Tacitus described in the late first century as the German's weapon of choice, gave way to the iron axe and sword, first looted from Roman soldiers then copied by German smiths.[100] Iron working became "the most important and sophisticated craft of the Germanic peoples" by the close of the first century AD. The blades produced by German smiths were "far superior to the equipment of the Roman troops."[101] Roman mail garments and metal helmets begin to crop up in archeological sites in later centuries. By the fourth century the armament of the western Germans, especially the Franks and Alamanni, was difficult to distinguish from that of the frontier armies of Rome. "Indeed, such a distinction may not realistically be attempted since the Roman forces were themselves largely composed of barbarian troops."[102]

By the late second century AD, Germania's population may have begun to outstretch available resources. Demographic stress in turn may have stimulated technological innovation and political consolidation, as well as raiding and piracy. By the late third century, the availability of rich, uncultivated land in Gaul proved irresistible.[103] But the reforms of Diocletian and Constantine the Great succeeded in restoring territorial integrity to the empire for another two generations.

---

[95] Silvanus, for example, was appointed commander of the infantry, though was later put to death for intrigues with German tribes. Ternes, *Römisches Deutschland*, p. 136; Petrikovits, *Altertum*, pp. 189, 221.

[96] Petrikovits, *Altertum*, p. 205. See also, more generally, Petrikovits, *Altertum*, p. 274.

[97] Geary, *Before France and Germany*, p. 62.

[98] Wightman, *Gallia Belgica*, p. 215. See Geary, *Before France and Germany*, pp. 20–6.

[99] Todd, *The Northern Barbarians*, p. 139.   [100] See Tacitus, *Germania* VI.

[101] Both citations from Geary, *Before France and Germany*, p. 49.

[102] Todd, *The Northern Barbarians*, p. 161.

[103] On warlords, see Tacitus, *Germania* XIV. Cf. place of warlords in pre-Roman Gaul, discussed *supra*. On the Germanic peoples' attraction to the empire see Petrikovits, *Altertum*, p. 237.

In 313, Constantine waged war on the Franks and the Saxons who joined them in piracy along the North Sea coast, and was sufficiently victorious to award himself a triumph over the enemies of *ultima barbaria*.[104] But following Constantine's death in 337, internal rivalries between his sons, successors, and other claimants to the throne weakened the empire.[105] In 351, Franks and Alamanni began to cross the Rhine on a broad front. The emperor Julian defeated the Alamanni in 357, only to find himself ruler of a land that was now durably cultivated by barbarians.[106] He signed a treaty with the Frankish Chamavi in 358 that allowed transportation of Roman foodstuffs on the lower Rhine. He signed a treaty of peace with the Alamanni that, among other things, provided Rome with the wood and tools it needed to reconstruct the *limes* on the right bank, the ostensible purpose of which was to keep the Alamanni out![107] Valentinian, following victories in 364 and 368 that avenged the fall of Mainz, restored the Agri Decumates to Roman rule for a brief time and set out once again to rebuild and fortify the *limes*. But as Rome negotiated, it simultaneously pursued a policy of intimidation by punishing Germanic incursions into Roman territory with retaliatory strikes. Retaliation precluded accommodation. Persistent unrest in the late fourth century discouraged economic activity, destroyed infrastructure, and frightened Romanized inhabitants into migrating south.[108] Frankish arrivals replaced those who fled, often assuring the survival of Roman industries, especially in wine, glass, and ceramics.[109] Production of ceramic tableware decorated with Christian motifs continued, for example at Châtel-Chéréhy, into the Frankish period, with only gradual change in style and firing techniques. The production and sale of Cologne glassware was essentially unaffected by the upheavals.[110]

The incursion of Goths into Thrace sent the legions scurrying eastward, opening the door to an Alamannic counter-offensive. Internal rivalries

---

[104] Ternes, *Römisches Deutschland*, p. 135.

[105] Barbarian incursions had already developed a pattern of responding to internal imperial turmoil. See, e.g., Petrikovits, *Altertum*, p. 181, on the disturbances accompanying Constantine's rise to power.

[106] Petrikovits, *Altertum*, pp. 196, 239.   [107] Petrikovits, *Altertum*, pp. 198–9.

[108] Petrikovits, *Altertum*, pp. 201–2, 240–5. On Roman arrogance, see account of Alamannic diplomatic mission to Valentinian in Petrikovits, *Altertum*, p. 203.

[109] Todd, *The Northern Barbarians*, p. 9. But compare with Petrikovits, *Altertum*, pp. 249–50. Petrikovits underscores the industrial decline of the Rhineland cities, but notes the resistance of artisanal industries in the hinterland, along the Meuse and the Sambre, and in the Argonne (where economic development in the high middle ages would accelerate). See Petrikovits, *Altertum*, p. 290. See Wightman, *Gallia Belgica*, pp. 239–42.

[110] Wightman, *Gallia Belgica*, p. 276.

following Gratian's assassination (in 383) encouraged the Franks to invade along the lower Rhine. The Frankish commander of the Roman army, Arbogast, negotiated peace with the Frankish princes before falling victim himself to imperial court intrigue.[111] After the death of Theodosius in 395, the defenses of the western empire were breached on a wide front. Visigoths invaded Greece in 397, sacked Rome in 410, then settled in Provincia, nominally as *foederati*. Rome abandoned the imperial court of Trier and the fortresses of the *limes* sometime before 400. Alans, Suebi, and Vandals crossed the Rhine in 406–7. Cologne was *hostibus plena* – full of foreigners/enemies – according to a document of the mid-fifth century.[112] In 455, Rome surrendered control of the upper Rhine to the Alamanni. Burgundians invested Sapaudia – Savoy – then occupied the historic capital of Gaul, Lugdunum (Lyons), in 461. The barbarians laid siege to cities, destroyed or expropriated *villae*, and expelled the peasants.[113] "The rich tried to reach the properties they held in other parts of the Empire, emigrating to Africa, Carthage, Egypt, or Syria. The poor did what they could."[114] Armies, marauders, refugees, herds of sheep and cattle clogged Rome's military roads.

Despite the upheaval, there is significant evidence of continuity in the Greater Rhineland.[115] Though episcopal vacancies between about 435 and about 550 at Tongeren-Maastricht, Mainz, Worms, Speyer, and Strasburg confirm the flight of the Roman elite, a Gallo-Roman element endured at Cologne and a Roman senatorial family survived at Trier, where there are no gaps in the line of episcopal succession.[116] Cologne, "hostibus plena," was not pillaged, perhaps because the Franks who occupied it were *foederati* of Rome. Trier, frequently besieged, was never abandoned. Its new Frankish masters preserved its baths and palaces. Barbarians – probably Huns – destroyed Mainz in about 450, but within a century its river port was active again.[117] In the countryside Frankish settlers replaced Gallo-Roman populations that had fled or fallen to more general factors of demographic decline, shifting the "German/Latin linguistic frontier," a notion that would only become politically meaningful in the nineteenth

---

[111] Petrikovits, *Altertum*, pp. 269–71.
[112] Eugen Ewig, *Die Rheinlande in fränkischer Zeit* (Düsseldorf: Schwann, 1980), p. 10. The Latin term permits both translations.
[113] Doehaerd, *Le haut moyen âge occidental*, pp. 148–9.
[114] Doehaerd, *Le haut moyen âge occidental*, p. 53.   [115] Wightman, *Gallia Belgica*, p. 256.
[116] Ewig, *Die Rheinlande in fränkischer Zeit*, pp. 55–7.
[117] Ewig, *Die Rheinlande in fränkischer Zeit*, pp. 36–43. The Huns included in their ranks numerous Germanic peoples, including Ripuarian Franks.

century, about 30 miles west of the Rhine and about 100 miles south of the river's lower, east–west course.[118] But Latin resisted in cities such as Tournai and Trier and in pockets of the Moselle valley.[119] Franks and Alamanni on the Rhine, already participants in the political economy of the Roman west, never threatened the existence of the empire per se, but took up its defense against marauding war parties of Visigoths, Vandals, Alans, Burgundians, and Huns.[120] Rome, inversely, could no longer defend the Greater Rhineland and withdrew behind the Alps.[121]

The enduring myth of separation

The myth of the Rhineland frontier was born, Minerva-like, full-blown from the head of Julius Caesar. "Caesar changed the ... historical geography of Europe."[122] Although the image is harsh, it is not mere bravado to call his legacy a kind of discursive Caesarian section, an act of verbal violence, a *coup de force* that gave birth to the warring twins, France and Germany, and defined the river wall that was supposed to separate them. That act left a discursive scar, an ontopology of separation and animosity, a geography of separation where geographic *fact* revealed an economy (*oikos*: house, or household) of encounter, transaction, and creativity. Caesar's performative speech act would repeatedly disrupt Greater Rhineland political, economic, and cultural space in subsequent generations, and one day elicit the revolutionary therapeutic intervention that is European Union.

Literature of the Roman era reveals the tension between foundational myth and political and economic fact. Tacitus recounts the rebellion of Germanic auxiliary troops in AD 69 and their attempt to establish an

---

[118] The trace of Frankish migrations and settlements is fossilized in place names. See Albert Demangeon and Lucien Febvre, *Le Rhin* (Paris: Armand Colin, 1935), pp. 48–9. See also Charles Rostaing, *Les noms de lieux* (Paris: Presses Universitaires de France, 1974), ch. 6.

[119] Wightman, *Gallia Belgica*, pp. 245, 310. The right bank lost population, and would not experience growth until the eighth century. Geary, *Before France and Germany*, p. 108. See Petrikovits, *Altertum*, p. 287.

[120] Ternes, *Römisches Deutschland*, p. 155; Petrikovits, *Altertum*, pp. 272–4, 286; Geary, *Before France and Germany*, pp. 62–73.

[121] Petrikovits, *Altertum*, p. 268. I do not want to suggest that the destructions and disruptions of the fifth-century invasions were not important. The population of Trier might have fallen by as much as two thirds by the beginning of the fifth century. Inversely, economic activity was not disrupted to the point where technologies were lost, and archeological evidence shows continuity through the seventh century. See Ternes, *Römisches Deutschland*, pp. 183, 257.

[122] Dyson, *The Creation of the Roman Frontier*, p. 126.

independent Gallic empire with the support of Gallic and Germanic tribes of the lower Rhine.[123] The Tencteri, who lived opposite the Ubii of Cologne, resented and envied their prosperous Romanized cousins and incited them to join the rebellion, to pull down the walls of the town, and to slaughter its Roman inhabitants.

> The Tencteri ... sent an embassy with orders to present their demands in an assembly of the people of Cologne. These demands the most violent of the delegates set forth thus: "We give thanks to our common gods and to Mars before all others that you have returned to the body of the German peoples and to the German name, and we congratulate you that at last you are going to be free men among free men; for until today the Romans have closed (*clauserant*) rivers and lands, and in a fashion *heaven itself*, to keep us from meeting and conferring together, or else – and this is a severer insult to men born to arms – to make us meet unarmed and almost naked, under guard and paying a price [an entry tax] for the privilege. But to secure forever our friendship and alliance, we demand that ... both we and you ... have the right to live on both banks, as our fathers once did. Even as Nature has always made the light of day free to all mankind, so she has made all lands open to the brave. Resume the manners and customs of your fathers, cutting off those pleasures which give the Romans more power over their subjects than their arms bestow. A people pure, untainted, forgetting your servitude, you will live the equals of any or will rule others."[124]

The Tencteri dismiss as folly Rome's attempt to *close off* "sacred" space, as if they could parcel out the light of day.[125] They debunk the myth of separation and attribute its influence to unmanly luxury. The

---

[123] The Batavii, like the Mattiaci, entered into alliance with Rome while inhabiting the right bank of the Rhine, "for the greatness of the Roman nation has projected the awe felt for our Empire beyond the Rhine, and beyond the long-established frontier (*terminos*)." Tacitus, *Germania* XXIX.

[124] *Histories* IV.64.

[125] Cologne, as Roman colony, would have been sacred space of a sort. Its founder, draped in a toga, would have read auspices from the entrails of birds, then gripped the twin handles of a bronze-tipped plow drawn by a white heifer and a white bull, and cut a furrow that would mark the limits of the city. He would have lifted the plow to leave a passage for the sacred ways, the *cardo* and *decumanus*, to return to the point of departure. At this point, the city was born. From the rent ground surged earth's divinities to take possession of the limit and render it impenetrable. The line of demarcation, the *pomerium*, made sacred the space that it enclosed. The imperial *limes*, one could say, was the forward military protection of a mosaic of space that was, in similar fashion, consecrated in the social imaginary. See Pierre Grimal, *Les villes romaines* (Paris: Presses Universitaires de France, 1966), pp. 7–9, 14–18.

Roman commanders meet the argument by cultivating distrust and fear of the right bank barbarian. Gaul, after all, was peaceful and prosperous:

> The Germans always have the same reasons for crossing into the Gallic provinces – lust, avarice, and their longing to change their homes, that they may leave behind their swamps and deserts, and become masters of this most fertile soil and of you yourselves: freedom, however, and specious names are their pretexts; but no man has ever been ambitious to enslave another or to win dominion for himself without using those very same words.

(IV.73)

But the contrast between a pacified and prosperous "Gaul" and an untamed and jealous "Germania" was not sufficient to carry the debate. The Roman commander explains (anticipating Thomas Hobbes) that the frontier serves to protect the inhabitants from the enemy *within*: "For, if the Romans are driven out ... what will follow except universal war of all against all (*bella omnium inter se*)?" (IV.74: translation modified). It is a curious admission, for it suggests that there was tension between the advocates of material privilege and those of barbarian liberties *inside* the bounds of Gaul. The Rhine, by this reading, was irrelevant to the task of keeping disputants apart. It merely marked the territorial limit of Rome's legal authority, its coercive peace.

Three centuries later, Ausonius, Prefect of the Gauls (second to the Caesar) under the western emperor Gratian, wrote this hymn to the Moselle:

> Now spread thy azure folds and glass-green robe, O Rhine, and measure out a space for thy new stream [the Moselle]: a brother's waters come to swell thee. Nor is his treasure waters alone, but also that, coming from the walls of the imperial city [Trier], he has beheld the united triumphs of father and son [Valentinian and Gratian in 368] over foes vanquished beyond Nicer [Neckar] and Lupodunum [Ladenburg?] and Ister's [Danube's] source, unknown to Latin chronicles [though it lay within the Agri Decumates]. This laureate dispatch which tells of their o'erwhelming arms is but now come to thee: hereafter others and yet others shall he bring. Press on united both, and with twin streams drive back the deep-blue sea. Nor do thou fear to lose esteem, most beauteous Rhine: a host has naught of jealousy. Thou shalt enjoy endless fame: do thou, assured of renown, take to thyself a brother ... So shalt thou gain strength to make Franks and Chamavii and Germans quake: then shalt thou be held their boundary indeed (*tunc verus habebere limes*).[126]

---

[126] Ausonius, *Mosella* 418–35, translated by Hugh G. Evelyn White (Cambridge: Harvard Loeb editions, 1919). See discussion by Ternes, *Römisches Deutschland*, pp. 144–5, 147–52.

The poem celebrates Valentinian's and Gratian's military success against the barbarians, the forward positioning of Roman arms, the recovery and reinforcement of the Rhineland *limes*, the promise of conquests to come ("yet others shall he bring") presumably on the right bank, and the establishment of the imperial government at Trier, "proxima Rheno."[127] The image is one of triumph. Yet the imperial government, as shown above, was importing, settling, organizing, and arming Frankish warriors, and promoting the ascendance of Frankish chieftains to the highest ranks of power in order to defend the frontier against invasion by ... the Franks. As Rome invested again in the fortification and adornment of the frontier, it not only stimulated the desire of the barbarians living beyond the *limes* to gain entry by violence, but invited them in through service. "The strongest factor of Germanization of the Rhineland and northern Gaul was the [Roman] military."[128] In this restless and troubled scene the Rhine is "host" and stabilizing frontier. And yet Ausonius' imagery is not one of quiet, of settlement, but of movement, of battle, of currents and tides. The Rhine "drives." But its energy does not drive barbarian hordes; it drives the "deep blue sea."

Ambiguity of vision informed ambiguity of deed. The internal dynamics of empire still spurred ambitious Roman warlords to seek moral authority and troop loyalty – the *auctoritas* of the *Augustus* – in military victory.[129] Rapid campaigns among the barbarians remained the strategy of choice, and the *limes* the El Dorado of political fortune. Success meant storming the barbarian hinterland in the same way the waters of the Rhine, in the imagery of Ausonius, stormed the great formless sea. The politics of warlord competition, however, destabilized the instrument of geopolitical pacification that the Rhine frontier was supposed to be.[130] The empire could not sustain the glaring incompatibility between Roman dependence on Germanic troops for frontier defense and Roman dependence on Germanic victims for career advancement. Gratian

---

[127] "... near the Rhine," in Ausonius, *Treveris*, in *Ordo Urbium Nobilium* VI. Cf. J. Caesar, discussed above.

[128] Petrikovits, *Altertum*, p. 237; see also p. 266. "The military in the Rhineland, once the primary agent of Romanization, had become by the late third century the primary agent of barbarization." Geary, *Before France and Germany*, p. 14.

[129] See Petrikovits, *Altertum*, p. 264; Wightman, *Gallia Belgica*, p. 191; Rougé, *Les institutions romaines*, pp. 103–5; Petit, *La paix romaine*, pp. 125–7. Petit notes, pp. 132–4, that of sixteen emperors from Augustus to Commodus, nine ascended the throne through regular dynastic succession.

[130] Wightman, *Gallia Belgica*, p. 209.

showed favoritism toward the Alamannic military units he raised even as Valentinian II was bribing Huns and Alans to invade the Alamanni.[131] Commenting on such cross-purposes, Ternes writes:

> It is tragic that Rome, in the end, for reasons of politics ... and even *Weltanschauung,* no longer possessed the power to let willing newcomers participate durably in the mutual enjoyment (*Nutzen*) of the *fata imperii,* the destiny of empire. The frequent indecisiveness of the Romans ... and their brutal attempts to achieve through raw force what they could no longer work out with patience and wit, demonstrate that the principle of the Triumph without (true, pacifying) Victory, so deplored by Tacitus, remained in effect to the very end.[132]

Habits of thought and action, born of myth, produced unintended consequences. For Patrick Geary, "The Roman creation of the barbarian world was not simply a perceptual one in which the Romans processed the data of contact with barbarians through the grid of Roman values. Roman perceptions and influences, both active and passive, transformed and structured this world even while trying to understand it to an extent only recently beginning to be recognized."[133] The barbarian world evolved through contact with the urban, commercial political economy of the Greater Rhineland, which thrived (relative to other regions) even as the empire stagnated. Rome endowed its creation, the *limes,* with a vital, *deconstructive* tension – it deconstructed the opposition between self and other even as it instituted that opposition. That tension was the logical effect of the dual-natured *limes: limes*-as-frontier; *limes*-as-vector-of-peoples.

---

[131] Petrikovits, *Altertum,* p. 267.   [132] Ternes, *Römisches Deutschland,* p. 136.
[133] Geary, *Before France and Germany,* p. vii.

3

A "principality of priests": the inauguration of Europe

If Trier embodies the Rhineland of the Romans, Aachen embodies the Rhineland of the Franks, who once ruled a territory almost coterminous with that of the six signatory states of the 1957 Treaty of Rome from this small city lodged today at the intersection of the German, Belgian, and Dutch borders. Its octagonal Imperial Cathedral, site of Charlemagne's throne, was, at the time of its construction, the tallest edifice north of the Alps (see plate 3.1). Its innovative fusion of Roman and Byzantine styles influenced western architecture for centuries. The late eighth and early ninth centuries were a time of prodigious ecclesiastical construction. New construction "brought to light" a political space that restored, and was legitimated by, the twin legacies of the old and new Rome – the old Rome of classical Latin speech and rational administration, and the new, Constantinian Rome of God and Church. It was an ambitious and costly enterprise, inaugurated by the *coup de force* of forged evidence that posited a close, cooperative relationship between the bishop of Rome and an emperor whom he "restored" to power to govern and evangelize Gaul and the northern barbarian march. Rhineland commercial links with the Baltic Sea and central Asia helped finance this vast enterprise. Discursive revolution and Rhineland commerce forged, in mutual resonance, a new myth of place, a new ontopology called "Europe."

This chapter interrogates this ontopology by tracing it to the *coup de force* that engendered it, the "Donation of Constantine." This text, drafted by an anonymous, eighth-century monk, asserted papal supremacy over the secular government of the western empire. It advanced the idea of an alliance between pope and emperor that would inform political ambition from the ninth to the thirteenth century. This chapter, like the previous one, examines grounds for suspicion regarding the "naturalness," or the "determinacy," of European ontopology by reconstructing the political motivations from which the text emerged, and by contrasting

Plate 3.1 The Imperial Cathedral at Aachen

the political geography implicit in the ontopology with the geographic resources that realized it as fact. The ontopology of "Europe" – Carolingian ontopology – "hid from view" the regional economy that substantiated it. Efforts to rule "Europe" from Rome, its mythical center, left the Greater Rhineland core nameless and politically fragmented. The forged text that memorializes the *coup de force* is, like Caesar's geographical *pronuciamento*, a living text. It names the place that EU seeks to unify, while consigning to namelessness, to invisibility, the geopolitics and regional economy that evoked the project and assured its success.

The Frankish restoration of Roman Gaul

As Roman power collapsed before them, the Franks elaborated their military and political ambitions within a discursive universe still stamped by Gallia as ontopology. Their actions either sought or were justified post hoc by reference to that ontopology, that is, by the preservation of the unity of the place named Gaul. Merovich "the sea-born," eponymous founder of the Merovingian dynasty, though he emerged from the northerly, pagan fringes of the Frankish confederacy, commanded the Salian Franks of the lower Rhine as Rome's ally against Attila the Hun. His grandson Clovis inherited a reputation as defender of Roman Gaul, its institutions, and its aristocratic interests.[1] Remigius, bishop of Reims and principal representative of a Gallo-Roman aristocracy that, through its Christian bishops, preserved Roman administration in the cities even as the empire crumbled around them, formally recognized Clovis as "administrator" of "Roman Belgium."[2] Clovis converted to Catholicism (in 495 or 508), and received a consular office from the eastern emperor Anastasius.[3] By that conversion, the Franks became the defenders of Catholic orthodoxy against Arian invaders – Visigoths, Burgundians, and Alemmans.[4] "The unique achievement of Clovis and his successors was that, through his conquest and conversion, he was able to begin to reunite these two splintered halves [Gallic and Frankish] of the Roman heritage."[5] Clovis and his followers ruled peripatetically from the towns controlled by their Gallo-Roman patrons. Paris, Soissons, Metz, Verdun, Toul, and Reims all served as sites of the Frankish court (see figure 3.1).[6] Christianity's influence and the bishop's centrality in public affairs kept the city alive. From this "Belgian" province Clovis undertook the conquest of all of Gaul, beginning with the Ripuarian Franks of the middle Rhine and "Alsace," the land of the Alemannic *Alesaciones*. Cologne, Worms, Mainz, and Trier were added to the list of cities that hosted the royal suite. Clovis subdued the Burgundians and Visigoths, and his successors wrested Provence from the Ostrogoths.[7] By 537, The Franks had reunited the erstwhile provinces of Roman Gaul under their rule.

Merovingian legislation, exemplified by the *decretio Childeberti* of 594–6, reprised many elements of Roman civil law and attests to the survival of a Roman lettered aristocracy.[8] Most royal officials were literate. Kings of the Merovingian period "were unquestionably literate, which is more than can be said for many later medieval rulers."[9] Roman

---

[1] Ian Wood, *The Merovingian Kingdoms: 150–751* (London and New York: Longman, 1994), pp. 40–1.

[2] Eugen Ewig, *Frühes Mittelalter*, vol. I part 2 of Franz Petri and Georg Droege, *Rheinische Geschichte* (Düsseldorf: Schwann, 1978), pp. 46–7.

[3] Wood, *The Merovingian Kingdoms*, p. 165.

[4] Norman Davies, *Europe: A History* (Oxford: Oxford University Press, 1996), p. 276.

[5] Patrick J. Geary, *Before France and Germany: The Creation and Transformation of the Merovingian World* (New York and Oxford: Oxford University Press, 1988), p. 93. Renée Doehaerd, *Le haut moyen âge occidental* (Paris: Presses Universitaires de France, 1971), p. 56.

[6] Wood, *The Merovingian Kingdoms*, p. 153. Ewig, *Frühes Mittelalter*, pp. 20–4. Trier, Cologne, and Mainz, it is relevant to note, lost their circuses during the invasions: Doehaerd, *Le haut moyen âge occidental*, p. 118.

[7] Davies, *Europe*, p. 232.   [8] Wood, *The Merovingian Kingdoms*, pp. 107, 262, 24–32.

[9] Wood, *The Merovingian Kingdoms*, pp. 153, 240–1, 250.

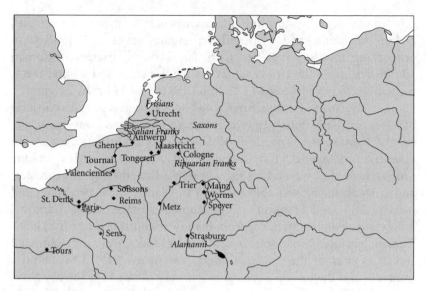

Figure 3.1 Merovingian Gaul

roads and waterways remained passable until the tenth century. River towns, like Huy on the Meuse, show "signs of continuous artisanal activity from late Roman into Merovingian times."[10] Syrian, Greek, and Jewish merchants plied the roads of Gaul, sometimes in camel caravans, providing Frankish leaders with luxury goods with which to cultivate clienteles – like Gallic chieftains and Roman warlords before them. Mediterranean tableware from the period is found in the British Isles and northern Europe.[11] Frankish kings financed games and circuses. Chilperic built amphitheaters in Paris and Soissons, inviting unkind comparisons with Nero – a last admiring mimetic gesture to the Mediterranean civilization of Rome.

> Two distinct, and at first sight contradictory, trends can be ... clearly seen in the north. On the one hand, the day of cities in the Mediterranean sense was already over, even though remnants of Roman civic administration did survive. At the same time, the last feature of the city to spread out from the Mediterranean, the ecclesiastical diocese, was just

[10] Edith Mary Wightman, *Gallia Belgica* (Berkeley and Los Angeles: University of California Press, 1985), p. 241.

[11] Richard Hodges and David Whitehouse, *Mohammed, Charlemagne, and the Origins of Europe: Archeology and the Pirenne Thesis* (Ithaca: Cornell University Press, 1983), p. 32.

completing its conquest, and the hybrid product of these processes was to give birth to the medieval town.[12]

Rhineland resurgence

Christianity, however, problematized Roman ontopology and prepared the discursive terrain for the *coup de force* that would give birth to "Europe." Monasticism in some form or other had existed in Gaul since the fourth century when a Roman centurion, Martin, converted to Christianity, won authority as an evangelist, served as bishop of Tours, then retired as an anchorite to the cavernous cliffs overlooking the Loire. His hermitage metamorphosed into a de facto monastic community (monastic rules, such as those of St. Benedict or St. Augustine, did not yet exist in the west). A century later, Clovis, following his conversion to Catholicism, declared that Martin, now venerated as a saint, would be honored as patron of the royal household. Clerics among his retinue preserved the saint's military cape or *cappa* as a holy relic, and so acquired the moniker *capella*, whence our "chapel." Clovis's son Childebert I established many religious communities, mostly in the southern, Roman cities of Provence, Aquitaine, and Burgundy.

At this time, monasticism was the preserve of the Gallo-Roman aristocracy. Monasteries at Marseilles and on the isle of Lérins, which followed the eastern monastic rule of St. Andrew, were hatcheries of Gallo-Roman bishops.[13] But the monks of Lérins unwittingly undermined the Gallo-Roman lock on ecclesiastical power when they introduced monasticism to the non-Romanized, non-urbanized wilds of Ireland, where it assumed a new form. "Unlike monasteries on the Continent, which were communities of men or women determined to escape the world, these Irish monasteries were the centers of Christian life and the primary religious institutions around which lay religious practice focused and on which it was modeled." Around 590, Columbanus introduced Irish monasticism, untainted by Gallo-Roman culture and unattached to the Gallic Church, to Gaul. The impact on the Frankish aristocracy "can scarcely be overestimated."[14] Powerful Frankish families established monasteries on the Irish model, generally away from the city and often on uncultivated land that the monks cleared. They decorated them

---

[12] Wightman, *Gallia Belgica*, p. 242. See Doehaerd, *Le haut moyen âge occidental*, p. 121.

[13] Wood, *The Merovingian Kingdoms*, pp. 22–4.

[14] Geary, *Before France and Germany*, p. 171; Ewig, *Frühes Mittelalter*, pp. 68–9; Wood, *The Merovingian Kingdoms*, ch. 11.

richly, and supplied them with holy relics that legitimated their power in the countryside. The number of such foundations grew rapidly in northern Gaul.[15] The Frankish nobility began to turn out its own saints, whose hagiographies, unlike those of their Gallo-Roman counterparts, made great case of their secular connections and accomplishments. "For the first time in Western history the tide of religious culture had reversed. After centuries of the Mediterranean forms of Christianity gradually penetrating north, a new and vigorous form of Christianity, closely tied to royal and aristocratic interests and power bases, was spreading out from the north and gradually transforming the Romanized south."[16]

Monasticism fostered the emergence of new named spaces. The cultivation of western *saltus*, particularly in the Paris basin where the monks of St. Denis, St. Germain, and Ste. Geneviève doubled the area placed under the plow, conditioned Paris' rise to power as the core of the "new provinces," Neustria, centered on the Seine and Oise. The term appears in texts from 575, and gestures toward its other, the "older," eastern provinces of Austrasia, centered on the Rhine, Meuse, and Moselle. Royal immunities exempted the monasteries from episcopal and secular intervention, and curtailed the power and influence of the urban bishops. In the early seventh century other powerful monasteries were established: St. Médard at Soissons, St. Pierre at Sens, and St. Aignan at Orleans.[17] The Merovingian court also invested heavily in the establishment of monasteries in the lower Rhine–Meuse delta – St. Amand, St. Pierre, and St. Bavon near Ghent and Antwerp. Columbanus himself evangelized the peoples of the River Scheldt. Dagobert established the church of Utrecht and enrolled Bishop Cunibert of Cologne in the evangelization of the enterprising Frisians who inhabited the Rhine delta, in the hope of bringing them under Frankish dominion.[18]

The multiplication of monasteries along the lower Rhine and its affluents pushed commercial activity north. Cereals, wine, and salt were shipped down the Rhine from Mainz to the coastal marshlands. Inversely, Christian obligation stimulated demand up-river for salted fish from the North Sea.[19] Valenciennes, on the Scheldt, appears in the

[15] Wood, *The Merovingian Kingdoms*, p. 191.

[16] Geary, *Before France and Germany*, p. 178; Ewig, *Frühes Mittelalter*, pp. 64–72.

[17] Wood, *The Merovingian Kingdoms*, pp. 155, 200.

[18] Wood, *The Merovingian Kingdoms*, p. 161.

[19] Guy Fourquin, *Histoire économique de l'occident médiéval* (Paris: Armand Colin, 1969), pp. 108–9.

texts at this time as *vicus* and *portus*, and Ghent as *portus* serving the monasteries of St. Pierre and St. Bavon, already engaged in the cross-channel trade in wool and woolen textiles that would one day enrich all of Flanders. By 700 Maastricht appears in the texts as *oppidum*, *urbs*, and *civitas*. Namur and Dinant, on the Meuse, acquired mints and the right to levy a tariff.[20] Frisian merchants developed a commercial network that reached out to Paris, London, Cologne, and the regions between the Scheldt and the Weser. Late in the seventh century one encounters references to a specifically Rhenish territory: *Francia rinensis*, Rhineland Francia.[21]

Monastic and commercial development in the Greater Rhineland conditioned the rise of the Pippinids, whose territorial roots were in the lower Rhine and the Meuse valleys – Utrecht, Nijmegen, Tongeren, Maastricht, as well as Reims (see figure 3.2).[22] Like other powerful families, the Pippinids leveraged Irish monastic energies into family power and prestige. They cultivated the loyalty of the regional aristocracy, as well as the dukes of Alsace and noble families in the duchy of Ripuaria, in the vicinity of Cologne. They made lavish use of ecclesiastical lands to grant their followers precarial tenure.[23] In the late eighth century, the Pippinid monastery of St. Wandrille possessed 4,264 properties (*mansus*) throughout Gaul, of which well over half had been granted as benefices to allies or alienated on other terms. Noble families like the Pippinids harbored court ambitions and vied for regional power. They competed for control of the imperial treasury, for episcopal power, and above all, for the position of Mayor of the Palace, or *maior domo*, who, by the late Merovingian period, had assumed responsibility for the day-to-day affairs of the realm.[24] Pepin of Herstal, duke of Austrasia, defeated the Mayor of the Neustrian Palace at the battle of Tertry in 687 and became *maior domo* of the Frankish kingdom in its entirety. But his bastard son, Charles Martel, made it his priority to consolidate his power base on the Rhine, where he undertook difficult but successful campaigns against the Frisians, the Alamans (who had gained considerable independence under the last Merovingians) and the Saxons on the Weser. The ascendancy of the Pippinids culminated in Martel's victories over Chilperic II in 716 and 717, the last of the Merovingians to exercise effective rule.[25] Once Mayor of the Palace in

[20] Doehaerd, *Le haut moyen âge occidental*, p. 262.   [21] Ewig, *Frühes Mittelalter*, p. 9.
[22] Wood, *The Merovingian Kingdoms*, ch. 13, esp. pp. 257–9.
[23] Wood, *The Merovingian Kingdoms*, pp. 264–5.
[24] Geary, *Before France and Germany*, p. 181.   [25] Wood, *The Merovingian Kingdoms*, p. 271.

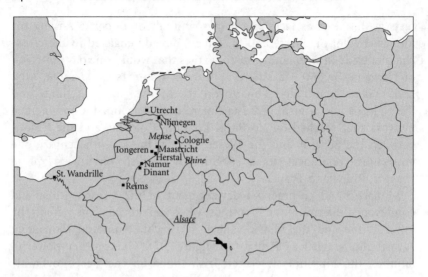

Figure 3.2 The Pippinids

both Austrasia and Neustria, Martel appointed family members and supporters everywhere he could.[26] His clientele consisted perhaps of thirty noble families who, through intermarriage, spawned a European aristocracy that, by the ninth century, was supplying the leaders of all the regional principalities.[27] As long as the conquests continued, the Pippinids could count on aristocratic support. They knew the nobility, its needs, its desires, and its cupidity.[28]

Coup de force: the Donation of Constantine

The *coup de force* that brought Europe to light as ontopology was conditioned by two further historical developments besides the rise to prominence of Rhineland (Pippinid) warlords. The first was the subversion of Byzantine and patriarchal authority by Islam. Byzantium was on the defensive, unable to rule or defend its western provinces. Though the population of Rome had fallen to about 30,000, the loss of three patriarchates to Islam – Alexandria, Jerusalem, and Antioch – reinforced the Roman papacy's claims to leadership in the Christian world. Whereas

[26] Wood, *The Merovingian Kingdoms*, pp. 277–80, 160–3.
[27] Pierre Riché, *The Carolingians: A Family Who Forged Europe*, trans. Michael Idomir Allen (Philadelphia: University of Pennsylvania Press, 1993), p. 137.
[28] Riché, *The Carolingians*, p. 88.

previously the bishop of Rome "spoke with one Latin voice against four Greeks; after Islam, it was one to one." This was the time, Norman Davies observes, "when the papacy was born."[29] Islam's success, moreover, fomented the iconoclast persecution in Byzantium that further undermined the empire's political and religious authority in the west. By contrast, Charles Martel's victory over the Saracens at Poitiers sometime around 732, which returned Aquitaine to the Merovingian realm, had earned Martel a reputation as defender of *Christianitas*.[30] The temptation to equate Christendom with "Europe," which, as of the mid-eighth century, had still not acquired its contemporary signification, was great.

The second development was the emergence of new evangelical energy, this time in Anglo-Saxon Britain, which paved the way for an alliance between Rhineland warlord and Roman pope, by conferring on the former a divine, legitimating mission. When British missionaries sought Frankish support to convert their Saxon kindred on the continent, Pepin of Herstal responded by founding three monasteries on the Meuse north of Maastricht (Odilienberg, Susteren, and Aldeneyck), while his ally Liutwin established new abbeys at Echternach and Mettlach, near the old Roman capital of Trier. Charles Martel helped the English monk Boniface create abbeys near Gotha in Thuringia, as well as new diocesan sees in Würzburg, Buraburg, and Erfurt (see figure 3.3). The Visigoth monk Pirmin accomplished similar work in Alamannia, reinforcing Martel's hold on the right bank.[31] Carloman, Martel's successor, named Boniface archbishop of Mainz and placed newly elevated missionary bishops under his authority.[32]

Unlike the Irish church, the English church was tightly organized and accustomed to working with a royal court. Anglo-Saxon monasticism was Benedictine, regulated by and loyal to Rome. Its combination of "old monastic traditions [and ancient Rome's] military spirit"[33] made it ideally suited to bring European Christendom under Rome's authority.[34] Together, English missionaries and the Pippinid court brought unity and obedience to the Frankish church.[35] Relations between Rome and the Frankish court prospered, such that the pope, in conflict with

---

[29] Davies, *Europe*, pp. 266, 273: "The title of *papa*," for example, "had once been affectionately applied to all bishops. Henceforth it was reserved exclusively for the bishop of Rome."
[30] Wood, *The Merovingian Kingdoms*, pp. 281–4.
[31] See Riché, *The Carolingians*, pp. 41–2. [32] Ewig, *Frühes Mittelalter*, p. 100.
[33] Hans Küng, *The Catholic Church: A Short History*, trans. John Bowdon (New York: Modern Library, 2001), p. 66.
[34] Geary, *Before France and Germany*, p. 216. [35] Riché, *The Carolingians*, pp. 55–8.

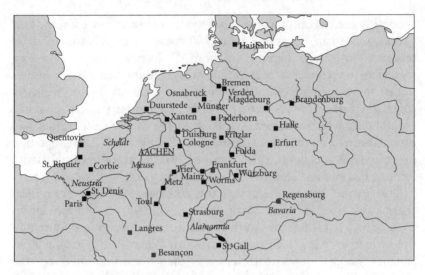

Figure 3.3 The Carolingian Rhineland and eastward expansion

the expansionist Arian Lombard kingdom in northern Italy, turned for aid not to the imperial court at Byzantium, but to the Franks. Charles' successor Pepin III saw the opportunity to accede to the throne, still occupied formally by descendents of Merovich and Clovis even though decades had passed without a Merovingian serving even as a figurehead king.[36] Pepin laid claim to the throne in 751. Though he had the support of the nobility, he justified his claim not by aristocratic election, but by divine providence. Pope Stephen II granted Pepin's petition, applied the chrism to his sons Carloman II and Charles (the future Charlemagne), and declared the selection of a king from outside the Pippinid family to be an offense punishable by excommunication. Pepin's coronation made ample use of biblical and ecclesiastical symbolism – "never before had a [Frankish] king been confirmed in his office by ecclesiastical ritual."[37] In recognition of the pope's support, Pepin wrested Ravenna and much of central Italy from the Lombards (in 755), which he "returned" to the pope.

The forged "Donation of Constantine" enters the story at this point as the instrument that gave the pope the legal standing to name the emperor.[38] The document, about ten pages long, explains that the

[36] Riché, *The Carolingians*, pp. 65–8.
[37] Geary, *Before France and Germany*, p. 220. See Riché, *The Carolingians*, p. 67.
[38] Davies, *Europe*, p. 302.

division of the empire into eastern and western halves by Constantine was intended to benefit the papacy. It recounts Constantine's conversion and gratitude to the bishop of Rome as "vicar of the Son of God" and successor to "the prince of apostles." Constantine declares it his wish to confer on the papacy, whose principate is of heavenly origin, a power greater than he, the emperor, holds by the mere benevolence of men, and thus "to attribute to it the power, the dignity, the means to act and the imperial honors, that is to say, primacy over the four principal sees of Antioch, Alexandria, Constantinople, and Jerusalem, and over all the churches of the entire world."

> So that the pontifical dignity shall not be abased, but that it should be honored in glory and in power even more than the dignity of the earthly empire, we give to the most blessed pontiff, Sylvester, our Holy Father, universal pope, and abandon to him and to his successors not only our palace [the Lateran], but the city of Rome and all the provinces, all the localities, all the cities in all of Italy as in all the western regions, and, by a firm decision of our imperial authority, by virtue of this sacred edict and this enactment, we do attribute them in full possession to the holy Roman Church, that it may benefit from them in perpetuity. Thus we have judged opportune to transfer our empire and the exercise of our authority to the eastern regions, to edify in the province of Byzantium, in a place particularly favorable, a city that shall have our name and there to constitute our empire. For there where the principality of priests and the capital of the Christian religion has been instituted by the celestial Empire, it is not just that the earthly empire should exercise its power.[39]

By asserting the primacy of Rome over western Christendom and by exiling "secular" power to the east, the Donation inaugurated habits of speech and thought that would, for centuries, endow Latin Christendom with an ontopology. The document "revealed" the enduring reality, inscribed in celestial metaphysics, of the Roman empire *of the west*, once ruled from Trier, now ruled from Aachen, 50 miles away, through the agency of the Pippinids with the divine authorization of Christ's vicar in Rome. The Donation of Constantine is the discursive *coup de force* that brought "Europe" to light, that made it visible and available to speech.

---

[39] Louis Halphen, *Charlemagne et l'empire Carolingien* (Paris: Albin Michel, 1947), p. 36. The Donation was one in a series of ninth-century forgeries legitimating the primacy and power of the bishop of Rome. See Küng, *The Catholic Church*, pp. 74–5.

The chroniclers of Charlemagne's Christmas day, 800, coronation in Rome portray the event as a *renovatio imperii*, a restoration of the empire. The pope proclaimed Charles "Augustus, crowned by God, great and pacific emperor of the Romans." Charles was reluctant to use the title "Emperor of the Romans," and preferred to call himself king of the Franks and Lombards, or "Augustus, ruler of the Roman Empire," but his successors had no such scruples. Pope John VIII proclaimed Charles the Bald, last of the great Carolingian monarchs, the (secular) leader of "Christianitas" before a synod at Rome in 875, and anointed, crowned, and acclaimed him emperor of the Romans. Charles returned to Gaul flanked by papal legates and the papal vicar for Gaul and Germania. He wore Byzantine imperial dress and sealed imperial correspondence with the words *renovatio imperii Romanorum et Francorum*.[40] The spiritual leaders of Roman Christianity, meanwhile, assumed quite literally the mantle of the Caesars, since the forged Donation awarded the popes the power to create "patricians and consuls," the right to wear the imperial diadem, the purple chlamys, and the scarlet tunic, and to bear the scepter.[41] The resurrected empire of the west was, in the terms of the Donation, "a principality of priests." "Imperial politics was church politics and church politics was imperial politics."[42]

Between the eighth and tenth centuries, the name that, with growing frequency, was assigned to the site of this *renovatio imperii* was "Europe." An anonymous poet of Cordoba celebrated the victory of Martel's "men of Europe" at Poitiers in 732.[43] Pepin's successor, Charlemagne, was heralded "head of the world and summit of Europe, the new Augustus who reigns in a New Rome."[44] The Paderborn epic styled Charlemagne the "beacon of Europe."[45] His successor, Louis the Pious, "by order of Divine Providence, Emperor and Augustus," dropped all reference to the Franks, the *people* of which he was king, in order to rule over a *geographic* site chosen by God to become the divine city. Charles the Bald was the "prince of Europe," and the Saxon Otto I the "emperor of all Europe."[46] The reference fell from use when the empire crumbled, but was resurrected again in the twelfth century by the Ottonians.

The empire invested money and manpower in making "Europe" as Christendom discernible, visible, audible, tangible, by resurrecting the

[40] Riché, *The Carolingians*, p. 202.
[41] Davies, *Europe*, p. 292; Halphen, *Charlemagne*, p. 36.
[42] Küng, *The Catholic Church*, p. 70.   [43] Riché, *The Carolingians*, p. 44.
[44] Riché, *The Carolingians*, p. 124.   [45] Riché, The *Carolingians*, p. 140.
[46] Jean-Baptiste Duroselle, *L'Europe, histoire de ses peuples* (Paris: Hachette, 1995), p. 156.

language, administrative rationality, and monumental architecture of Constantine's Rome. Latin was confirmed as the language not only of learning but of administration throughout the realm. Schools labored to expunge the language of barbarisms that had entered the language since the invasions. Exposure to the Lombard court had shown the Franks a style of rule that was, like that of the early Merovingians, closely patterned on Roman practice and dependent on Roman-style administration by well-qualified clerics. Pepin adopted that style of rule and promoted clerics of the royal chapel to the highest positions of his council and administration. "From this date until the end of the thirteenth century, laymen were largely excluded from the direction of the royal administration."[47] The Carolingians attached importance to the education of clerics who would provide the administrative backbone of the new empire. "The goal," however, was not simply "the resurrection of an earlier historical condition, but the realization of transhistorical norms and laws legislated by God in all areas of life, including in the political sphere."[48] Alcuin, director of the cathedral school in York and a leading theological and philosophical figure, was made abbot of St. Martin of Tours in 796. Einhard, of the monastery school of Fulda, became palace chaplain. Intellectual talents assembled by the emperor spearheaded a cultural renaissance. Ecclesiastical schools multiplied.[49] The education they provided produced an elite that was homogeneous, Christian, and humanistic.[50] That elite controlled perhaps two hundred of the most powerful abbeys, which it placed at the disposal of the king.[51] The Carolingians founded monasteries, often at personal expense, and renovated and aggrandized Merovingian churches on a staggering scale.[52]

Aachen was the "new Rome" of the restored empire. The early Pippinids, like their Merovingian patrons, situated government in the old Roman cities, especially Metz, Cologne, and Worms. Charles Martel, however, elected residence in the family homeland near Herstal, not far from Liège. Charlemagne's encounter with the Lombard capital at Pavia inspired him to construct the capital complex at nearby Aachen on the site of the Roman spa Aquisgranium, "Waters of Apollo Granus." Aachen became the permanent residence of the emperor and his successor Louis, and the hub of a network of palaces that extended from

[47] Riché, The Carolingians, p. 81.   [48] Ewig, Frühes Mittelalter, p. 101.
[49] Riché, The Carolingians, p. 330.   [50] Ewig, Frühes Mittelalter, p. 102.
[51] Riché, The Carolingians, p. 129.
[52] Ewig, Frühes Mittelalter, pp. 120–5; Hodges and Whitehouse, Mohammed, Charlemagne, and the Origins of Europe, p. 104.

Plate 3.2 The Throne of Charlemagne

the Seine and the Oise to Austrasia and Saxony to the east.[53] Documents refer to the palace as the *Lateranum*, after the residence of the first Christian emperors according to the Donation of Constantine. The designation conveyed the claim that the Frankish emperor was Constantine's successor, and Aachen the new Rome.[54] The palace was probably modeled on the Constantinian *aula* at Trier. The gilt chapel of the cathedral, completed in 805, served as throne room (see plate 3.2).

[53] Ewig, *Frühes Mittelalter*, p. 95.   [54] Ewig, *Frühes Mittelalter*, pp. 142–3.

The close intermingling of the secular and the religious recalled Hagia Sophia, and, mythically, the temple of Jerusalem. San Vitale at Ravenna probably served as the model for the chapel, or possibly the Sergius and Bacchus church built by Justinian at Constantinople, the most important in that city prior to the construction of Hagia Sophia. The ambo was encrusted with fragments of Roman pottery and glass, and decorated with a Roman eagle cameo. The Egyptian columns from Ravenna in green and rose porphyry celebrated the rivalry with Byzantium. The altar panel, in solid gold, portrayed the Passion in classic Roman relief. Above the cross was the portrait cameo of the emperor Augustus.[55]

The nameless core

From its Greater Rhineland core, the empire extended south and west to Gaul, and east and north across the Rhine to the Baltic, where Charlemagne waged a savage, thirty-year campaign to reduce the Saxons to obedience. He founded a monastery at Corvey, established a diocese at Münster, and built strongholds at Magdeburg on the Elbe and Halle on the Saale to anchor a new *limes sorabicus*, or Sorbian March.[56] Rhineland support was crucial to securing this march for Rome and *Christianitas*. The archdiocese of Cologne underwrote the new diocese of Münster, and later those of Bremen and Osnabrück. Cologne also played a central role in the pacification of Frisia.[57] Mainz initiated the foundation of the important monasteries of Paderborn and Verden, as well as those along the southern frontier of Saxony – Fulda, Hersfeld, Fritzlar, and Lul. Mainz's province, one of the largest of medieval Christianity, covered most of the territory between the Rhine, the Danube, and the Elbe.

Conquest placed the Greater Rhineland, with its economy and political energy, at the center of the *imperium*. It subverted Caesarian ontopology, which placed the Rhine at the edge of pacified political space. But discursive habit and perhaps appeal to the legitimating political geography dictated by Rome conspired to ratify Caesarian ontopology, even within the framework of the new "Europe" that was being constructed. As Frankish arms subdued the Saxons and consolidated the emperor's hold on both the Weser and the Danube, what had been a boundless barbarian space became an organized,

[55] Davies, *Europe*, p. 305.   [56] Riché, *The Carolingians*, pp. 103–10.
[57] Ewig, *Frühes Mittelalter*, p. 112.

structured province. Mainz, on the Rhine, became the *Metropolis Germaniae*, the episcopal center of the right bank, the representative of *lingua theodisca*. The province did not cover Saxony, nor the lands of *lingua theodisca* on the left bank, but its creation preserved the *nominal* distinction between Gaul and German.[58] In so doing it left "unrevealed" the core regional economy that enabled the imperial project. Belgian historian Henri Pirenne argued famously that Islamic expansion had conditioned vigorous economic growth in northern Europe by isolating it from the Mediterranean. "Without Mohammed Charlemagne would have been inconceivable."[59] But modern historians, while acknowledging the brilliance of Pirenne's thesis, have reversed the causal arrows, ascribing Muslim incursions to Mediterranean economic collapse rather than vice versa. The change of perspective is important. The Greater Rhineland's relative prosperity, its relative immunity from the factors that engendered economic decay and demographic depression in the Mediterranean, bears witness to the region's privileged geography and its central importance to Europe's emergence as a political and discursive entity.

At the death of Justinian in 565, Europe's political economy was centered on a Mediterranean world in dramatic decline.[60] Commercial crops – wine and olive oil – were abandoned.[61] North Africa experienced a dark age that lasted until the tenth century.[62] By the middle of the seventh century Byzantium had lost Carthage to Islam. In 717 it blockaded shipping in the Mediterranean to defend Corsica, Sicily, and the Adriatic.[63] Byzantium entered a long eclipse as relations among peoples inhabiting the Mediterranean basin "were reduced to an almost 'prehistoric' scale."[64] By contrast, the evangelization of England in the seventh century and Frisia and Saxony in the eighth century had conditioned the rise of a "Mediterranean of the North" that encompassed the English Channel, the North Sea, and the Baltic. Roman roads remained passable along the middle Rhine and around Trier. The waterways of the Scheldt, the Rhine, and the Meuse linked markets in the lower Rhineland.

---

[58] Ewig, *Frühes Mittelalter*, pp. 112–13.
[59] Hodges and Whitehouse, *Mohammed, Charlemagne, and the Origins of Europe*, p. 4. See Davies, *Europe*, p. 258.
[60] Hodges and Whitehouse, *Mohammed, Charlemagne, and the Origins of Europe*, p. 91.
[61] Hodges and Whitehouse, *Mohammed, Charlemagne, and the Origins of Europe*, pp. 54–8.
[62] Hodges and Whitehouse, *Mohammed, Charlemagne, and the Origins of Europe*, p. 71.
[63] Doehaerd, *Le haut moyen âge occidental*, p. 275.
[64] Hodges and Whitehouse, *Mohammed, Charlemagne, and the Origins of Europe*, p. 75.

Wheat, wine, salt, and fish continued to make their way up and down the Rhine and Meuse rivers. Merchants established permanent settlements outside the walls of monasteries, "veritable cities unto themselves."[65] The monasteries were "the inheritors of Roman traditions, and they developed into the major *foci* of settlement in Carolingian Europe."[66] The most imposing among them – Corvey, St. Riquier, St. Denis – may have housed thousands of monks and lay workers. In Bonn, Mainz, and Worms, local markets arose near the cathedral. The royal court authorized *emporia* on the Scheldt at Valenciennes, Tournai, and Ghent, and on the Rhine at Mainz. Pepin established a monastery near Xanten that rejuvenated the city. Settlements at Namur, Huy, and Maastricht were granted mints. Cologne, Trier, and Mainz still produced glass. Trier still produced tableware.[67]

Innovations in northern agriculture contributed to the region's prosperity. Texts from the eighth century reveal the spread of a new triennial crop rotation that produced a second summer harvest in addition to the usual fall harvest. Summer wheat became common on the large estates of Neustria, the Rhineland, and Bavaria in the ninth century. A heavier plow, with coulter and moldboard, made it possible to cultivate the heavy bottomlands of humid northern Europe. A new type of harness that facilitated the improved plow's adoption was in use in Trier by the year 800. The plow, in turn, spurred smiths to supply coulters, spade-tips, and sickles.[68] The practice of using iron to shoe horses, known in Gaul since the fourth century BC, became widespread only in Carolingian times.[69] "By the early ninth century all the major interlocking elements of [an agricultural] revolution had been developed: the heavy plough, the open fields, the modern harness, the triennial rotation."[70] Together they engendered a more "balanced system of animal and cereal production ... [that] was apparently developed into a normal and accepted system during the seventh century in the Frankish heartland. It helps to account for the relative

---

[65] Riché, *The Carolingians*, p. 345.

[66] Hodges and Whitehouse, *Mohammed, Charlemagne, and the Origins of Europe*, p. 85.

[67] Ewig, *Frühes Mittelalter*, pp. 149–56. Regional production nevertheless followed the general trend away from the city and into the countryside.

[68] The plow was known to Pliny, who described its use by the peasants of Rhaetia, but it cannot safely be dated earlier than the sixth century. It became widespread only in the tenth century. Doehaerd, *Le haut moyen âge occidental*, pp. 67–9. Lynn White, *Medieval Technology and Social Change* (Oxford: Oxford University Press, 1962), pp. 41–57.

[69] Doehaerd, *Le haut moyen âge occidental*, pp. 84–5.

[70] White, *Medieval Technology*, p. 78.

prosperity and vigor of the Carolingian Age."[71] Technological innovation conditioned population growth and a new assault on forests. The capitulary of Aix of 801–813 enjoined the overseers of royal estates to clear and cultivate *ubicumque inveniunt homines utiles*. Deforestation was methodical in Germany, especially in Bavaria "where one can speak of a veritable colonizing thrust."[72] But it is also well attested along the middle Rhine and in northern Germany. It was also in the seventh and eighth centuries that the marshes of Flanders, west of the Scheldt, were drained.[73] Population growth, particularly in the Greater Rhineland, fueled "the bursting vitality of the Carolingian realm in the eighth century."

Frisian merchants plied the waters between the Rhineland and markets in the North Sea and the Baltic. Duurstede had been the chief *emporium* for Baltic trade since Frisia's conquest by Charles Martel, following the arrival of British missionaries in about 690. Frisian merchants traded at Birka, on Lake Mälar, and Old Uppsala, transporting goods across the Danish peninsula through the *emporium* of Haithabu. South of Duurstede, merchants made their way up the Rhine, Meuse, and Moselle rivers and traversed the northern French plain to the annual trade fair at St. Denis.[74] The Frisians also maintained permanent settlements in several interior sites: Duisburg, Xanten, Cologne, Strasburg, and Mainz.[75] Texts from the period show Frisians transporting cereals, wines from Alsace and the Rheingau, fabrics of various colors, especially Frisian cloth, and slaves. Wine sold as far away as Scandinavia. Treveran glass found markets in Sweden. Rhineland iron smiths learned to produce Frankish swords in quantity early in the seventh century and exported them widely.[76] Other goods included furs, jewelry, and querns (stone hand-mills) from the Rhine gorge south of Bonn, sorely needed in the stone-poor lowlands. The exporting mills and workshops were concentrated along the Meuse, Moselle, and Rhine. The left bank of the Rhine supplied wine while the right bank, especially the Main valley, supplied cereals.[77] Coins minted in the cities of the middle Rhine have turned up in Lyons, Vienne, Arles, Chur, Milan, Pavia, and Venice. But this commercial renaissance was

---

[71] White, *Medieval Technology*, p. 56. The spread of such innovations was gradual, however. Doehaerd does not date their generalization until the eleventh century and even later for the use of the horse to draw the plow.

[72] Doehaerd, *Le haut moyen âge occidental*, p. 106. See also Geary, *Before France and Germany*, p. 163.

[73] Doehaerd, *Le haut moyen âge occidental*, pp. 103–13.

[74] Riché, *The Carolingians*, p. 82.   [75] Riché, *The Carolingians*, p. 318.

[76] Geary, *Before France and Germany*, p. 101; Ewig, *Frühes Mittelalter*, p. 44.

[77] Ewig, *Frühes Mittelalter*, p. 149.

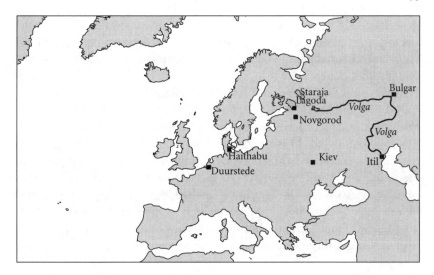

Figure 3.4 Duurstede, Haithabu, Mesopotamia

confined to the Greater Rhineland and its North Sea and Baltic markets. Central Gaul, the Loire valley, Aquitania, and Marseilles did not participate directly.[78]

The foundation of Baghdad in 762 whipped Frisian trade with the Baltic into a brilliant but short-lived frenzy. The extravagant construction of the capital of the caliphate was financed with silver from mines in Afghanistan.[79] The courts of Harun al-Rashid and al-Mamun stimulated commerce throughout the Indian Ocean, as evidenced by the ruins of vast *emporia* at Siraf on the Persian Gulf, Banbhore at the mouth of the Indus, and Kilwa in Tanzania. Archeological digs at Siraf reveal trade links with China, probably through Sri Lanka, and with Africa, as a source of wood, ivory, and slaves. Byzantium's conflict with the caliphate and the Roman west closed the Mediterranean to traffic at a time when demand at Baghdad was unusually high. That action enabled northern barbarian merchants to take the trade away from Mediterranean merchants.

Duurstede, founded at Pippinid initiative, was the Rhineland anchor of the northern trade route (see figure 3.4). At its zenith, the *portus* covered about 50 hectares, an area larger than most Carolingian cities. Its Baltic orientation, combined with the explosive growth the *portus*

[78] Ewig, *Frühes Mittelalter*, p. 147.
[79] Hodges and Whitehouse, *Mohammed, Charlemagne, and the Origins of Europe*, p. 129.

experienced in the period 780–820, attests to its mediation between the two upstart palaces at Aachen and Baghdad. The archeological trail leads from Duurstede to Haithabu, first mentioned in a text of 804, and one of the richest archeological digs in all of Europe. Graves near Haithabu contain important stores of Islamic coin, which are also found further east at Staraja Lagoda, near St. Petersburg, and Bulgar on the Volga. Along this route Scandinavian traders sold furs, slaves, and possibly metals to Muslim traders in exchange for silver dirhems. Merchants exchanged the silver for Rhineland manufactured goods in Haithabu and Duurstede. Archeologists suspect that Frisians – pagans or new converts to Christianity – melted the dirhems of the infidel before introducing them into the priestly principality.[80] Such "money laundering" would explain both the absence of dirhems in Carolingian digs and the mint at Duurstede.

Commercial decline and imperial collapse

The Greater Rhineland regional economy enabled European ontopology. Abbasid silver helped make European ontopology present to the imaginary by financing the *renovatio imperii* as cultural project, through church construction, the foundation of new monasteries, and the education and sustenance of an imperial clerical class. The collapse of that economy conditioned the empire's downfall. Under Harun al-Rashid, whose reign (775–809) was coterminous with that of Charlemagne, the caliphate's coffers overflowed and silver spilled into the Baltic. But the flow stopped. Political instability and extravagant spending – notably the construction of the lavish capital city at Samarra – caused economic ruin. Trade at Duurstede fell off rapidly after 830. Long-distance trade entered a steep decline. Hard times may have stimulated Viking raids, which, though documented as early as 789 when growing North Sea trade invited piracy, multiplied dramatically in the 830s. Northmen, especially Danes threatened by the decline of Baltic trade, pushed up the valleys of the Rhine, Scheldt, Somme, Seine, and Loire in search of booty. They sacked Paris, Utrecht, and other river cities. In 843, they mounted a full-scale invasion of Carolingian Europe, and established themselves securely in coastal areas. Duurstede's inhabitants fled in 863 never to return, following the seventh raid in a generation. Other

---

[80] Hodges and Whitehouse, *Mohammed, Charlemagne, and the Origins of Europe*, ch. 5. Cf. Doehaerd, *Le haut moyen âge occidental*, pp. 285–9. See also Riché, *The Carolingians*, p. 113.

emporia – Quentovic in France and Hamwih in England – were also abandoned. Mints shut down; money became rare.

The loss of income from caliphate trade contributed to the break-up of the empire by undermining the Carolingian court's powers of administration and legitimation through munificence. Charlemagne bequeathed his throne to an undisputed heir, Louis the Pious. But Louis was unable to do the same. He crowned his oldest son Lothair co-emperor according to a principle of primogeniture that was still alien to Frankish practice. Rebellions and counter-rebellions marked the reigns of Louis and Lothair. Lothair's brothers, Charles in Neustria and Louis in Germania, allied against him.[81] The Treaty of Verdun in 843 ratified the break-up of the empire by redistributing the core territories of the Rhine–Meuse basin among the three pretendants.[82] It acknowledged Charles' rule west of a line that followed the Scheldt, Meuse, Saône, and Rhône rivers. Louis acquired everything east of the Rhine and north of the Alps.[83] Lothair retained the imperial title and a strip of land that bordered the left bank of the Rhine and then extended south through Burgundy to Italy. The Rhine was once again a political frontier (see figure 3.5).

The settlement created an ontopological entity, Lotharingia, as nominal container of the Carolingian heartland. But Lotharingia would not endure. Lothair and his son, Lothair II, reigned briefly over this "middle kingdom." When Lothair II died without a legitimate heir, the Kingdom was surrendered to his uncles, Charles the Bald and Louis the German. The dioceses of Cologne, Strasburg, and Basle went to Louis, along with the eastern part of the diocese of Utrecht, Liège (east of the Meuse), Trier, Metz, Toul, Besançon, and Langres. Lotharingia was no longer the center of an empire, but a frontier province.

In a replay of Rome's last days, Charles III's brother-in-law Hugo allied with Norsemen to win possession of Lotharingia. The "Great Army" marched on Ghent in 878, laid waste the valleys of the Seine and the Rhine in 879, and in 881 marched up the Meuse and plundered

---

[81] Ewig, *Frühes Mittelalter*, p. 161. The Treaty of Verdun divided the Carolingian core, the territories of the Meuse and lower Rhine, among the three contending successors. Charlemagne, as he pondered at one time how to divide his empire among three sons, kept the core territory intact, from the Loire to the Elbe.

[82] Riché, *The Carolingians*, pp. 160–6.

[83] Riché, *The Carolingians*, pp. 166–7. Louis of Bavaria, who, from 833, referred to himself as *rex in orientalis francia* (Ewig, *Frühes Mittelalter*, p. 157), also received land on the left bank of the Rhine, particularly that which was tied to the trans-rhenish dioceses of Mainz, Worms, and Speyer. Ewig, *Frühes Mittelalter*, p. 160. Personal loyalties, not "national sentiment," determined the division.

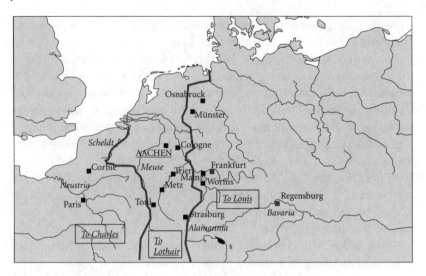

Figure 3.5 Disintegration of Carolingian space

Maastricht, Tongres, Liège, Cologne, the monastery of Stavelot-Malmédy, and the palace of Aachen itself.[84] In Trier, the Norsemen reduced the cathedral of Constantine – a survivor of the Frankish invasions of the fifth century – to rubble and ashes. Meanwhile, in the southeast, Magyars – horsemen of the steppes – cut a path of destruction up the Danube to the Rhineland and Burgundy. Dukes and counts – not the empire, diminished by fiscal distress and political dissension – rallied resistance. Arnolf, a Carolingian, count of Karnten and Pannonia, led a Bavarian contingent against the Vikings in 882. The count of Paris, not Carolingian, directed the defense against the Vikings in the same year. His success stirred the Neustrian nobility to elect him king in 888. Imperial notables would soon elect a Saxon duke to an imperial throne deprived of Neustrian lands.

Europe, as ontopology, faded from discourse as political space atomized. As the empire crumbled, the practice of vassalage, whereby men placed themselves in the service of powerful landlords in exchange for protection and land, the *beneficium,* preserved local political cohesion. The Celtic term *vassus* first appeared in eighth-century Bavarian and Alamannic texts. Charlemagne exploited the practice to forge the backbone of his army, the *vassi dominici*. The capitulary of Mersen (847) required all free men to pledge service, and the capitulary

---

[84] Ewig, *Frühes Mittelalter*, p. 149.

of Quierzy (877) made the *beneficium* hereditary. In the Greater Rhineland, the practice enabled a few powerful men, typically descended from counts established by the Pippinids, to impose feudal control over significant expanses of territory. New provinces, new named territories – ontopologies – like Flanders, emerged in texts of this period. Baldwin, count of Flanders, whose Alsatian ancestors were established in the province by Charlemagne, ruled as a veritable monarch, erecting wooden citadels at St. Omer, Bruges, Ghent, and Courtrai, expropriating lands abandoned by royal and ecclesiastical administrators, and protecting *emporia* that controlled trade with England. Robert the Strong leveraged fiefs granted to his family by Charlemagne into effective control of all of Neustria. In like manner, Richard, count of Autun, achieved supremacy in Burgundy. "Lothringen," however, would disaggregate into a half-dozen or more named counties and duchies: Brabant, Hainaut, Luxemburg, Zealand, Holland, Alsace, etc. Lorraine, Lotharingia's etymological survivor, would become a province of modest dimensions.

The Ottonian restoration

Europe as ontopology, in the ninth century as in the twentieth, was made accessible to discernment, was made "tangible" or "real," by the investment of Greater Rhineland wealth. The irony of European ontopology – then as now – is that it denies accessibility to the discernment, fails to make "tangible" or "real," the regional economy that sustains it. When Carolingian imperial discourse reemerged in the eleventh century, Greater Rhineland resources again lent "visibility" to that discourse, as is manifest in the grandiose cathedrals of Worms and Speyer. But Carolingian discourse conditioned the political atomization of Greater Rhineland space by enabling, as political ambition, quixotic attempts to transfer the center of imperial rule to Rome.

When the Carolingian dynasty fell in 911, the nobility offered the crown first to Conrad, duke of Franconia, then to Henry the Fowler, duke of Saxony.[85] Henry's territorial base extended north to the Weser, the Elbe, and the Mark of Branibor or Brandenburg. Henry sought to increase the resources needed to rule by annexing Haithabu and creating the port of Hamburg in order to tap the commercial riches of the Baltic. But Henry's Saxon roots did not spell disinterest in the

---

[85] Ewig, *Frühes Mittelalter*, p. 202.

Carolingian core. "Henry ... valued the former kingdom of Lothair as the richest and most developed in the west," and sought to assert his presence there by forming an alliance with one of its leading noble houses, the Matfriede, to which he awarded a countship and the bishoprics of Cologne, Liège, and Verdun.[86] He also crafted alliances upstream and downstream by granting dukedoms to allies in Frisia and Alsace. But Otto, Henry's son and successor, neglected Saxony and the interests of the local elite to pursue the mythical ideal of empire. He revived support among the high clergy by restoring immunities and naming bishops to local countships.[87] He led an army into Italy and won election as king of the Franks and the Lombards. Victory over the Magyars in 955 won him vast spoils and the title of emperor. He married his son, the future Otto II, to the daughter of the Byzantine emperor, Theophano, and established his court at Aachen. Otto III (983–991), the son of Theophano, pursued the imperial ideal with greater energy, electing residence at Rome, which he restored at great expense. Ottonian Germany experienced

> a full-fledged classic Renaissance, simultaneously Italian and Oriental, which, charging the Rhenish cities with productive energy, combined its effects with that of an active commercial rebound – of continuous passage of Byzantine goods through Passau, Lorch, Regensburg to Hamburg and Bremen; or merchandise from Italy through Augsburg and the Lech to Cologne and the Frisian shores.[88]

Otto III named his preceptor, Gerbert of Aurillac, to the papacy (as Sylvester II), in obedience to the Carolingian myth of imperial government in the name of Christ's vicar in Rome. He adopted Byzantine titles and rituals, and stamped coins with the motto *renovatio imperii romani*. His absence in Rome, however, enabled feudal lords in the north to consolidate their power. Fiefdoms became hereditary under Otto's successor Henry II (1002–24). The collateral Salian or Franconian line succeeded to the throne in 1024, with strong regional attachments to the middle and upper Rhine (see figure 3.6). The Salians, however, were equally enthralled by the myth of empire, though one more Augustan than Carolingian in inspiration. They reasserted imperial supremacy by creating *ministeriales*, bondsmen lacking the power and

---

[86] Riché, *The Carolingians*, pp. 243, 274.
[87] Riché, *The Carolingians*, p. 259. René Fédou, *L'état au moyen âge* (Paris: Presses Universitaires de France, 1971), pp. 66–7.
[88] Albert Demangeon and Lucien Febvre, *Le Rhin* (Paris: Armand Colin, 1935), p. 70.

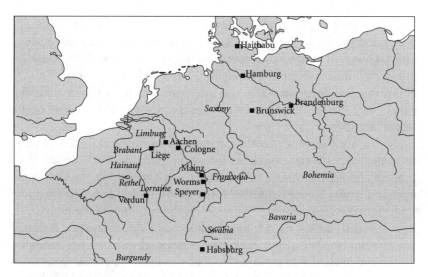

Figure 3.6 The Ottonian Rhineland

privileges of vassals who formed a royal administration that was "independent of the aristocracy and devoted to the service of the crown."[89] The Salians used Roman law, which experienced a revival in the eleventh and twelfth centuries, to seat the authority of the emperor as *dominus mundi*, without reference to Christianity or the papacy, even as they redefined the empire, in 1157, as "holy" and "Roman": *sacrum imperium romanum*.[90]

Conflict with the Church over the nomination of bishops brought the emperor into conflict with both the Church and the aristocracy for whom Church office was a source of power. At Henry's death, the Church, led by the archbishops of Mainz and Cologne, entered into discord with the Salians' collateral descendents, the Hohenstaufen of Swabia, over the imperial succession. Frederick I of Hohenstaufen, "Barbarossa" (1152–90), one of medieval Europe's most brilliant monarchs, attempted to consolidate a power base that associated his home province of Swabia with Burgundy and the commercial cities of Lombardy. To achieve this, he bought peace with the great feudal lords of the Greater Rhineland by multiplying their privileges and allowing

[89] Sidney Painter, *Medieval Society* (Ithaca: Cornell University Press, 1951), p. 96.

[90] Roland Axtmann, "State Formation and Supranationalism in Europe: The Case of the Holy Roman Empire of the German Nation," in Mabel Berezin and Martin Schain, eds., *Europe without Borders: Remapping Territory, Citizenship, and Identity in a Transnational Age* (Baltimore: Johns Hopkins University Press, 2003), p. 127.

them to appropriate imperial lands.[91] His successor, Frederick II, continued the policy of placating the German aristocracy in order to assert power in Rome, conceding privileges that turned the German monarchy into a simple presidency "of a federation of princes."[92] Following his death in 1250, an interregnum and conflict with the papacy saw the princes confiscate yet more power at the expense of the imperial crown.

By the late thirteenth century, the forces of dissolution in Germany had effectively overwhelmed the forces of centralization. "Rather than prepare the reconstitution of royalty, feudal monarchy [in Germany] opened the way to the definitive constitution of *Landeshoheit* (regional sovereignty). German unity shattered on the empire and the church."[93] Power settled among the regional aristocracies: the Ascanians, dukes of Saxony; the Guelfs in Brunswick; the Wittelsbachs in Bavaria. Administration and justice fell to the dukes, to the towns, and even to secret societies like the League of the Holy Court, the *Heilige Fehme*.[94] The Habsburgs, who succeeded to the imperial dignity, turned their back on imperial restoration in order to cultivate their dynastic territorial base along the upper Rhine. When victory over Bohemia established the dynasty on the Danube, they turned their attention to consolidating power there, where they would rule until World War I. The emperor Rudolf von Habsburg, by suffixing (in 1474) *nationis teutonicae* to *sacrum imperium romanum* – Holy Roman Empire of the German Nation – abandoned any imperial pretensions to universal, "European" rule.[95]

Enduring ontopologies

Carolingian ontopology survived the failure of the *renovatio imperii* as an ideal, an ambition, an abstraction, as the imaginary province of clerics and philosophers. Christianity, through conquest and evangelization, had reached the shores of the Baltic, the Vistula, and the lower Danube by the new millennium. The spatial referent of the signifier "Europe" grew to embrace all the lands won to the bishop of Rome,

---

[91] Painter *Medieval Society*, p. 109.   [92] Fédou, *L'état au moyen âge*, pp. 66–7.
[93] Fédou, *L'état au moyen âge*, pp. 66–7.   [94] Davies, *Europe*, p. 352.
[95] Bernard Guénée, *L'Occident aux XIVe et XVe siècles: les états* (Paris: Presses Universitaires de France, 1971), p. 68. Geoffrey Barraclough, *The Origins of Modern Germany* (New York: Norton, 1984), p. 368. A century thereafter, jurists referred to the German king as "emperor in his kingdom" in the French and English manner (see next chapter). Nevertheless, ambiguity and political tension endured. Emperor Sigismund, visiting Louis XI in Paris, presided over a session of the Paris Parlement, as emperor, without invitation.

including Scandinavia, Poland, Bohemia, and Hungary, though the use of the term receded before its synonym, *Christianitas.*[96] The expulsion of Muslim pirates from the Mediterranean in about 915 stimulated commerce and inaugurated a new era of city-building. By the end of the tenth century, Trier was actively restoring its antique splendor. Cologne was again a center of learning and culture.[97] Carolingian ontopology was kept alive as a visible ideal by the adoption of the *Westwerke* of the Carolingian cathedral as the model for the west fronts of Romanesque and Gothic cathedrals.[98]

But by the thirteenth century, theorists of European political unity had abandoned hope in imperial restoration and begun to consider the possibility of uniting western Christendom through a league of sovereign princes. Pierre Dubois, in a mid-thirteenth-century tract entitled *De Recuperatione Sanctae,* ostensibly an appeal to King Philip III of France to lead a crusade, concluded with an appeal to establish a European league of princes that would enforce peace through common military and economic action, and settle disputes by judicial methods.[99] Monarchs, inversely, worked to enlist the myth of Carolingian Europe to legitimate their territorial rule. In Germany, eleventh- and twelfth-century rivals for the imperial throne wrapped themselves in Carolingian iconography. On the feast of Pentecost, in the year 1000, Otto III "discovered" Charlemagne's tomb at Aachen and declared himself custodian of his "holy" relics. Frederick Barbarossa, who showed little political interest in the Rhineland, oversaw Charlemagne's canonization in Rome in 1165. Philippe Auguste, Capetian king of France, invented a Carolingian pedigree for himself. In 1369 the French king Charles V conferred the privileges of French subjects on the inhabitants of Aachen, keepers of the tomb of St. Charlemagne, "who formerly ruled the kingdom of France." In 1469, Louis XI declared the feast day of "Monseigneur Saint Charlemagne" to be a holiday in France.[100]

Charlemagne's empire endured as a kind of Camelot. Nineteenth-century French and German nationalists alike, but separately, hailed

---

[96] Christer Jönsson, Sven Tägil, and Gunnar Törnqvist, *Organizing European Space* (London: Sage, 2000), p. 115. William Chester Jordan, "'Europe' in the Middle Ages," in Anthony Pagden, ed., *The Idea of Europe* (Cambridge and New York: Cambridge University Press and Woodrow Wilson Center, 2002), p. 74.

[97] Riché, *The Carolingians*, p. 355.

[98] Riché, *The Carolingians*, pp. 341ff; Ewig, *Frühes Mittelalter*, pp. 120–5.

[99] See Derek Heater, *The Idea of European Unity* (New York: St. Martin's Press, 1992), ch. 1.

[100] Guénée, *L'Occident*, p. 119.

Charlemagne as their nation's king. "His example was invoked at Napoleon's imperial coronation in 1804. His portrait occupies the first place in the gallery of the German emperors painted in 1838–52 in the Kaisersaal at Frankfurt." "In 1943, when the Nazis formed a new division of French volunteers for the Waffen SS or in 1955 when the Council of Europe funded a Prize 'for services to the cause of European unity,' the organizers appealed to the same name – to Charlemagne."[101] Inversely, Lotharingia, though site of the regional economy that made possible the realization of Carolingian ontopology, did not survive as a named place. Just as the term "Austrasia" receded before the reality of empire, "Lotharingia" as a named place was lost in the atomization of imperial space following the empire's collapse. No *coup de force* "brought it to light" as motivating myth, as "geographical form," to inform and guide political ambition. Documents of the eleventh century still referred to Lotharingia's inhabitants as *Lotharienses, Lotharingi,* or *Lutharii,* and placed them beside other named provincials – Saxons, Bavarians, and Alamanni. The region's politics, made chaotic by the repeated interventions of princely rivals for the imperial throne, even gave birth to a "national" reputation. The Ottonian historian, Widukind of Corvey, described the *Lotharingi* as "Gens varia ... et artibus assueta, bellis prompta mobilisque ad rerum novitates."[102] But feudal atomization partitioned Lotharingia into a dozen counties and duchies: Brabant, Hainaut, Rethel, Limburg, and others. By the sixteenth century, all that remained of Lothringen/Lorraine was a duchy of undistinguished dimensions.

The Donation of Constantine, like Caesar's geography of Gaul, is a living text. In the twentieth century, Europe would become once again the site of a project of moral improvement. European federalist literature in the 1950s would evince a new "evangelism," or, perhaps more appropriately, a "salvationism." Europe, as surveyed from the Berlaymont – as from Aachen – would become once again a "principality of priests." Once again, however, the discourse of Europe, the Carolingian representation of political space, would, in the twentieth century as in the ninth, find no words with which to bring to presence, "to light," the regional economy that made that representation tangible.

---

[101] Davies, *Europe,* p. 307.
[102] Ewig, *Frühes Mittelalter,* p. 208; passage quoted on p. 210. "A fickle people, familiar with the higher pursuits but inclined and even prompt to revolution."

4

Anonymity and prosperity

Bruges' belfry and *hallen*, or cloth hall, stand as monuments to an urban civilization that flourished between Flanders and the Alps under the conditions of political atomization that characterized post-Ottonian western Europe. The belfry's dimensions and its centrality, in contrast to the more modest dimensions and curious eccentricity of the city's four churches, attest to the importance of commerce and capital in the life of the city (see plate 4.1). Bruges' Michelangelo, its Flemish primitives – Jan van Eyck, Hans Memling, Rogier van der Weyden – remind us of Flanders' vigorous participation in the gestation of Renaissance art and learning. Erasmus, the fifteenth century's most influential thinker, wandered the Greater Rhineland peripatetically from Rotterdam and Cambridge in the north to Basle and Freiburg in the south. The Mainz/Strasburg goldsmith Johannes Gutenberg assembled the contraption – Europe's first movable-type printing press – that would come to define modernity.

The next two chapters examine the interplay between regional economy and the political anonymity that was the enduring effect of *coups de force* that begat Greater Rhineland ontopology. The medieval Rhineland, in prosperity and power, was at least equal to the monarchical states – France, England, Denmark, and the Habsburg domain – that were beginning to take shape around it. But the region itself, though a "civilization" by its economic life, political organization, and even physical, architectural veneer, failed to coalesce as state. No discursive frame made the region present, as "place," as ontopology, to the political imagination. No discursive frame made it available, as space, to receive a state. The medieval Rhineland, at peak economic prosperity, was left, for want of a text, politically formless, a place without a name. Yet the legacy of this nameless *power* is potentially suggestive of political possibilities for EU construction in our time. Medieval Rhineland civilization, with its towns, merchants, diasporas, and non-hierarchical organization, offers itself to us not as a model to be imitated, but as a

Plate 4.1 Bruges' *hallen* and belfry

representation of space that is neither rent by a river frontier, nor dependent for its emergence on a signifier, "Europe," that gestures toward a vaguely perceived but contested future.

The Greater Rhineland economy

The technological inventiveness that characterized the Carolingian period survived the invasions, continued through the middle ages, and indeed through modernity into our time. By 1300, "the greatest agricultural novelty of the Middle Ages," the three-year crop rotation (two years of crops and one year of fallow), was widespread.[1] The triennial rotation made it possible to cultivate oats, which in turn made it possible to harness the faster and more powerful horse rather than oxen to the cart and the plow.[2] It also favored the cultivation of vegetable proteins: peas and beans. Georges Duby calculates that the agricultural yield doubled on average between the eleventh and fourteenth centuries.[3] Greater productivity enabled greater diversity of production, which resulted in growing consumption of meat and dairy products. For Lynn White, "it was not merely the new quantity of food produced by improved agricultural methods, but the new type of food supply which goes far toward explaining, *for northern Europe at least*, the startling expansion of population, the growth and multiplication of cities, the rise in industrial production, the outreach of commerce, and the new exuberance of spirits which enlivened that age."[4]

Agricultural innovation and growth spurred the reconstruction of Rhineland towns and the establishment of new towns in England, northern Germany, and the Rhine estuary. Although the *Vita Burchardi* reports of ninth-century Worms that "wolves penetrate and escape with impunity," Ermold the Black describes ninth-century Strasburg as flourishing with a new prosperity, hence its German name: "because it is the route whereby everyone passes." Mainz, Cologne, and Trier rebuilt their Roman walls.[5] The bishops of Mainz and Cologne authorized new markets. By the tenth century, merchant settlements were sprouting up again outside the walls of abbeys and castles, laying the foundation for new towns like Bruges, Ghent, and Ypres.[6] Namur, Huy, Liège, and Maastricht constructed stone bridges across the Meuse in the eleventh and twelfth centuries. New roads were laid as Roman roads were abandoned because they bypassed new settlements.

---

[1] Lynn White, Jr., *Medieval Technology and Social Change* (Oxford: Oxford University Press, 1962), p. 69.

[2] White, *Medieval Technology*, p. 62.

[3] Guy Fourquin, *Histoire économique de l'occident médiéval* (Paris: Armand Colin, 1969), p. 161.

[4] White, *Medieval Technology*, p. 76, emphasis added. Climate change, in the form of a global warming that lasted into the fourteenth century, is also credited for economic growth.

[5] Eugen Ewig, *Frühes Mittelalter*, vol. I part 2 of Franz Petri and Georg Droege, *Rheinische Geschichte* (Düsseldorf: Schwann, 1978), pp. 134, 149, 154–6.

[6] Renée Doehaerd, *Le haut moyen âge occidental* (Paris: Presses Universitaires de France, 1971), pp. 132–3. William Chester Jordan, "'Europe' in the Middle Ages," in Anthony Pagden, ed., *The Idea of Europe* (Cambridge and New York: Cambridge University Press and Woodrow Wilson Center, 2002).

The Christianization of Scandinavia in the tenth and eleventh centuries restored stability and trade to the Baltic and the North Sea. Merchants traveled long distances to attend trade fairs established under local military protection. Fairs in England (Winchester, Boston, Northampton, St. Ives, Stamford) dealt in wool; fairs in Flanders (Ypres, Lille, Bruges, Messines, Thourons) specialized in wool and fabrics; the fairs of Champagne (Lagny, Provins, Bar-sur-Aube, Troyes), heirs to the *portus* of the Remi, dealt in finished textiles. The counts of Champagne, and in 1209 the French monarch Philippe Auguste, placed merchants coming and going to the fairs of Champagne under their personal protection.

The growth of the towns in the twelfth and thirteenth centuries was prodigious. Trade with the eastern Mediterranean reopened. Merchants exchanged wood and slaves for Arabian, Indian, and Far Eastern spices – pepper, cinnamon, cloves, nutmeg, and cane sugar. Venice, Pisa, and Genoa flourished. Genoa dominated a northern trade route through Byzantium that avoided Muslim intermediaries. Its merchants imported wheat, salt, lumber, and furs from the northeast Mediterranean and Black Sea, and silk conveyed on the Mongolian Road. As the textile industry developed in the Rhine estuary, the Genoese cornered the market for alum, a component of textile dyes, which it marketed in Bruges. Venice, by contrast, traded with Muslim merchants primarily in Beirut and Alexandria, whence they imported cotton and spices, especially cinnamon, nutmeg, and pepper, for which Venice held a near-monopoly. Its principal export was silver mined in Bohemia and Serbia.[7]

By the twelfth century, the Italian commercial cities were dealing heavily in Flemish textiles, demand for which repaid the cost of shipping over long distances. The towns of Flanders were the leading edge of a manufacturing revolution that animated, even defined, the medieval Rhineland economy. The spinning wheel (the first machine to employ belt transmission) appeared in the thirteenth century, followed by the geared wheel and the watermill, used for fulling. Windmills became a characteristic feature of the lower Rhineland landscape at about this time.[8] The rise of manufacturing spurred long-distance trade in bulky commodities like cereals, wine, salt, wood, hay, fruit and wool, forcing trade to migrate from the inland fairs to sea and river ports,

[7] Jacques Heers, *L'Occident aux XIVe et XVe siècles* (Paris: Presses Universitaires de France, 1961), pp. 170–5.
[8] White, *Medieval Technology*, p. 88.

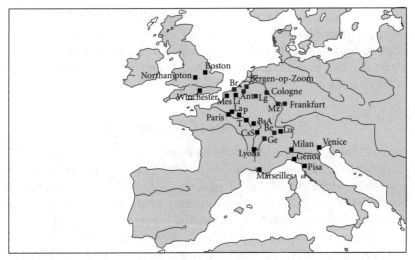

Br = Bruges Mes = Messines Li = Lille Ant = Antwerp Lg = Liège La = Langres P = Provins T = Troyes
BsA = Bar-sur-Aube CsS = Chalon-sur-Saône Ge = Geneva Be = Berne Lu = Lucerne Mz = Mainz

Figure 4.1 North–south trade patterns shift east, from fairs to towns, from Champagne to the Rhine

specifically from Champagne to the Rhine (see figure 4.1). Flemish merchants constructed canals, *vaarten*, to link waterways and seaports. Technical innovations improved shipping on the high seas. The astrolabe was in use by Italian seamen by the eleventh century, the compass by the twelfth.[9] The late thirteenth-century invention of the sternpost rudder gave ships greater stability and maneuverability. This period also saw the development of banks and credit.

New technologies drove a wedge between the towns of the commercial core, like Venice, Genoa, and Bruges, deeply invested in long-distance trade, and satellite towns of regional reach along the Adriatic, the western Mediterranean, and the North Sea. Flanders, especially Bruges, became the northern pole of a Eurasian economy based on manufacturing and long-distance trade. Venice and Genoa formed the southern pole. Between the poles, Berne and Lucerne opened new routes across the Alps, diverting trade from the Rhône, the Saône, Champagne and its fairs northward and eastward to the Rhine and its cities: Bruges, Antwerp, Bergen-op-Zoom, Frankfurt, and Geneva where the Greater Rhineland linked up with the Rhône. The duke of Burgundy tried to lure commerce back to the Saône–Rhône axis by establishing a fair at

[9] Fourquin, *Histoire économique*, pp. 170–1.

Chalon-sur-Saône. Louis XI of France established a fair at Lyons. Both efforts, though successful, were hampered by the fact that Marseilles, as seaport, was eccentric relative to eastern Mediterranean markets. Marseilles had become little more than a supplier of Provençal grains to Italy's commercial cities.

The monarchies of the periphery

Of the cities outside the Rhine corridor, only Paris matched (and in fact surpassed) the Rhineland cities in growth. Paris' dynamism, however, was the product not of commercial expansion, but of administrative power. That power in turn was the fruit of the king's efforts to free himself from the bonds of a feudal system that sustained but constrained monarchical authority. If monarchy survived the initial feudal atomization of Carolingian space, it was, writes the historian Sidney Painter, because "no one had any great interest in overthrowing it." But the kings, beginning with Louis VI (1108–37), asserted their independence by placing lesser nobles, clerics, and even merchants in positions of administrative and judicial power. They extended the reach of royal courts by establishing a high court, or *Parlement*, to hear appeals of decisions handed down by feudal lords or their agents. They strengthened royal authority in the provinces by sending permanent representatives, *baillis* and *seneschaux*, backed by itinerant *enquêteurs*, to assure the application of the king's decrees. By the late thirteenth century, administrators trained in Roman law at Bologna and Montpellier were defending the judicial supremacy of the royal courts. Endemic war-making engendered permanent taxation. Charles V, in the early phases of a Hundred Years War (1338–1453) that was as much a struggle between monarchy and nobility as between the rival dynastic houses of Capet and Lancaster, prolonged emergency fiscal impositions *sine die* and endowed state finances with the organization they would retain until the 1789 Revolution. French kings, however, like other European monarchs, adopted practices that had been elaborated by the city-states of northern Italy, especially Milan, Venice, and Florence, to reform and modernize their administrations. Charles VII (1429–61) gathered representatives of the various social strata of the realm, the "Estates General," to ratify the principle of permanent taxation. Regular fiscal income enabled him to establish a permanent army, composed of elite cavalry, a professional infantry housed in barracks, an auxiliary force of archers, and artillery. Fiscal stability made it possible to hire mercenaries to reduce towns and fortifications to submission through long sieges.[10] Louis XI (1461–83) ratified yet again the principle of permanent taxation and further rationalized the financial administration, using the income to develop a costly royal artillery. When the Estates General met in 1469 – their last meeting before the Revolution – they surrendered all financial and legislative authority to the monarch. Louis took the decisive step of requiring his *grands seigneurs* to conduct themselves not as loyal vassals, obligated by bonds of personal fidelity, but as loyal subjects, obligated by the law of the realm.[11]

Administrative needs resulting from permanent taxation and the management of a standing army gave rise to a new socio-professional class of bureaucrats recruited from the lettered bourgeoisie. The bureaucracy grew rapidly. France numbered four *conseillers aux requêtes* in 1314, but twenty-nine in 1343; twenty *conseillers au parlement* in 1314, but sixty-two in 1343; ten *maîtres des comptes* in 1338, but nineteen in 1484; ten *notaires* in the chancellery in 1286, but 120 by the end of the fifteenth century.[12] By the middle of the fifteenth century, the royal chancellery was sending out 17,000–18,000 sealed letters annually, copies of which had to be preserved in archives. Administrators and archives needed work- and storage-space. State development pitted bureaucrats against masons in a race without end. The apposition in 1370 of the clock seen today on the northeast tower of the Palais de la Cité publicized both the timeless and the regulatory character of the new monarchical state. The concentration of wealth made Paris an important financial center, brimming with Italian expatriates. The Seine was the conduit of a vibrant trade in wine that linked the vineyards of Burgundy and the Loire valley with the capital and foreign markets. Beyond the basin of the Seine, however, France participated little in the kind of manufacturing and long-distance trade that characterized the Rhineland core.

Administrative rationalization presented a semantic challenge. There was no word for "state." Scholastics used *civitates et regna*, whence Machiavelli derived *città e regni*. But whereas *civitas* captures the institutional permanence of the city, *regna*, an accusative neuter plural, an object, assumes the existence of a subject. It assumes the action of a flesh and blood *rex*. *Regnum* does not convey the idea of institutional permanence, that is,

---

[10] Sidney Painter, *Medieval Society* (Ithaca: Cornell University Press, 1951), p. 17.
[11] Bernard Guénée, *L'Occident aux XIVe et XVe siècles: les états* (Paris: Presses Universitaires de France, 1971) p. 229.
[12] René Fédou, *L'état au moyen âge* (Paris: Presses Universitaires de France, 1971), pp. 129; Guénée, *L'Occident*, pp. 195–201.

of a kingdom unaffected in its existence by the disappearance of its mortal king. Thirteenth-century jurists experimented with *status coronae*, where *status* referred to the "state" or "condition" (as in "state of the Union") of the "crown." One also finds *status imperii* and *status rei publicae*. But such references to empire and republic left unexpressed the non-imperial, non-republican (in the Roman sense) legitimacy of the royal monarch. In the second half of the same century French and Italian jurists began to use *status regis*, the state or fortune of the king. By the end of the fifteenth century, writers converged on *status regis et regni*, the "state" of the king and kingdom. Finally, exhausted, they settled on the abbreviated *status* to designate whatever it was they were trying to designate, and the modern state, as ontological entity, was born.[13]

The emergence of the medieval monarchies subverted the Carolingian ideal of European imperial unity. Kings laid claim, in the territories they ruled, to the functions, rights, and duties of the emperor. Louis VI, in the early eleventh century, had already styled himself *imperator franciae*; Henry I of England was *rex, legatus apostolicus, patriarcha, imperator*. Innocent III, in 1202, declared the king of France to be without secular superior (*superiorem in temporalibus minime recognoscat ...*). In the second half of the thirteenth century, jurists converged on the formula: *rex in regno suo est imperator* (the king is emperor in his kingdom).[14] Legal scholarship, meanwhile, resurrected the Roman ideal of secular rule, as opposed to the Carolingian ideal of a sacred *imperium*.

The towns of the core

The Greater Rhineland's urban civilization, beyond the reach of the monarchical states that were taking shape on the periphery, was one of towns, merchants, diasporas, and non-hierarchical organization that looks familiar when set beside the *Lebenswelt* of the modern EU citizen. It emerged in the eleventh and twelfth centuries, when towns everywhere were voicing demands for freedoms and privileges. Pisa petitioned the pope in 1075 to ratify its municipal code. The French crown, cultivating allies against the landed barons, granted charters to the towns of Le Mans, St. Quentin, and Beauvais in the late eleventh

---

[13] See also Fédou, *L'état au moyen âge*, pp. 5–7; Guénée, *L'Occident*, pp. 60–2: *stato* for Machiavelli almost always refers to the power of command, not to the institutions that supply the power.

[14] Guénée, *L'Occident*, pp. 63–8.

century. Venice forced the Byzantine emperor to recognize its autonomy. St. Omer, Bruges, and Ghent in Flanders, and Lübeck and Hamburg in the Holy Roman Empire all received charters in the twelfth century.[15] In the thirteenth century, the towns of the northern Italian and Rhineland core began to band together to defend their new autonomy. The towns of the periphery, by contrast, often (not always) welcomed monarchical rule. The vassals of the bishops in Italy took advantage of the long conflict between pope and emperor to renounce their obedience and form sworn associations, or communes, which turned Lombardy into a land of city-states governed by the urban nobility. When the emperor Frederick I Barbarossa challenged the autonomy of the towns, they formed the Lombard League and defeated Frederick at the battle of Legnano in 1176. In Germany, when interregnum weakness (1250–72) emboldened barons to assert local power, the Rhineland towns, particularly those proximate to the middle Rhine heartland of the Hohenstaufen dynasty, banded together in 1254 to form the League of Rhineland Cities for the "salvation of the people and the country" (see figure 4.2). The League's ostensible purpose was to protect the empire against aristocratic rebellion by opposing the reforms of the Diet of Mainz, which augmented the powers of the German princes. In doing so, however, they were acting to safeguard Rhenish trade, threatened by the multiplication of duties and taxes by barons now unconstrained by imperial law.

> If the cities of the Rhine could acknowledge and serve the cause of a superior political formation situated above them – it was the empire, the germanic Holy Roman Empire to which they were attached by affection; to this cosmopolitan empire that gestured toward Italy and the Burgundian lands as well as the Rhineland and the lands that were properly Germanic. It was to this empire, whose principal strength was located by a twelfth-century chronicle in the country that extends from Basle to Mainz: *ubi maxima vis regni esse noscitur.*[16]

But as Geoffrey Barraclough observes, when the towns "proclaimed their desire to have the emperor as lord, this often meant, by the fourteenth century, little more than a desire to have no effective lord at all."[17]

---

[15] Norman Davies, *Europe: A History* (Oxford: Oxford University Press, 1996), p. 342; Guénée, *L'Occident*, pp. 235–7.

[16] Albert Demangeon and Lucien Febvre, *Le Rhin* (Paris: Armand Colin, 1935), pp. 81–2. "Where the authority of dominion (or kingly government) is most greatly acknowledged."

[17] Geoffrey Barraclough, *The Origins of Modern Germany* (New York: Norton, 1984), p. 335.

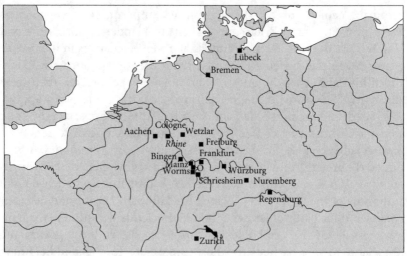

Legend: O = Oppenheim

Figure 4.2 The League of Rhenish Cities of 1254

Outside the Greater Rhineland core, the towns, adapted to monarchical rule more readily. Kings enrolled them as allies in their struggle to short-circuit agrarian lords and win administrative and judicial control over the countryside. They did so in part by taxing commercial transactions between the towns and their hinterland, which freed them from military dependence on their vassals by enabling them to support standing armies or rent mercenaries. As the king amassed military power he tamed the countryside, further facilitating the expropriation of revenues. Unlike the towns of the commercial core, which did business primarily with one another, the towns of the periphery did business primarily with their hinterlands.

> Only those shipping or receiving goods in bulk, to or from distant points of intensive production or wholesale distribution, [were] involved in [long-distance] commerce. The traffic in luxuries that developed between the cities of northern Italy and northern Europe originally flowed through the geographic corridor that lies between the Rhône–Seine systems to the west and the Elbe to the east. Within this broad Rhineland path, new towns tended to be commercial, but to either side, their counterparts were seldom more than agricultural market centers.[18]

[18] Edward Whiting Fox, *History in Geographic Perspective: The Other France* (New York: Norton, 1971), p. 45.

Differences of economic activity fostered (but did not determine) differences in politics. Burghers of the periphery, whose commercial horizons were restricted, found service in state administration attractive. Burghers of the core, by contrast, pursued profits from long-distance trade and opposed the taxes and mercantilist restrictions that the monarchs typically imposed.

The distinction between the two kinds of political economy remains visible today in the very physical appearance of the two kinds of town. As the historian Edward Fox writes: "any alert observer driving across France and into the lower Rhineland will be struck by the physical difference between the towns of the two areas," for "many of the most famous commercial cities . . . were located between, rather than within, the rising monarchies."[19] The French monarchy celebrated its triumphs in Gothic. Brilliant, striking, rich, and royal, the Gothic cathedral that dominates so many French towns celebrated not only divine glory but monarchical power.[20] With the exception of Strasburg and Cologne, the cathedral towns of the Rhineland eschewed the new style and preserved Ottonian Romanesque. Inversely, one seldom encounters in France the great market halls that dominate the trading cities of the corridor. "In the towns of northern France and Flanders, the great market hall, like the village church in the countryside, rising in the main square, attracted all social and political activities." It served as depot, commercial center, and meeting place for the merchant guild and town government. The towns adorned the guild and market halls with magnificent clocks and belfries (*Bergfriede*: towers of peace, tranquility, harmony, but also the medieval watchtower or *donjon*) that exalted their merchant civilization. "The market hall, with its belfry, its bells, its clock, signified the vital heart of a vast urban complex toward which everything converged."[21]

The civilization of the merchant towns was polyglot and multicultural. The towns of Italy vied to lure weavers from Flanders and Brabant, silk workers from Luca, goldsmiths from Germany. The merchant elite in Italy was generally local, but much of the working population, skilled and unskilled, came from afar.[22] In the trading towns of the Rhineland

---

[19] Fox, *History in Geographic Perspective*, pp. 33, 55.

[20] See Henry Adams' 1905 classic *Mont Saint-Michel and Chartres* (New York: Heritage, 1957).

[21] Both passages quoted in Heers, *L'Occident*, p. 100. Town halls, as seats of town government, as found in Italy, were introduced to Bruges, Ghent, Brussels, and other towns of the north only in the sixteenth century.

[22] Heers, *L'Occident*, p. 273.

corridor, by contrast, foreign businessmen – Italian, German, or Flemish merchants, financiers, and bankers – constituted large, prosperous, generally organized, and often segregated communities that convened and deliberated in their own meeting houses.[23] Many of the Rhineland cities of Roman foundation, moreover, were the site of powerful archdioceses, whose universities drew students from far and wide. The University of Cologne matriculated students from Langres, Nancy, Lunéville, Toul, Valenciennes, and Metz. Cambrai sent as many students as a nearby Rhenish diocese. Reims, Amiens, and especially Liège, and every Rhenish city – Chur, Constance, Basle, Strasburg, Speyer, Worms, Mainz, Trier, Utrecht, and of course Cologne – are represented.[24] Artists solicited contracts and patronage in these merchant and episcopal cities, migrating from Holland and Flanders to Cologne, Mainz, and Strasburg. Foreign merchants everywhere, by their very presence, their purchases, their commercialization of art, and the fads they initiated, animated cultural as well as commercial life. Italians and Frenchmen of the Midi brought home large quantities of art from the towns of Flanders. The role of German merchants appears to have been especially important.[25] Artistically, the towns of southern Germany were a second Italy. "Foreigners marvel repeatedly (*s'exclament à l'envi*) at the wealth, the power of these Rhineland cities."[26]

The towns of the commercial core, from Venice to Bruges, were populous. Milan and Venice probably numbered more than 200,000 inhabitants in 1300. Ghent and Bruges numbered about 50,000. The old Roman *civitas* of Cologne probably had a population of 40,000. Arras, Ypres, Lübeck, and Strasburg may have numbered 20,000. Outside the core, only the capital cities of Paris, with a population of 200,000, and London, with 40,000, compared.[27] New walls had to be erected in the mid-fourteenth century at Leuven, Ghent, and Brussels to make room for the growing population.[28]

Because of the striking economic, political, and even civilizational differences between the Rhineland core and its periphery, it has been tempting to assign causal importance to political economic difference. Stein Rokkan, in an analysis that has become a classic, observed that state formation occurred at the "periphery of a network of strong and independent cities." The fortune of the monarchical states, he

[23] Heers, *L'Occident*, p. 338.   [24] Demangeon and Febvre, *Le Rhin*, pp. 86–7.
[25] Heers, *L'Occident*, p. 340.   [26] Demangeon and Febvre, *Le Rhin*, p. 83.
[27] Fourquin, *Histoire économique de l'occident médiéval*, p. 233.
[28] Heers, *L'Occident*, p. 108. Genoa, in contrast, covered only 120 hectares.

theorized, depended on their ability to control and to exploit the movement of goods and persons across frontiers. They were therefore opposed by the merchant city-states whose prosperity was predicated on the ease and openness of such movement. The resultant incompatibility of interests nourished the desire of monarchs to extend their control, and, wherever "the cities were weak and isolated, the territorial centralizers succeeded."[29] The historian Edward Whiting Fox accounted for the same observation by contrasting the military logic of territorial control with the commercial logic of market access. Mounted warriors needed land to support horses and armies, whereas town merchants needed rivers and roads for commerce. Under feudalism, the two kinds of political economy coexisted peacefully. "More important than the precise nature of these characteristics within either of the two major types of society ... [was] their mutual independence. Even as they evolved into increasingly complex structures, they manifested no tendency to lose their separate identities."[30] Because the political economy of the commercial town was dominant in the Rhineland corridor, territorial consolidation did not occur there. Consolidation yielded no profits. Disinterest in the hinterland distinguished the Rhineland commercial town "from the self-sufficient agricultural market towns [of the periphery]."[31] The Rhineland towns bound themselves by ties of interdependence with one another in an expandable network.

But such attempts to explain Rhineland specificity by political economy ignore the fact that the towns and commerce of the Greater Rhineland have always flourished regardless of political organization. The towns appreciated and defended their autonomy, but they had already proved their ability to flourish as subject cities of vast territorial dominions, Roman, Carolingian, and Ottonian. With the exception of the eighteenth century, examined in a subsequent chapter, the Greater Rhineland *always* displayed economic dynamism. As for the towns' supposed disinterest in territorial control, one should recall that in Italy the towns struggled to carve out territorial city-states endowed with a hinterland, a *contado*. The great merchant towns of the north, as they defended their immunities from monarchical jurisdiction and taxation,

---

[29] Stein Rokkan, "Dimensions of State Formation and Nation-Building: A Possible Paradigm for Research on Variations within Europe," in Charles Tilly, ed., *The Formation of National States in Western Europe* (Princeton: Princeton University Press, 1975). Passages quoted on pp. 576–7, 589.

[30] Fox, *History in Geographic Perspective*, p. 38.

[31] Fox, *History in Geographic Perspective*, p. 37.

sought simultaneously to impose an organized monopoly on European markets, a kind of territorial control. The Hanseatic League, examined below, assembled an impressive navy to wrest territorial control of the Baltic from the king of Denmark. "Territorial" ambition, moreover, produced stable alliances with royal courts. The Hansa enjoyed good relations with the English monarchy. The territorial principality of the Teutonic Order in Prussia was admitted to the League. Finally, when social discontent in the weaving towns, bred by the growth of a proto-industrial, indebted urban proletariat, stirred political disorder, the merchant elite appealed to the territorial prince for help.[32] The merchant elite of the Flemish towns had a complicated relationship with the dukes of Burgundy, *against* whom they defended their autonomy, but *with* whom they coerced social peace in the city.

Just as dynamism in the Greater Rhineland has its source in the *fact* of physical geography, not in some deterritorialized logic of political economy type, so does town autonomy – in the Middle Ages – have its source in ontopological myth, not simply or solely in political struggle. Ontopology lured the imperial dynasties to rule from Rome, which, in that quixotic venture, facilitated and approved feudal atomization in the Greater Rhineland. Inversely, ontopology – the existence of a place called Gallia, now recast as Francia (see below) – lent legitimacy to the French monarch's efforts to counter feudal freedoms with adminis-trative and judicial constraints. Ontopology as "myth of place" conferred an aura of legitimacy and "naturalness," as understood by natural law theologians, on France and the empire, and lent legitimacy and even sanctity to kings and emperors. The French king, up to the time of Louis XIV, was popularly thought to possess healing powers. The mythological construction of named places legitimated social hierarchies. Warriors, whose divine calling was to protect natural, named political space and bring justice to that space, showed disdain for merchants, who moved stuff for profit. The career of the dukes of Burgundy, discussed below, exemplifies that disdain. Habits of thought inaugurated by the *coups de force* that begat Gallia, Germania, and the European *imperium* retained their authority as the Greater Rhineland economy reached the zenith of its prosperity. The Rhineland as Europe's commercial core generated tremendous resources, cultural influence, and political energy. But its ability to coalesce as a politically organized territorial entity was undermined, despite cultural and economic

[32] Heers, *L'Occident*, pp. 277–82. See Fourquin, *Histoire économique*, pp. 236, 249.

homogeneity, by the non-existence of a word – a name – that brought the region "to daylight" in speech as a political corporeality. The name the towns used, Germania, like "Europe," or *imperium*, obfuscated specificity of place by gesturing toward a broader, vaguely delimited and atomized territorial entity.

Bruges, Cologne, and the Hansa

The careers of the Hanseatic League and the duchy of Burgundy shed light on the relationship between the Rhineland towns and state consolidation, and between political economy and the mythical discourse in which politics was framed. They illuminate the importance of linguistic habit, of place name, in the fracturing of European space and the ratification of the Rhine as frontier.

The Hansa's roots go back to the "Frankish" realm's eastward expansion that from the eleventh to the fourteenth century saw thousands upon thousands of Westphalians, Rhinelanders, Hollanders, Flemings, and Franconians migrate to new settlements in the east. The Teutonic Knights, a north German crusading order, shifted its mission from the Holy Land to the eastern marches of the Baltic in order to undertake the systematic conquest, colonization, and evangelization of Prussia. Merchants followed soldiers and peasants as colonization engendered regional markets and new towns like Breslau, Dresden, and Wismar.[33] Commerce in the Baltic spawned new ports at Rostock, Stettin, and Stralsund. In 1201 Albert, bishop of Bremen, founded Riga as a missionary and commercial outpost and created a military order, the *fratres militiae Christi*, to defend it. Riga brought merchants into contact with Russian towns along the upper Dvina and with Smolensk on the Dniepr, resurrecting the trade route to the Black Sea and Mesopotamia.

During this same period "Lotharingian" merchants in the eleventh century and "Flemish" merchants thereafter (the distinction is purely nominal) began to displace "Frisian" merchants from their dominant position on the North Sea. "Flemish" merchants from the "French"-speaking towns of the Meuse – Huy, Liège, Nivelles, and Dinant – played a significant role in this development. Merchants from Cologne and Bremen entered the fray following the bishop of Cologne's authorization of an important staple market in the twelfth century. In

---

[33] See Fourquin, *Histoire économique*, pp. 131–3; Heers, *L'Occident*, p. 103.

1161 merchants of the German empire (which at the time would have excluded merchants from the French duchy of Flanders, including Bruges) created the United Gotland Travelers of the Holy Roman Empire to police the Baltic. In 1237, merchants from Visby gained admission to markets in England and French Flanders. By the thirteenth century Cologne and Bruges, in the west, were well connected by overland routes, which Cologne's merchants were quick to dominate, with the new towns of the Elbe, Oder, and Vistula.

In the mid-thirteenth century the countess of Flanders conferred privileges on imperial merchants in Bruges that included favorable customs duties, legal rights, and, later, a voice in city government. The merchants rewarded the countess' liberality by establishing a *Kontor*, or clearing house, at Bruges in 1252, which rapidly became the command center for the whole of North Sea trade. At about the same time, the English court lured merchants from Cologne and Dinant to London to establish a second *Kontor*. Merchants later created a third *Kontor* at Novgorod and a fourth at Bergen. The four *Kontore* gave the merchants a management structure that enabled them to dominate northern European commerce.

The development of town leagues at about the same time reinforced the merchant towns' economic power. The Rhenish league was established in 1254. A Westphalian league and a Saxon league were formed in 1256. That same year saw the creation of a league of Wendish towns (Lübeck, Stralsund, Wismar, Rostock, and Lüneburg), built on the foundation of a 1241 association between Lübeck, Hamburg, and Kiel. Lübeck joined forces with Riga and Visby in the late thirteenth century to combat piracy. Wendish, Saxon, and Westphalian leagues consulted on matters of mutual interest, not merely security but joint action to coerce non-member towns to grant them rights of anchorage, storage, residence and local immunity by threatening them with commercial boycott, or *Verhansung*. In England in 1282, German merchants of the Westphalian and Wendish leagues joined their Cologne partners in wresting from the crown a veritable monopoly on wool exports (see figure 4.3).[34]

The leagues organized the merchant cities of northern Germany and the Greater Rhineland into three, sometimes four, regional organizations, called *hansa*, each of which was more or less autonomous. Lübeck provided a general secretariat and a legal code, but there were no central

---

[34] Heers, *L'Occident*, p. 180.

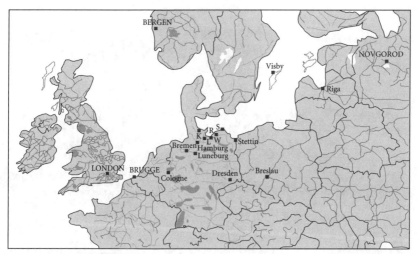

Legend: K=Kiel L=Lübeck R=Rostock S=Stralsund W=Wismar <u>LONDON</u> = *Kontor*

Figure 4.3 The Hansa

Hansa officials apart from the consulates to the four *Kontore* and the annual herring market at Fasterbo.[35] The Hansa organized commerce in the North Sea and Baltic, between the eastern reaches which provided timber, pitch, tar, turpentine, iron, copper, livestock, salt fish, leather, hides, wool, grain, and beer, and the west, especially Flanders, which supplied textiles and spices from Venice.

The twelfth-century Frisian invention of the *kogge* facilitated transport of bulky, heavy cargoes both on the high seas and up the Rhine to Cologne.[36] But trade in cheap, bulky commodities, which barely repaid the risks of shipping, required more than large vessels. It required market regulation, which in turn required political organization, which in turn required the coordinating power of a metropolitan core. That metropolitan core was Bruges. The fine textiles produced by Flemish industry, and which represented more than 75 percent of Flemish exports, served as a kind of international currency. Bruges' importance as a textile town attracted Italian, Iberian, French, and English merchants. With the establishment of the *Kontor*, Bruges became the chief

---

[35] Heers, *L'Occident*, pp. 181–2. "Vers 1400, on estimait la pêche de Scanie à environ huit mille tonnes de harengs, soit plusieurs fois la pêche actuelle."

[36] The *kogge*, at 200 metric tonnes, multiplied by ten the capacity of previous boats. In the fourteenth century the larger *julk* and in the fifteenth the three-masted, 400 tonne Mediterranean *krawel* (or caravelle) replaced the *kogge*. Philippe Dollinger, *The German Hansa* (Stanford: Stanford University Press, 1970), pp. 141–2.

Figure 4.4 The Cologne Hansa

commercial center of the North, the clearing house for grain and German beer, the import market for spices and fruits, the northern hub of the Genoese alum trade, and the market that organized commerce throughout the North Sea.[37] Bruges' importance as a commercial center and clearing house enabled it to prosper long after textile manufacturing had disseminated throughout Flanders and Brabant, and even after silting in the River Zwynn closed its port to large cargo.[38]

Cologne was also a central player in the Hansa. Until the middle of the fourteenth century, it was the only town on the Rhine to hold Hansa membership. But the Hansa, at Cologne's demand, admitted other Rhine towns – Duisburg, Düsseldorf, Solingen, and Neuss, and Dinant, Cologne's "French"-speaking partner on the Meuse (see figure 4.4). By the middle of the fifteenth century, about twenty towns of the lower Rhine basin belonged to Cologne's regional association. Cologne, like Bruges, wielded great power, in part thanks to its control of the London *Kontor* and its relationship with the English court, and in part thanks to its location on the Rhine, which made it the supplier of Rhine and Burgundy wines to wealthy markets – capital cities like London or other merchant cities of the core. Wine, like luxury textiles, was a universally accepted medium of exchange. Cologne's Rhenish situation also placed it astride both land and water routes, endowing it with a

[37] Heers, *L'Occident*, pp. 183–4.   [38] Dollinger, *The German Hansa*, pp. 246–8.

rich array of interests that allowed it to shift coalitions and act as power-broker.[39]

The power to make and unmake coalitions was important. The Hansa's influence depended on its cohesion. When the king of Denmark captured Visby and tried to break the Hansa's herring monopoly, the Hansa summoned a diet to Cologne, at which seventy-seven towns joined to form the Cologne Confederation. They pooled resources, built a navy, and waged war. The Peace of Stralsund (1370) gave the Hansa not only control over traffic between the North Sea and the Baltic, but veto power over succession to the Danish throne. After its victory the Cologne Confederation quickly lapsed. But in the 1390s the Hansa again assembled a fleet of eighty-four ships and 4,000 men to clear the Baltic of pirates.[40]

Despite the victory against Denmark, political disorganization placed the Hansa at a disadvantage as monarchical states began to challenge its monopoly power. The duke of Burgundy's expanding territorial base in the lowlands, in particular (see below), threatened the Hansa by subverting its influence in Flanders. On several occasions the Hansa, in disagreement with Bruges' policies, threatened to move its *Kontor* elsewhere.[41] The Hansa reduced Bruges to submission in 1388 with just this kind of threat. But the same threat proved empty in 1450 when Burgundy, whose power now extended across the entire Rhine–Meuse estuary, militarily opposed a threat to move the *Kontor* to Utrecht. Although negotiations ended in compromise, "it was the general opinion that the community had suffered a defeat ... The unpalatable truth was that the transfer of the *Kontor* and even a blockade, weapons so effective in earlier times, were useless against a power which had control over the greater part of the Low Countries."[42]

Burgundy's active support of Dutch manufacturing and trade was probably the single most important factor in the Hansa's decline. When weavers in Flanders forced their way into town government and regulated the industry to their advantage, merchants, to escape regulation, diffused looms throughout Hainaut, Brabant, and Holland, and eastward to Liège and Maastricht.[43] Holland's textile industry developed rapidly, especially in Delft and Leyden. The duke of Burgundy chartered associations of

---

[39] The value of Lübeck's inland trade with Cologne, Frankfurt, and Nuremberg exceeded that of its maritime trade. Dollinger, *The German Hansa*, p. 224.

[40] Dollinger, *The German Hansa*, p. 80.

[41] Dollinger, *The German Hansa*, pp. 48, 62, 76–7.

[42] Dollinger, *The German Hansa*, p. 302.   [43] Fourquin, *Histoire économique*, pp. 360–7.

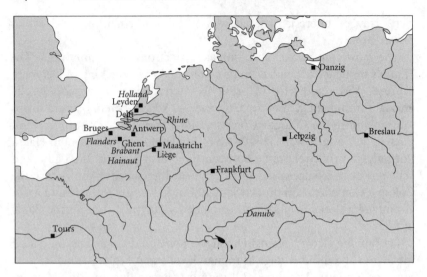

Figure 4.5 Challenge to the Hansa

Dutch merchants to market Dutch textiles in Bruges, Antwerp, and even Leipzig and Breslau (see figure 4.5). By the early fifteenth century, Amsterdam and Rotterdam were sending merchant fleets to Norway, Danzig, and the towns of the Baltic.[44] English merchants mounted a similar challenge to Hanseatic power. "Merchant Adventurers," primarily from Bristol, complained to their king of the unfair and "unpatriotic" privileges granted to German merchants. The king annulled those privileges in 1447.[45] Soon thereafter, English ships were also plying the waters of the Baltic.

Loosely organized and traversed by divergent interests, the towns of the Hansa were unable to muster a unified response to either the Dutch or the English challenge. Danzig imposed an embargo on Dutch trade, but the Grand Master of the Teutonic Order and the Livonian towns welcomed the Dutch monopoly-busters.[46] Cologne, with land routes across the great plain and export markets in England, refused to comply with Hanseatic efforts to close Flemish markets to English exports. Cologne merchants peddled English textiles up and down the Rhine valley, at the fair in Frankfurt, in the towns of southern Germany, and along the Danube. When the Hansa tried to shut them down, the city appealed to the duke of Burgundy, who, no friend of the Hansa, sided

---

[44] Heers, L'Occident, p. 188.   [45] Heers, L'Occident, p. 187.
[46] Dollinger, The German Hansa, p. 195.

with Cologne (1467). When war broke out between England and the Hansa, Cologne remained neutral. The English rewarded the city by restoring its privileges in London. The duke of Burgundy, in turn, granted safe passage to Cologne merchants peddling English wool in Flanders. The Hansa formally excluded Cologne in 1471, but was later forced to concede to the Dutch the right to trade in the Baltic.[47] The French crown, meanwhile, began to contest Burgundian prosperity with mercantilist policies of its own. Louis XI established silk manufactures in Tours and Lyons to stem imports from Burgundy's allies in Italy (see below).[48] To promote French exports, Louis organized an exhibition of French goods in London, and established a trade fair at Lyons that he hoped would draw business away from Geneva, the Rhine corridor, and Antwerp (which had begun to overtake Bruges as the Rhine estuary's principal maritime port). The Lyons fair rapidly outstripped Antwerp's. By the early sixteenth century, "the counselors of Francis I were capable of giving all the elements of a veritable mercantilist doctrine."[49]

Hendrik Spruyt and others have closely examined the comparative advantages of the urban league and the monarchical state.[50] As Spruyt observes, the monarchical state did not emerge unproblematically from the dissolution of feudal order. On the contrary, feudal decay spawned a variety of political orders, of which the state and the urban league were two (the Italian city-state being a third). In time, the monarchical state supplanted the league, Spruyt argues, because it possessed a more rational institutional organization. "Sovereign authority proved to be more adept at preventing freeriding, standardizing weights and coinage, and establishing uniform adjudication."[51] But Spruyt's analysis and others like it, however compelling, do not address the prior question, why some *places* had states and others did not. As stated above, the Greater Rhineland's history, including that of the Hansa, reveals no

---

[47] Dollinger, *The German Hansa*, pp. 305–9.

[48] Fédou, *L'état au moyen âge*, p. 194; Guénée, *L'Occident*, pp. 221–4.

[49] Guénée, *L'Occident*, p. 224. Antwerp owed its recent good fortune to Burgundy's efforts to diminish the power of the Hansa and its Flemish allies, as well as from the silting of the Zwynn.

[50] Hendrik Spruyt, *The Sovereign State and Its Competitors* (Princeton: Princeton University Press, 1994). The literature on the formation of the modern state is vast, and Spruyt's work is chosen as representative of efforts to understand the emergence of the state as a historically contingent phenomenon, without positing some teleological, evolutionary, or "modernizing" process. See in this same spirit the analysis of Charles Tilly, *Coercion, Capital, and European States, AD 990–1990* (Cambridge, MA: Blackwell, 1992).

[51] Spruyt, *The Sovereign State*, p. 6.

essential allergy to state-like territorial organization. Spruyt's observation that "states … increasingly only recognized similar units as legitimate actors in international relations" makes sense only with reference to customary legitimating myths, which in turn assume meaning only within a geography organized by ontopological legacy and the *coups de force* that fostered it.[52] Spruyt appears to admit as much when he observes that the Hansa "lacked a theory legitimating sovereign power."[53] The fact that the trading towns lacked discursive representation as an element of legitimate (indeed, divine) political order reinforced the vices of decentralized decision-making that Spruyt dissects. "Material" analyses help us understand the strategic interactions of centers of power as extant entities, but stumble on the emergence of the *places* that locate those entities, and are thus prone to falsely deterministic distinctions between territorial states and merchant towns.

Avatars of the Middle Kingdom: the duchy of Burgundy

The medieval Rhineland, despite its political disunity, occupied a central position not only in European commerce and industry, but in European politics as well. But the region failed to coalesce as political space for want of a discursive frame that made it present, as "place," as ontopology, to the political imagination. The merciless struggle for dominance in the Greater Rhineland that opposed the towns and the duchy of Burgundy in the fifteenth century tells a similar story, though one that starts from the premise of prior integration rather than from one of atomization.

When Burgundy escheated to the king of France in 1361, John II surrendered it to his son Philip as an "apanage," a revocable territorial trust that would assure a living to royal offspring.[54] Philip's marriage to Margaret, daughter and heiress of the duke of Flanders, extended Burgundy's authority not only to Flanders, but to Franche-Comté (the imperial county of "Burgundy"), Artois, Nevers, and Rethel. A subsequent marriage with the Wittelsbach family added Hainaut, Holland, and Zealand. Burgundy's marital politics thus reconstructed much of Carolingian Lotharingia. The addition of the core Carolingian territories of Alsace, Lorraine, and the episcopal cities of Trier and Cologne would have completed Lotharingia's resurrection. The first dukes of Burgundy,

---

[52] Spruyt, *The Sovereign State*, p. 6.   [53] Spruyt, *The Sovereign State*, p. 166.
[54] See Fédou, *L'état au moyen âge*, pp. 44–5.

however, showed no interest in establishing such a kingdom. As scions of the French royal family, their political horizons were Parisian, not "Lotharingian." They participated in the power struggle provoked by the insanity of King Charles VI. During the minority of Charles VII, when "English" armies occupied half of France, they struck up an alliance with the Lancaster claimants to the French throne. French military victories led to the peace of Arras of 1435, which put an end to the English–Burgundian alliance but rewarded Philip of Burgundy with recognition as a sovereign prince. When Charles the Bold succeeded to the dukedom in 1467, he looked no longer to Paris but to the Holy Roman Empire for opportunities to climb in power and prestige. He first set his sights on Alsace. Burgundian influence had been growing there since the early fifteenth century when Alsatian lands, notably Breisach (site of the only bridge across the Rhine between Basle and Strasburg), figured in negotiations with the imperial house. Charles later advanced claims on the imperial lands of Lorraine and Frisia. Diplomacy and Charles' ties to the bishop of Metz won him Lorraine, while his ties to the counts of Holland brought success in Frisia.[55]

Two-thirds of the duke's territories now lay within the formal boundaries of the empire. The duke, as prince of the Holy Roman Empire, sent deputies to the imperial diet and struck alliances with Frederick I, Elector Palatine of the Rhine, the most powerful prince in western Germany, and his brother Ruprecht, archbishop of Cologne, both of the house of Wittelsbach, rivals of the Habsburgs.[56] Charles began to nurture designs on the imperial crown. He proposed a marriage alliance with the Habsburgs in return for his recognition as King of the Romans, but negotiations collapsed, complicated by territorial and political tensions between Charles and the Wittelsbach Elector Palatine.[57] The duke then lowered his sights and contemplated the title of "King of Burgundy." That title would have resurrected the ontopology of the short-lived kingdom of Burgundy, established by Germanic invaders when Rome fell. Again negotiations unraveled, in no small part because the title itself, to borrow a term from Walter Benjamin, lacked an "aura."[58] For Benjamin the term signifies the prestige of an original work, say a painting. It is that aspect of the original that cannot be

[55] Richard Vaughan, *Charles the Bold: The Last Valois Duke of Burgundy* (London: Longman, 1973), pp. 100–7.

[56] Vaughan, *Charles the Bold*, p. 124   [57] Vaughan, *Charles the Bold*, p. 131

[58] See Walter Benjamin, "Das Kunstwerk im Zeitalter seiner technischen Reproduzierbarkeit," in *Gesammelte Schriften* (Frankfurt: Suhrkampf, 1972–89), vol. VII.

captured in a reproduction – its material embodiment of history, of tradition, of cultural meaning. Burgundy had been a "kingdom" only intermittently, following the fall of Rome and during the period of anarchy separating the death of Charles the Bald (877) and the accession of Henry I of Saxony to the imperial throne (919). The duke's realm, by its material resources and capabilities, looked like a kingdom. It was a rich principality and a formidable military power. The dukes of Burgundy had rationalized state administration on the French and Italian models, and developed an efficient system of tax collection.[59] Its tax revenues amounted to about a third of those of France, by far the richest kingdom in Europe. The northern textile provinces of Flanders and Artois alone produced half that revenue, enabling the duke to employ large armies of Italian mercenaries and English archers and new-fangled siege artillery to win his neighbors' fear and respect. But such advantages were useless to the duke if they did not buy him the legitimacy, the "aura" of rule over an "acknowledged" ontopology, a *real* crown. The term "Burgundy" lacked that aura. It referred specifically only to the lands situated to the left and right of the River Saône, leaving the rest of the "kingdom" unnamed. Only the duke himself, who provided it with unity of rule, brought the realm to light. If the duke did not exist, neither would the "kingdom" of Burgundy.

Charles' expansionist ambitions, though frustrated, brought conflict with the towns of the Greater Rhineland. The dukes of Burgundy had always treated the towns with aristocratic disdain. It was Burgundy's troops that repressed the weavers' rebellion of 1382. Philip the Good (1396–1467) boasted on his epitaph that he had restored civil order in Liège, Bruges, and Ghent. The boast was a bloated one, since in all cases he had acted in cooperation with a merchant elite engaged in bitter class warfare. But it made plain the duke's tense and often violent relations with the towns. As for Charles the Bold, he opened his reign by repressing an uprising, in Liège in 1469, with a brutality that "sent a chill" throughout the commercial world, and spurred Hanseatic merchants at Bruges to write to Lübeck to urge solidarity.[60] Frankfurt, which Charles had accused of harboring refugees, wrote with alarm to Aachen and Cologne. Although historians have tended to focus on Burgundy's conflicts with the French monarchy, it is the antagonism of the towns that is emblematic of Charles' reign.

---

[59] Vaughan, *Charles the Bold*, pp. 185, 213, 222, 230.
[60] Vaughan, *Charles the Bold*, pp. 34–7.

Legend: Fr Cte = Franche-Comté

Figure 4.6 The Burgundian Middle Kingdom

> The real enemy of Duke Charles the Bold, opposing him with a bitter and
> consistent hatred, was urban ... In particular, it was that mosaic of city-
> states which had been brought into existence by the avaricious, grasping
> and dynamic merchant communities of the great borderland [*sic*] of the
> Europe of those days, where the French and German speaking worlds
> met and merged.[61]

In the wars against Burgundy, "the first initiatives were urban; the
finances were urban, and the armies ... were primarily recruited in or
by the towns." The historian Richard Vaughan reminds us that the first
league of Rhineland towns, formed in 1254, comprised many of the
cities that banded together in the fifteenth century to stop Burgundy's
expansion (see figure 4.6).

The clash was one not of interests but of culture. Economically, the
towns and the dukes thought alike. For all the Greater Rhineland's
political, economic, and civilizational specificity, its towns were not
averse to "seeing like a state," to paraphrase James Scott.[62] Both towns

---

[61] Vaughan, *Charles the Bold*, p. 40. I follow Vaughan's carefully documented refutation
of the common sense that the chief factor in Burgundy's collapse was conflict with
Louis XI.

[62] The reference is to James C. Scott, *Seeing Like a State* (New Haven: Yale Univesity Press,
1998).

and kingdoms displayed greater mutual understanding than either Rokkan or Fox attribute to them, notably in their similar efforts to use commerce to impose rule and to use rule to generate commerce. As Bruges' entanglements with the Hansa illustrate, they were capable of acting in alliance. In 1470 the duke, in conflict with Louis XI, mimicked Hansa-style mercantilism by confiscating the property of French merchants passing through the duchy. In 1474, he canceled safe-conducts to French merchants and prohibited trade with the hostile towns of Cologne, Strasburg, and Basle, and the guardian towns of the Alpine passes. He banned the import of Rhine wines in 1476.[63] But just as the duke and the towns were joined agonistically by similar but incompatible interests, they were separated by cultural disdain. Following his defeat by the Swiss at Murten, Charles confessed to a Milanese ambassador his desire to wreak vengeance on "these bestial people."[64] The crass, aristocratic contempt of Charles' legate in Strasburg caused rebellion and provoked the legate's assassination. Strasburg never wavered in its opposition to the duke, and amply returned the aristocrat's disdain with scorn for the "Welsche," its "French"-speaking, aristocratic adversaries and interlopers in imperial politics.[65] The epithet did not express nationalist prejudice, which would not emerge in a recognizably modern form for several centuries. The duke's armies were mercenary and multilingual. The term, derived from the Latin *Gallus*, gestured broadly toward all those who lived "beyond the *limes*." In the context of the period, monarchical court culture lay "beyond the *limes*." The town's disdain expressed contempt not for the soldiers that besieged its walls, but for the army's employers, the alien, aristocratic class that ruled the agrarian periphery and was seeking to impose its rule on the autonomous imperial and ecclesiastic cities of the Greater Rhineland, as it had done in France. Strasburg, in particular, would prove to be a relentless opponent. It exercised a kind of protectorate over the trade routes of the upper Rhine to the fairs downstream at Frankfurt and Cologne and, upstream, through neighboring Basle, to the Alpine passes, Geneva, the Rhône, and Italy. Together, Strasburg and Basle established the League of Constance in 1474 to keep Charles the Bold out of the upper Rhineland.[66]

---

[63] Vaughan, *Charles the Bold*, pp. 66, 125, 405. The duke generally showed great interest in the wine trade, for nearly all the wine consumed by the prosperous lowlands arrived by the Rhine, even when exported from Burgundy.

[64] Vaughan, *Charles the Bold*, p. 387.

[65] Welsche, like Wallen or Walloon, derives from the Latin *Gallus*.

[66] Vaughan, *Charles the Bold*, pp. 302, 306, 297.

The heart of the Greater Rhineland's opposition to Burgundian expansion, however, lay in the Swiss Confederation, the origins of which go back to about 1230, and the opening of the St. Gothard Pass that linked Schaffhausen on the Rhine to Milan and Italy via Lucerne. The pass had enriched the towns of Berne, Lucerne, and Zurich, whose wealth aroused the cupidity of the emperor, Frederick II. To defend their control of the passes, the towns formed a union modeled on the 1254 Rhineland League. This confederation prevailed in war, expanded, and ultimately endowed itself with a diet in 1460.[67] Under Berne's leadership, the confederation was dynamic, expansionist, and aggressive. But expansionism brought the confederation into conflict with Burgundy, first in the Vaud, and then in the Valais. Through the Vaud passed the road from the upper Rhine to the Rhône and the fairs of Geneva and Lyons. Burgundy's allies, the dukes of Savoy, had imposed strict and onerous rules governing access to this important trade route.[68] Berne advanced militarily against Savoy, but in so doing endangered Burgundy's garrisons in Franche-Comté. Southward expansion toward the Valais also brought Swiss troops within proximity of the Great St. Bernard Pass, which was vital to Charles' Italian mercenary armies.

War broke out in 1474, when an uprising against Charles' ally, the archbishop of Cologne, provided the duke with a pretext to parade his military might up and down the Rhine valley to frighten the towns into submission. Charles laid siege to Neuss. But the support of Strasburg, Frankfurt, and other towns emboldened Neuss' resistance, forcing Charles to lift the siege. Charles then turned south to dispel the threat posed by the League of Constance and the Swiss Confederation to Franche-Comté and Savoy. Despite failure at Neuss, Burgundian military prestige was high, and Charles' southern campaign filled the towns with terror.

> The great city of Strasburg, seized with near panic, made ... costly and crippling preparations for a Burgundian siege. A committee of eight leading citizens reported early in November that only the systematic demolition of buildings outside the walls could enable Strasburg to withstand Charles the Bold. The work continued through the winter until five monasteries and 620 houses had been destroyed and a two-mile wide belt of open flat ground surrounded the walls ... Powder and artillery were bought in from Nürnberg ... Never did [Charles'] reputation as a successful and ambitious conqueror stand higher than at this time. Politically, too, his position

---

[67] Guénée, *L'Occident*, pp. 292–6.   [68] Vaughan, *Charles the Bold*, p. 361.

seemed more assured than ever. He had made an advantageous settlement with Louis XI and peace with the emperor . . . Leaving some of his troops to garrison the principal towns of the duchy, he set off on 11 January 1475 on his ill-starred expedition in support of Savoy against Berne and her allies. For it was Berne, not Strasburg, against which Charles the Bold now hoped to lead his victorious army.[69]

The Swiss citizen army, unlike the mercenary armies of the duke, could not afford a lengthy war of attrition. It therefore maneuvered aggressively and struck decisively, placing hope in the effect of surprise. In two decisive encounters at Grandson and Murten, the Swiss and their allies, fighting for the first time behind the white cross on a red field, defeated Burgundy's armies. Charles lost a third of his army, "the victim of one of the most destructive and decisive battles in the military history of the middle ages."[70] The victories of the Swiss emboldened the burghers of Nancy to rebel, threatening the duke's hold on Lorraine. Charles hurried to regain control of the city and province, but the Swiss pursued him, defeated his army in battle, and took his life. Unable to keep prisoners of war, the Swiss alarmed the royal courts by their savagery on the field. At Murten and Nancy, in particular, the carnage was extensive. At Nancy

> it took two days of careful searching through the frozen and dis-membered corpses littering the field of battle before the body of the forty-four year old duke was found. It had been stripped of clothes and jewels and the face was mangled, cut open, and partly eaten by dogs or wolves, but it was identified by its long nails and battle scars. Apparently Charles the Bold's horse had failed to clear a stream in the general flight. He had fallen, perhaps already wounded, and was then dispatched with a blow which cut open his head. With him fell the Burgundian state which his great grandfather Philip the Bold had founded.[71]

Nothing more exotic than botched maneuvers on the battlefield caused the duke's defeat. His mercenary army, which comprised French-speaking Burgundians and Picards, Dutch-speaking infantry-men from Flanders and Holland, English archers, and Italian mercenaries, may have suffered from linguistic confusion on the field. The Swiss forces, in contrast, though German- and French-speaking, were united by a strong sense of purpose and urgency. "It was . . . an

---

[69] Vaughan, *Charles the Bold*, pp. 357–8.   [70] Vaughan, *Charles the Bold*, p. 394.
[71] Vaughan, *Charles the Bold*, p. 432.

army of townsmen which defeated the Burgundians at Grandson and Murten; an army of townsmen opposed by a prince, a territorial ruler whose entire political career was dominated ... by his opposition to the towns and their opposition to him."[72]

Charles' defeat did not cause the collapse of his proto-kingdom, but rather its "evaporation." The duke's well-oiled administration financed the war efficiently to the very end and survived military defeat. But following Charles' death, French Burgundy proper and imperial Franche-Comté escheated to the French crown, while Flanders, through marital ties, went to the Habsburgs. Two peripheral dynasties, Habsburg and Valois, touched henceforth at several points in the Greater Rhineland, transforming "Lotharingia" into a frontier land wedged (nominally) between monarchical states. It is idle to speculate how things "might have turned out" had Charles been less dismissive of Swiss military skills, less arrogant in his dealings with the towns, more interested in swapping a king's crown for an emperor's, or blessed with a son who could inherit both the duchy and the Burgundian project, even in defeat, rather than a daughter who could not. If we are to understand the deconstruction of the Rhineland frontier in the present it is important to observe that nothing in the Rhineland's past fated it to become a frontier. Nothing, that is, but ontopological myth, discursive habit, and Rhineland namelessness. The history of both the Hanseatic League and the duchy of Burgundy remind us how close the Greater Rhineland came to possessing its own cohesive, territorial organization, whether in the form of a monarchical state or an urban confederation. Indeed, the towns of the lower and upper Rhine, that is the United Provinces of the Netherlands and the Swiss Confederation (discussed in the following chapter), successfully forged urban associations, defended them, and, by the 1648 Treaty of Westphalia, won sovereignty rights equal to those of the agrarian monarchies. But the Greater Rhineland, as economic region and civilizational site, did not coalesce for want of a name, a legitimating ontopology, a *coup de force* to "give birth" to such an ontopology.

Discursive habit and (il)legitimacy of place

From the thirteenth to the fifteenth century the rival political economies and civilizations of commercial town and agrarian monarchy existed side

---

[72] Vaughan, *Charles the Bold*, p. 398.

by side, each in its own space. The former occupied the Rhineland corridor, the commercial and economic core of western Europe, while the latter occupied the periphery. By contrast, the towns of the core were important players in the politics of monarchical consolidation in the ninth century. The cities of the Roman Rhineland subsidized Carolingian consolidation with revenues from trade, and provided it with administration and symbolic (ecclesiastical) legitimation. Two centuries later, the towns were central actors in the Ottonian *renovatio*. The importance that Rokkan and Fox attribute to political economy, therefore, would appear overly deterministic. Difference in political economy is explained by Rhineland geography. There was no fundamental sociopolitical incompatibility between town and state. The political history of the Greater Rhineland in the middle ages provides a demonstration not of economic determinism but of the force of discursive habit, of place names as legitimators of power. It demonstrates the "force" of *nominalism*, of the location of a geography's ontology in the *name* that fashions it.

In the centuries separating Charlemagne from the Ottonians and Capetians, places received new names, which, in time, congealed as discursive habit. Under the Merovingians, the term Francia designated only the core territories of Frankish conquest between the Seine and the Rhine. Francia was the *regnum* and *patria* of the Franks, as distinct from other *regna* located in modern French space: Aquitaine, Burgundy, or Gothia. In the tenth century, Francia, when employed by educated clerics, referred nostalgically to Charlemagne's empire. For the commoner, however, it still signified only the northern fringe of a kingdom ruled from Paris. Reference was still made, moreover, to the Merovingian *regna*, Austrasia and Neustria.[73] These names fell from use as the French monarchy was consolidated and the German empire disintegrated. Francia endured, however, but not in its original sense. It came to designate all territories, north and south of the Loire, that owed allegiance to the Capetian and Valois kings. The king of France is called *Franciae rex* for the first time in 1204, and we first encounter the term *regnum Francie* in 1205. *Teutonicus* appeared in the ninth century and gained currency in the tenth to refer to Ottonian territories. It excluded the Germanophone Flemish and Frisians, however, who, after being called "Lotharingians" in the tenth and eleventh centuries, had begun to acquire their more specific appellations. Inversely, the adjective *teutonicus* included the Alamannic peoples of Alsace and Swabia, and

[73] Fédou, *L'état au moyen âge*, p. 139.

the rebellious Swiss. *Teutonia* became a place name in the twelfth century, at about the same time as Francia acquired its modern meaning.

The development of place names began to nourish a mythology of patriotism, at least among the literate classes. Until the sixteenth century, one's "country," or "pays," was "for a monk his monastery, for a peasant his village, for a bourgeois, his town."[74] Myths of origin, composed during this period, provided discursive elements for the development of nationalism in later centuries. The monks of St. Denis, at the end of the twelfth century, had compiled a *Historia regum francorum*, which was translated into French a century later. But the title designated kings of a people, not kings of a place. The fifteenth-century *Grandes chroniques de France*, by contrast, centered on a place, not a people. It portrayed Clovis as the new Constantine, Paris (not Aachen) as the new Rome, and acquired quasi-biblical prestige among French readers. The myth of Trojan origins, a Frankish gloss on Vergil, emerges throughout the Greater Rhineland in the middle ages. Just as Aeneus founded Rome, so "Francion" (unknown to Vergil) founded Sicambria, whose inhabitants established Lutetia, renamed Paris not with reference to the Gallic Parisi, but in honor of Helen's abductor. In Germany, Priam himself was supposed to have founded Xanten, where Trojans intermarried with Teutons to give rise to Rome's siblings: its "Germani." Myths of origin nourished myths of difference. The fifteenth-century humanist Jacob Wimpheling, a Strasburger who had witnessed the mortal struggle with Burgundy, wrote an *Epitome rerum germanicorum* which claimed that Germans differed from the French not only by their language, their character and their customs, but by the color of their hair and their physiognomy. It is significant that Wimpheling's treatise drew a sharp rebuke from a fellow Strasburger, the Franciscan humanist and satirist Thomas Murner, who would shortly become one of Martin Luther's most redoubtable critics. But such debates were the province of a literate few. The village would remain the *patrie* of peasants for many centuries to come. The literary class was, throughout the middle ages, strikingly cosmopolitan by twentieth-century standards. Murner, for example, studied, taught, or preached in Paris, Cracow, Basle, and Lucerne, as well as Strasburg. The epithets, moreover, were not applied to "nations" in the modern sense of the term. As noted above, the *Welsche* of the Strasburgers were scions of the Burgundian court and the motley, multilingual gang of mercenaries that fought for them. The

---

[74] Guénée, *L'Occident*, p. 120.

term did not apply to a "nation in arms," which simply did not exist in the modern sense of the term. Nor did nation refer to a monolingual people. In 1439, the archbishop of Salzburg complained of the great difficulty he had reading a letter from a Rhineland colleague. In effect, the archbishop's Tyrolean dialect would have been more distant from the speech of Cologne than Flemish, which, at this time, was also called *Diets (Deutsch)* by its literary adepts, even though it was not spoken in the space called *Teutonia*.[75]

In the fifteenth century, monarchs began to identify with the named "nations" they ruled. This is not to say they identified with the "peoples" they ruled. The congruity of "people" and "nation," which would become political fact in the nineteenth century (see chapter 6), was far from acknowledged in the fifteenth. Congruity characterized the relationship, not between people and nation, but between a king's rule and God's plan. The nation manifested "naturalness" of rule, legitimation *by place*, by *named* place, and therefore, according to the Scholasticism of the times, by divine will. Nature was divinely created, and *natio* was nature (both terms derive from the Latin *nascor*: to be born, begin life, be produced, proceed, be begotten). The nation existed *by virtue of* the king's rule, as legitimized by *custom*, as manifested by *place name*, as sign of God's disposition. It did not exist by virtue of language or culture. Armies, though multilingual and often mercenary, began to fight under "national" flags in application of this concept. Joan of Arc goaded Charles VII to resist England's "unnatural" rule in France. And it was in France that the word "frontier" made its first appearance in 1315 to designate the line of separation – however obscured by the survival of confused and contested feudal loyalties – between territories that *customarily* owed obedience to the monarch.[76] The French court defined that line of separation, not by culture or language, but by "natural" geophysical limits: the Rhône, the Saône, the Meuse, and the Scheldt.[77] "Dutch"-speaking Flanders, west of the Scheldt, was part of the French "nation." Meanwhile, humanist scholarship was reviving the classic ontopologies, Gallia and Germania, which were used only by monks in the post-Carolingian period before falling from use altogether. By the time of the Thirty Years War (1618–48), however, it was Gallia that would become the embodiment of "nature,"

---

[75] Guénée, *L'Occident*, pp. 117–18.   [76] Fédou, *L'état au moyen âge*, p. 149.
[77] Paul Guichonnet and Claude Raffestin, *Géographie des frontières* (Paris: Presses Universitaires de France, 1974), pp. 93–4.

divine ordinance, and God's pleasure in the French king's claims to the Rhine's left bank.

The name Lotharingia fell into disuse except to designate the lands drained by the upper Moselle. The former middle kingdom disintegrated into a multiplicity of named provinces and cities: Flanders, Lorraine, Brabant, Hainaut, Metz, Liège, and others. Many of the provinces were "bilingual," and "existed" only by custom, by virtue of having a name. They existed as ontopologies. Ontopology, however, was denied to the Greater Rhineland as a whole, as "Lotharingia," as a middle kingdom. There was no constitutive text, no *coup de force* that intervened to lend it coherence and existence in speech and thought, to give it representation in deliberations and debates regarding the political organization of Greater Rhineland space. Lotharingia did not cohere long enough to acquire a customary name. In the words of historian Bernard Guénée, "the fact that neither the states nor the subjects of the duke of Burgundy had a *common name* was more threatening to Charles the Bold" than the machinations of his most determined adversaries.[78]

Despite its "ontology" as, according to Charles Fox and Stein Rokkan, a political economy and civilizational type, the Greater Rhineland had no name. It did not exist, as such. But anonymity implies a framework of named space. The Greater Rhineland, then as now, owed its anonymity to the existence of a name that diverted the gaze toward loftier horizons: "Europe" in our day, "empire" in the fifteenth century. "Empire" was the towns' nominal home. It had been so from time immemorial, from Caesar, to Charlemagne, to Charles V (see chapter 5). The two regions of the Greater Rhineland that succeeded in "graduating" to ontopological status, Switzerland at the Rhine's source, and the Netherlands at the Rhine's estuary (see chapter 5), did so by rebelling against the "empire." The term "Switzeri" or "Zwitsois," variations on the name of the rural canton *Schwyz*, came into use toward the end of the fifteenth century, along with the red and white flag, just as the Swiss cities were mounting their challenge against Burgundian power. The name, however, was conferred on them by others. The Swiss themselves referred to their confederation rather ponderously as the "Grosse Bund Oberdeutschen Länder," or "Liga Alamanie Superioris," despite the fact that it was composed of towns that were not exclusively *Deutsch* or Alamannic, and despite the fact that *Oberdeutsch* and Alamannic are not strict

---

[78] Guénée, *L'Occident*, p. 115, emphasis added.

synonyms.[79] But it was the term Switzeri that brought the league "to daylight" as an ontopology, even though it did not coalesce as a political entity until the nineteenth century. The towns of the middle Rhine, by contrast – the towns of the League of Constance and its allies downstream – had no dispute with the emperor and therefore no reason to reject or secede from their nominal home. Both the League of Constance and the Hanseatic League appealed to the broadest of categories to express their political identities, that of a kind of linguistic affiliation, *Teutonicus*, and of subjection to the Holy Roman Empire. The emperor's political remoteness, after all, made the name easy to bear. The anonymity of the Greater Rhineland, understood as a coherent political, economic, and civilizational space, must therefore be understood as the counterpart, even the consequence, of the customary legitimacy and discursive force of *habitual names*, such that town leaders of the fifteenth century were no more able than historians of the twentieth to conceptualize the Greater Rhineland outside the framework of existing ontopologies. No moniker like the term "Swiss" would emerge to turn them into an "entity," bring them "to daylight" as the commercial and political animators of a "place" that one could imagine as something more than the simple and occasional sum of its parts.

The possibility of cause–effect relationships between "ideational factors" such as myths and names, on the one hand, and historical outcomes, on the other (and vice versa), is a legitimate and fascinating topic of research and speculation. It is not, however, the topic of this book. This is not a book of forward-flowing history, but one of backward-gazing critique, which seeks to trace commonsense representations of space in the present to their emergence in the past in flights of fancy and imagination. In this perspective, the conclusions to be drawn from the struggle that opposed Burgundy's effort to resurrect a middle kingdom and the Rhineland towns that allied to prevent it do not concern causality, but the referential power of myths of place. There is no political-economic, cultural, or topographical logic to the distribution of place names. Despite the fact that Burgundy's career and Burgundy's defeat at the hand of the Greater Rhineland's commercial towns illustrate and underscore the power and potential cohesiveness of the Greater Rhineland political economy, that power did not find

---

[79] *Grosse Bund Oberdeustchen Länder* translates as "Great Alliance of the Higher Teutonic Lands (Countries, or Territories)." *Liga Alamanie Superioris* translates as "League of Higher Alamannia."

ontopological expression. Even contemporary historiography is firmly inscribed within the habitual discursive framework of nationhood. The mind, as discussed in chapter 1, was and is "imprisoned" by ontopological habit. When Burgundy fell, it ceased to exist, *even in language.* Nothing about Burgundy's partition by Valois and Habsburg was seen as illegitimate. It did not occur to the mind to save or resurrect the Burgundian kingdom. It could not have occurred to the mind to resurrect something that is not present "to," present "in," the mind. The absence of an ontopology, the Greater Rhineland's "non-presence" to the mind as ontopology, deprived the duchy of "aura" and legitimacy, just as it dulled the imagination of the townsmen who fought the duchy and obscured the path to political consolidation. By contrast, France in 1430, its court banished from the capital, its core territory occupied by armies loyal to the king of England, its coffers empty, never ceased to "exist." France's existence as ontopology made conceivable, legitimate, and mobilizing as myth and vision, the restoration of the Valois to power in Paris. That restoration needed nothing more than the spark of charisma provided by a teenage maiden.

Again, the point is not to advance a causal argument, even though I attribute effect to nominal cause in the above illustrations in order to stress a point. What I wish to emphasize is this: by recovering the history of the Greater Rhineland as nameless place, one "opens the mind" to rival representations of space that oppose, that have the effect of relativizing, habitual discourse. By doing so, one becomes absorbed by the suspicion that *fortuity* assigned name to place, and that caprice positioned the regional economy of the Greater Rhineland at the *edge* of named spaces. That suspicion enables us to see that "edge" as the site of a rival representation of political space, which might frame, embolden, energize new thinking about the purposes and possibilities of European Union. The EU emerged, after all, from efforts to unmake that "edge." Then as now, the Greater Rhineland was the core regional economy of western Europe. Then as now, one encounters power in the absence of hierarchical governance. Then as now, one discovers a region articulated and represented culturally, discursively by its towns and cities, in contrast to the monarchical periphery, articulated and represented culturally by its capitals and palaces. The Greater Rhineland, then as now, was marked by commercial activity on a "global" scale, by capitalism, mercantilism, class conflict, but also by cosmopolitanism, as well as technical and intellectual invention.

5

The great antecedent cracking

The Greater Rhineland regional economy, which flourished against the backdrop of a Hundred Years War opposing the dynastic monarchs of France and England, fell victim, in the seventeenth century, to a hundred years war of its own. War erupted in 1619 and persisted with little respite until 1714, leaving the region in ruins and its economy durably depressed. Although the towns of Switzerland, at the source of the Rhine, and the towns of the Netherlands, at the mouth of the Rhine, negotiated their transition from urban league to sovereign state, the violence marginalized Flanders and the towns of the middle Rhineland, from Freiburg to Liège, and Antwerp to Frankfurt. Religious conflict subverted the ontopology of empire. *Christianitas*, as a geographical term, awakened suspicion. "Europe" was redefined as a territorial home to sovereign princes. Rhineland frontier mythology reemerged, relegating Europe's core regional economy to the edges of a "nation-state" system that we still inhabit, and that European Union seeks to reform or transcend.

The Greater Rhineland and the Reformation

The Hansa, in fact if not by law, disaggregated in the fifteenth century, a victim of class struggle, conflict with the dukes of Burgundy, Dutch competition, and new trade patterns arising from European maritime expansion.[1] The wars with Burgundy left Cologne deeply in debt. The expansion (through dynastic inheritance and marriage) of the duchy of Cleves threatened Trier's autonomy. Mainz anxiously observed the growing power of the Elector Count Palatine who ruled from Heidelberg.[2] But the economic impact of such developments was not

---

[1] The Hansa would endure as a formal, though hollow, organization until the Thirty Years War.

[2] Franz Petri, *Im Zeitalter des Glaubenskämpfe*, vol. II, *Neuzeit*, of Franz Petri and Georg Droege, eds., *Rheinische Geschichte* (Düsseldorf: Schwann, 1976), p. 10.

immediately apparent. Bruges continued to export tapestries, cloths, and linens as far away as Spain and Italy. Flanders lost its preeminence as an industrial and commercial center but was replaced by its neighbor Brabant, whose rise to prosperity is reflected in the architecture of Brussels' magnificent Grand-Place. The first mercantile exchanges or *bourses* (from Flemish *beurs*: purse) were established in Bruges and Antwerp. Inside the towns, demographic growth following the plague-ridden fourteenth century made labor more plentiful, causing the political fortunes of the merchant oligarchy to rise at the expense of the craftsmen, vulnerable to labor abundance. In the foothills of the Ardennes, miners and metal workers experimented with new technologies.[3] A peasant activity in the Middle Ages, mining became increasingly industrial and capitalistic. Liège had a blast furnace in 1400. By the mid sixteenth century, tunnels, winches, windlasses, watermills, and windmills made for a recognizably modern industrial landscape. Investor associations financed the capital-hungry mining companies. Stock became negotiable. Investor associations were transformed into joint stock companies. France's economy, by comparison with that of the Greater Rhineland, was backward. Agriculture produced miserly rents. Demographic recovery from plague and war failed to stimulate trade and industry. Inhibited by the military ambitions of extravagant monarchs, capital accumulated slowly.

Religious and political turmoil occasioned by the Reformation – for Demangeon and Febvre, the "great antecedent cracking" – would cause the medieval Greater Rhineland economy to collapse.[4] It would durably subvert the discursive authority of Carolingian ontopology, and condition the absorption of the Greater Rhineland's towns by emergent, monarchical states. The event that sparked the turmoil occurred in the Rhineland city of Mainz. In 1517 Pope Leo X authorized the sale of indulgences to pay for the installation of Albert of Hohenzollern as archbishop. An Augustinian monk, Martin Luther, protested that such authorization was an abuse of the sacrament of absolution. The dispute grew venomous. Luther penned provocative treatises – "Concerning Christian Liberty" (1520), "A Treatise on Good Works" (1520), and "An Open Letter to the Christian Nobility of the German Nation" (1520) – that proposed new understandings of justification and the

---

[3] Guy Fourquin, *Histoire économique de l'occident médiéval* (Paris: Armand Colin, 1969), pp. 368–78.
[4] Albert Demangeon and Lucien Febvre, *Le Rhin* (Paris: Armand Colin, 1935), pp. 111–14.

priesthood, and inspired many ecclesiastics and their faithful to question the authority of the Roman bishop. Luther's influence grew not merely because of the force of his ideas and rhetorical style, but because of the rise, particularly in the towns and cities of the Greater Rhineland, of new religious sensibilities – more private, less institutionally mediated – nourished by the writings of Meister Eckhart, Dietrich of Strasburg, and Thomas à Kempis. The Church throughout the Greater Rhineland, moreover, was confronting a number of festering institutional challenges engendered by demographic growth and dependence on church office for livings.[5] Those challenges kindled disobedience.

The anxious spirit of the times is reflected in the writings of that most influential of late medieval Rhinelanders, Desiderius Erasmus. Born in Rotterdam in about 1469 and educated at the University of Paris, Desiderius participated in the "renaissance" of classical "humanism." He embraced the life of the peripatetic scholar and traveled the length and breadth of the present-day EU's "golden triangle," from Cambridge to Rome, Venice, Paris, Basle, and Leuven (see figure 5.1). An outspoken critic of Scholastic philosophy and the formal, institutional Church that Scholasticism legitimated, he exhorted Christians to return to the textual foundation of their faith and undertook the systematic examination of biblical manuscripts. Published in Basle in 1516, Erasmus' New Testament, a new Latin translation based on a critical edition of the Greek text, became the basis of scholarly study, and, in England, of the "King James" English translation. Erasmus later wrote the widely translated and disseminated *Paraphrases of the New Testament*, which promoted a kind of spiritual life that was respectful but independent of the institutional Church. He advocated a "philosophy of Christ" located "more truly in the disposition of the mind than in syllogisms," and energized religious scholarship by translating, editing, and commenting on the works of Church fathers: Saints Ambrose, Augustine, Basil, and John Chrysostom.[6] He also wrote commentary on Aristotle and Cicero and published pamphlets, notably *In Praise of Folly* (1511), in which he ridiculed the doctrines and practices of the Church with the verve, though not always the subtlety, of a Voltaire.

---

[5] Petri, *Im Zeitalter des Glaubenskämpfe*, pp. 18–19.
[6] Léon E. Halkin, *Erasmus: A Critical Biography* (Oxford: Blackwell, 1993), p. 284.

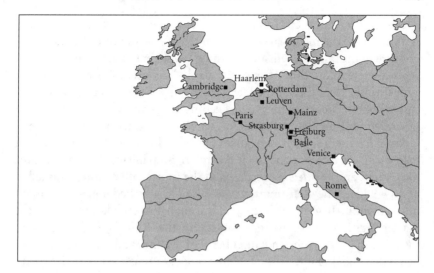

Figure 5.1 The Erasmian corridor

Erasmus' scholarly edition of the New Testament appeared only months before Martin Luther's public demands for reform. Though he corresponded with Luther and was sympathetic to reform, Erasmus never pronounced himself formally in favor of the Reformation. He sought rather to defend his scholarly independence and discourage dogmatic claims, whether Catholic or Protestant, and engaged in debate with great hesitation yet with humor and rhetorical brilliance in pamphlets such as *De Libero Arbitrio* (1524) and in his scholarly edition (1530) of a medieval treatise by Algerus on the sacraments, in which he affirmed his faith in the orthodox doctrine of the real presence of Christ in the Eucharist while acknowledging room for disagreement by reasonable people. It was a position that did not please enthusiasts, either orthodox or reformist. "I am," he declared, "a Ghibelline to the Guelfs and a Guelf to the Ghibellines."[7] In his 1536 work *De Puritate Ecclesiae Christianae*, he attempted to map common ground between the orthodox and reform positions. But when Basle reformed in 1529, Erasmus felt compelled to leave for the neighboring imperial and Catholic town of Freiburg. But he returned to Basle in 1535 to spend his final years in the company of Protestant friends. At his death, the Roman Catholic Church placed his works on the Index of prohibited books.

[7] Halkin, *Erasmus*, p. 287.

Erasmus' career is emblematic of the non-hierarchical, town-centered civilization of the medieval Greater Rhineland, devoid of frontiers, either political, cultural, or linguistic. Erasmus "spoke out, with calm boldness, against the exploitation of national names" as exemplified by Luther's appeal to the "nobility of the German nation." "These names were 'very stupid labels,' because they had become the names of factions. They separated and divided, whereas the scholar, the Christian and the man ignored frontiers . . . 'My own wish is to be a citizen of the world, to be a fellow-citizen to all men . . .' "[8] Erasmian humanism, like the *béguine* movement and the *devotio moderna* in the fourteenth century, was a fact of town life. The Reformation was also, in the beginning, an urban phenomenon. It grew in large part through the circulation of printed matter from town to town, enabled by the Rhineland invention of movable type by Johann Gutenberg of Mainz and Strasburg, Peter Schoeffer and Johann Fust of Mainz, and Lourens Coster of Haarlem. Huldrych Zwingli, who brought the Reformation to Zurich, and Martin Bucer, who made Strasburg one of its principal centers, infused the movement with urban communalism and autonomy. Zwingli and Bucer emphasized lay participation, democracy in government, and tolerance of doctrinal diversity.[9] The Zwinglians were particularly influential among the guilds. The towns of the middle and lower Rhine, especially the cathedral towns, were slower to embrace the Reform. But Mainz was ultimately receptive, as was Trier, with its university and humanist traditions where, according to one professor, Latomus, writing in 1523: "everyone speaks and debates about theological questions, the butcher, the tailor, the candlestick-maker, the innkeeper, and the peasants."[10] Even episcopal Cologne was absorbed in tense debate. The openness of the towns of the Greater Rhineland to new thinking was such that two-thirds of the imperial cities embraced the reform movement in either its Lutheran or Zwinglian form by 1535 (see figure 5.2).

Reformation politics would ultimately undermine the political influence and autonomy of the towns. The reform movement occurred at a time of imperial revival. At the death of Charles the Bold, the imperial lands of Burgundy – Franche-Comté, Luxemburg, and the Netherlands – fell to Philip, the son of Mary of Burgundy and the Habsburg emperor Maximilian I. At Philip's death in 1506, the Burgundian heritage fell to

---

[8] Halkin, *Erasmus*, p. 281.

[9] G. R. Elton, *Reformation Europe: 1517–1559* (New York: Harper, 1963), p. 71.

[10] Petri, *Im Zeitalter des Glaubenskämpfe*, p. 28.

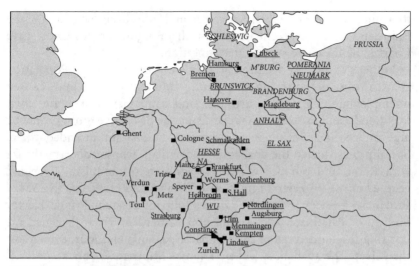

PROTESTANT PRINCIPALITIES: *M'BURG* = Mecklenburg *NA* = Nassau <u>Towns</u> and <u>PRINCIPALITIES</u> of the 1531 Protestant (Schmalkalden) League. <u>PA</u> = Palatinate <u>WU</u> = Württemberg <u>EL SAX</u> = Electorate of Saxony <u>S.Hall</u> = Schwäbische Hall

Figure 5.2 The reform movement in 1535

his son Charles, born in Ghent of Joanna of Spain, the daughter of Ferdinand of Aragon and Isabella of Castille. Charles became duke of imperial Burgundy in 1515, and king of Aragon and Castille and all of Spain's lands in Italy and America in 1516. In 1519, Emperor Maximilian died, leaving to Charles the Habsburg domains on the Danube and the upper Rhine as well as the expectation of an imperial crown. Charles' election was hotly contested by Francis I, king of France, but Fugger money and dynastic legitimacy won him the empire. As emperor, Charles V was, at the age of twenty, the titular ruler of lands more extensive than those of Charlemagne. Moreover, unlike his Habsburg predecessors, Charles "quite consciously thought of himself as the heir of Charlemagne, the secular head of a united Christendom, God's vicar side by side with the pope whose spiritual rule it was his duty to defend."[11] At the Diet of Worms, called to reform the government of the empire as well as to settle the dispute with Luther, the young emperor declared it his intention to impose political unity: "The empire from of old has had not many masters, but one, and it is our intention

[11] Elton, *Reformation Europe*, p. 37.

to be that one."[12] More than Aztec gold and Inca silver, the wealth of the Rhineland cities, especially those of the Burgundian lowlands, gave Charles the means to pursue that ambition.

Luther's campaign occurred at a time of peasant unrest. Population growth put pressure on the land, inflated prices, and caused unemployment. Peasants, artisans, and craftsmen feared for their livelihoods, and expressed that fear using the discursive tools, prophetic and millenarian, with which reformist enthusiasm provided them. Social protest fueled the anabaptist movement, whose adherents broke with Rome and pursued a kind of agrarian communism. Rebellion erupted in the Rhineland provinces of Swabia and Franconia in 1524.[13] Provincial princes, especially Duke Philip of Hessen, Prince Elector Ludwig of Palatinate, and Archbishop Richard of Trier, drowned the uprising in blood. Tens of thousands of peasants and journeymen lost their lives. The anabaptist leader, Thomas Münzer, was put to death.[14] The rebellion proved to Luther that humanity in its fall from grace had lost the capacity for moral and political improvement. He developed an Augustinian sensitivity regarding humanity's need for government. That conviction triggered the great cataclysm in Greater Rhineland political history. Because the towns had neither the legal right nor perhaps the political desire to pacify the countryside, and because Luther could not appeal to the emperor to intervene – Charles V, at the Diet of Worms, had placed Luther on imperial ban – Luther threw in his lot with the German princes, local potentates who were bristling at the young emperor's imperial ambitions and who were anxious to assert their privileges. The principalities of Hesse and Brandenburg-Ansbach and the dukes of Brunswick and Schleswig embraced the Protestant cause. Luther's appeal provided them with legitimation. In A. J. P. Taylor's forceful judgment:

> Luther crept under the wing of the princes of northern Germany, who became protestant not as the most advanced, but as the most backward, section of German society. Luther gave to Germany a consciousness of national existence and, through his translation of the Bible, a national

---

[12] Geoffrey Barraclough, *The Origins of Modern Germany* (New York and London: W. W. Norton, 1984), p. 365.

[13] Petri, *Im Zeitalter des Glaubenskämpfe*, p. 33.

[14] The movement, however, endured, and indeed met with success in the Netherlands, whence it relocated to the New World as Amish, Mennonites, and Pennsylvania "Dutch" (Teutsch).

tongue; but he also gave to Germany the divine right of kings, or rather the divine right of any established authority.[15]

The Reformation's success among princes rekindled conflict between the empire and princely particularism. In 1526, Protestant princes at the Diet of Speyer proposed the settlement that would ultimately prevail at the Diet of Augsburg in 1555, and a century later at Westphalia, which was to locate authority over religious questions in acknowledged territorial rulers rather than in emperor and pope. Charles, by contrast, defended the cause of Carolingian-style imperial and confessional unity. The multiplication of reformed churches in the 1540s, notably along the economically vital lower Rhine, seemed to augur ill for the imperial cause. A 1539 uprising in Ghent, Charles' birth place, required his intervention with a sizable army. In 1542, Hermann von Wied, archbishop of Cologne, one of the cities most loyal to Church and emperor, alarmed Charles by asking the Strasburg reformer, Martin Bucer, to reform his diocese.[16] Frederick II of Palatinate also welcomed Lutheran proselytizers in 1544. Charles was able to suppress the uprising in Ghent and force Hermann von Wied from office. The following year he defeated a league of Protestant princes in battle, using Spanish troops. In 1546 Luther died. Charles was victorious. Ironically, however, victory engendered tensions with the pope, who feared the emperor's military power and ecclesiastical pretensions. When the Church called a Council at Trent to restore confessional unity, the emperor pressed it to make a gesture toward the Reform so as to weaken the appeal of the schismatics. But the Council focused principally on doctrine, and thus exacerbated rather than reconciled its differences with the Reform.

Church intransigence fueled a Protestant resurgence under the able military leadership of Maurice of Saxony. The struggle brought the French monarchy into Greater Rhineland politics. Protestant princes appealed to the French king, Henry II (1547–59), to intervene, declaring that Charles V intended to occupy the three episcopal seats of Lorraine – Metz, Toul, and Verdun – as well as Strasburg and other towns of the Rhine.[17] Henry II occupied the three bishoprics and laid siege to

---

[15] A. J. P. Taylor, *The Course of German History* (New York: Capricorn Books, 1962), p. 18.

[16] Petri, *Im Zeitalter des Glaubenskämpfe*, pp. 36–43.

[17] Albert Sorel, *Europe and the French Revolution: The Political Traditions of the Old Régime*, ed. and trans. Alfred Cobban and J. W. Hunt (Garden City, NY: Anchor Books, 1971), p. 259.

Strasburg and Speyer. The towns, "better able than the princes to grasp how much the French campaign on the Rhine augured a world-historical change (*weltgeschichtliche Tendenzwende*),"[18] favored the emperor, particularly after the fall of Metz, with which they were in close economic and cultural relationship via the Moselle. At the same time, vulnerability to French arms inclined the towns to prudence, an attitude that makes plain their political debilitation when contrasted with their daring defense against Burgundy a half-century earlier.

The Diet of Augsburg, in 1555, was attended by neither emperor nor papal representative, nor even most German princes. In the face of enduring princely resistance and autonomy, the Holy Roman Empire began to revert to its more nominal existence. The delegates, however, did succeed in forging a peace that would last until the outbreak of the Thirty Years War in 1618 by agreeing that the issue of religious confession would be settled by the effective territorial ruler. The famous clause that summarized this arrangement, *cuius regio, eius religio*, did not appear in the text of the settlement, nor did it appear explicitly in the European settlement of Westphalia in 1648, but it inaugurated the era of state sovereignty and the eclipse of the mythical ideal of European imperial unity. In October 1555, Charles V abdicated. The Habsburg empire was divided into Spanish and Austrian components; the Netherlands were awarded to Spain, now the preponderant power in the estuary of the Rhine as well as the Mediterranean.

The turmoil of war pushed the towns to the political margin, but, for the time being, spared their economic prosperity. The region's population climbed throughout the sixteenth century.[19] Trier had a population of about 5,500, Speyer 7,000–8,000, Frankfurt and Aachen 10,000–20,000. Cologne, at 40,000, remained the most important commercial center of the lower Rhine, "hardly affected [economically] by the Reformation."[20] Its glass, textile, metallurgical, and leather manufacturing were intact, and the volume of its trade surpassed that of the previous century. Religious refugees, particularly from the Habsburg lowlands where religious repression was severe, invigorated the Rhine towns' economies. Exiles brought new skills in cloth and silk manufacturing not only to Cologne, but to Aachen, Neuss, Wesel, and Duisburg. In 1585, a wave of refugee merchants – Portuguese converts

---

[18] Petri, *Im Zeitalter des Glaubenskämpfe*, p. 57.
[19] Petri, *Im Zeitalter des Glaubenskämpfe*, p. 157.
[20] Petri, *Im Zeitalter des Glaubenskämpfe*, p. 161.

from Judaism and Dutch-speaking Protestants – turned Cologne into a European banking center.[21] The old imperial town of Aachen received a significant influx of Calvinist Dutch- and French-speaking weavers and artisans, who preserved their faith and, for many generations, even their language.[22] But the princely courts had become the new center of political life, and would soon excite career ambitions even among the burghers as the mercantile oligarchies of the towns lost their independence and influence.

Switzerland and the United Provinces

Unlike the towns of the middle Rhineland, the towns of the Rhine's headwaters and estuary negotiated the transition from urban league to sovereign territorial state. The Swiss Confederation's victory over Burgundy won it immense prestige and new members: Freiburg, Soloturn, Basle, Appenzell, and the Rhine town of Schaffhausen. France entered into formal alliance, enabling the Confederation to settle remaining differences with the Habsburgs on the battlefield. By the 1499 Treaty of Basle the Empire recognized de facto the independence of a Swiss Confederation that stretched from the Jura to Tyrol and ruled extensive "subject" territories that included the Vaud, Valais, Ticino, and Grisons (see figure 5.3). Subsequent wars with France for control of northern Italy did not threaten Swiss independence. The Protestant reform, however, brought violent conflict between Catholic cantons led by Lucerne and Zwinglian cantons led by Zurich, turning confederal unity into an empty formalism for most of the sixteenth century. The Federal Diet did not meet. Swiss mercenaries fought on opposing sides in the wars between France and Habsburg Spain. The confederation nevertheless retained its legal unity and neutrality in the Thirty Years War, at the conclusion of which the Peace of Westphalia gave it full diplomatic status. The Confederation was a sovereign entity, but hardly a "nation." Its borders betrayed no logic of physical geography, or linguistic or religious uniformity. It remained (and remains) a federation of cantons whose frontier is defined by the customary limits of its members.

The northern Netherlands also won its independence – in this case from Habsburg Spain – on the battlefield. Its towns had occupied a central position in the Greater Rhineland political economy since the ninth century when Frisians provided Francia's commercial link to

[21] Petri, *Im Zeitalter des Glaubenskämpfe*, p. 163.
[22] Petri, *Im Zeitalter des Glaubenskämpfe*, p. 73.

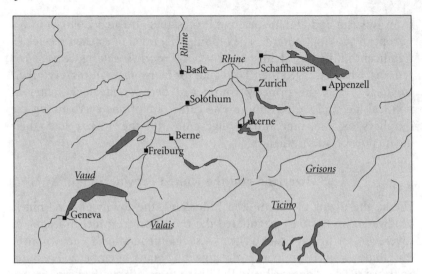

Figure 5.3 The expansion of the Swiss Confederation

the Baltic. Some of the northern towns – Arnhem, Nijmegen, Utrecht – were of Roman foundation. Many towns, however – Haarlem, Delft, Alkmaar – were, throughout the period of Bruges' and Antwerp's commercial dominance, fishing villages perched among the dunes fronting the North Sea. Dordrecht, situated on the estuary, was the only northern port of importance. Subsequent commercial growth in the late middle ages brought increasing prosperity to entrepôts such as Rotterdam and Amsterdam. But it did not bring territorial consolidation, nor did it foreshadow modern imagery of Dutch political space (see figure 5.4).

> Any description of Holland's early history belies the popular mis-
> conception that Europe's later nations must already have existed in
> embryo in the medieval period ... Familiar terms such as "Holland,"
> "Dutch," and "Netherlands" all possessed different connotations from
> those which they later acquired. The modern myth about the permanent
> union of a "nation" and its "soil" was plainly irrelevant.[23]

Under Habsburg rule, the towns of the Rhine–Meuse estuary controlled perhaps 50 percent of Europe's trade, generating tax revenues

---

[23] Norman Davies, *Europe: A History* (Oxford and New York: Oxford University Press, 1996), p. 379. The word "Dutch" is English, and corresponds to the German *Deutsch*, from the root *Teutonicus*. The Dutch have no word for Dutch, but employ *nederlands*, low-lander.

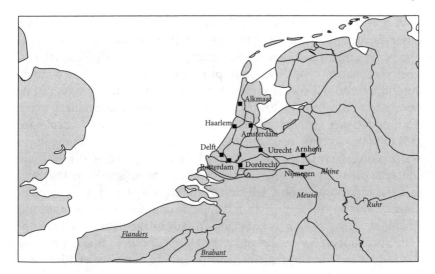

Figure 5.4 The United Provinces

worth seven times as much as the gold bullion produced by the mines of Spanish America.[24] But rule by the Spanish Habsburg court, religiously intolerant and dismissive of town privileges, provoked insurrection. Spanish armies repressed the rebellion by sacking Maastricht, Ghent, and Antwerp in 1576. The poorer northern provinces persevered in the struggle, forging institutions of permanent confederation in 1584. Maurice of Nassau, Prince of Orange (1567–1625), named Captain General of Holland and Zealand in 1585, persuaded the towns to adopt the *trace italienne*, thick earthen fortifications that deflected artillery barrages of city walls and exposed attacking forces to cross-fire.[25] He imposed military drill, based on a Taylor-like analysis of the basic motions of marching, advancing in rank, loading and shooting, and established Europe's first officer training academy in 1619. Nassau wrested dozens of fortified towns from Spanish Habsburg control, conducting maneuvers "with a technical precision and dispatch never attained before."[26] The financial burden of fighting in the Rhineland was more than the Spanish treasury could bear. Philip II repudiated his debts on four separate occasions.

[24] Davies, *Europe*, p. 536.
[25] William H. McNeill, *The Pursuit of Power: Technology, Armed Force, and Society since A.D. 1000* (Chicago: University of Chicago Press, 1982), pp. 90–4.
[26] McNeill, *The Pursuit of Power*, p. 134.

War was also a trial for the Dutch. The Dutch towns, Hans Blom observes, struggled internally to retain their freedoms and commercial prosperity under conditions of war mobilization.[27] But the Netherlands' prowess cautions against conceptualizing the struggle for town autonomy and Greater Rhineland political cohesion as one pitting poorly armed merchant towns against well-armed monarchical states. The dominance of the monarchical state is sometimes explained teleologically as the consequence of technological developments in war-making. New technology "entailed far-ranging changes in war and statecraft, favoring the larger states north of the Alps, especially France and the Habsburg empire, which had the scale to absorb the increased costs."[28] But on closer inspection it appears that the Dutch Republic was hardly at a material or technological disadvantage in its war with the Habsburg monarchy. As shown by the Hansa at war with Denmark and the Swiss Confederation at war with Burgundy, the Greater Rhineland towns often had the strategic and technological advantage. Indeed, the Greater Rhineland was a principal site of military goods production. Liège's metallurgists, having learned to cast cannon from iron, became Europe's principal producer of artillery, thanks in part to the Machiavellian savvy of its archbishop, who disarmed the city and declared it neutral during the Burgundian wars. In the early seventeenth century, the towns of Holland profited from Liège's good fortune by commercializing its guns throughout Europe. Louis de Geer, a Liège native, built an arms industry empire that extended to Sweden, managed from his base in Holland.[29] New war-making technology probably favored some kind of territorial consolidation, but it did not, per se, threaten the political autonomy of Greater Rhineland towns, as demonstrated by the success of the Swiss Confederation and the United Provinces, and, in contrast, by the Habsburgs' inability to assert their rule in Germany. As argued in the previous chapter, the obstacle to territorial consolidation among the towns of the Greater Rhineland was not political economy, but ontopological legacy – the want of a word that might have brought their existence "to light" as territorial entity.

[27] See Hans W. Blom, "The Republican Mirror: The Dutch Idea of Europe," in Anthony Pagden, ed., *The Idea of Europe* (Cambridge and New York: Cambridge University Press and Woodrow Wilson Center, 2002).

[28] Christer Jönsson, Sven Tägil, and Gunar Törnqvist, *Organizing European Space* (London: Sage, 2000), pp. 25, 68.

[29] McNeill, *The Pursuit of Power*, p. 122.

Gallia redux

Religious strife pushed the commercial towns from the center of Greater Rhineland politics, creating a political vacuum that the French court, in competition with a resurgent Habsburg dynasty, struggled to fill. Discursively, the pretensions of Charles V to rule as emperor spurred the French court to resurrect Caesarian myth to legitimate its political claims. It was a significant move in French diplomatic rhetoric, clearly discernible in Albert Sorel's classic diplomatic history, even though the historian himself was unresponsive to it. Well into the fourteenth century the court had typically evoked imperial, European mythology to justify claims in the Greater Rhineland. Philip IV the Fair (1285–1314) was "obsessed by the memory of Charlemagne, whose heir he claimed to be,"[30] and his court was "nourished on the popular poetry of the Carolingian *chansons de geste*," accepted as historical fact.[31] Pierre du Bois, a royal counselor and author of *De Recuperatione Terrae Sanctae*, aspired to see the imperial crown, "which had been transferred from the Greeks to the Germans in the person of Charlemagne,"[32] placed on Philip's head. The French monarchy asserted its rights to the bishoprics of Toul in 1281 and Metz in 1297. Philip IV extended the court's legal competence and protection over Valenciennes, Tournai, and Quesnoy, imperial towns of Hainaut. In 1299, France tried to negotiate a marriage between the sister of Philip and the son of Albrecht of Austria that would have transferred Alsace to the French king and placed the kingdom's frontier on the Rhine. Philip's successor, Louis X (1314–16), placed Verdun under royal protection, and Philip VI (1328–50) garrisoned Cambrai with French troops (see figure 5.5).

But in the fifteenth century, in response first to Burgundian prosperity, and thereafter to Habsburg power, the myth of Gallia reemerged as a motivating and justificatory myth alongside and in agonistic encounter with that of imperial Europe. In 1444, Charles VII (1422–61) summoned the cities between the Meuse and the Vosges to submit to his authority in application of "the rights of the kingdom of Gaul, which extended to the Rhine." He called on the "provinces, lordships, cities and towns which, being situated on this side of the Rhine, ought by ancient right to appertain to the kings of France" to cease their (and the emperor's) usurpation of French authority. "We have entered into the marches of Bar and Lorraine,"

---

[30] Sorel, *Europe and the French Revolution*, p. 242.
[31] Sorel, *Europe and the French Revolution*, p. 243.
[32] Sorel, *Europe and the French Revolution*, p. 244.

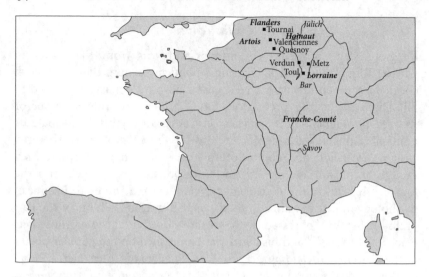

Figure 5.5 French expansion

he declared, "and toward the Germanies for great matters touching us and our Lordship, and especially to provide a remedy for various usurpations and attacks on the rights of our kingdom and the crown of France in the several provinces, seignories, cities and towns being on the side of the Rhine, which from olden times used to belong to our predecessors, the kings of France."[33] Toul and Verdun acquiesced. Metz resisted, arguing confusion between the competing claims of king and emperor, in order to defend its independence from both. The Dauphin, the future Louis XI (1461–83), while advancing on the Swiss Confederation, turned north toward Alsace to "assert the rights of the Kingdom of the Gauls which extends up to the Rhine."[34] Upon the death of Philip the Bold of Burgundy, Louis launched a general attack on the duke's lowland possessions, making an unusual appeal (for the times) to linguistic sentiment: "You Walloons, who speak French, need a French ruler, not a German."[35]

Henry II's campaign against a Habsburg empire in disarray, discussed above, was framed within this same mythical discourse of motivation and justification. The king's chronicler, Rabutin, gave his history a thoroughly

---

[33] Sorel, *Europe and the French Revolution*, p. 251.
[34] Sorel, *Europe and the French Revolution*, p. 250.
[35] Sorel, *Europe and the French Revolution*, p. 252.

Caesarian title, *Commentaires des dernières guerres en la Gaule belgique.*[36] Caesarian discourse, however, did not displace but accompanied Carolingian legacy. The myth of Gallia reemerged as the source, foundation, and legitimator of the myth of empire. The Maréchal de Vieilleville refused advancement in order to pursue the campaign "right into the kingdom of Austrasia, which was the first crown of our former kings." The son of one of Henry's counselors faulted the king for not occupying Alsace in order to resurrect "the kingdom of Austrasia."[37] Coligny, counselor to Charles IX (1560–74), pressed the king to complete the annexation. Sully, as counselor to Henri IV (1589–1610), claimed that "the sole and only means to restore France to its ancient glory and to make it greater than all the rest of Christendom" was to assert its rule over territories that "formerly belonged to it and seem to be properly within its limits, namely Savoy, Franche-Comté, Lorraine, Artois, Hainaut, and the provinces of the low countries including Jülich and Cleves." Henry, according to his adviser Théodore d'Aubigné, was prepared to invade Flanders, place the frontier of France on the Rhine, and put "the imperial crown on his head with a single effort."[38]

By the time of the Thirty Years War the *re-presentation* of France as heir to Gaul had become the principal justificatory and motivating myth of French action in the Greater Rhineland. Historians rightly emphasize the *Realpolitik* of Cardinal Richelieu, minister to Louis XIII, and of his successor, Cardinal Mazarin, chief counselor during the regency of Louis XIV. In the words of the German historian Franz Petri, "It would be beside the point to attribute French policy and results to Richelieu's offensive on the 'natural frontiers' . . . The perspectives in Richelieu's and Mazarin's policies were not annexations, alliances, or guarantees, but the security and durability of a future peace based on the firm solidarity of France's allies: Sweden, the United Provinces, and the German Protestants." France's realist prudence and desire to cultivate alliances explain, Petri continues, why French annexations were limited to Habsburg possessions along the upper Rhine.[39] Nevertheless, though the cardinals' *Realpolitik* is uncontestable, brilliant strategizing occurred within, and assumed meaning within, a discursive world marked by the new authority of the myth of Gallia, a resurrected ontopology that had

---

[36] Sorel, *Europe and the French Revolution*, p. 260.

[37] Sorel, *Europe and the French Revolution*, p. 260.

[38] Sorel, *Europe and the French Revolution*, p. 263. On Sully's "Grand Design," see Derek Heater, *The Idea of European Unity* (New York: St. Martin's Press, 1992), ch. 2.

[39] Petri, *Im Zeitalter des Glaubenskämpfe*, p. 153.

little or no meaning in the middle ages when political space could not be conceptualized independently of the loyalty networks that characterized feudalism, but which reemerged to justify the claims of an absolutist monarchy to rule in the Greater Rhineland. It was within this resurrected discursive space that it became possible to imagine possibilities and concoct strategies. To claim that Richelieu and Mazarin were "realists" is simply to say that they were prudent and realistic in their pursuit of ends, the attractiveness of which becomes understandable only when replaced within the mythological discourse that framed their thinking. Mythology legitimated strategy, justified diplomatic argument, and lent brilliance and nobility. Richelieu himself is reported to have been a great admirer of John Barclay's romance *Argenis* (1621), in which Poliarque, "King of the Gauls," is told by a seer that "the Rhine will see you victorious on one side and the Ocean on the other."[40] Richelieu declared that "the emperor has no rights in the lands on this side of the Rhine except by usurpation, and all the less because the river was the boundary of France."[41] Richelieu financed publicists to defend France's territorial claims. One of these, Chantereaux-Lefèvre, authored a 1642 pamphlet, *Considérations historiques sur la généalogie de la Maison de Lorraine*, that claimed that restoration of Frankish Gaul, bounded by the Rhine, would "restore an honorable and sure peace, to France and the whole of Christendom."[42] Jacques de Cassan, a publicist writing in 1643, advanced French claims to Flanders and the Low Countries, not only because they were Caesar's legacy, but because the Rhine, the Pyrenees, and the Alps defined limits that "nature" seemed to have drawn with her own hand. The image of the Rhine as a "natural frontier" also emerges from the *Testamentum Politicum* of Richelieu, in which one reads: "the aim of my ministry has been to give back to Gaul the frontiers destined by nature, to give the Gauls a Gallic king, to identify France with Gaul, and to re-establish new Gaul wherever the old one had been."[43] The authenticity of the text is disputed, but the Donation of Constantine shows that texts do not have to be authentic to generate mythological truths.

---

[40] Sorel, *Europe and the French Revolution*, p. 268. *Argenis* had a large international following that included Grotius, Leibniz, and Jonson. Barclay was a native of Pont-à-Mousson, on the Moselle (between Metz and Nancy), but left for England with his father at an early age. The greater part of his literary life was shared between London and Rome.

[41] Sorel, *Europe and the French Revolution*, p. 269.

[42] Sorel, *Europe and the French Revolution*, p. 271.

[43] Sorel, *Europe and the French Revolution*, p. 273.

The arguments of the pamphleteers employed a discourse that departed from medieval representations of political space as a territorial assemblage of monarchical claims to aristocratic fidelity. The new discourse referred back to the myth of Gaul, as "atomic" territory, impervious to division, a "natural entity" that placed no territorial or aristocratic intermediaries between ruler and ruled, which existed before Rome's conquest and was preserved by Roman arms. The discourse re-presented political space for absolutist rule. By the time of the settlement of Westphalia, France's claims on Lorraine and Alsace as "lost territory" typically accompanied and justified more technical, legal claims grounded in dynastic or feudal rights. A 1648 pamphlet, *Les affaires qui sont aujourd'hui entre les Maisons de France et d'Autriche*, assigned "Celtic and Belgic Gaul" to the French monarchy and justified the annexation of Lorraine as a province "usurped from France."[44]

The reemergence of Gallia places in discursive, ontopological perspective the observations of those who, like Rodney Hall, analyze the shift away from legitimating norms grounded in dynastic legitimacy to norms that legitimated action designed to consolidate territory. Hall formulates that observation in terms borrowed from Evan Luard:

> Dynastic claims to territory based upon custom or ancient privilege no longer held the sway they once had. As these claims could now be contended, territory was desired "to create readily defensible and powerful states" with rounded frontiers "to create more self-sufficient units" of sovereignty. Territorial sovereigns had thus developed a passion for continuous, defensible territories, and many conflicts were fought in order to unite divided dynastic holdings.[45]

The observation, accurate at a certain level, nevertheless misses the discursive *re-presentation* of political space (and the king's duties and opportunities within that space) that took place. One does not encounter unadorned geopolitical or strategic reflection. The appeal is not to "rounded frontiers," but to the *restoration* of a rightful political order.[46] The myth of a Gaul *restored* to its legitimate frontiers justified expansionist policy in the seventeenth century and beyond. If it were

---

[44] Sorel, *Europe and the French Revolution*, p. 272.

[45] Quoted in Rodney Bruce Hall, *National Collective Identity: Social Constructs and International Systems* (New York: Columbia University Press, 1999), p. 99.

[46] See Hall, *National Collective Identity*. Hall bases his argument largely on the Austro-Prussian struggle over control of Silesia.

simply a matter of "rounding frontiers," there was, again, no reason to prefer the Rhine to the Meuse.

The Westphalian edge

The seventeenth century was one of warfare in the Greater Rhineland, a kind of hundred years war that brought ruin, obliterated memories of the region's autonomous merchant town civilization, and turned the Rhineland into a frontierland of great power rivalry. War erupted in 1619 when Protestant opponents of Ferdinand II, the Habsburg emperor, deposed him as king of Bohemia and offered the crown to Frederick V, the Elector Palatine. Ferdinand repressed the rebellion while Habsburg Spain, from its lowland base, marched up the Rhine to lay waste to the Palatinate.[47] Austria fought as a member of a Catholic League led by Maximilian, duke of Bavaria, which placed its armies under the command of Jan t'Serclaes, baron of Tilly in Brabant. The League defeated the rebellion and Frederick fled to Holland. But hostilities resumed in 1625 when the king of Denmark, as imperial duke of Holstein, took up the Protestant cause. Imperial armies knocked Denmark out of the war, but drew in Sweden's Gustavus II Adolphus, whose kingdom encompassed much of the Baltic region. Richelieu, a Roman Catholic cardinal but forever attentive to opportunities to weaken the Catholic Habsburgs, subsidized the Protestant Swedes and Saxons. Gustavus defeated the League at Leipzig in 1631. Following the deaths of Gustavus Adolphus in 1632 and the Protestant leader Bernhard of Saxe-Weimar in 1639, France entered the war directly. It occupied the Meuse and Moselle valleys, including Saarbrücken, Ehrenbreitstein, near Koblenz, and Philippsburg, south of Speyer. French troops devastated the region in order to disrupt the lines of communication between Spain's Italian and lowland territories.[48] From bridgeheads on the Rhine, French armies joined the Swedes to fight imperial forces in Bavaria.

The Thirty Years War was extraordinarily destructive. Following the battle of Leipzig, 16,000 Swedish troops entered Mainz and exacted a heavy tribute of 80,000 talents from the town and 81,000 talents from the Church. Hunger and pestilence killed off half the population. Speyer and Darmstadt lost more than half their population; Trier, three-fifths.

---

[47] Petri, *Im Zeitalter des Glaubenskämpfe*, p. 135.
[48] Petri, *Im Zeitalter des Glaubenskämpfe*, pp. 143–6.

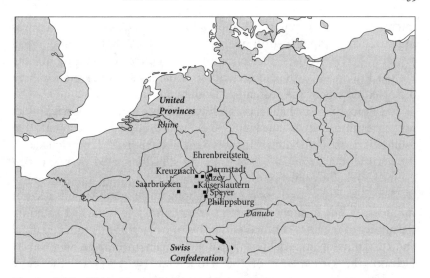

Figure 5.6 The Thirty Years War

Downstream, cities that saw important military engagements, such as Düren and Cleves, also suffered significant losses. Cologne, Aachen, Wesel, Essen, Elberfeld, Düsseldorf, and Bonn suffered little population loss, but in many parts of the Palatinate it reached 60 and even 70 percent.[49] The population of Kaiserslautern fell from 2,000 to 350. The populations of Alzney and Kreuznach fell by half. Bingen lost 10 percent of its inhabitants. Mainz and Trier were occupied (see figure 5.6). Cologne, though fortunate in comparison with other towns, strained under the burden of a massive influx of refugees.[50]

The Treaties of Westphalia restored a provisional peace to the Greater Rhineland. They acknowledged France's possession of the three diocesan cities of Lorraine – Metz, Toul, and Verdun – which it had annexed militarily in 1552. France also won Upper and Lower Alsace and ten of Alsace's imperial cities. Finally, the treaties installed French troops in two bridgehead towns on the right bank of the Rhine: Breisach, north of Basle, and Philippsburg. The treaties confirmed the territorial autonomy, *Landeshoheit*, of the states of the empire, including the right to conclude alliances on condition they not be directed against the empire. Both France and Sweden had an "entrenched

---

[49] Petri, *Im Zeitalter des Glaubenskämpfe*, p. 158.
[50] Petri, *Im Zeitalter des Glaubenskämpfe*, p. 228.

interest in seeing a system [of imperial governance] sustained that was organized around the institutional and geographical dispersal of political power."[51] The treaties recognized the complete sovereignty of the United Provinces of the Netherlands and the Swiss Confederation, and dissolved all ties of subordination to the empire.

The Peace of Westphalia has exercised theorists of international politics for generations. It is considered the "constitutional" document that founded the modern international system of territorially sovereign states, the "crucial demarcation between an era still dominated by competing claims to religious universalism and hierarchical authority and an era of secular competition and cooperation among autonomous political communities."[52] The formula *cuius regio*, which made the territorial authority the arbiter of religious conflicts within his or her territory, brought a final end to claims of imperial and papal supremacy in Europe. For Robert Jackson, the *Grundnorm* of the nation-state system was "the basic prohibition against foreign intervention which simultaneously imposes a duty of forbearance and confers a right of independence on all statesmen."[53] But Stephen Krasner has objected that this "constitutional" reading of Westphalia is a back-projected myth. As Krasner observes, the "Westphalian" concept of sovereignty received no explicit treatment until philosophers and jurists like the Leibnitzian Christian von Wolff and the Swiss natural law theorist Emerich de Vattel began to treat it as foundational in the mid eighteenth century. Westphalia appears to have had little appreciable impact on the thinking of Louis XIV (1643–1715), who surveyed the world not from the perspective of modern sovereignty discourse, but through the mythical lens formed by representations of Gallia and empire. Westphalia, for Louis, was simply proof that the construction of Europe had decayed to the point that Habsburg claims to the imperial throne, given their inability to govern, had no legitimate foundation. In his memoirs, he went "out of his way

---

[51] Roland Axtmann, "State Formation and Supranationalism in Europe: The Case of the Holy Roman Empire of the German Nation," in Mabel Berezin and Martin Schain, eds., *Europe without Borders: Remapping Territory, Citizenship, and Identity in a Transnational Age* (Baltimore: Johns Hopkins University Press, 2003), p. 132. The empire did retain a formal constitution. See *ibid.*, pp. 131–7.

[52] R. B. J. Walker, quoted in Jönssen *et al.*, *Organizing European Space*, p. 65.

[53] Quoted in Stephen D. Krasner, *Sovereignty: Organized Hypocrisy* (Princeton: Princeton University Press, 1999), pp. 20–1. Note, however, that the treaty referred to the status quo of 1624, and did not expressly or technically assign new powers to the sovereigns. Pufendorf and Bijnkershoek wrote during Louis XIV's lifetime. It is arguable whether their thought occurs within a recognizably Westphalian framework.

to stress his contempt ... of the Habsburg ruler. Charlemagne, he announced, had been the only real ruler of Europe – and the king of France must be his successor."[54] From such a perspective, *cuius regio*, far from awarding sovereignty to German princes, merely revealed the illegitimacy of the constitutional arrangements that existed between the empire and its largely autonomous provincial and town governments. That illegitimacy justified French intervention, both to restore the ancient frontiers of Roman Gallia and ultimately to resurrect the empire with Gallia as its foundation. Westphalia, in other words, inaugurated an era not of French respect for the sovereignty of German towns and princes, but of French expansionism in the Greater Rhineland. The three bishoprics of Lorraine (Verdun, Metz, Toul), Philippsburg, Ehrenbreitstein, Kaub, Mainz, Mannheim, and Alsace were all in French hands. Trier was suspended anxiously between the threat of Spanish intrusion from its base in Brussels, and French annexation from its base in Metz. French armies threatened the Palatinate from bridgeheads in Philippsburg. The French court negotiated a defensive treaty with Cologne. The duke of Hanau-Lichtenberg petitioned the court for protection. "France found more clients than enemies in Germany"[55] not only because it guaranteed the independence of local princelings vis-à-vis Vienna but because it bought their support with generous subsidies. Under French protection, imperial princes further consolidated their power at the expense of the towns.[56]

Louis XIV first set his sights on the Spanish lowlands, justifying his designs by claiming rights to the inheritance of his queen, Maria Theresa of Spain. She had renounced those rights to enable the marriage alliance, but Louis discovered a law specific to the province of Brabant – the law of devolution – that enabled him to claim the renunciation was invalid. French armies entered Brabant. Dutch armies, once France's allies in the struggle against Spain, marched to oppose them. The United Provinces, an upstart urban republic in Louis' eyes, without historical or institutional legitimacy – without "aura," despite Westphalia – now became his principal adversary. In language reminiscent of Burgundy's, the French court dismissed the Dutch as "beasts, not men."[57] The Netherlands by this time had succeeded Flanders as the core commercial economy and financial center of Europe, and, like the Burgundian lowlands two centuries earlier,

---

[54] Maurice Ashley, *Louis XIV and the Greatness of France* (London: The English Universities Press, 1967), p. 42.

[55] Sorel, *Europe and the French Revolution*, p. 276.

[56] Petri, *Im Zeitalter des Glaubenskämpfe*, p. 231.   [57] Ashley, *Louis XIV*, p. 73.

was a center of artistic and intellectual creativity of the first order. Among Louis' beasts were Franz Hals, Meyndaert Hobbema, Jacob Ruysdael, Jan Vermeer, Rembrandt of the Rhine (van Rijn), and philosophers Hugo van Groot (Grotius) and Baruch Spinoza. Immanuel Wallerstein has gone so far as to characterize seventeenth-century Netherlands as "hegemonic" in the world political economy.[58] Its preeminence had several sources: the destruction of the Hansa's monopoly in the Baltic, as related in the previous chapter; the flight of artisans, merchants, and capitalists from Spanish Flanders and Brabant, discussed above; and finally, European colonial expansion. Portugal had opened new sea routes to the Indian Ocean in the fifteenth century, and, with Spain, had colonized the Americas. When Portugal fell under the sway of the Spanish Habsburgs (1580–1640), Dutch merchants, now excluded from formerly Portuguese ports, showed the same independence of spirit and intensity of purpose they had shown against the Hansa. They developed their own trade routes to the Indies, creating the Dutch East India Company in 1602, and the Dutch West India Company in 1621. They displaced the Portuguese in the Indian Ocean and the Straits of Sumatra. They policed the waters off south Africa from their base in the Cape. They established themselves in the Caribbean, attempted to conquer Brazil, and defended their maritime supremacy in war, first with the Spanish and Portuguese, then with the English (1652–67).

The Netherlands' wars with France, however, were not about maritime supremacy, but about its survival as a sovereign entity. The French court began its assault by imposing prohibitive tariff duties on Dutch imports in 1667, and assembling a merchant marine to challenge its commercial supremacy. The Treaty of Aachen (or Aix-la-Chapelle, 1668) transferred twelve fortified towns including Lille, Tournay, and Oudenarde, all captured in the campaign against Spain, to France. French diplomats, meanwhile, purchased the neutrality of Rhineland princelings with subsidies. The Elector of Cologne contributed 18,000 troops to the campaign against the United Provinces, while the emperor agreed to remain neutral. The Dutch, under the hereditary *Stadhouder* William III of Orange, deployed their small forces against an army of more than 100,000 men, "probably the largest mass of troops ever seen in the modern West."[59] The French cleared the left bank of the Rhine in 1672.

---

[58] Immanuel Wallerstein, *The Modern World System*, vol. II, *Mercantilism and the Consolidation of the World Economy, 1600–1750* (New York: Academic Press, 1980), ch. 2.
[59] Ashley, *Louis XIV*, p. 70.

Figure 5.7 The wars of Louis XIV

Neuss, which had resisted Charles the Bold, fell to Louis XIV. Louis took possession of the town personally, becoming the first French king to set foot in the Greater Rhineland in centuries.[60] French troops then occupied Saarbrücken and Trier and laid waste to the land around Philippsburg (see figure 5.7). The French advanced rapidly down the Rhine toward Amsterdam. In one of the few effective uses of the natural defensive aptitudes of the Rhine river in history, the Dutch pierced the dykes and flooded the polders that separated Amsterdam from the French in Utrecht. Amsterdam's dramatic defense, coupled with Dutch victories at sea, stalled the French advance and won Holland an alliance with its erstwhile enemy, Spain, and with the Habsburg emperor and some German princes. William of Orange concluded an alliance with Holland's other erstwhile enemy, Great Britain, by marrying the English king's niece. In seeking "to overthrow the Dutch Republic ... [thus] thrusting the protestant Dutch ... into the arms of the Catholic Habsburgs, Louis made a fatal, if not exceptional, mistake."[61] The countervailing coalition contained the French advance. The Treaty of Nijmegen abolished the discriminatory tariff on Dutch commerce and deprived the French of some of the towns they had won in previous campaigns. Louis, despite the results, rejoiced in his "good luck and clever conduct whereby I was able

[60] Petri, *Im Zeitalter des Glaubenskämpfe*, p. 246.   [61] Ashley, *Louis XIV*, p. 61.

to profit from every opportunity I found to extend the boundaries of my kingdom at the expense of my enemies."[62]

Louis turned from the lower to the upper Rhine, where the Treaty of Westphalia had granted him Alsatian fiefdoms. Louis sought to annex the entire province by challenging legal claims in French courts, the "chambers of reunion," established expressly for this purpose in Metz, Besançon, Breisach, and Tournai in the lowlands. "The idea was to make use of the rather complicated structure of territorial sovereignty which survived from the Middle Ages in the countries bordering on France."[63] One hundred and forty thousand troops stood ready to enforce the chambers' decisions. By 1680, Strasburg, still an autonomous town, was virtually the only remaining independent entity in Alsace. Louis, emboldened by rebellion in the Habsburg territories and a Turkish invasion, occupied the city in 1681.

In 1683, French troops occupied the Flemish towns of Courtrai and Dixmuide, and ravaged the country around Bruges and Brussels. They seized Liège and occupied the territory of the Elector of Cologne. A second countervailing alliance arose in 1687–8, composed of Austria, Sweden, Spain, Bavaria, Saxony, the Palatinate, England, and the Netherlands. To defend against invasion, the French adopted a scorched earth policy in the Palatinate.

> Beyond the Rhine the French army was to create a wilderness, denying fortifications, shelter and food to any advancing enemy. In the depth of winter, villagers, the inhabitants of towns, the occupants of châteaux fled before the French terror. Over a thousand villages and small towns were put to the torch, crops and livestock taken or destroyed. The devastation spread beyond the Electorate proper – to Württemberg and various Rhineland principalities. The whole region burned. Nearly a dozen cities and major towns suffered serious damage. At Heidelberg the magnificent Renaissance palace was shattered by explosives. Then, as the army finally drew back behind the Rhine in the early summer of 1689, they meted out the same fate to the cathedral towns of Trier, Worms, and Speyer.[64]

Social discontent at home and Holland's victory at Namur produced the compromise treaty of Ryswick in 1698, whereby France retained Alsace and Strasburg, but acquiesced in the Dutch occupation of towns in the Spanish lowlands to defend against French invasion. But a disputed succession to the Spanish throne brought war to the Rhineland again

---

[62] Ashley, *Louis XIV*, p. 77.   [63] Ashley, *Louis XIV*, p. 98.
[64] Heater, *The Idea of European Unity*, p. 41.

in 1701. Louis seized towns occupied by the Dutch – Namur, Mons, and Ostend – and crossed the Rhine to join anti-Habsburg forces led by the Elector of Bavaria. But as the Franco-Bavarian army marched on Vienna, the English under the duke of Marlborough moved quickly up the Rhine to inflict a stunning defeat on Louis' forces at Blenheim in 1704. Louis was forced to withdraw troops from Spain and Italy to defend his northern frontier. England and Holland signed the Barrier Treaty of 1709 whereby England subscribed to Holland's annexation of the Habsburg lowlands as a defense against French armies. French diplomacy took England out of the war by surrendering Gibraltar and recognizing England's monopoly on the triangular slave trade in exchange for England's recognition of French claims to the Spanish crown. France then made peace with Austria by agreeing to transfer rule of the Spanish lowlands to the Austrian Habsburgs. Finally, France acquiesced in Holland's occupation of Habsburg towns. France retained Alsace, including Strasburg, but lost Lorraine.

A measure of peace returned to the Greater Rhineland in the eighteenth century. Religious persecution receded by about 1750. The first oil well in Pechelbronn, in Alsace, foreshadowed the renaissance of the Rhineland economy in the industrial age. The geographic scope of war moved eastward, sparing the Rhineland the destructions of the previous century. The French laid claim again to the formerly Spanish but now Austrian Netherlands. Their armies, under the command of their ally, the Maréchal de Saxe, won control of the territory in two battles, Fontenoy (1745) and Raucoux (1746). But Russia entered the fray and a treaty negotiated in the old imperial town of Aachen restored the lands to the emperor. In 1756, in a stunning diplomatic reversal, the French and Austrian Habsburg courts entered into alliance to oppose growing Prussian influence in Germany. It was also inspired by growing French and English rivalry in the new world. The "Third Silesian" or "Seven Years" War again saw French armies cross the Rhine. But the principal theaters of war were in Silesia, Saxony, and North America, rather than the Greater Rhineland.

Although the region slowly recovered from its "hundred years" war, the Greater Rhineland of Erasmus had ceased to exist. The towns were under the influence or rule of princes. Cosmopolitanism was imperiled by a new discourse of closure. The regional economy, so brilliant in the middle ages, lay in ruin. The middle Rhine was devastated. The Rhine as conduit between the North Sea and the Mediterranean declined in importance as the towns of Italy lost their eastern Mediterranean markets to the Ottomans. Colonial expansion shifted economic activity to the sea ports of the Atlantic, Bordeaux and Liverpool. By 1789, colonial trade accounted for a third of France's commerce with the rest of the world and about half of Britain's.[65] The ports of the lower Rhine, if not the towns of Rhineland Germany, were able to participate in this development. The United Provinces became one of the principal colonial powers. Belgium, which would become a "nation"-state in 1830, would seize colonies in Africa. But the Rhineland political economy as civilization-type, as described in the previous chapter, was no longer. The representation of Greater Rhineland political space as a network of largely autonomous towns lost all hold on the social imaginary. The empire as ontopology, legacy of Charlemagne and titular home to the towns, had long since lost rhetorical effect. William of Orange, in response to French efforts to justify expansion by ontopological legacy – by a kind of *renovatio* of an imagined map of Europe organized as an empire anchored by a reemergent Gaul – ordered his pamphleteers to delete references to *Christianitas*, the redemptive legitimator of that ontopology, and use instead the term "Europe" to designate the topographical site of Westphalian sovereignty.[66] But the signifier "Europe" was not easily dissociated from its salvationist *telos*. Voltaire and Kant imagined Europe as a great republic that would allow states committed to peace to coexist under the rule of law. Novalis (Friedrich Leopold von Hardenberg), German romantic poet and mystic, penned a tract, *Europe or Christendom*, that foresaw the regeneration of Europe's spiritual unity and purpose. Europe, as place, acquired a history in the eighteenth century thanks to the efforts of Gibbon and Voltaire, of Raynal and Diderot. It became a "character," or family of characters, in a salvationist drama (or, in the case of Gibbon, in a cautionary tale about the dangers of salvationism).[67] Despite these literary efforts to keep Carolingia alive, the seeds of a new, more authoritative representation of Greater Rhineland space had been sown by Louis XIV's armies. A landscape of disturbing, inspiring nostalgia would emerge from the middle Rhineland's devastation in the late

---

[65] Evan Luard, *The Balance of Power: The System of International Relations, 1648–1815* (London: Macmillan, 1992), p. 228.

[66] Etienne Balibar, *Nous, citoyens d'Europe: les frontières, l'état, le peuple* (Paris: Découverte, 2001), p. 22.

[67] See Anthony Pagden, "Europe: Conceptualizing a Continent," in Pagden, ed., *The Idea of Europe*, pp. 62ff. See James Tully, "The Kantian Idea of Europe," in *ibid.*, which will be reprised by Woodrow Wilson.

eighteenth century, a landscape of Romanesque cathedrals; of razed castles, entwined in foliage, that guarded the memory of a collapsed civilization; of river rapids that evoked lost youth; of vineyards that unlocked memories of happier times; of aspirations that lived on as matter decayed. Those images would engender *Rheinromantik* in the nineteenth century, the fertile ground from which would germinate a new *re-presentation* of Rhineland space as the cradle of a German nation, defined by its refusal to surrender its cultural authenticity to "Welsch" – Roman, then French – expansionism. Thus would the Reformation and the passions it unleashed transform the "river of nations" into a "wager (*enjeu*) between ... nations."[68]

[68] Demangeon and Febvre, *Le Rhin*, p. 114.

6

Coups de force: Ossian and the département

About 3 million visitors cram into Rüdesheim's cuckoo-clock alleys each year to wallow in wine culture and *Rheinromantik*. A viscous slurry of peoples, languages, and wine oozes through the narrow *Drosselgasse* as bits and pieces of polka emanate from open doors and windows. Cable cars lift off with a hum from a village square to convey passengers across hillsides combed in Riesling. A Romanesque-style church – memorial to medieval polymath Hildegard of Bingen – rises in the distance. At the top, a wooded path leads to the towering figure of *Germania*, erected in 1883 to celebrate German nationhood. Engraved on its base, one reads:

> Es braust ein Ruf wie Donnerhall
> Wie Schwertgeklirr und Wogenprall:
> Zum Rhein, zum Rhein, zum deutschen Rhein!
> Wer will des Stromes Hüter sein?
> Lieb Vaterland, magst ruhig sein;
> Fest steht und treu die Wacht, die Wacht am Rhein!
>
> A voice resounds like thunder-peal,
> 'Mid dashing waves and clang of steel:
> The Rhine, the Rhine, the German Rhine!
> Who guards to-day my stream divine?
> Dear Fatherland, no danger thine;
> Firm stand thy sons to watch the Rhine![1]

The tone of defiance, like *Germania*'s brazen-faced vigilance, seems incongruous in its setting (see plates 6.1a and 6.1b). Vintners on the hillside below potter among their vines, patiently coaxing into existence a world commodity export. The village on the banks prepares for

---

[1] Eva March Tappan, ed., *The World's Story: A History of the World in Story, Song and Art*, 14 vols. (Boston: Houghton Mifflin, 1914), vol. VII: *Germany, the Netherlands, and Switzerland*, pp. 249–50.

Plate 6.1a *Germania*

night-time revelry. An incessant drone rises from the valley as trains, barges, ships, and automobiles inscribe their itinerary in the Rhine's timeless logs of travel, commerce, industry, and cultural encounter. But *Germania*'s incongruent insolence is itself a monument to the ontopological revolution that occurred here. The wars of the seventeenth century had turned the Greater Rhineland into a frontierland disputed by monarchical powers – France, Austria, and Prussia. The monarchical states, however, were not "nation-states." The ontology of the monarchical state was predicated on the unicity of

Plate 6.1b *Germania* with Riesling

the ruler: "monarchy."[2] The ontology of the "nation-state," in contrast, was (and is) predicated on the unicity of the ruled, a unicity grounded in the existence of a common legacy, or inheritance, which the ruled assume as a birthright, as *natio*, or nation (from *natus*, like *natura*, from *nasci*: to be born). The myth of nationhood *re-presented* the state as the emanation and protector of a people defined by its participation – *always already* in the language of Heidegger and Derrida; a fact of

---

[2] See Anthony Smith, *Myths and Memories of the Nation* (Oxford: Oxford University Press, 1999), p. 111.

birth – in the transmission from generation to generation of a common language, culture, and territory. People, culture, language, and land merged to form an *ethnoscape*, to borrow Anthony Smith's felicitous term.[3] According to this mythical representation, the survival of the nation as legacy demanded feats of arms, which the nation memorialized in bronze monuments like *Germania*, erected in grateful recognition of the sacrifice of fallen sons, brothers, and fathers. It was the struggle to secure the survival of the nation as legacy, rather than as divine ordinance as in the past, that legitimated rule. The struggle to preserve the legacy of nationhood provided, in Max Weber's term, the *Vorstellung*, literally the presentation, the offering, the "placing before" (or, more abstractly, conception, idea, or even performance – translated tendentiously by Talcott Parsons as "belief") of a legitimate order.[4]

The nation-state, inscribed in bronze and political practice, emerged from a revolution in the conceptualization of political space – a revolution in the sense not of armed insurrection, but of artistic representational style, of *Vorstellung*, of performance. In the words of Anne-Marie Thiesse, the nation was the product of a "conscious and militant willfulness." The nation was born when "a handful of individuals declared that it exists and undertook to prove it."[5] Two texts inaugurate this revolutionary shift in spatial representation: the epics of Ossian and the constitutional decree that created the French *département*. The first unleashed a literary campaign to retrieve or reconstruct an array of linguistic and cultural "legacies" that, it was imagined, had been eclipsed by the classical pretensions of the French (or French-style) court and salon. The second washed away all but the memory of the antecedent spatial representation – composed of duchies, counties, cities, and kingdoms – that had once situated local ontopologies and often substantial administrative and fiscal privileges. The *département*, in other words, erased ontopologies that had arguably become "customary." The new administrative map authorized, as names of *départements*, only "natural," topographical features. By cleansing territory of its particularisms, the *département* cleared a space in the imagination for the nation. Unified within and protected by its "natural frontiers" – the oceans, the Alps, the Pyrenees, and the Rhine – the

---

[3] Smith, *Myths and Memories of the Nation*, ch. 5.

[4] Max Weber, *The Theory of Social and Economic Organization*, trans. A. M. Henderson and Talcott Parsons (London: Collier-Macmillan, 1964), p. 124. See Albert Demangeon and Lucien Febvre, *Le Rhin* (Paris: Armand Colin, 1935), pp. 124–5.

[5] Anne-Marie Thiesse, *La création des identités nationales: Europe XVIIIe–XXe siècle* (Paris: Seuil, 1999), pp. 11, 16.

"old France" as geographical space defined by claims to loyalty by a dynastic house gave way to a "new France" as topographical container of a linguistically and culturally homogeneous nation. Within the new discursive framework, the extension of France's frontiers to the Rhine became, in the first half of the nineteenth century, a kind of manifest destiny. Inversely, the defense of the Rhine, as mythical cradle of German civilization, became, *Germania* tells us, the German nation's moral obligation.

In this chapter I examine the two texts that inaugurate this representational revolution. In the next chapter, I examine the state's efforts to construct – through education, cultural initiative, and military conscription – the nation that the state, so says the myth, was established to preserve. As in the previous chapters, one must caution against a deterministic, or even casually causal reading of this discursive history. The self-destruction of the medieval Rhineland town civilization conditioned, but did not determine, the discursive violence that would "give birth" to the modern nation. The nation, in turn, would inaugurate discursive practices and prejudices that would assume a life of their own, framing, enabling, and constraining political action. But the purpose of this chapter is not to explain the rupture of Greater Rhineland space by nations, but to bear witness to that rupture so as to interrogate the vocabulary that, today, frames, enables, and constrains deliberation about European Union.

Ossian

James Macpherson, the son of a Scottish farmer, aspired to be a poet. Early success earned him a position as preceptor in one of Edinburgh's influential families. Because his countryside childhood gave him fluency in Gaelic, his employer's literary friends asked him to translate some Gaelic songs into English. These appeared in 1760 under the title, *Fragments of Ancient Poetry, collected in the Highlands of Scotland and translated from the Gaelic or Erse language by James Macpherson.* One of his benefactors, Hugh Blair, believed the poems were fragments of an epic poem, "our epic," composed by an ancient Celtic bard to memorialize the exploits of a great warrior named Fingal. Blair and other literati raised funds for Macpherson to recover more fragments, compile them, and reconstruct the epic.

The interest in home-grown epics was not new or unique to Scotland. It expressed a widespread urge among writers and intellectuals to challenge cultural hegemonies – English hegemony in Scotland, French hegemony on the continent. The proximate literary cause, however, was the 1735 publication of Thomas Blackwell's *Enquiry into the Life and Writings of Homer*. The book was hardly a critical essay, but following its publication "the search was on, in Scotland as elsewhere in Europe, to find the truly national poet."[6] Early contenders for the title in Scotland were Dr. Thomas Blalock, the "Scottish Pindar," John Home, the "Scottish Shakespeare," and William Wilkie, one of Macpherson's supporters, a (if not the) "Scottish Homer." Macpherson therefore made for the Highlands to interview pastors, peasants, and landlords, collecting material that he worked into a 1761 publication, *Fingal, an Ancient Epic Poem, in Six Books, together with several other Poems, composed by Ossian, the son of Fingal; translated from the Gaelic language by James Macpherson*. The poem begins:

> Cuchullin sat by Tura's wall; by the tree of the rustling leaf. His spear leaned against the mossy rock. His shield lay by him on the grass. As he thought of mighty Carbar, a hero whom he slew in war; the scout of ocean came Moran the son of Fithil.
>
> Rise, said the youth, Cuchullin, rise; I see the ships of Swaran. Cuchullin, many are the foe: many the heroes of the dark-rolling sea.
>
> (*Fingal*, 1–2)

Macpherson claimed to translate, not compose, verses penned by a third-century bard named Ossian. The epics' adepts received the poems as the work of "a 'natural genius,' whom men of unquestioned literary sagacity placed next to and even above Homer."[7] But the epics spurred controversy. Macpherson, for some, was an unscrupulous counterfeitor. Samuel Johnson asked pointedly what third-century Caledonians might have used for an alphabet. The dispute was intense, and stoked scorn for what was at the time an abused minority. Macpherson promised but failed to produce documentation to support his claim. The "Highland Societies" of Edinburgh and London named an expert committee shortly after Macpherson's death to settle the question of the epics' authenticity. In 1807 this committee produced a three-volume analysis that, for whatever reason, juxtaposed modern Gaelic and Latin translations of the English original with commentary. The commission did not find Macpherson's "originals," but it did interview witnesses who attested to their existence. Summarizing the controversy one

---

[6] Howard Gaskill, ed., *Ossian Revisited* (Edinburgh: Edinburgh University Press, 1991), p. 73.
[7] Rudolf Tombo, "Ossian in Germany," PhD thesis, Columbia University, 1901. Published also as no. 2, vol. I of the Columbia University Germanic Studies, p. 66.

hundred years later, a sympathetic Ossian *aficionado* characterized Macpherson as a "'skillful artificer,' who took a few crude scattered fragments of Irish – not distinctively Scotch – folksongs as his foundation, and not only lengthened them into more elaborate and refined poems, but built up long epics, which, although accepted as genuine by a credulous age in a moment of blind enthusiasm, have not been able to withstand the scrutiny of the unprejudiced scholar."[8]

The "moment of blind enthusiasm" was conditioned by contemporary developments in European literary life. Expansionist Europe had acquired a fascination with the exotic. Twenty years before *Fingal*, William Collins composed a book of *Oriental Eclogues*, which he marketed, like Macpherson, as the work of an obscure, natural genius: "I received [the poems] at the hands of a merchant, who had made it his business to enrich himself with the learning, as well as the silks and carpets, of the Persians." Collins equated the exotic with *national* style:

> It is with the writings of mankind, in some measure, as with their complexions or their dress, each nation hath a peculiarity in all these, to distinguish it from the rest of the world. The gravity of the Spaniard and the levity of the Frenchman are as evident in all their productions as in their persons themselves; and the style of my countrymen is as naturally strong and nervous as that of an Arabian or Persian is rich and figurative.[9]

Europe had also developed a new appreciation of sentiment and sentimentality in its interrogation of classical standards and universalistic reasoning. That interrogation fueled demand for a new literary genre, the romantic novel. Ossian's manipulation of sentiment recalls writings by Laurence Sterne (*Tristram Shandy* and *A Sentimental Journey through France and Italy*), Abbé Prévost (*Manon Lescaut*) and, above all, Jean-Jacques Rousseau (*Emile* and *La Nouvelle Héloïse*). Regard for sentiment was evident as well in the philosophical works of two other Scotsmen, David Hume and Adam Smith, as in the writings of Denis Diderot on the continent. Ossian's "joy of grief," the bittersweet longing that Ossian's characters (and public) expressed on hearing tales of a lost golden age, exerted great influence on the Romantic movement.

> But I am sad, forlorn, and blind; and no more the companion of heroes. Give, lovely maid, to me thy tears, for I have seen the tombs of all my friends …

---

[8] Tombo, "Ossian in Germany," pp. 66–7; see Gaskill, *Ossian Revisited*, p. 1.
[9] Fiona Stafford and Howard Gaskill, eds., *From Gaelic to Romantic: Ossianic Translations* (Amsterdam: Rodopi, 1998), p. 32.

I, often, joined the bards, and sung of battles of the spear. – battles! Where I often fought; but now I fight no more. The fame of my former actions is ceased; and I sit forlorn at the tombs of my friends.[10]

Finally, Ossian participated in a literary rebellion. *Fingal*, with its epigraph *fortia facta patrum* – "more valiant the deeds of our forefathers" – challenged English cultural hegemony in the north by giving voice to "Caledonians" who, unlike their neighbors to the south, successfully resisted Rome's armies. The preface by Blair vaunted primitive virtues, unsoftened by civilization's blandishments, with near-Rousseauian imagery:

> I shall ... only observe, that the general poverty of a nation has not the same influence, that the indigence of individuals, in an opulent country, has, upon the manners of the community. The idea of meanness, which is now connected with a narrow fortune, had its rise after commerce had thrown too much property into the hands of the few; for the poorer sort, imitating the vices of the rich, were obliged to have recourse to roguery and circumvention, in order to supply their extravagance, so that they were, not without reason, reckoned, in more than one sense, the worst of people.[11]

In sum, the "Rousseau-like natural refinement of the Ossianic heroes, as well as that 'joy of grief' which arose from the contemplation of an irretrievably lost past; the strange and sometimes dazzling imagery and style similar to that found in the Bible; the rhythmical language of its poetic prose, which, freed from classical rigor, seemed to bear witness to the force of expression ascribed to the earliest stages of society; and the almost mythical portrayal of a people and its culture, which apparently took on the role of a model society along the lines of a new philosophical primitivism and a yearning for freedom from the restraints of absolutism," all conspired to win for the bard a large and enthusiastic readership.[12]

Herder

As early as 1763 Melchiore Cesarotti, classicist and translator of Homer, produced an Italian version of the epics. The Viennese Jesuit, Michael Denis, working initially from Cesarotti's translation, produced a German version in 1768.[13] When Denis submitted his translation for

---

[10] Cited in Stafford and Gaskill, *From Gaelic to Romantic*, pp. 61–2.
[11] Gaskill, *Ossian Revisited*, p. 82. [12] Gaskill, *Ossian Revisited*, p. 74.
[13] Gaskill, *Ossian Revisited*, p. 77. See Stafford and Gaskill, *From Gaelic to Romantic*, p. 163.

publication he feared it would prove too "unmodern" to be popular, but the reviews were enthusiastic. The most influential of these appeared in the *Allgemeine Deutsche Bibliothek* under the name of Johann Gottfried Herder, who called the poem a "priceless survival of the ancient Celtic or Gallic language."[14] Herder even set about rewriting parts of it, finding Denis' vocabulary too polished – too Latin – and the rhythm too regular. Reprising an enduring confusion between Celts and Germans (see chapter 2), Herder exclaimed "Was Ossian not our brother? And what good fortune, what a durable service it would have been to have translated (*verdeutschen*) him as if he had been a German, which, of course, he was by half."[15]

Ossian's impact on German literary life was profound. "There was scarcely a writer of note who did not at some time or other fall under [Ossian's] spell."[16] Goethe, who gave Herder his own copy of the English text, developed a deep interest in the bard, having read Macpherson's texts in Leipzig as a student (1765–8). With Herder's encouragement, he translated Ossian during his student days in Strasburg (1770–1). Ossian's "Songs of Selma" became, in his 1774 novel, *The Sorrows of Young Werther*, the vehicle whereby Werther and Lotte lamented their ill-fated love.[17] The novel turned Ossian into popular reading in Germany.[18]

Ossian's epics also found favor among literati seeking to develop a style that was distinctly "German," yet legitimated, like the classicism of the fifteenth-century humanists, by antique wisdom and cultural achievement. In 1749, the Osnabrück lawyer Justus Möser wrote *Arminius*, a celebration of the first-century defeat of Rome's legions. Johann Jakob Bodmer founded a literary society in Zurich to promote

---

[14] Tombo, "Ossian in Germany," pp. 120–2: *diese kostbaren Ueberbleibsel aus der alten celtischen oder gallischen Sprache.*

[15] Tombo, "Ossian in Germany," p. 123. The putative brotherhood of Ossian and the German nation was accepted both in Germany and in Scotland. At the same page one finds this genealogical fantasy: "The family of Keith ... derives its origin from the Catti, people of Germany ... in the time of Tiberius they were entirely routed by Germanicus ... part of the Germani submitted to the Roman yoke ... But the most part, under the conduct of their leader Battus ... settled about the mouth of the Rhine [whence Batavia] ... the Batavian Catti sent a colony to Britain. Being separated in a storm, part of them arrived in the Thames, and the rest were driven to the northern parts of Scotland, and landed in that part called Caithness; which name took its rise from Catti."

[16] Tombo, "Ossian in Germany," p. 67.

[17] Gaskill, *Ossian Revisited*, p. 86; Stafford and Gaskill, *From Gaelic to Romantic*, p. 100.

[18] Gaskill, *Ossian Revisited*, p. 80; on Goethe, see A. Tedeschi, *Ossian: "l'Homère du Nord" en France* (Milan: Tipografia Sociale, 1911), p. 9. But cf. Stafford and Gaskill, *From Gaelic to Romantic*, p. 97.

German literature, and, while Macpherson was "reconstructing" Ossian's epics, published fragments of the thirteenth-century *Nibelungenlied*, later heralded as the German *Iliad*. In 1755, the Swiss essayist Paul-Henri Mallet published an influential work much praised in later years by Germaine de Staël (see below) and the Swiss socialist historian Léonard Sismondi, entitled *Introduction à l'histoire de Danemarc*. The title of its supplement – "Survivals of the Mythology and Poetry of the Celts and particularly the Ancient Scandinavians" (*Monumens de la mythologie et de la poësie des Celtes et particulièrement des Anciens Scandinaves*) – reprised yet again the confusion between "Germans" and "Celts" inherited from Posidonius and Dio Cassius. In effect, Ossian's admirers asserted that the Celtic bard and the Germanic Skald were one and the same, as "proved" by Tacitus' use of the term *barditus* to refer to the battle chant of the Germans. Klopstock, like Herder, claimed Ossian for Germany, honoring the Caledonians' resistance to Rome, which, like France, was the militaristic bearer of a hegemonic culture:

> You, whose descendants even now inhabit the mountains of Scotland,
> Caledonians whom Rome never overcame,
> You are of German stock. Thus to us as well,
> And even more than to the land of the Angles,
> Does the bard and warrior Ossian belong.[19]

Poets, inspired by Ossian's success, tried their own hand at writing epics, making wholesale use of Ossianic tropes – strumming harps, echoing groves, ghosts and druids. They even assumed bardic names. The playwright Friedrich Gottlieb Klopstock, a leader of the movement, adopted the *nom de plume* of "Werdomar"; Heinrich von Gerstenberg, Klopstock's close friend and early adept of *Sturm und Drang*, became "Thorlaug"; Denis himself wrote under the anagram "Sined," and Karl Friedrich Kretschmann assumed the name "Rhingulph."[20] Although von Gerstenberg considered Ossian a forgery, for which he was taken to task by Herder, he produced his own, influential epic in 1766, the *Gedicht eines Skalden*.[21] That work inspired Kretschmann's – Rhingulph's – *Der Gesang Rhingulphs des barden als Varus geschlagen war*, which appeared

---

[19] Tombo, "Ossian in Germany," p. 86: *Sie, deren Enkel jetzt auf Schottlands Bergen wohnen,/ Die von den Römern nicht provinzten Kaledonen,/Sind deutschen Stamms. Daher gehört auch uns mit an/ Der Bard und Krieger Ossian,/Und mehr noch als den Engelländern an.*

[20] Tombo, "Ossian in Germany," p. 103.   [21] Tombo, "Ossian in Germany," p. 106.

in 1768. The genre turned precious and was soon the target of derision. But even as the bards fell from favor, Ossian's influence was still at work in the earliest dramas of Schiller, in Goethe's work, mentioned above, and in general among writers of the *Sturm und Drang* movement, which drew energy from the writings of this "ancient genius" who observed no rules. The philosopher and philologist Friedrich von Schlegel and the French Enlightenment figure Friedrich Melchior Grimm engaged in fervent debate about the epic's authenticity. "It [is] almost impossible," writes a literary historian, "to overestimate the favor which the poems of Ossian once enjoyed in Germany."[22]

Ossian's most influential admirer was the East Prussian native Johann Gottfried Herder (1744–1803). Though a correspondent of Kant, d'Alembert, and Diderot, Herder's enlightenment was more Rousseauian than Kantian. He discerned in Ossian's poetry "the majesty, purity, simplicity, energy and blessedness of human existence."[23] The encounter with Ossian informed his supremely influential theory of popular poetry and culture. For Herder, folklore revealed a way of life untainted by courtly, cosmopolitan pretensions. He exhorted the artist to go to the countryside (as Macpherson had done), to immerse himself in the people, to write in the language of the people, the living, organic expression of the spirit of a people. "Without a *territorial* mother tongue in which all the social classes are perceived as offshoots of the same tree and in which they receive the same education, there is no veritable understanding of hearts; no common patriotic formation, no communication or communion of impressions, no proper public."[24] In his 1772 *Treatise on the Origins of Language* he elaborated the concept of *Sprachkultur*, of culture located in speech – in tales, folksongs, and legends – rather than in the studied, written compositions of high culture. He collected folksongs and published them under the title "Voices of the Peoples in Song" (*Stimmen der Völker in Liedern*, 1779). In his *Ideas on the Philosophy of History* (1784–91) Herder evoked the union of language (*Sprache*) and people (*Volk*). His enthusiasm for folk culture, far from the exclusivist, reactionary enterprise it would become a century later, expressed a strong faith in the virtues of the "common man" and in the *nation* as the site of a "proper public." Herder welcomed revolution in France, and wrote a hymn to the storming of the Bastille.

---

[22] Tombo, "Ossian in Germany," p. 67.   [23] Gaskill, *Ossian Revisited*, p. 84.
[24] Thiesse, *La création des identités nationales*, p. 38. I have stressed the term "territorial," which appears almost as an but vital in Herder's claim.

The concept of "people," "nation," or *Volk* began to assume a specificity and depth of meaning that it had not possessed hitherto. Kant famously described humanity as parceled out among tribes or nations in his treatise on perpetual peace.[25] But the term nation translated the Latin *gens,* a "generative" site of human coexistence whose geometry varied – alternately family, clan, or tribe. Herder's *Volk* shared more than space and progeny. It shared customs, language, religion, feelings, and a social imaginary. Kant's "nation," by contrast, allowed for historical contingency – it could assimilate, it could separate. Herder's *Volk* battled contingency to defend its essential unity.[26] For Kant, the nation was a natural kind, but not a legitimating foundation of political order. In his *Anthropology from a Pragmatic Point of View* Kant portrayed the emergence of political order among "a mass of people" (*Menge Menschen*) sharing a "region" or "tract of land" (*Landstrich*), united by a common origin or trunk (*gemeinschaftliche Abstammung*), which *as whole or in part* organized itself as a civil whole (*bürgerlichen Ganzen*). Kant left room for a savage component of the *gens* or nation, a *wilde Menge in diesem Volk,* the *vulgus,* or *Pöbel,* that hived off from the rule of law. Kant's nation was the clay from which political society – and its leftover scraps – was formed through the admixture of reason and creativity. Herder's *Volk* was not clay. He likened it to a "natural plant." Political society was legitimated by its capacity to nurture that plant, which was *always already* present, to reprise the Heideggerian/Derridean formula. The most natural state is one sustained by (and which sustains) a coherent *Volk,* endowed with a coherent "national character" (*Nationalcharakter*).

The influence of Herder's theories of "natural society" and "natural political society" spread beyond the bounds of the German-speaking world.[27] They informed debate in Norway between proponents of *boksmaal* and *landsmaal.* They inspired efforts to normalize Yiddish, to retrieve the ancient literary traditions of Serbia, and to systematize written Serbian.[28] The construction of national culture was, by Herder's

---

[25] Hans Reiss, ed., *Kant: Political Writings* (Cambridge: Cambridge University Press, 1991), p. 111.

[26] Marc Crépon, Barbara Cassin, and Claudia Moatti, "Peuple," in Barbara Cassin, ed., *Vocabulaire européen des philosophies* (Paris: Seuil, Dictionnaires Le Robert, 2004).

[27] Thiesse, *La création des identités nationales,* pp. 34–8. In 1800, for example, the University of Copenhagen sponsored a competition for best essay on the question of whether ancient Scandinavian mythology should not replace Greco-Latin mythology as a tool of education.

[28] Thiesse, *La création des identités nationales,* chs. 2 and 3.

understanding, an internationalist project. It engendered a "new cultural theory ... that made it possible to propose nationality as the generative principle (*principe créateur*) of modernity."[29] It gave birth to a new representation of cultural space, according to which territory was distributed among authentic, and culturally and linguistically homogeneous nations contained by discernible borders, lines of cultural separation that, ideally, defined the limits of political space. The concept of frontier, present to the medieval imagination as a space of progressively diminishing (and therefore progressively contested) loyalties to a feudal lord, receded before an image of abrupt (and potentially violent) encounter between peoples differing by language and culture.

Ossian in Paris

The invention of Ossian's epics was a *coup de force* that revolutionized the discursive representation of cultural space. Although the imagined partition of Greater Rhineland space between "Gallic" and "Teutonic" was centuries-old, it had little political significance. Language segmented the region's inhabitants not spatially, but socially. The princely aristocracy, in the eighteenth century, spoke French, as did their intellectual sycophants. Townsmen – merchants, professionals, and bureaucrats – spoke the commercial and administrative lingua franca, *Hochdeutsch* or French in Germany, French in France. Latin remained the "business" idiom of much of the clergy as well as the university. The peasants spoke locally circumscribed dialects, as did the burghers at home and among one another. The *coup de force*, however, evoked a space that was not multilingual, but monolingual. The *coup de force* consecrated language – "national" language – as the site of cultural authenticity and political destiny. European space became a patchwork of monolingual, monocultural peoples, or nations.

Though Ossianic myth justified the rejection of French as the language of privilege, cultural hegemony, and above all inauthenticity, the bard's career in France was only moderately less brilliant than in Germany. Ossian was introduced to France by Jacques Turgot, an encyclopedist and adept of a proto-liberal doctrine that sought to free the economy from aristocratic privileges. The aristocracy opposed him

---

[29] Thiesse, *La création des identités nationales*, p. 23.

energetically and would force him out of office as Louis XVI's finance minister. Turgot's reformism might explain his interest in things "English," which, in turn, prompted the encounter with Ossian. Two months after their appearance in the *London Chronicle* in 1760, Turgot translated two of Macpherson's poems for the *Journal Etranger*, directed by Jean-Baptiste Suard, friend and translator of the Scottish philosopher David Hume. Both Suard and Hume had become Ossian enthusiasts.[30] Other journals, notably the *Gazette Littéraire de l'Europe*, created by Suard in 1764, and the *Journal des Savants*, devoted space to the bard.[31] Diderot was asked to provide a translation of "Shiric and Vinvela," but it never appeared. Voltaire, who provided a sympathetic but critical appraisal in his *Dictionnaire philosophique*, was too much the classicist to indulge in the new enthusiasm. Inversely, the court aristocracy, though hostile to Turgot, was impervious to Ossian's subversive appeal, at war with England, and forever eager to conform to fad, and so adopted the Scottish bard enthusiastically. "The *promeneurs* of Versailles and Trianon were soon making their way through the forests and heaths of Morven, to the strumming of Ossian's harp."[32] A complete French translation appeared in 1776, the same year as a French translation of Goethe's *Werther.*

Ossian's French career peaked under Napoleon, when the bard's champions ranged from the emperor himself to Germaine de Staël, an outspoken liberal critic of the empire, to François René de Chateaubriand, a legitimist exile and a leading voice of French Romanticism. De Staël never doubted Ossian's authenticity and devoted a chapter to the bard in *De la littérature*, published in 1800, in which she argued that the literary tradition of the "North" (represented by Ossian) was, compared to the classicism of the "South," philosophically more profound, more sincerely Christian in moral sentiment, and more compatible with Enlightenment values. "Long before the English knew about the theory of constitutions and the advantages of representative government," she wrote, "the warrior spirit that the Erse and Scandinavian poets sang with such enthusiasm gave man a prodigious idea of his power as an individual and his power of will. Independence existed for each, before liberty was constituted for all." Chateaubriand became a vocal champion of the bard during his years in London. Unlike de Staël, he represented the "two literary traditions" of

---

[30] Tedeschi, *Ossian: "l'Homère du Nord" en France*, pp. 16–20.
[31] Gaskill, *Ossian Revisited*, p. 156.
[32] Tedeschi, *Ossian: "l'Homère du Nord" en France*, p. 22.

"North and South" as complementary, and was less inclined to call the classical heritage corrupt.

> I like to imagine the two blind poets, Homer and Ossian, one on the summit of a mountain in Scotland, bald, his beard damp with dew, his harp under his arm, shrouded in mist, setting down his laws to the entire poetic people of Germania (*Germanie*); the other, sitting on the summit of Mount Pindus, surrounded by the muses who hold his lyre, lifting his crowned forehead in the bright sun of Greece, and, holding in his hand a scepter adorned with laurel, governing the fatherland (*patrie*) of Tasso and that of Racine.[33]

Napoleon was as susceptible to exoticism as others of his generation (witness the Egyptian campaign), and did not fault the anglophobia of the bard's defenders.[34] Cesarotti's Italian translation, heavily annotated, is said to have accompanied him on his campaigns "as the Iliad and Odyssey accompanied Alexander."[35] The neo-classical artist Anne-Louis Girodet presented Napoleon with a canvas that portrayed, not St. Peter, but Fingal and Ossian greeting the spirits of French military leaders slain in battle – Desaix, Kléber, Dampierre, Dugommier, Hoche, Championnet, and Joubert. Also portrayed was Théophile de La Tour d'Auvergne, who, in 1792, authored the book *Nouvelles recherches sur la langue, l'origine et les antiquités des Bretons* that inaugurated the field of "Celtic studies" in France. François Gérard, painter of the monumental "Bataille d'Austerlitz," presented the emperor with a "portrait" of Ossian. In 1804, the composer Jean-François Le Sueur, Berlioz's master, premiered his opera *Les Bardes* to Napoleon's praise: a "pièce brillante, héroïque, et vraiment ossianique!"[36] In 1805, Napoleon chartered the Académie Celtique to uncover France's Celtic roots, which, it was claimed, endured in the language and customs of Brittany. The Academy's research not only served to delegitimate Bourbon rule by ratifying the myth of France as fundamentally a Celtic nation subjugated by Frankish-Germanic warrior-aristocrats (see below), but demonstrated that Celtic culture, by its antiquity and survival in Brittany, undermined England's claims to Ossianic authenticity and cast suspicion on the English language as cultural usurper.[37]

---

[33] Tedeschi, *Ossian: "l'Homère du Nord" en France*, p. 4.
[34] Stafford and Gaskill, *From Gaelic to Romantic*, p. 154.
[35] Tedeschi, *Ossian: "l'Homère du Nord" en France*, p. 69. The claim, in the absence of evidence, may be apocryphal.
[36] Stafford and Gaskill, *From Gaelic to Romantic*, p. 161. The work has since retired "to those encyclopaedic Elysian Fields from whose bourn no opera returns to the stage."
[37] Thiesse, *La création des identités nationales*, p. 52.

Languages and peoples at the time of Ossian

Herder's claim that "*every* people is a nation (*jedes* Volk ist Volk)," that every people "has *its* national culture (Bildung), and *its* language," would, within a century of Ossian's epics, express a commonsense observation about Europe.[38] Herder's dictum reflects the impact of the discursive, literary *coup de force* that interrupted historical plot and launched an ontopological revolution. The revolutionary character of that act becomes apparent by recalling the origins and evolution of the languages that Ossianic myth made "sacred" – from *sacer*: dedicated, consecrated, from a root that means "fasten," "attach," as it appears in *saepes*: hedge or fence – as markers of cultural authenticity and political destiny. The image is one of consecration and boundary. But the languages of national, Ossianic Europe emerged in fact from mongrel idioms elaborated in the thirteenth and fourteenth centuries by tax collectors, which were subsequently gussied up by court poets, and, in the case of French, standardized by Dutch printers.

Old Low Franconian, as spoken by the sixth-century Frankish masters of the Rhine, probably bore more resemblance to modern Dutch than to modern German. But as it followed Frankish rule up the Rhine it mixed with Hessian and other dialects to produce local variants (see figure 6.1).[39] In Swabia and Alsace, the speech of the ruling Frankish aristocracy was transformed by the encounter with Alamannic peoples. As it migrated down the Danube, the dialectical encounter with non-Germanic peoples of the Alps, Celts and non-Indo-European Rhaetians, produced the sound shifts that later became characteristic of High German (the shift from dorp to dorf, or ik to ich, for example). These sound shifts then made their way partially and selectively back down the Rhine, in the direction of Old Franconian's geographic core, producing dozens of regionally specific idioms (see figure 6.1).

Today linguists mark a somewhat arbitrary boundary, downstream from Cologne, between High and Low German, the latter having been largely unaffected by the sound shifts. Old Franconian in the north was more affected by its encounter with Frisian and Saxon dialects. Overall differences among southern and northern dialects were greater than the differences between modern-day Spanish, Portuguese, and Italian.[40]

---

[38] Quoted in Benedict Anderson, *Imagined Communities* (London: Verso, 1983), pp. 67–8.

[39] W. B. Lockwood, *An Informal History of the German Language* (London: André Deutsch, 1976), p. 12.

[40] Lockwood, *An Informal History of the German Language*, pp. 6, 7.

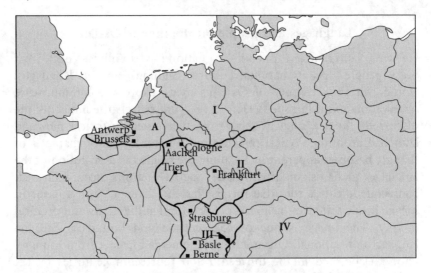

I. Low German, characterized by the gradual encounter of Old Franconian and Saxon dialectal families, as well as by immunity from the sound shifts characteristic of standard High German, is demarcated territorially by the ik/ich and the maken/machen linguistic frontier.

IA: The Rhine-Meuse or *Rheinmaasländischen* subgroup includes Flemish and Dutch dialects and low Saxon dialects of the eastern Netherlands, which extend with variations to Bremen and Hamburg and beyond.

II. Middle German dialects, derived from Old Franconian and spoken from French Lorraine and Luxemburg to the German Rhineland and eastward, are characterized by the general absence of appropriations from Saxon dialects and the progressive adoption of the sound shifts of standard High German. The dorp/dorf distinction emerges south of Cologne; the wat/was distinction surfaces east of the Saarland and extends east of Cologne; the appel/apfel distinction emerges yet farther to the east and gestures toward the dialects of Bavaria.

III. The Alemannic sphere includes the dialects of Alsace, the Schwäbisch dialects of Württemberg and western Bavaria, and the various subdialects of Swiss German. Alemannic dialects are subject to similar sound shifts as Franconian. *Kind* in Alsace, for example, becomes the more gutteral *Chind* of Switzerland.

IV. The Bavarian dialectal sphere.

The differences between dialects can be considerable. "Were you shopping in the marketplace" translates into Dutch as "*Was jij op de market aan het winkelen?*"; into High standard German as: "*Warst du auf dem Markt einkaufen?*"; and into the Alemannic dialect as employed in the vicinity of Basle and Freiburg as: "*Bisch uff'm Märt go iigchaufe gsi?*"

Figure 6.1 Old High German dialects

Despite the differences, the common denomination *theodiscus* (from the Old Franconian root *theod*: tribe or people) was adopted in the late eighth century, in deference to Caesarian ontopology which brought to light the *place* called Germania. It was in *theodisca lingua* that Charles the Bald recited the oath of Strasburg of 842, so as to be understood by the retinue of Louis the German (see inset 6.1).

Inset 6.1

The Oaths of Strasburg. Source: P. Riché and G. Tate, eds., Textes et documents d'histoire du moyen âge: Ve–Xe siècles *(Paris: Société d'Edition d'Enseignement Supérieur, 1974), pp. 431–2.*

Louis: Pro Deo amur et pro Christian poblo et nostro commun salvament, d'ist di in avant, in quant Deus savir et podir me dunat, si salvarai eo cist meon fradre Karlo et in aiudha cosa, si cum om per dreit son fradra salvar dift, in o quid il mi altresi fazet et ab Ludher nul plaid numquam prindrai, qui, meon vol, cist meon fradre Karle in damno sit.

Charles: In godes minna ind thes christianes folches ind unser bedhero gehaltnissi, fon thesemo dage frammordes so fram so mir got giuuizci indi mahd furgibit so haldih thesan minan bruodhir soso man mit rehtu sinan bruher scal in thiu thaz er mig so sama duo indi mit Ludheren in nohheiniu thing ne gegango the minan uuillon imo ce scadhen vuerdhen.

Translation: For the love of God and for the Christian people and our common salvation, from this day forward, as God shall give me knowledge and power, I will assist my brother Charles, here present, with my means and in all things, as one must assist one's brother, in all fairness, on condition that he do the same for me, and I will never enter into any treaty with Lothair that, of my will, might be prejudicial to my bother Charles.

Louis the German, inversely, took the oath in *rustica romana lingua* so as to be understood by the retinue of Charles. It was a Latin dialect in which daily contact with Old Franconian had produced significant changes in phonetics, syntax, and vocabulary, making it entirely foreign to speakers of the Latin vernaculars of the Mediterranean.[41] The Carolingian monarchs were bilingual. The Frankish nobility in France

---

[41] Peter Rickard, *A History of the French Language* (London: Routledge, 1989), p. 27.

did not abandon Old Franconian until the end of the tenth century, Hugh Capet being the first French king unable to speak it.[42] The Capetian court, as a site of artistic patronage, fostered the elevation of its Germano-Latin mongrel *patois* into a literary language.[43] Texts first referred to this literary tongue as *roman*, or *romanz*, but, reflecting its idiosyncrasy, the Frankish marker soon supplanted the Latin one and it became known as *franceis*, or *françois*. Thirteenth-century crusaders spread the idiom among the ruling and intellectual classes of the Mediterranean. *François* became a literary medium in northern Italy. Not only did copies of French epics and romances circulate in Italy, Italians themselves composed in French.[44] Rustichello da Pisa's 1298 account of Marco Polo's travels, for example, was composed in *françois*. But it was hardly a standardized language. The opulent court of the counts of Champagne, enriched by the trade fairs, favored literature composed in a rival dialect, closer to the *patois* of Picardie and Wallonie, and still in use as late as the fourteenth century, as attested by the chronicles of Jean Froissart (see figure 6.1).[45]

The Ottonian court, like its Capetian counterpart, also elevated its court idiom – medieval or Middle High German – to the status of a literary language. The *Niebelungenlied*, for example, was composed in this idiom.[46] South of the Rhine gorge it became the standard of elite speech.[47] When the Ottonian court took up residence in Italy, however, literary Middle High German fell into disuse. In its wake there emerged a multiplicity of vernacular High German dialects. By the early fourteenth century, a kind of lingua franca known as *Kanzleideutsch* was broadly used in administration and understood by the merchant class. *Kanzleideutsch* nevertheless displayed marked regional peculiarities. Three variants were in use in the Greater Rhineland alone: Swiss, Swabian (both marked by Alemannic survivals), and Rhenish-Franconian. But settlement of lands east of the Elbe and the Saale by colonists from many parts of the empire favored a fusion of dialects and the emergence of a variant of *Kanzleideutsch* that would set a standard, at least outside the Habsburg lands.[48]

---

[42] Rickard, *A History of the French Language*, pp. 18–20, 29, 35.
[43] Rickard, *A History of the French Language*, p. 29.
[44] Rickard, *A History of the French Language*, p. 59
[45] Rickard, *A History of the French Language*, pp. 46, 62.
[46] Lockwood, *An Informal History of the German Language*, p. 57.
[47] Lockwood, *An Informal History of the German Language*, p. 58.
[48] Lockwood, *An Informal History of the German Language*, pp. 89, 108–12.

Luther, a Thuringian, found it natural and expedient to adopt this eastern Chancery German in his writings. His impact on the development of modern High German was profound. One third of all publications in Germany between 1518 and 1523 bore Luther's name. One hundred thousand copies of his Bible appeared between 1534 and 1574. "Never before had any man exercised such influence through the medium of writing."[49] Nevertheless, the unifying effect on the German language was not immediate. Editors and printers had their say in the presentation of the printed text, and, as seen in inset 6.2, considerable differences made their way into the various editions. Over time, however, Luther's Bible had the effect of promoting a standard literary idiom beyond its original geographic home. Reformed regions – the Low German towns of the Hansa and Alemannic Switzerland – were more receptive to the new lingua franca than Bavaria and much of the Rhineland. In 1663, Justus Georg Schottel published an influential grammar, the *Ausführliche Arbeit von der teutschen Haubtsprache*. The Leipzig book fair and the Saxon court, as they became centers of cultural production and dissemination following the decline of the Rhineland towns, further promoted the use of this lingua franca. By the seventeenth century, High German had become a common, educated speech freed of significant dialectical influences. As a literary and administrative medium, it was well established in Protestant Swabia by 1650, in Switzerland by 1700, in Habsburg Vienna by about 1750. But it would become dominant in Catholic Bavaria and the Rhineland only in the nineteenth century.[50]

In the north, High German had already begun to displace Low German in the fifteenth century. Low German had been a written language of administration throughout the Hanseatic sphere and had exercised great influence on the evolution of the Scandinavian languages.[51] But in the fifteenth and sixteenth centuries, with the decline of the Hansa, and the rise of the courts and the trading and mining towns of the south and east, Chancery High German gradually replaced Low German. Halle's last official document in Low German dates from 1417. Berlin abandoned the administrative use of Low German in 1504. Magdeburg switched in the mid sixteenth century. The three dominant towns of the Hansa – Lübeck,

---

[49] Lockwood, *An Informal History of the German Language*, p. 112.

[50] John T. Waterman, *A History of the German Language* (Seattle: University of Washington Press, 1966), p. 76.

[51] Lockwood, *An Informal History of the German Language*, p. 79.

Bremen, and Hamburg – had all abandoned Low German as an administrative and literary medium by 1650. "If the north had maintained its traditional cohesion and prosperity into modern times, it would most likely have developed into an independent state with its own standard Low German as the official language, which would have differed as much from standard High German as Dutch does."[52]

Inset 6.2

Varieties of Biblical German (Matthew 10.5). Source:
W. B. Lockwood, An Informal History of the German Language *(Cambridge: Heffer and Sons, 1965), pp. 106–8.*

Luther's Bible, 1522 edition:
Dise tzwelffe sandte Jhesus, vnd gepott yhn und sprach, Geht nit auff die strasse der heyden, vnd zihet nit yn die stedte der Samariter, Sondern gehet hyn tzu den verloren schaffen aus dem haus Israel.

Luther's Bible, 1546 edition:
Djese zwelffe sandte Jhesus, gebot jnen, vnd sprach, Gehet nicht auff der Heiden strassen, vnd ziehet nicht in der Samariter stedte, Sondern gehet hin zu den verloren Schafen, aus dem hause Israel.

Modern rendition of Luther's prose:
Diese zwölf sandte Jesus, gebot ihnen, und sprach: Gehet nicht auf der Heiden Straße, und ziehet nicht in der Samariter Städte, sondern gehet hin zu den verlorenen Schafen aus dem Hause Israel.

Hermann Menge's 1926 translation:
Diese Zwölf sandte Jesus aus, nachdem er ihnen folgende Weisungen gegeben hatte: "Den Weg zu den Heidenvölkern schlagt nicht ein und tretet auch in keine Samariterstadt ein, geht vielmehr zu den verlorenen Schafen des Hauses Israel."

Occitanian dialects in France suffered a more violent fate. A courtly and literary medium in the middle ages, Occitanian fell from use as a literary medium when Languedoc's aristocracy was ousted by northerners

---

[52] Lockwood, *An Informal History of the German Language*, p. 78. *Pace* Adrian Hastings, *The Construction of Nationhood* (Cambridge: Cambridge University Press, 1997), Luther's Bible did not cause Low German's decline. Low German translations were available as early as 1523. The last Low German Bible was published in 1621. See Lockwood, *An Informal History of the German Language*, pp. 124–8.

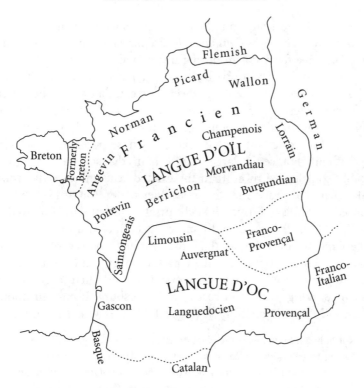

Figure 6.2 French dialects *c.*1200
Source: Peter Rickard, *A History of the French Language*, 2nd edn (London: Routledge, 1989) p. 40.

in the wake of the Albigensian crusade (figure 6.2).[53] The fourteenth and fifteenth centuries saw the triumph of a standard literary French. Its grammar and spelling were systematized. Latin terms were imported to enrich its vocabulary, even as Latin lost standing as a written medium (in no small part because Renaissance enthusiasts, like Erasmus who labored to purify its vocabulary and syntax and restore its classical pronunciation, turned it into a museum piece). University scholars began to lecture in French rather than Latin. But this did not prevent French, like all living languages, from mixing its "genetic code" with that of other idioms. As Italian scholarship, art, and money spread north to Lyons, Paris, and the châteaux of the Loire, so did Italian speech. "Lyons was almost an Italian city, as well as a staging post for Italian artists, poets,

[53] Rickard, *A History of the French Language*, pp. 63, 116.

architects and musicians on their way to Paris or Fontainebleau."[54] Dozens of everyday terms – *attaquer, briller, manquer, réussir* – entered the French language from Italian during this period.

In 1539 the French court, by the *Ordonnances de Villers Cotterets*, required that all court proceedings, deeds, and court judgments be recorded "en langue maternel françois et non aultrement."[55] In 1635, Richelieu established the Académie Française to formalize and systematize the language. But Protestant Dutch printers, whose books were smuggled into Catholic France in large numbers in the seventeenth century, probably contributed more than the exalted academy to standardizing the language by adopting the poet Pierre de Ronsard's (1524–85) proposed spelling reforms. French printers eventually followed the Dutch lead.[56] In the seventeenth and eighteenth centuries, the opulence of the French court, more than the (limited) power of its armies, caused French to supplant Italian as the courtly and even administrative lingua franca of much of Europe. It was adopted throughout the German-speaking world and east to St. Petersburg. It entered upon its career as diplomatic medium with the 1678 Treaty of Nijmegen.

> Not only did French take the place of Latin as the language of diplomacy during this period; it also replaced it as the language of international communication between men of letters, heads of state, scientists and intellectuals of all nations. Frederick of Prussia, Catherine the Great of Russia, the German philosopher [Friedrich] Grimm, the English economist [Robert] Walpole and the Italian economist [Ferdinando] Galiani all wrote elegant French.[57]

Meanwhile, Dutch bookmakers, as they were setting type for French books and pamphlets, were upbraiding their apprentices in a Germanic idiom that could trace its roots to the language of Charlemagne. But because no Old Low Franconian texts have come down to us, little is known of Charlemagne's dialect other than its immunity to the sound shifts that characterize High German. Yet the medieval prosperity and cultural energy of the lowland towns transformed the "Dutch dialects" into a literary language. The thirteenth-century Bruges poet Jacob van Maerlant composed knightly romances, philosophical treatises in verse, and biblical tales in an idiom called *Diets*, a designation derived from

---

[54] Rickard, *A History of the French Language*, p. 87.
[55] Rickard, *A History of the French Language*, p. 83.
[56] Rickard, *A History of the French Language*, p. 107.
[57] Rickard, *A History of the French Language*, p. 118.

the omnipresent *teutonicus*. Bruges, Ghent, and, later, Brussels and Antwerp all produced Dutch literature. When the Spanish occupation put an end to the cultural hegemony of Flanders and Brabant, the center of Dutch literary production moved north to Holland, where Joost van den Vondel, a friend of Hugo Grotius and one of the Netherlands' most influential poets, helped establish the northern idiom as a literary standard. By the time of the French Revolution, both medieval Flanders' cultural achievements and Holland's resistance to Spanish rule had turned Dutch, in contrast to its Low German cousin, into a literary and administrative language.[58]

Nothing in the history of the Greater Rhineland's "national languages" reveals a pedigree. None emerges recognizable from, say, some epic of Caesar's, much less Homer's era. Linguistic husbandry of the type championed by the Académie Française was an invention of the seventeenth century. National governments in the nineteenth century tried their hand at purifying the linguistic pedigree, but showed neither the energy nor the skill of breeders of dogs and dairy cows. Bilingualism – the frequent use of both "official language" and mother dialect – continued to characterize much of France into the twentieth century, and continues to characterize much of Germany, Flanders, and the Netherlands in the twenty-first. Despite Herder's interest in *Sprachkultur*, the search for legitimating roots in antiquity had the effect of marginalizing regional dialects, as spoken by the "people," as corrupt variations of a putative *Ursprache*, or antique language. The Ossianic representation of European space, in its final form, exalted the literary language as the vehicle of cultural authenticity.[59] Regional dialects were subjugated to the hegemonic idiom. Though Ossianic myth emerged from the meeting between poets and peasant dialects, it ultimately extolled the *national* language, the medium of state administrative power as the highway to authenticity and freedom.

The *département*

The Ossianic *coup de force* conditioned the emergence of our modern understanding of the nation. It redirected spatial signifiers to refer no longer to the space ruled by a monarch, but to the language, culture,

[58] Lockwood, *An Informal History of the German Language*, pp. 184–7.
[59] See Bernhard Giesen, *Intellectuals and the German Nation: Collective Identity in a German Axial Age*, trans. Nicholas Levis (Cambridge: Cambridge University Press, 1998), p. 94.

and even "character" of the people that inhabited that space. The simultaneous *coup de force* that created the French *département* "cleared a space" for the nation by enabling the repression, the erasure, the humiliation of the regional ontopologies and dialects that undermined the nation's claim to linguistic and cultural identity.

The *département* emerged from the political revolution that located sovereignty in the "people," as signified in French by two terms, *peuple* and *nation*. Both terms, as Marc Crépon and his collaborators observe, harbor a "redoutable polysémie." The term *peuple* was generally understood sociologically, signifying people who were neither aristocrats nor clergymen, but members of a remainder, "third estate," the *tiers état*. It also designated, sociologically, the subset of the *tiers état* whom poverty marginalized from political life. Jean-Jacques Rousseau did not ignore the sociological understanding of *peuple* as an entity "present" prior to the act of political creation, characterized by its exclusion from the exercise of power, but nevertheless somehow "definable," or bounded. But he endowed the term with new political significance. A *peuple* was a political creation. The term designated a population that came to be by entering into political contract.

The term *nation* was theoretically even more burdensome. "One of the strongest [terms of] revolutionary vocabulary, [it was] also one of the most enigmatic."[60] Under absolutism the *nation* designated the subjects of the king, represented and embodied by the king. The glory of the *nation* and that of the king who ruled it were of a piece. In an act of philosophical sedition, however, the *Encyclopédie* defined the nation as the source of sovereignty, the proprietor of the crown, and of government and public authority. Abbé Emmanuel Sieyès, the Revolution's theorist, conceptualized the nation as an *association* of people who agreed to submit to a common law established by their representatives. Like Rousseau's *peuple*, it was both source and outcome of a political emergence.[61] As source and outcome, it was more than the sum of its individual participants, more than a grab-bag of people who convened to form an association. Romantic notions of common destiny – a common language, a common culture, and a common history – floated just below the surface of Rousseau's and Sieyès' Enlightenment rationalism. Freedom, for Rousseau as for Herder, was indissociable from authenticity. Authenticity, understood as appreciable fidelity to an origin, was the

[60] François Furet, *Revolutionary France* (Cambridge, MA and Oxford: Blackwell, 1992), p. 50.
[61] See Crépon *et al.*, "Peuple."

well-spring that washed the people of its subjugation to a superficial, contrived hegemonic culture, and from oppression by the power that that culture sought to legitimate. A half century later, Jules Michelet (1798–1874), prominent historian and prophet of an anticlerical, republican, yet romantic nationalism, would write an epochal *Histoire de la révolution française* in which he would portray the insurrection as an awakening of a people and a nation, *a melding of people and nation* into a unitary entity through the (re)appropriation of sovereignty.[62]

Anxieties about the character and coherence of the nation were voiced from the earliest days of the Revolution in debates over administrative reform. The *ancien régime* was a mosaic of provinces, customary ontopologies. Some enjoyed their own specific legal codes and institutions. Customs, laws, weights, and measures varied from region to region. Regional particularism was particularly strong in the periphery, in provinces such as Brittany, Languedoc, Provence, Burgundy, and Franche-Comté (see figure 6.3). The monarchy had attempted to rationalize territorial administration by establishing the *généralité*, a territory made subject to the immediate authority of the king's personal representative, the bounds of which sometimes respected the frontiers of provinces, as in Brittany, but often did not. Normandy was divided into three *généralités*. The *généralité* of Auch covered part of the province of Guyenne and part of the province of Gascogne. Royal administrators looked for ways to further rationalize the administrative map. In 1764 comte d'Argenson, the *lieutenant général de police*, proposed to divide the kingdom into "départements" of approximately equal dimensions. Enlightenment fascination with mathematics produced a proposal by the geographer Letrône in 1777 to divide the territory into twenty-five *généralités*, divided in turn into perfectly square *arrondissements*. In 1780, Robert de Hesseln proposed a geometric grid of 9 *régions*, 9^2 *pays*, and 9^3 *cantons*. Condorcet, in 1787, argued for an administrative map that was more respectful of local custom, but, in keeping with his physiocratic leanings, emphasized that subjects should be able to pay their taxes without traveling more than a day's journey to reach the nearest administrative center.

---

[62] Furet, *Revolutionary France*, p. 374. Contrast Rogers Brubaker's treatment in *Citizenship and Nationhood in France and Germany* (Cambridge, MA: Harvard University Press, 1992), p. 35. Brubaker's emphasis on the "assimilationist" power of French nationhood ignores its exclusivist potential.

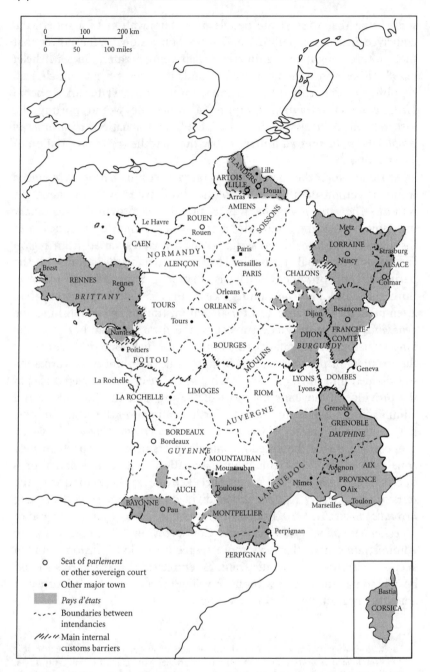

Figure 6.3 Pre-revolutionary France: principal administrative, judicial, and fiscal subdivisions.

Source: William Doyle, *The Oxford History of the French Revolution* (Oxford: Clarendon Press; New York: Oxford University Press, 1989).

The Revolution reprised such proposals, not only to rationalize local administration but to bring the institutions and practices of republican governance closer to the people, to the "nation." Adrien Duport, representative of the judicial nobility and ally of Sieyès, resuscitated d'Argenson's proposal in July 1789. Lally-Tollendal, opposed politically to Sieyès and Duport, proposed a map in August that distributed the population more equally among administrative units. Sieyès himself produced a map of fifty provinces, each with forty *arrondissements* comprising twenty parishes each. He later proposed a second map of eighty-nine *départements*. The Assembly charged Jacques Guillaume Thouret with the task of examining these proposals and making a recommendation. Thouret drew on all his scientific skills to examine population distributions, revenue collections, and geographic area. He proposed a map that divided France into eighty-one, or 9^2, *départements*, which, in the spirit of Letrône, formed perfect squares of some 72 kilometers on a side, and 9^3 districts, or *communes*, 24 kilometers on a side, which were in turn divided into *cantons* that were somehow expected to contain 680 active electors. Deputies objected that some of Thouret's *départements* had in fact a million inhabitants while others had fewer than 200,000. The most heated objections arose from representatives of towns and cities that Thouret had not designated as departmental centers, or *chefs-lieux*. Mirabeau criticized its abstract, impractical geometry, and advanced his own proposal for 120 *départements*. The Assembly dodged controversy by naming a committee (among whose members was the physiocrat Pierre-Samuel Dupont de Nemours, father of the American industrialist). Having concluded that mathematical elegance should submit to cartographical practicality, the committee recommended dividing large provinces up and gathering smaller provinces together, but otherwise to respect provincial boundaries. But respect for customary boundaries was qualified by the more revolutionary proposal that the customary *names* of provinces be erased. The committee recommended naming the new *départements* with reference to geographical features such as mountains and rivers – Meurthe-et-Moselle, Maine-et-Loire, Jura, etc. Customary provincial designations – Bar, Anjou, Franche-Comté – would lose all administrative significance. The texts read:

> Decree of 15 January, 1790
>
> The National Assembly, upon the report of the committee on the constitution, after having heard the deputies of all the provinces of the realm (*royaume*), decrees that France is divided into 83 departments.

This laconic text is followed a month later by:

Decree of 26 February, 1790
The National Assembly decrees that the committee on the constitution is charged with giving names [*dénominations*] to the 83 departments.

Decree of 26 February, 1790
The National Assembly, upon the report of the committee on the constitution, after having heard the deputies of all the provinces of the realm, has decreed, that France is divided into 83 departments, the account (*état*) of which follows:

Provence 3
Dauphiné 3
Franche-Comté 3
Alsace 2
Lorraine, les 3 évêchés, Barrois 4
Lyonnais, Forez, et Beaujolais 1
Bourbonnais 1
Périgord 1

[and so on]

Title One
The liberty, reserved for the electors of several departments or districts by different decrees of the National Assembly, regarding the choice of *chefs-lieux*, and the location (*l'emplacement*) of divers establishments, is that of deliberating about these, and proposing to the National Assembly or to the legislative bodies that will succeed it, that which shall appear most in conformity with the general interest of those who are subject to [their] administration and jurisprudence (*administrés et juridiciables*).

Title Two Division of the Realm
Departments

I. Department of the Ain. The assembly of this department will be held in the city of Bourg. It is divided into 9 districts, of which the *chefs-lieux* are . . .

II. Department of the Aisne. The first assembly of the electors of this department shall be held at Chauny, and they will propose one of the two cities, Laon or Soissons, as *chef-lieu* of the department. This department is divided into 6 districts, of which three *chefs-lieux* are . . .

III. Department of the Allier. The assembly of this department will be held in the city of Moulins. It is divided into 7 districts, of which the *chefs-lieux* are . . .

[and so on]

The logic that sought to eliminate customary representations of place also informed the Civil Constitution of the Clergy of July 1790. It abolished the 137 dioceses inherited from the *ancien régime* and made the Catholic diocese coterminous with the new *département*. It also provided for the election of Catholic bishops by the electors of the *département* (regardless of religious confession!), and required bishops to swear allegiance to the Constitution. The pope retained only the right to be informed of the results of such elections. The text reads:

> Series of Decrees on the Civil Constitution of the Clergy of 12 July 1790
> The National Assembly, after having heard the Report of the Ecclesiastical Committee, has decreed and decrees the following, as constitutional articles:
>
> Title One of the Ecclesiastical Offices
> Article I
>
> Each department shall form a single (*un seul*) Diocese, and each Diocese shall have the same extent and limits as the Department.
> [and so on]

In a third attack on the customary representation of French cultural and political space, the Assembly, in 1790, having decided that "the unity of speech (*idiome*) is an integral part of the revolution," commissioned the abbé Henri Grégoire to survey the parishes regarding the use of French. His report, "On the necessity and means of exterminating (*anéantir*) the *patois* and universalizing (*universaliser*) the use of the French language," established that at least 6 million of France's 25 million inhabitants, living principally south of the Loire, knew no French, while another 6 million knew some, but not enough to carry on sustained conversation. Only 3 million could speak it fluently. His report called for the elimination of "the diversity of idioms that extended the infancy of reason and prolonged obsolescent prejudices" and recommended that each commune, or parish, be required to maintain a primary school, the principal charge of which would be to teach French. It concluded: "to extirpate all prejudice, develop all truths, talents, virtues, and mold (*fondre*) all citizens into the national mass (*la masse nationale*), simplify the mechanism and facilitate the workings (*jeu*) of the political machine, there must be unity of speech (*il faut identité de langage*)."[63] The Convention acted to abolish dialects

---

[63] Eugen Weber, *Peasants into Frenchmen: The Modernization of Rural France, 1870–1914* (Stanford: Stanford University Press, 1976), p. 72; Rickard, *A History of the French Language*, p. 120.

and replace them with the official language of the Republic, "the language of the Declaration of Rights," and decreed that throughout the Republic children must learn "to speak, read and write in the French language," and that everywhere "instruction should take place only in French." "Reactionaries," complained a representative, referring to the Vendée counter-revolution, "speak *bas-breton*."[64] The three reforms together sought to construct a national space that was unified and coherent not only in its administration, but in language and culture as well. "The profound reason for this revolution, for it is one, and an enormous one, for it modifies profoundly certain habits of daily life, was clearly (*apparaît*) to renovate (as in *renovatio*, the operative term of the Carolingian ontopological revolution or *res novae*) everything and to destroy the last traces of the *Ancien Régime*."[65]

The two *coups de force*, Ossian and the *département*, revolutionized the representation of Greater Rhineland space, now distributed among "ancient nations," conceived as *essentially* – linguistically and culturally – homogeneous. The trading towns of the middle ages were discursively if not materially erased, politically suppressed, and absorbed by the nation. The town, marginalized politically by the Reformation, was further marginalized, discursively and politically, by the Revolution. Just as Ossian invited intellectuals to venture to the countryside to uncover and restore the national heritage, the *département* sought purposely to humble the city, a foreign presence in the *corps* of the nation, a site of cosmopolitanism and unpatriotic finance. When representatives of Marseilles proposed to establish a maritime *département* of which their city would be the *chef-lieu*, the Assembly rejected the proposal and placed the administrative center inland, at Aix-en-Provence. St. Malo, Bayonne, and Dunkirk, maritime banking cities, formulated similar demands and suffered the same reception. The Assembly, despite its mythological characterization as the instrument of a "bourgeois" revolution, was "doubly suspicious of the large city, its influence, as a danger to 'virtue,' and even more suspicious of ports, their cosmopolitanism and merchant wealth, suspect *a priori* because wealth ... can only be acquired badly ... It was the first indication that revolutionary France was turning its back on the sea."[66] The sea, one might add for the purpose of this book, into which

---

[64] Weber, *Peasants into Frenchmen*, p. 72; Thiesse, *La création des identités nationales*, p. 58.

[65] Jean Meyer and André Corvisier, *La Révolution française*, vol. I (Paris: Presses Universitaires de France, 1991), p. 384. See also Furet, *Revolutionary France*, p. 87.

[66] Meyer and Corvisier, *La Révolution française*, p. 386. Cf. the similar "flight from the city" that occurred in Andrew Jackson's America.

flowed the river Rhine. Suspicion of the city was characteristic of provincial representatives, rural notables, whether trained in the law or propertied *rentiers*, whose horizons were parochial, and who approached reform with "an incurable distrust of the modern world."[67] Suspicion of the city and idealization of the countryside would become emblematic of nineteenth-century nationhood.[68] The representation of political space that emerged from the *coup de force* would prove amenable, despite its apparently modernist, progressive inspiration, to a romantic, nostalgic, and exclusivist project. It conceptualized political space as the site of the defense and cultivation of a linguistically, historically, and culturally totalizing nation. The countryside and peasant dress, not the city and bourgeois banality, would make the nation present – bring it to light – in the social imaginary. The Rhineland of Erasmus was a distant memory.

The Rhine as "natural frontier"

The *coups de force* from which emerged national space gave rise to the *re-presentation* of the Rhine that framed geopolitical strategizing from the mid nineteenth to the mid twentieth century. That representation reprised and naturalized the Caesarean construction of the Rhine-as-frontier, now *re-presented* as the natural edge not of Caesar's legacy but of the French nation's *natural* topographical container.

Antecedent efforts by French monarchs to clarify and rationalize the frontiers of the realm conditioned the "French nation's" claims to the Rhine as its "natural" container and defense. Henri IV inaugurated the policy with the 1601 Treaty of Lyons, which subsequently informed the Treaty of the Pyrenees in 1659 and the Treaty of the Alps in 1713. Although it was still quite rare in the seventeenth century, as Louis André observes, "to encounter an author ... who defended the theory of natural frontiers," no fewer than ten *traités des limites* were negotiated and signed in the eighteenth century.[69] In the diplomatic commotion the question of France's claims to the Rhine arose as a matter of course. Dom Martin Bouquet's 1738 *Recueil des historiens des Gaules et de la France* recalled that "our Gaul ... was bounded by the Ocean, the Mediterranean

---

[67] Meyer and Corvisier, *La révolution française*, p. 388.

[68] See Celia Applegate, *A Nation of Provincials: The German Idea of Heimat* (Berkeley and Los Angeles: University of California Press, 1990), p. 104.

[69] Louis André, *Louis XIV et l'Europe* (Paris: Albin Michel, 1950), p. 2. Quoted in Paul Guichonnet and Claude Raffestin, *Géographie des frontières* (Paris: Presses Universitaires de France, 1974), pp. 19, 94.

and the Alps, and stretched from the Pyrenees to the banks of the Rhine." The *Bibliothèque historique* of Père Lelong summarized the traditional catalogue of legal – dynastic and feudal – claims to the Rhine. Père Bourgeant, in his history of the Peace of Westphalia, asserted that Richelieu and Mazarin had sought to locate France's frontier on the Rhine, and in 1764 Forcemagne published Richelieu's *Testament politique*, discussed in the preceding chapter. But it was Jean-Jacques Rousseau, theorist of emancipation and prophet of "natural" political order, who authored the clearest articulation of the "natural frontier":

> The situation of the mountains, seas and rivers of Europe, which serve as frontiers to the nations that inhabit it, seem to have determined the number and size of . . . nations. It might be said that the political order of this part of the world is, in some respects, the work of nature . . . This is not to say that the Alps, the Rhine, the sea, the Pyrenees, are insurmountable obstacles to ambition, but these obstacles are supported by others which strengthen them or bring back the nations to the same limits when temporary struggles have overridden them.[70]

Despite literary assertions regarding the existence of a natural frontier on the Rhine, eighteenth-century French diplomacy maintained a prudent silence on the matter. The wars of Louis XIV had left France exhausted. The fortifications of maréchal de Vauban (1633–1707), Louis XIV's military engineer and strategist, provided better security than either rivers or mountains. Vauban emphasized the need to court Greater Rhineland diplomatic support in the dynastic contest with the Habsburgs. He insisted that conquests be limited to Strasburg, Luxemburg, and a line extending from Ypres to Courtrai. By the middle of the eighteenth century, both Montesquieu and the comte d'Argenson, an Enlightenment figure and diplomat, were proclaiming that the time for conquests had passed. Vergennes, foreign minister to Louis XVI, adhered to the same principle in reaction to the failed policies of Louis XV (1723–74), who alienated the German states by allying with the Habsburgs in the hope of winning the lowlands and routing the English in the colonies. The policy ended in defeat and embarrassment in 1763.

In the early days of the Revolution, Mirabeau and Talleyrand prolonged the cautious policies of Vauban and Vergennes. Mirabeau's

[70] Albert Sorel, *Europe and the French Revolution: The Political Traditions of the Old Régime*, ed. and trans. Alfred Cobban and J. W. Hunt (Garden City, NY: Anchor Books, 1971), p. 319.

motives were ideological and principled. He wrote in 1788 in *De la monarchie prussienne sous Frédéric le Grand* that "to effect territorial exchanges without consulting the inhabitants is an act of violence and tyranny."[71] The Preamble to the Constitution of 1791 made the renunciation of conquests a fundamental law. Emigré aristocrats, however, were pressing foreign governments to suppress the Revolution, and German princes were demanding compensation for privileges lost in Alsace. The Pillnitz agreement of August 1791, between Frederick William II of Prussia and Leopold II of Austria, raised the specter of a counter-revolutionary coalition. The French Assembly declared war in April 1792. Revolutionary forces defeated the Prussian army at Valmy. While not militarily significant, the victory energized the revolutionary cause and entered mythology as the foundational act of the French Republic. The French pushed the Prussians across the Rhine and occupied Brussels and the Austrian Netherlands in November (see figure 6.4).[72]

The French advance raised anew the question of the Rhine frontier. The Assembly, after examining claims to compensation in Alsace advanced by the bishops of Speyer and Trier, had already declared Alsace French, not by right of conquest or diplomatic agreement, but "by its voluntary membership in the great federation of provinces of 1789–90."[73] Frontiers, by this reasoning, were legitimated by the will of the people. The people could theoretically will to establish no frontiers at all. Indeed, Jacques-Pierre Brissot, a Girondin leader of the *Convention*, exhorted his compatriots to "set fire to the whole of Europe," while the *communard* Pierre-Gaspard Chaumette proclaimed that "the land which separates Paris from Petersburg will soon be *gallicized* [a fascinating use of a signifier of "national roots" to designate a political mission], municipalized, jacobinized."[74] Revolutionary troops entered Mainz in April 1792. In November 1792, following Valmy and the abolition

---

[71] Sorel, *Europe and the French Revolution*, pp. 311–12.
[72] See Sanjay Seth, "Nationalism in/and Modernity," in Joseph A. Camilleri, Anthony P. Jarvis, and Albert J. Paolini, *The State in Transition* (Boulder, CO: Lynne Rienner, 1995), pp. 42–4.
[73] Furet, *Revolutionary France*, p. 101. The dispute opposed the imperial notion of *Landeshoheit* with the evolving revolutionary concept of national sovereignty. See discussion in Rodney Bruce Hall, *National Collective Identity: Social Constructs and International Systems* (New York: Columbia University Press, 1999), pp. 140–5, and Paul Schroeder, *The Transformation of European Politics 1763–1848* (Oxford: Clarendon Press, 1994), pp. 67–72.
[74] Furet, *Revolutionary France*, p. 104. See also Guichonnet and Raffestin, *Géographie des frontières*, pp. 19–21.

Figure 6.4 Departmentalized space expands toward the Rhine

Source: William Doyle, *The Oxford History of the French Revolution* (Oxford: Clarendon Press; New York: Oxford University Press, 1989), p. 127.

of the monarchy, the revolutionary government offered its assistance to all "peoples" who wished to overthrow their despotic rulers. Mainz played host to a Rhineland Convention whose members, representing the left bank between Landau and Bingen, formally seceded from the Habsburg empire and asked, in March 1793, to be admitted to the French Republic.[75] Four new *départements* were created in the east: Roer, with Aachen as its administrative *chef-lieu*; Rhin-et-Moselle around Koblenz; Sarre; and Mont-Tonnerre around Mainz.

> Let us survey some of the formulae of the times: "Give us to France, as you have given liberty to us," said those of Crefeld. But those of Aachen: "The masculine (*le*) Rhine is made to fraternise with the (*la*) Seine, the (*la*) Garonne, the (*la*) Loire – and Nature gave it its north–south course only to provide with legitimate bounds (*borner légitimement*) the *départemental* checker-board of France." "We are burning with the ardent desire," they added, "to see ourselves reunited by an act of legislature with our ancient brothers the Gauls."[76]

The revolutionary government, however, did not embrace its "Frankish" brothers on the Rhine without debate. Representatives concurred that the Republic required boundaries, if only to "close ranks in the hour of invasion ... when public safety was in jeopardy."[77] But there was difference of opinion regarding the most expedient placement of those boundaries. Lazare Carnot, one of the principal architects of the republican army, favored the customary limit, the Meuse. Others advanced the Vosges. The Girondins, before their physical elimination from government in 1793, rejected permanent revolution and made the recovery of France's "natural frontier" on the Rhine, and the disposition of the lands beyond the Rhine as the "cordon of a federal republic," the goal of revolutionary policy. Georges-Jacques Danton, one of Carnot's military collaborators, was an outspoken advocate of this position.

> The [revolutionary government], at the very moment when they were decreeing the Constitution of the Republic, settled, by another decree, its definitive frontiers. *Since the rights of the nation come from nature, the exercise of these rights could only stop at the point where nature itself had drawn the line.* The same doctrine that derived the laws of Republican

---

[75] Demangeon and Febvre, *Le Rhin*, pp. 127–32.
[76] Demangeon and Febvre, *Le Rhin*, pp. 131–2.
[77] Furet, *Revolutionary France*, p. 103.

France from the law of nature grounded international law in the principle of natural frontiers ... These frontiers, traced by nature, were precisely those indicated by legend and delineated by history for centuries [*sic*]. What the study of the past suggested to statesmen, abstract reason suggested to the *philosophes*; the empiricism of the former led to the same conclusions as the rationalism of the latter.[78]

If physical geography supplied natural frontiers, it followed that the societies that inhabited the space delimited by those frontiers were unified and coherent. The frontier had to enclose one political space, not several. If that were not the case, the natural barrier would not qualify as a frontier. But what discourse would "bring to light" that space in its oneness? Political will and contract did not suffice. As is the case of the European Union in our day, there is no geographical limit that legitimates a republic's refusal to enter into contract with a people that will it. Physical geography can impose only arbitrary limits on political deliberation. The discourse that emerged to "bring to light" political space in its oneness was not philosophical, but mythological. Ossianic imagery made the French nation, as it revealed itself in revolution, visible to the imagination. Apologists of the Revolution advanced the claim, first made in 1732 by Henri, comte de Boulainvilliers, that two "nations" coexisted on French territory – the first a Germanic, Frankish nation that, in its triumph, begat the aristocracy, the second a Celtic nation which endured as the *peuple* to be governed and protected. Republican theorists used Boulainvilliers' formula to legitimate revolution, popular sovereignty, and national unity. Abbé Sieyès in his 1789 pamphlet *Qu'est-ce que le Tiers Etat?* exhorted the *peuple* to "send back" (*renvoyer*) the aristocrats to the "forests of Franconia." Constantin Boisgirais, comte de Volney, orientalist, philologist, and friend of Benjamin Franklin, encouraged his students at the Ecole Normale Supérieure in 1795 to overcome their deference to French culture's classical pretensions and discover the Gallic nation's "Celtic" origins. The Ossianic myth of French republicanism's ethnic roots survived into the nineteenth century, informing the historiography of such liberal-minded scholars as Augustin Thierry (1795–1856), historian and Saint-Simonian, and François Guizot

---

[78] Sorel, *Europe and the French Revolution*, p. 319, emphasis added. Walter Platzhoff, "Die Französische Ausdehnungspolitik von 1250 bis zur Gegenwart," in Rudolf Kautzsch, Walter Platzhoff, Fedor Schneider, Franz Schulz, and Georg Wolfram, *Frankreich und der Rhein: Beiträge zur Geschichte und geistigen Kultur des Rheinlandes* (Frankfurt: Englert and Schloffer, 1925), p. 54. See, in same volume, the chapter by Georg Künzel, p. 84.

(1787–1874), historian and reformist education minister, who in 1829 depicted the Revolution as, in essence, an ethnic conflict.[79]

In June 1794 the French reinforced their hold on Habsburg Belgium at the battle of Fleurus. They occupied the United Provinces, which, previously "nameless," received the appellation "Batavian Republic" in application of the Ossianic *re-presentation* of Greater Rhineland space. Prussia sued for peace and formally surrendered its left bank possessions to France. By then, writes Albert Sorel, "the *Constituants* of 1789 had long disappeared from the scene and nothing remained of their outlook. The men who now ruled were powerful jurists, armed and armored, direct descendants of the *chevaliers ès lois* of Philippe le Bel, exaggerated rivals of Richelieu, immoderate successors to Louvois. They transferred to the *peuple* all the ideas that their predecessors had applied to the majesty of the king."[80] France's possession of the left bank was ratified by the treaties of Campo Formio (1796) and Lunéville (1801).

As Ossianic ontopology reinforced its hold on the discursive framework within which contemporaries struggled to make sense of events and possibilities, France's presence on the Rhine conditioned the brief but potent reemergence of a mythical Carolingia, the resurrection of the myth of empire – an empire ruled once again, legitimately, from Gaul. After the fall of the radical left in 1794, the government of France fell to a five-person *Directoire*, of which Napoleon Bonaparte was a member. Following his return in 1799 from the disastrous campaign in Egypt, Bonaparte overthrew the *Directoire* with the aid of Sieyès and assumed dictatorial powers under the *Roman* title of *Consul*. In 1804 he declared himself Emperor, appealing liberally to Carolingian imagery to legitimate his action by recalling "a past which was not the detested *ancien régime*, but a venerable tradition."[81] He assembled relics of Charlemagne's rule, and meditated on his tomb at Aachen. Like Pepin and Charlemagne, he crowned himself in the presence of the pope, in Paris on December 2. His coronation luxuriated in Carolingian symbolism. "There was a golden crown, fashioned in accordance with old designs . . . a sword . . . a sceptre. Napoleon's honors . . . included an object unprecedented in the coronation of former kings: an imperial globe, to evoke the Holy Roman

---

[79] Thiesse, *La création des identités nationales*, p. 50. See Smith, *Myths and Memories of the Nation*, p. 75. The passage from Sieyès reads: "Pourquoi ne renverrait-il pas dans les forêts de la Franconie toutes ces familles qui conservent la folle prétention d'être issues de la race des conquérants et d'avoir succédé à leurs droits?"

[80] Sorel, *Europe and the French Revolution*, p. 313.

[81] Furet, *Revolutionary France*, p. 245.

Empire. When the emperor arrived in the cathedral, the marshals carried the honors to the altar, where they laid them down; then they stood just opposite, where they can still be seen, immortalized in David's painting of the event."[82]

The old Holy Roman Empire disintegrated. Only fourteen of the hundred or so members of the college of princes and only eight of the fifty-one imperial cities bothered to show up at the Diet of 1789. When Napoleon defeated the combined armies of Austria and Russia at Austerlitz in December 1805, Bavaria, Baden, Württemberg, and fourteen smaller principalities seceded from the Holy Roman Empire to form a "Confederation of the Rhine" under French "protection." At the Imperial Diet of Regensburg, the French delegate announced that Napoleon "consented" to become the Confederation's protector, and no longer recognized the existence of the Holy Roman Empire. By then the Habsburgs had already abandoned claims to rule outside the bounds of their dynastic territories. In 1804 Francis II was styling himself "hereditary emperor of Austria" and in 1806 formally forswore the crown of the Holy Roman Empire.[83]

The Revolution was generally welcomed in the Greater Rhineland. In 1790, revolutionaries proclaimed Belgium's independence from the Habsburgs and established the *Etats Belgiques-Unis*, again providing one of the Greater Rhineland's nameless provinces with a *name* that was Ossianic by its reference to an ancient "people." Mainz, as mentioned above, embraced revolution and the Republic in 1793. Student clubs propagated revolutionary ideas and anticipated the success of French armies. "When the first French troops entered the Rhineland in 1792, they were welcomed as liberators and *neo-frankish brothers*," stirring yet more discursive complexity within the framework of the new Ossianic *re-presentation* of space.[84] Even as the Republic turned dictatorial, Rhineland cities applauded arrangements that placed constraints on the liberties of the princes, and integrated left bank businesses into a single market that extended from Hamburg to Spain, untrammeled by the multiplicity of tolls and duties that characterized antediluvian

---

[82] Furet, *Revolutionary France*, pp. 245–6. For a rival interpretation, see Biancamaria Fontana, "The Napoleonic Empire and the Europe of Nations," in Anthony Pagden, ed., *The Idea of Europe* (Cambridge and New York: Cambridge University Press and Woodrow Wilson Center, 2002), p. 122.

[83] Geoffrey Barraclough, *The Origins of Modern Germany* (New York and London: W. W. Norton, 1984), pp. 404–5.

[84] Barraclough, *The Origins of Modern Germany*, p. 407, emphasis added.

Rhineland space.[85] Freedom of the press, legal security, the dismantling of class (*Stand*) privileges, the promotion of a system of education, and economic prosperity all made French rule bearable, and even attractive to some. Moreover, Napoleon's policy of religious tolerance comforted the Protestant minority of this generally Catholic region. Cologne and the Rhineland gave Napoleon a hero's welcome in 1804, and again in 1811.

Napoleon's rule, however redolent of Enlightenment principle, nevertheless completed the discursive and cultural task of erasing the Greater Rhineland's political and civilizational specificity by further suppressing town autonomy. Autonomous towns had no place in departmentalized space. "The confused mosaic of the Holy Roman Empire outraged [revolutionary France's] logical minds. The quasi-sovereign *noblesse* and all the feudal paraphernalia shocked their legal spirits. Followers of the *philosophes* could not endure the sight of ecclesiastical principalities."[86] Many of the Holy Roman Empire's ecclesiastical and imperial cities were placed under the rule of larger states according to a process called *médiatisation*. Napoleon compensated the duke of Württemberg for ceding the left bank of the Rhine, for example, by awarding him rule over imperial cities like Esslingen and Reutlingen and ecclesiastical lands like those of the Grand Master of the Teutonic Order. The annexations quadrupled the duchy's size, and presaged the monarchical reorganization of German space by the Vienna treaty.

Cradle of the German nation

Following Napoleon's defeat, the Treaty of Vienna (1815) established a German federation composed of thirty-five independent, sovereign states, *Mittelstaaten,* and four free cities. France retained Alsace and Lorraine. England's insistence on a buffer against French expansionism produced a new Kingdom of the Netherlands that united Napoleon's "Batavian Republic," the United Provinces of old, with previously Habsburg Belgium. The treaty also established Prussia on the left bank of the Rhine between Bingen and the Dutch border. The French negotiator Talleyrand, seeking to convince the victors that Bourbon France was a

[85] Gertrud Milkereit, "Sozial- und Wirtschaftsentwicklung der südlichen Rheinlande seit 1815," in Franz Petri and Georg Droege, eds., *Rheinische Geschichte*, vol. III, *Wirtschaft und Kultur im 19. und 20. Jahrhundert* (Düsseldorf: Schwann, 1979), p. 199.

[86] Sorel, *Europe and the French Revolution*, p. 320.

viable partner in the post-Napoleonic concert of European powers, worked diligently and secretly with England and Austria to "dose" Prussia's presence on the Rhine in a way that gave England satisfaction, safeguarded Austria's influence in the new Confederation, and nourished France's hope to reconstitute a right bank clientele.

> Unconsciousness? Calculation? French diplomacy seemed satisfied with a situation that culminated in the creation of an enlarged Prussia "but deprived of real force." It was hoped that the very structure of the new Prussia would provoke numerous difficulties, require heavy military expenditures, and in that way contain Berlin's claims to dominate the German-speaking world.[87]

Talleyrand's calculations were not unreasonable. Napoleon's victory at Jena had provoked calls for German unity. Johann Gottlieb Fichte's (1762–1814) 1806 "Address to the German Nation" proclaimed the awakening of a German national consciousness. Fichte called for the construction of institutions that expressed the national character and connected the people with its cultural and historical traditions.[88] Uprisings, inspired by popular resistance to French occupation in Spain, erupted in 1808 and 1809 in Tyrol, Prussia, and Brunswick. In 1813, as Napoleon's army retreated from Moscow, Frederick William III exhorted his people to form volunteer corps to free Prussia. The response was enthusiastic.

But, once victorious, Prussia showed no more interest in German national unity. Its agrarian aristocracy – Junkers – clung to their privileges and regional autonomy. Nationhood was an idea of the left, one of revolution and citizenship. Prussia looked on with disapproval as voluntary associations formed to support the cause of national unity. Gymnastic and sharpshooter associations nurtured patriotic and military values. Choral societies cultivated a German musical esthetic.[89] The Prussian ruling class feared the free-thinking liberals who were advocating national unification. Prussia's occupation of the Rhineland reinforced rather than weakened perceptions of regional difference. The Rhineland's town culture and Napoleonic reform had brought forth "'Rhenish institutions,' as they came to be called, [which] represented the height of progress, the most radical political transformation of the time."[90]

---

[87] Raymond Poidevin and Jacques Bariéty, Les relations franco-allemandes, 1815–1975 (Paris, Armand Colin, 1977), p. 10.
[88] Abigail Green, Fatherlands: State-Building and Nationhood in Nineteenth-Century Germany (Cambridge: Cambridge University Press, 2001), p. 272.
[89] Green, Fatherlands, pp. 98–104.   [90] Applegate, A Nation of Provincials, p. 23.

Rhinelanders experienced the Prussian annexation as a foreign occupation. They called the Prussian troops "Litauer" – Lithuanians – and greeted them with a mix of superciliousness and anxiety. "The conviction that the German people as a whole had the right and the duty to construct a national state as the sure refuge (*sicheren Hort*) of its own culture was not heard loudly" in the Rhineland.[91] The nationalist historian Heinrich von Treitschke (1834–96) would later write of the "hard work [that was] needed to integrate this land of half-Frenchified papists (*halbverwaelschten Krummstabslande*) into German life!"[92]

But the Rhenish landscape secured the survival of Ossianic tropes and imagery in literature, and nurtured the language of nationhood even as nationalism was repressed. Poets reveled in the romantic vistas of the Rhine river gorge, and the "joyful sorrow" induced by the contemplation of its monumental ruins. "The Rhine actually discovered, indeed one could say created, romanticism"[93] as a celebration in art of primitive virtues and sentiments, of loyalty and sacrifice, of nostalgia for a lost people and its heroes. Romanticism nurtured nationhood. Johann Georg Forster, the Mainz revolutionary and companion of Captain James Cook, had found his boat trip through the gorge so "melancholy and horrible (*Schauderhaft*)" that he plunged his nose into a book to escape it.[94] But Friedrich Schlegel, eighteenth-century classicist, philologist, and early champion of Romantic literature admired, in his "Letters on a trip through the Netherlands, the Rhineland, Switzerland, and parts of France," the "wild cliffs" of the gorge and the "audacious castles (*kühne Burgen*)," its monuments from heroic times (*Heldenzeit*), which resembled less an incidental landscape than a "framed painting and a conceptualized work of art."[95] He celebrated the gorge in his ballad "The Sunken Castle." Goethe wrote on the Rhineland in his 1814

[91] Horst-Johannes Tümmers, *Der Rhein: Ein Europäischer Fluss und seine Geschichte* (Munich: Verlag C. H. Beck, 1994), p. 218, quoting the historian Max Braubuch. Norbert Oellers, "Geschichte der Literatur in den Rheinlanden seit 1815," in Petri and Droege, *Rheinische Geschichte*, III, pp. 570–1.

[92] Tümmers, *Der Rhein*, p. 221.

[93] Norbert Oellers, quoting Ricarda Huch, an early twentieth-century student of romanticism, in "Geschichte der Literatur in den Rheinlanden," Petri and Droege, *Rheinische Geschichte*, vol. III, p. 567.

[94] Oellers, "Geschichte der Literatur in den Rheinlanden," p. 568.

[95] Tümmers, *Der Rhein*, p. 209, and Oellers, "Geschichte der Literatur in den Rheinlanden," p. 568.

"Über Kunst und Alterthum in den Rhein und Mayn Gegenden."[96] The historian and poet Ernst Moritz Arndt, an opponent of Napoleon, wrote bitterly of the destruction left by the passage of Louis XIV's armies in his 1798 travelogue, *Reisen durch einen Theil Deutschlands*. A native of Koblenz, Joseph von Görres, a fervent admirer of the French Revolution, welcomed Koblenz's annexation in 1794 and participated in the proclamation of a Rhenish Republic in 1797. He led a delegation of "Rhineland patriots" to Paris in 1799 to plead for the establishment of an independent Rhineland Republic. Unsuccessful, he sought consolation in the study of medieval German literature, and, in 1806, assumed duties at the University of Heidelberg where he befriended Achim von Arnim and another Koblenz native, Clemens Brentano. Arnim and Brentano had met several years earlier during a youthful exploration of the towns, ruins, and vineyards near Rüdesheim, during which Arnim composed idyllic literary sketches of cliffs surmounted by ancient castle ruins and of vineyards that "sucked [the Rhine's] fiery blood."[97] In 1806, Arnim and Brentano published *Des Knaben Wunderhorn*, followed in 1807 by *Die Teutschen Volksbücher*. Arnim hoped that awareness of Germany's cultural roots would strengthen its resistance to Napoleon.[98] In 1810, Görres, having returned to Koblenz, called for a spiritual rebirth of the German nation (*Volk*), and in 1814 he founded *Der Rheinische Merkur*, a controversial but influential journal that championed German unification under a German emperor. Napoleon called the *Merkur* the "cinquième puissance" in the international coalition (Prussia, Austria, Russia, England) arrayed against him.[99] Görres opposed Prussian annexation and agitated for the creation of an independent Rhenish state. The publication in 1819 of *Teutschland und die Revolution* spurred the Prussian court to demand Görres' imprisonment. He pursued his campaign in exile, inveighing against Prussia's conservativism in pamphlets like *Europa und die Revolution* and *In Sachen der Rheinprovinzen*, which Prussian officials confiscated.[100] Arndt, whom the Prussian government also pursued for demagoguery, in an 1814 pamphlet "The Rhine,

---

[96] "Art and Antiquitiy in the Rhine and Main Regions." See Oellers, "Geschichte der Literatur in den Rheinlanden," p. 569.

[97] Tümmers, *Der Rhein*, p. 212.   [98] Thiesse, *La création des identités nationales*, p. 63.

[99] Oellers, "Geschichte der Literatur in den Rheinlanden," p. 572.

[100] Görres, in the course of the decade, evolved from nationalist to committed Roman Catholic ultramontanist and mystic. Brentano also embraced Catholic mysticism in the 1820s, and Arndt ended his life as a pious Protestant. Cf. Demangeon and Febvre, *Le Rhin*, pp. 142–3; Oellers, "Geschichte der Literatur in den Rheinlanden," pp. 570–4, 585–7.

Germany's River, not its Frontier" declared: "What do you see? What do you feel? ... you see the origins of your people, the oldest and most sacred memories of the empire of the Germans, the cradle of your culture (*Bildung*), the cities where your emperor was elected, crowned, and anointed ... the monuments of your glory and greatness."[101] As the Prussian armies under Blücher massed to cross the Rhine near Kaub on January 1, 1814, Max von Schenkendorf composed the "Lied vom Rhein":

> We do homage to our Lord,
> We drink his wine,
> May freedom be our star,
> May the watchword be the Rhine!
> We swear allegiance once again;
> We are obliged to it, that it be ours.
> From the bluffs it flows free, sublime,
> Flowing free toward God's bright sea.[102]

Brentano exclaimed: "Thou, a frontier? No! Not a frontier, thou old Rhine! Thou blood of life, flowing from the heart of Teutonia (*Teutoniens*)!" And August von Platen: "Speak, O Rhine! Ye currents, speak! Surely, as it is Heaven that guards you: We trust in our good right and our good sword!" Treitschke later wrote about the day, in May 1815, when the king of Prussia was anointed in the Carolingian cathedral of Aachen while taking possession of the territories conferred on him by the Treaty of Vienna: "from this beautiful land on the Rhine our history began to unfold one thousand years ago; now the mighty currents of German life flow back from the young colonial territories of the northeast [Prussia] to recover their old, silted (*verschüttetes*) bed."[103]

Perhaps the most influential figures in the elaboration of the discourse of nationhood were Jacob and Wilhelm Grimm. Jacob had studied old Germanic texts before joining up with Arnim and Brentano in 1804 to compile *Des Knaben Wunderhorn*. In 1808, in Paris, he was active in the Académie Celtique. That experience earned him an appointment as librarian to Jérôme Bonaparte, "King of Westphalia." His consuming interest in Germanic culture inspired his 1811 book *Über den altendeutschen Meistergesang*, in which he posited the existence of an "original" German language, the root of modern German dialects and culture. In 1812 he published the *Kinder- und Hausmärchen* with his brother Wilhelm,

---

[101] Oellers, "Geschichte der Literatur in den Rheinlanden," p. 572; Tümmers, *Der Rhein*, p. 261.
[102] Tümmers, *Der Rhein*, p. 220.   [103] Tümmers, *Der Rhein*, p. 222.

assembled from material provided by peasants of their native Hesse (and by Marie Hassenpflug, the daughter of an upper-class, French-speaking family, who, scholars speculate, may have "contaminated" the collection with themes and characters from Charles Perrault's 1697 French collection, *Ma Mère l'Oye*). Jacob Grimm was appointed professor at the University of Göttingen in 1829. The title of his inaugural lecture, *De Desiderio Patriae*, "Of longing for the fatherland," echoed the Ossianic "joy of sorrow."[104] The Grimms, however, were more systematic and rigorous in their research than Macpherson, and their efforts produced durable achievements: a German grammar (1819), a collection of ancient German legal documents (1828), *Deutsche Mythologie* (1835), and the first volumes of a German dictionary (1852). The Ossianic inspiration is discernible in *Deutsche Mythologie* (1835), in which Jacob Grimm traced fairy tales to primitive "Germanic" peoples, whose romanticized portrayal was colored by nostalgia for a heroic age.

The Grimms' scholarship was not contained by Germania's frontiers, but exhibited the "internationalism" of the first inventors of the new discourse of nationhood. When they began to suspect, following Schlegel, that the legends they collected might be pointing to a common "European" heritage, and possibly a common "European" idiom that would explain grammatical and verbal similarities across Europe's various languages, they turned their attention to other ancient literatures: Scandinavian, English, Finnish, Spanish, and Provençal. Their scholarship nurtured the republican internationalism that characterized the 1830s. Inversely, it also fed growing interest in Europe's "Indo-European" or "Aryan" roots, with fateful implications. Be that as it may, the breadth of their scholarship earned Jacob, on the recommendation of François Guizot, admission to the very Napoleonic Légion d'Honneur in 1841.

Rheinromantik retained its creative power through mid-century. The Lorelei, pure poetic invention, made its debut in Clemens Brentano's 1801 novel *Godwi*. Brentano's Koblenz childhood may have exposed him to tales of elves and dwarves that inhabited a grotto, the *Hanselsmann-sloch*, at the base of the Lurley, a precipice overlooking the rapids of the Rhine gorge (Lurley from *Leie*: cliff). Frances Trollope, an insistent debunker of *Rheinromantik*, wrote in 1833 of a prankster who spent his summers blowing on a horn to make echoes for tourists. Whatever the elements that became entwined in Brentano's imagination, they gave birth to the enchantress "Lore Ley," an inspiration to generations of

---

[104] Thiesse, *La création des identités nationales*, p. 64.

poets, composers, and painters (see plate 6.2). It was this figure of "ancient" ("aus alten Zeiten") legend that Heinrich Heine immortalized in his 1823 poem:[105]

> Ich weiss nicht was soll es bedeuten,
>
> Dass ich so traurig bin;
>
> Ein Märchen *aus alten Zeiten*,
>
> Das kommt mir nicht aus dem Sinn …

In 1837 the poet Karl Simrock (1802–76) of Bonn, a student of Schlegel and Arndt, published a popular collection of Rhine legends. He followed it with a collection of essays, *The Picturesque and Romantic Rhineland*, a litany of Ossianic "clichés, moonlit nights, mountains, wine, maidens' eyes, and the Fatherland."[106] But Simrock's most decisive contribution to *Rheinromantik* was his 1827 translation of the *Niebelungenlied*, a medieval epic that brought Franks and Burgundians together in an ambiguously "German" tale of Rhineland origins.

> Es wuchs in Burgonden
>
>> ein schönes Mägdelein,
>
> Wie in allen Landen
>
>> nichts schöners mochte sein.
>
> Kriemhild war sie geheissen
>
>> und war ein schönes Weib,
>
> Um dass viel Degen mussten
>
>> verlieren Leben und Leib …
>
> Zu Worms am Rhein wohnten
>
>> die Herrn mit ihrer Kraft.
>
> Von ihren Landen diente
>
>> viel stolze Ritterschaft
>
> Mit stolzlichen Ehren
>
>> all ihres Lebens Zeit,
>
> Bis jämmerlich sie starben
>
>> durch zweier edeln Frauen Neid.[107]

---

[105] Tümmers, *Der Rhein*, p. 248. "I know not what it means/ that I am so sad;/ a tale from olden times/ that I cannot get out of my head." On the legend's genealogy, see Oellers, "Geschichte der Literatur in den Rheinlanden," pp. 575–6.

[106] Tümmers, *Der Rhein*, p. 254.

[107] "In Burgundy there grew so noble a maid that in all the lands none fairer might there be. Kriemhild was she called; a comely woman she became, for whose sake many a knight must needs lose his life … At Worms upon the Rhine they dwelt with all their power. Proud knights from out their lands served them with honor, until their end was come. Thereafter they died grievously, through the hate of two noble dames."

Plate 6.2 Goldberg: *Loreley*, *c.*1865, after a Wügen painting. With the permission of the Stadt Museum Bonn.

A friend of Goethe, the art theorist and landscape artist Carl Gustav Carus, wrote of the Rhenish landscape:

> Certainly, I confess never to have had a feeling so unusual, so new, of patriotism. It was as if for the first time I had a fatherland, that I had found my fatherland. Here is in fact that same thing that grips us so powerfully in Italy: a sublime landscape, a land of world historical

importance and significant monuments, in which, standing or fallen, the many high moments of a great history had engraved such deeply meaningful words. Indeed, it is more to me than Italy; it is my country, it is Germany, and never will Roman architecture speak to our spirit as well as that mysteriously pure style, peculiar to our people, born within it, which still breathes within these vaults, and which continues to play in the smallest rose window.[108]

At mid-century, Wilhelm Heinrich Riehl, a native of Rhenish Pfalz, earned the title "father of German *Volkskunde*" (folklore studies, or more academically, anthropology) for the publication of his three-volume *Naturgeschichte des deutschen Volks* (Natural History of the German People). "Riehl's work had a grittiness and unpretentious sharpness of observation that brought him a wide audience. His opposition to cities, to industrial society, to France, all grew out of his objection to uniformity in social life."[109]

As *Rheinromantik* flourished as a literary fad, the machine age was bringing new energy and dynamism to the Greater Rhineland. The region was on the verge of reclaiming its place as one of the most productive and wealthiest regional economies of the world (see chapter 7). But the machine age had the ironic effect of enhancing the Rhineland's exoticism by turning *Rheinromantik* into a marketable commodity. In 1816, an English steamboat paddled its way up the Rhine, newly opened to English shipping by Napoleon's defeat. It astounded Rhinelanders by accomplishing the two-week journey from Rotterdam to Cologne in fewer than five days. In 1822, a Dutch company, the Niederländische Dampfschiffsreederei, scheduled a regular liaison between the two cities, foreshadowing the Netherlands' enduring dominance of Rhine river traffic.[110] In 1824, at the invitation of a German financier, a Dutch boat made the journey to Mainz to assess the feasibility of regular service to that city. A German engineer, Gerhard Moritz Roentgen, described the voyage in language redolent of Jules Verne: "it was like a magic spell. We found ourselves transferred all at once in the most foreign surroundings. The most elegant of Dutch and English appointments made for all manners of comfort, and yet the noise of the paddles reminded us that we were in a machine, a kind of

---

[108] Tümmers, *Der Rhein*, p. 212.

[109] Applegate, *A Nation of Provincials*, p. 34. See also Oellers, "Geschichte der Literatur in den Rheinlanden," pp. 607–8, 611.

[110] Hermann Kellenbenz, "Wirtschafts- und Sozialentwicklung der nördlichen Rheinlanden seit 1815," in Petri and Droege, *Rheinische Geschichte*, vol. III, p. 53.

swimming mill, fighting the currents."[111] River-dwellers swarmed the banks – at Koblenz in the rain, at St. Goar, Bacharach – to stare with dumb astonishment at the "mill ship" (*Mühlenschiff*). The following year, a steamboat vanquished the currents of the upper Rhine to reach Kehl, opposite Strasburg. Such achievements spurred the Prussian government in 1829 to charter a company that would assure regular service between Cologne and Mainz. It granted a similar concession to a Düsseldorf firm in 1836.

The Rhine became, with Italy and the Alps, a travel destination of choice.[112] *Rheinromantik* was big business. The Stolzenfels castle, atop the Rhine gorge, was refurbished in 1830. The first Baedeker – a guide to the Rhine – appeared in 1835. The castle of Liechtenstein, near the source of the Rhine, was restored in 1840. By 1844, the Cologne company, with twenty-three ships, was ferrying some 600,000 passengers up and down the Rhine each year. About half of these were Englishmen retracing the steps of Childe Harold.[113]

> Wisdom's world will be
> Within its own creation, or in thine,
> Maternal Nature! for who teems like thee,
> Thus on the banks of thy majestic Rhine?
> There Harold gazes on a work divine,
> A blending of all beauties; streams and dells,
> Fruit, foliage, crag, wood, cornfield, mountain, vine,
> And chiefless castles breathing stern farewells
> From gray but leafy walls, where Ruin greenly dwells.[114]

The Düsseldorf company, with ten ships, was conveying another 300,000 passengers. In 1853 the two companies merged to form the Köln-Düsseldorf Rheindampfschiffsgesellschaft, which continues to rule Rhine tourism in our day. A thriving travel industry, however, had the effect of reintroducing a palpable cosmopolitanism to the "brooding, romantic" Rhine in a way that clashed with its Ossianic *re-presentation*. Carl Simrock provides this glimpse of the "romantic Rhine" at mid-century:

> Nowhere is the traffic livelier. The hourly departure of the postal carriages, hauling trailers, the gleaming, golden steamboats, before whose rotating

---

[111] Tümmers, *Der Rhein*, p. 228.   [112] Tümmers, *Der Rhein*, p. 284.
[113] Oellers, "Geschichte der Literatur in den Rheinlanden," pp. 564, 568–9. Byron visited the Rhineland in 1816.
[114] Lord Byron, *Childe Harold's Pilgrimage*, Canto III, XLVI.

paddles the river never rests, the railways that run alongside both banks of the river, the spacious hotels, installed with the lavish splendor of a palace, which have learned how not to move the crowds of tourists too expeditiously, how not to decrease the number of foreigners ... one is no longer in Germany; one feels here as if one is out in the wide world (*man fühlt sich in der grossen Welt*).[115]

By the second half of the century, even as steel and chemical plants spilled their ample effluence into the Rhine's waters, steamboats were still carrying about a million passengers yearly.

The Ossianic *re-presentation* of France as nation

Scholars commonly mark the difference between the French and German concepts of nationhood. Rogers Brubaker contrasts "state-centered and assimilationist" France with "*Volk*-centered and differentialist" Germany. Anthony Smith uses the terms "civico-territorial" and "ethnico-genealogical" to make the same distinction, and John Plamenatz asserts that the French and German models reflect the more general contrast between western liberalism and a kind of oriental essentialism.[116] The contrast manifests itself most clearly in laws regulating the acquisition of nationality. French law evinces a greater effort to marry nationhood with Enlightenment universality. Inversely, the failure of social and political revolution in Germany, Brubaker argues, preserved the principle of filiation, *jus sanguinis*, in the transfer of class or caste privileges, and, as corollary, of national affiliation.[117]

---

[115] Tümmers, *Der Rhein*, p. 238; Kellenbenz, "Wirtschafts- und Sozialentwicklung der nördlichen Rheinlanden," pp. 2–3. See also Oellers, "Geschichte der Literatur in den Rheinlanden," pp. 593–4.

[116] Brubaker, *Citizenship and Nationhood in France and Germany*. See *ibid.*, ch. 4, and Patrick Weil, *Qu'est-ce qu'un Français? Histoire de la nationalité française depuis la Révolution* (Paris: Grasset, 2002). See Patrick Cabanel, *La question nationale au XIXe siècle* (Paris: Editions La Découverte, 1997), p. 9. Essentialism is not Plamenatz's term. For an analysis of the various theories of nationhood, see esp. Smith, *Myths and Memories of the Nation*, pp. 36–9.

[117] Brubaker, *Citizenship and Nationhood*, ch. 3. More precisely, p. 81, "Although based on *jus sanguinis*, French citizenship law incorporates substantial elements of *jus soli*." Note that the replacement of "the panoply of special law communities" by the "development of unitary internal sovereignty," p. 54, occurs in Prussia and does not take the analysis forward to the emergence of a sentiment of German nationhood. See esp. pp. 134–7. Left bank Pfalz, as analyzed by Applegate, *A Nation of Provincials*, pp. 8–9, is more durably affected in its understanding of citizenship by contact with French republicanism. But Bavarian rule after 1815 spawns a similar "territorialization" of citizenship.

But one should not conclude from this distinction that French discourse was not affected by the *coup de force* that conferred nationhood by lineage rather than by the accident of place of birth. When the Académie Celtique closed its doors after Napoleon's fall,[118] Ossianic discourse survived in literature and scholarship. Germaine de Staël, daughter of Louis XVI's reformist finance minister Jacques Necker and one of Napoleon's fiercest critics, sojourned in Weimar in 1803–4 and in Munich and Vienna in 1807–8. Her 1810 publication, *De l'Allemagne*, vaunted a primitive, Rousseauian freedom, an uncomplicated spiritualism, and frank sentimentalism. In her *Considérations sur la révolution française* she castigated Napoleon's efforts to bring homogeneity to Europe and saw in national difference the antidote to despotism.[119] A number of influential French intellectuals made the trek to Germany to witness firsthand the new ideas and literary styles that were evolving there. Edgar Quinet, who settled in Heidelberg in 1826 and lived in Germany for more than a decade, introduced his countrymen to Herder's philosophy of history and drew on the work of Görres to fashion his own religiously informed, historicist conceptualization of civilization. Jules Michelet, historian, and friend and ally of Quinet, studied in the Rhineland in 1828. A student of Herder and admirer of Grimm, Michelet felt the fascination of primitive legend, symbols, and myth, and developed a kind of totalizing historicist interpretation of culture and civilization. Victor Hugo explored the Rhine and, like de Staël, celebrated in writing of the "liberty of the German," his "noble, grave, serious" character, his "body in mist, his mind in chimera." Alfred de Musset, poet and playwright, lover of George Sand and admirer of Schiller, sojourned in Baden. Gérard de Nerval, peripatetic poet and translator of Goethe's *Faust*, exclaimed upon discovering the Black Forest that Germany was "the mother of us all, Teutonia!" Saint-Marc Girardin, a critic of the Romantics but admirer of German education, had high regard for the domesticity, the faith, and the sentimentalism of the German.[120] Literary journals, most notably the *Revue des Deux Mondes*, founded in 1829 to promote knowledge of America, became a vehicle for the diffusion of German thought in France.

---

[118] Thiesse, *La création des identités nationales*, p. 58.
[119] See Bianca Fontana, "The Napoleonic Empire and the Europe of Nations," in Anthony Pagden, ed., *The Idea of Europe* (Cambridge and New York: Cambridge University Press and Woodrow Wilson Center, 2002).
[120] Poidevin and Bariéty, *Les relations franco-allemandes*, p. 32.

While some sought inspiration in Germany, others continued to scour the Breton countryside for evidence of France's "Celtic origins." The holy grail of that quest was the presumed manuscript of a fifth-century bard named Guinclan. Théodore Hersart de la Villemarqué, who corresponded with the Grimm brothers, discovered manuscripts that served as the basis for his 1842 publication *Barzaz Breiz* (Songs of Brittany), an anthology of folk poems that included tales of King Arthur. In a report to the French government, Villemarqué proclaimed that the ancient language of the Gauls (which had so confused Julius Caesar by its variety) was in fact the same as that spoken in his day by Breton peasants. Villemarqué insisted that Welsh tales, particularly the Arthurian legends that were the talk of England, were in fact of Breton origin. Villemarqué was elected unanimously to the Academy of Berlin in 1851. At about the same time, the Ministry of Public Instruction established the Commission des Chants Religieux et Historiques de la France and the Comité de la Langue, de l'Histoire, et des Arts de la France, which resurrected the project of the Académie Celtique and extended it to Basque, Flemish, and Alsatian folklores.

The *Barzaz Breiz* inspired Eugène Sue's (1804–57) novel *Les mystères du peuple* (1849), which reprised the claim that France was home to two nations, Frankish and Celtic. Journalist, novelist, and one of the most widely read writers of melodramatic fiction of his time, Sue gained fame in the 1840s as author of *romans-feuilleton*, serial novels that appeared in newspapers. During the revolution of 1848, Sue was elected Socialist deputy to the National Assembly, a success that earned him exile after Louis Napoleon's *coup d'état*. *Les mystères du peuple*, reviewed critically by Karl Marx, is the story of a Paris merchant, Marik Le Brenn, who participates in the 1848 revolution. A native Breton-speaker, he is able to read "manuscripts" of ancient Gaul, and discovers in them a civilization that is democratic, feminist, wisely governed by druids, and bound by a religion that reveres a divinity named Hesus. One of Le Brenn's "ancestors" travels to Palestine in the year 33 AD and finds that Christ's teachings conform to the basic principles of Celtic religion. Napoleon III banned the book, but erected a monument to Vercingetorix in Alise-Sainte-Reine to shore up his own "Celtic" credentials.[121]

[121] Thiesse, *La création des identités nationales*, p. 126. Hesus was, in fact, the name of a Gallic deity.

Belgian exceptionalism

Ossianic ontopology turned named space – Gallia, Germania – into homes for nations. The place name existed as marker (long) before the nation that was constructed to inhabit the place. The struggle to bring to light the "thing" – the nation – that "corresponded" to the name "cracked" the nameless place that was the Greater Rhineland into pieces. The tension between Ossianic ontopology and Greater Rhineland anonymity was nowhere more apparent than in the struggle to bring to light the place called "Belgium," a state carved out of the Greater Rhineland heartland in 1830 (see below). Belgium was not a named place until "nation-states" began incising frontiers into Greater Rhineland space. Nineteenth-century Belgians might point proudly to Caesar's observation that the *Belgae* were the most warlike of the Gauls, but Belgium, like the Greater Rhineland as a whole, had traversed most of its history nameless. Twelfth-century designations were uniformly descriptive: *Avalterre, Pays d'En Bas, Basses Régions, Partes Inferiores, Partes Advallenses, Lage Lande by der See, Nederlant.*[122] After the fall of Burgundy, the Habsburg court referred to its lowland possessions as the "seventeen provinces." Dutch-speaking "Belgians" did not have a named language. In the sixteenth century its divers dialects were called *Nederduitsch*, low German, or *Nederlandsch*, "low landish." In French, the dialects of Flanders were called *Flameng*, but the term did not apply outside the duchy. The francophone populations of the Holy Roman Empire were collectively called "Wallons," which, like Welsh or *Welsche*, derived from the Latin *Gallus*, and referred to the peoples of Roman Gallia generally.

A discourse of place began to emerge at the time of the Reformation. Although Calvinism advanced as readily in the old towns of Flanders and Brabant as it did in those of Holland and Zealand, Spanish repression destroyed the Protestant cause in the south and, by provoking mass migration, strengthened it in the north. Fifteen thousand people fled Ghent following its destruction in 1584. Half the population of Antwerp, more than 40,000 people, abandoned the city when it fell in 1585. Many sought safety in Germany and England, but others joined the Protestant resistance that was taking shape north of the Rhine. The consequence was the emergence, by the end of the century, of a generally Catholic and "loyalist" south and a generally Protestant and "revolutionary" north.

---

[122] Jean Stengers, *Les racines de la Belgique: jusqu'à la révolution de 1830* (Brussels: Editions Racine, 2000), p. 69.

The distinction became etched in the landscape: the *Oude Kerken* were termed "typical" of the Protestant north; flamboyant Gothic dominated the Catholic south. Southerners fashioned the pejorative term *gueux* – from the Dutch *guit*, rogue – to refer to the schismatic northerners, who in turn embraced the epithet with pride. The term "Belgian," however, was first advanced in the hope of restoring unity to north and south. An anonymous brochure published in Leuven in 1602 exhorted lowlanders to conduct themselves as "vrays et naturelz belgeois." It continued: "Nous sommes patriotz, Belgeois, frères et sœurs, amys et parens, voires une mesme chair et sang par alliances infinies, pourquoy demourons-nous en ceste raige?"[123] But the language of difference durably colonized political and cultural discourse. Not merely religion, but rebellion, war, and colonial expansion legitimated patriotism in the north, whereas the language of patriotism – whether to Austria or "Belgium" – remained ambiguous if not foreign to the south. The Habsburg court adopted the term "Belgian" as an appellation of convenience (though it excluded the episcopal city of Liège and its dependants on the Meuse: Huy, Dinant, and St. Trond), but it did not displace *Pays-Bas* in common parlance. In the Dutch-speaking provinces, the term *België* was hardly used at all. The words *Nederland, de Nederlanden*, and *Nederlanders* remained the common denominations. The adjective *Flamand*, like the noun *Flameng*, applied only to the province of Flanders, west of the Scheldt.

Dutch- or more specifically Flemish-speaking Belgians were slower than their German Rhineland neighbors – who were not quick – to equate the promotion of the "national" idiom with political emancipation. French was widely used as a business and administrative lingua franca. "Flanders is the only region of Europe in which French penetrated the middle (*bourgeois*) class."[124] Toward the end of the seventeenth century, many Flemish-speaking inhabitants of the bilingual province of Brabant used French exclusively in law and public affairs. Jan Baptist Verlooy, a Brussels jurist and Voltairean critic of the Church and the Habsburg court, complained (in French) in 1788 that French had become the language of "all those who want to be something."[125] In Belgium, as in France a century later (see next chapter), women were among the most active agents of French linguistic hegemony.

---

[123] Stengers, *Les racines de la Belgique*, p. 107: "We are patriots, Belgians, brothers and sisters, friends and family, even a same flesh and blood by infinite alliances, why do we remain in this rage?"

[124] Stengers, *Les racines de la Belgique*, p. 162.

[125] Stengers, *Les racines de la Belgique*, p. 163.

Some were educated in Catholic convents where Dutch, the idiomatic vehicle of heresy, was forbidden. But more generally, as a resident of Mechelen observed: "How often do we hear ridiculous women say that there is something hard, heavy, uncultured (*boersch*) about the *Neder-landsche* language."[126] The use of French in administration was made official by the Napoleonic occupation. Dutch was no longer written in the formerly Habsburg lowlands, and dissolved into a multiplicity of mutually incomprehensible spoken dialects. A resident of Antwerp soon found it challenging to understand the Dutch of Bruges. Mutual incomprehensibility, in turn, further depreciated the status of Dutch in Belgium.

French linguistic hegemony was therefore an obstacle to the Ossianic *re-presentation* of "Belgian" space. "Belgium entered the period during which linguistic nationalism, originating in Germany, began to spread across Europe, with a single culture – French culture."[127] Linguistic nationalism did not appear until the mid-nineteenth century. Until then, the language of "national unification" was, for many, an instrumental language. It was not "sacred." Belgians could not ground their nationhood in myths of bards and warriors forging and defending a cultural legacy, a self, an identity. When Belgians surveyed the "national" past, they saw weavers and merchants. Their country's roots were not in misty, brooding, sacred groves, but in bustling, multilingual, bourgeois trading towns. One reads a reference to the lowlands' tradition of town autonomy in the anonymous revolutionary pamphlet *Le cri du peuple*:

> Ten centuries of prosperity and opulence ... have consecrated the excellence of the Belgian (*belgique*) constitution. It has always gloriously repelled the attacks of its most formidable neighbors, it has sometimes made them tremble in their very homes ... This imposing brilliance ... it owes not only to the fecundity of its fields, the activity of its inhabitants, and to its incredible population, but even more to its political constitution [reference to town autonomy] which ... leaves to the inhabitants of these fair lands this honest and precious liberty that makes them cherish the Fatherland, and which becomes the source of national felicity.[128]

Verlooy proclaimed (this time in Dutch):

> By its character, our people owes nothing, neither in grandeur, nor in nobility, nor in intelligence to any in the world. It is we who, by our

---

126 Stengers, *Les racines de la Belgique*, p. 164.
127 Stengers, *Les racines de la Belgique*, p. 167.
128 Stengers, *Les racines de la Belgique*, pp. 142–3.

antique courage and our love of liberty, by our navigation and our commerce so celebrated in the past with all peoples of the world, by our so useful and numerous creations ... it is we who deserve to be cited first in the march of savage humanity toward civilization (*in 'therzedigen van 't verwildert mensdom*).[129]

Verlooy's reference to "savage humanity" expresses indifference to or ignorance of Ossianic lore about nations grounded in primitive but accomplished civilizations. Even when Belgian poets sounded Ossianic themes, they seemed incapable of imagining Belgium's past as anything other than commercial and industrial. In 1807, when Belgium was an anonymous assemblage of French *départements*, a "national" poetry contest on the topic "The Belgians" produced these prize-winning lines by a certain De Borchgrave, a tax collector from Wakken:

> *Ik zing, ontvlamd van drift, myn' dierb're landgenooten!*
> *Ik zing het helden bloed, waar uit ik ben gesprooten!*
> *Kortom, ik zing den Belg, zyn onverschrokken trouw,*
> *Zyn kunst, zyn koopmanschap, zyn land- en akkerbouw!*[130]

> I sing, burning with passion, my beloved compatriots!
> I sing the blood of heroes from which I descend!
> In short, I sing the Belgian, his undaunted loyalty,
> His art, his business, his cultivated fields and agriculture!

No harps ... no druids ... but mills and merchants.

The conflicted ontopology of the Rhine frontier

However fragile the foundations of Ossianic discourse, however contestable the referential power of Ossianic mythology, revolution in Belgium in 1830 and the threat of war in 1840 made clear that a paradigmatic shift was occurring in the representation of Greater Rhineland space. The Treaty of Vienna, which restored Bourbon rule to France, did not end France's aspirations to reclaim its "natural frontier." France's counter-revolutionary intervention in Spain in 1823 restored trust among its legitimist neighbors. Chateaubriand, the French minister of foreign affairs (and erstwhile Ossian enthusiast), thought the time was ripe to advance claims on the Rhine.[131]

---

[129] Stengers, *Les racines de la Belgique*, pp. 143–4.
[130] Stengers, *Les racines de la Belgique*, p. 155.
[131] Poidevin and Bariéty, *Les relations franco-allemandes*, p. 16. Cf. Demangeon and Febvre, *Le Rhin*, p. 144.

French statesmen concocted diplomatic strategies to revise the 1815 settlement, the most serious of which was drafted by Jules-Armand de Polignac, Chateaubriand's successor at foreign affairs, which sought to piggy-back a revision of Rhineland frontiers on diplomatic efforts to resolve a crisis in the Near East. The plan called for the annexation of Belgium, the transfer of Prussia's Rhineland possessions to Saxony, compensation for Prussia in the east, and compensation for Russia in the Ottoman empire. The return of peace to the Orient dashed the scheme.

In July 1830, insurrectionists, among whom figured the marquis de Lafayette, deposed the French king Charles X. Louis Philippe, a representative of the cadet branch of the royal family and son of Philippe Egalité, supporter of Robespierre and Danton, was crowned his successor. French revolutionaries exhorted the subjugated nations of Germany and Poland to rise up to recover their liberty while, insensitive to the contradiction, exhorting the French to reclaim their rank in the European concert by annexing the left bank of the Rhine. Revolution in France awakened the national liberal movement in Germany from its Prussian-imposed slumber. *Burschenschaften* – liberal student fraternities that had formed in the nationalist fervor surrounding Napoleon's defeat – emerged from years of repression. Uprisings forced abdications in Brunswick, Saxony, and Hesse-Cassel. In 1832, tens of thousands of demonstrators gathered at Hambach, in Rhineland Palatinate, "the first and possibly the only large political demonstration of the liberal German Bourgeoisie," to toast France's Revolution and demand the creation of a democratic German republic.[132] German nationalism in the 1830s was typically pro-French. German intellectuals read and debated the works of Babœuf, Auguste Blanqui, and Saint Simon. Revolutionary intellectuals and authors of the "Young Germany" movement distanced themselves from the romance and folklore of *Rheinromantik*, seeking inspiration instead in literati such as Heinrich Heine, poet and satirist who wrote of the "sleeping sovereign," the "great, mysterious" Germany of the people,[133] and Heinrich Börne, a political philosopher who influenced Marx. Both lived in Paris, Heine as expatriate and Börne as political exile.

---

[132] Applegate, *A Nation of Provincials*, p. 27. See Oellers, "Geschichte der Literatur in den Rheinlanden," pp. 587–8.

[133] Giesen, *Intellectuals and the German Nation*, pp. 106–14; Oellers, "Geschichte der Literatur in den Rheinlanden," pp. 575–80, 592–3.

The revolutionary wave unleashed by the Parisians also spurred insurrection in Brussels. The 1815 creation of a greater Netherlands was, from the beginning, compromised by confessional and linguistic tensions between "Belgians" and their Dutch masters. The Dutch favored their dialect in administration, promoting its use even in the French-speaking provinces. In August 1830, Brussels' opening-night performance of Daniel François Auber's *La muette de Portici*, which celebrates a "national" uprising in 1647 Naples, ended in riot. As the musicians attacked the duet *Amour sacré de la Patrie*, the audience stormed into the streets and raised barricades. The insurrectionists were not entirely clear on what they wanted. Some talked of autonomy, others independence. But the Dutch bombardment of Antwerp in subsequent days tipped the scales in favor of independence. Crisis erupted when the French threatened to intervene on the side of the insurrection and the Prussians on the side of the Dutch. The British, ever sensitive to the geopolitics of the lower Rhine, called a conference of great powers in London which, indifferent to Westphalian principles of state sovereignty, dissolved the Kingdom of the Netherlands and brokered the divorce with "Belgium." The Dutch did not acquiesce in the creation of Belgium as "an independent and perpetually neutral state" until 1839, and then only because the great powers detached half of Luxemburg from Belgium and gave it to the king of Holland as an independent dukedom.

In 1840 there occurred a second event that revealed the change that was taking place in the commonsense representation of Greater Rhineland space, and, through that representation, in the discursive tools that enabled political judgment and ambition. A diplomatic crisis, occasioned once again by instability in the eastern Mediterranean, resurrected French designs on the left bank. Victor Hugo, the cosmopolitan, internationalist visionary who would one day call for the creation of a "United States of Europe," exhorted his countrymen to retake the Rhine, proclaiming that "the left bank belongs to France by nature (*appartient naturellement à la France*)." The Rhine embodied Europe, Hugo proclaimed, and France was not complete until it occupied its banks. Alphonse de Lamartine, who would later figure among the leaders of the 1848 revolution, brought the question of the Rhine frontier before the legislative chamber. Edgar Quinet seconded Hugo's and Lamartine's arguments in a pamphlet entitled *1815 et 1840*. Heinrich Heine, from his Parisian exile, reported to the *Augsburger Allgemeine* that French "national feeling is agitated to its most fundamental depths, and the great act of justice appears to the French as a rehabilitation of their lost national vanity, as an additional dressing upon the wounds of Waterloo."[134]

French agitation stirred emotions in the German Rhineland, whose inhabitants had once greeted Napoleon's troops as "neo-Frankish brothers," but who now reasoned and judged within a discourse that articulated the mythical image of a unified German nation. Hagen Schulze dates nationalism as a mass political phenomenon in Germany to this 1840 crisis.[135] Thomas Nipperdey, by contrast, suggests continuity between Rhineland attitudes toward a (distant) empire and an (equally distant) myth of German unity: "If people could no longer be Rhinelanders, then they wanted to be Germans, not Prussians or Bavarians."[136] But it is not the attitude, essentially unknowable, that matters, but the discursive imagery that invites definition, and that enables mobilization of self against other. The prince or heretic of the past became a Frenchman of the present. Arndt again took up his pen in a political cause to write:

> Das ganze Deutschland soll es sein!
> So klingt's vom Belt bis übern Rhein.
> Der Römer sank, der Römling sinkt,
> Wo Stahl in deutschen Fäusten blinkt.
> So soll es sein!
> So war, so soll mein Deutschland sein![137]

The term *Römling*, pejorative in its suggestion of imitation of what was the glory of Rome, not only was synonymous with *Welsche*, or Gaulish, but had assumed in the preceding decades the additional meaning of "Catholic," particularly ultramontanist Catholic, in other words the *ancien régime* negation of German nationhood, still prevalent in the Rhineland. The *Burschenschaften*, among whose members was the young Rhinelander Friedrich Engels, abandoned their sentiment of solidarity with France's revolutionary, republican left and pledged to defend, not the

---

[134] Tümmers, *Der Rhein*, pp. 222, 223.

[135] Hagen Schulze, *The Course of German Nationalism: From Frederick the Great to Bismarck 1763–1867* (Cambridge: Cambridge University Press, 1991), discussed by Green, *Fatherlands*, p. 6, footnote 12.

[136] Applegate, *A Nation of Provincials*, p. 27.

[137] "It shall the whole of Germany be!/So goes the clamor from the Belt to beyond the Rhine./The Roman fell, the "Römling" is falling,/Where steel in German fists is gleaming./ So shall it be!/As it was, so shall my Germany be!" Quoted in Oellers, "Geschichte der Literatur in den Rheinlanden," p. 591. See Oeller's discussion of the crisis, pp. 589–93.

town, as in the fifteenth century, but the *Rhine*.[138] The crisis spurred enthusiasm for the completion of the cathedral of Cologne, half-finished since the fourteenth century. *Dombauvereine*, "associations for the completion of the cathedral," were formed in the 1840s to finance the completion of this monument to "the brotherhood of all Germans."[139] The Protestant Prussian king, Frederick William IV, assumed sponsorship of the project in 1842. Franz Liszt staged benefit concerts. "Numerous princely personages came to Cologne to prove their sense of community."[140] The 1840 crisis also inspired efforts to raise, on a hill in the Teutoburger Wald above Detmold in Lower Saxony, a colossal monument to Hermann, Arminius, destroyer of Varrus' legions, depicted in "ancient German" costume (recall his service in the Roman cavalry), crushing the Roman eagle under foot.[141]

It was in the heat of the 1840 crisis that Max Schneckenburger composed the *Wacht am Rhein*, engraved on the base of *Germania*. That composition provoked this observation by Karl Simrock, revelatory of the new ontopology of the Greater Rhineland:

> when ... we come to the words '*am Rhein! Am Rhein!*', how all the voices join together loudly, how the glasses clink, how one German grasps the hand of another, how they come together in the festivities, however haphazardly they made their way here, in the awareness of having become friends and brothers by this most beloved stream![142]

It was also during this crisis that Hoffmann von Fallersleben, poet and collecter of German *lieder*, composed *Deutschland über Alles*. But it is not without significance that the ditty that met with greatest success was Nikolaus Becker's *Rheinlied*:

> No they shall not have it,
> The free, the German Rhine,
> Tho' they like greedy ravens
> Should e'en their throats shriek dry![143]

---

[138] Poidevin and Bariéty, *Les relations franco-allemandes*, p. 22. Engels haled from Barmen, near Wuppertal, where he lived until 1845.

[139] Tümmers, *Der Rhein*, p. 272.

[140] Oellers, "Geschichte der Literatur in den Rheinlanden," p. 59. The nave was completed in 1863, and the landmark steeples in 1880.

[141] Green, *Fatherlands*, pp. 123–8; Oellers, "Geschichte der Literatur in den Rheinlanden," p. 590.

[142] Tümmers, *Der Rhein*, p. 253.

[143] "Sie sollen ihn nicht haben/ Den freien deutschen Rhein,/ Ob sie wie gierge Raben/ Sich heiser danach schreien ..."

It appeared in the *Triersche Zeitung* in September 1840, was frequently republished, printed on flyers, and handed out in streets, to the point that the *Leipziger Zeitung* suggested that it be declared the national anthem of a united Germany under the name *La Colognaise*, Germany's rejoinder to *La Marseillaise*. The crisis faded without resolution, but its effect on the cultural *re-presentation* of the Rhineland endured. Editors of Lorelei songs were enriched. Two hundred arrangements appeared – eighty for voices – of which Robert Schumann's (whose Rhenish Symphony would premier in Düsseldorf in 1850) was the most successful. Singing clubs intoned patriotic songs at music festivals, as did, more informally but with greater gusto, university students in *Bier-* and *Weinstuben*. Germany, observes music historian H. J. Moser, was unified through song.[144]

In subsequent decades, nationalism would wax and wane, realism would supersede romanticism as a literary fad, and proletarian internationalism would seek to reconstruct an image of community not bounded by national frontiers. And yet the *re-presentation* of the Rhine as the site, indeed the fountainhead, of a specifically German culture endured. In his 1922 book *Der Rhein*, Ernst Bertram, friend of Carl Schmitt and Thomas Mann and collaborator of the Nietzschean poet Stefan George, reprises many of the old romantic tropes.[145] In 1925, a group of Frankfurt historians published *Frankreich und der Rhein* in the aftermath of the Ruhr occupation, using their professional training to demonstrate the Rhineland's essential Germanness, or *Deutschtum*. Part of that demonstration included a detailed proof that Lothringen was, prior to its annexation by France, never anything other than an imperial German duchy, never destined to become a "middle kingdom."[146]

---

[144] Tümmers, *Der Rhein*, p. 256.

[145] Ernst Bertram, *Der Rhein, ein Gedenkbuch* (Munich: Georg-Verlag, 1922). See Oellers, "Geschichte der Literatur in den Rheinlanden," p. 624. Though Bertram's writings were applauded in Nazi circles, he rejected any association with the movement and fled to Switzerland. Early twentieth-century elitism was ill at ease with the mass politics of modern nationalism, and some elitist thinkers, such as Ortega y Gasset (see chapter 8) became early adepts of European federation. Drieu la Rochelle was one such early adept. His fascination with and adherence to German National-Socialism developed in part because of the movement's promise to unite Europe and preserve "Europe's" cultural legacy from the corrupting influence of capitalism, bolshevism, and foreign, i.e. Jewish, influence.

[146] Rudolf Kautzsch, Walter Platzhoff, Fedor Schneider, Franz Schulz, and Georg Wolfram, *Frankreich und der Rhein: Beiträge zur Geschichte und geistigen Kultur des Rheinlandes* (Frankfurt: Englert und Schloffer, 1925). Platzhoff became a Nazi party official and university administrator.

Nationhood

For Derrida, the *coup de force*, the constitutive speech act, the naming and placing of political geography, the designation of the ontopological figure, is independent of and prior to the "existence" of the entity that the speech act claims only to describe. The description becomes "real" as it is acted upon. In the Greater Rhineland, the *coup de force* that was Ossian's epic posited the existence of *ancient* nations, culturally and linguistically homogeneous, that bequeathed language, culture, and homeland to successor generations. Language became a sacred trust, and monolingualism the educational ideal. The *coup de force* that was the French *département* completed the revision of spatial representation by showing how regional particularisms nesting within the national territory were mere palimpsests on the foundational, national parchment, easily erased. In 1815, despite mass mobilization against Napoleon's crumbling empire, the new representation still had little purchase on the social imaginary. But by 1840, through scholarship, political tracts, the press, and song, it had become "real."[147] At the dawn of the twentieth century, Ossianic space, as explicated in schools, made palpable through economic integration, and forcibly inserted into the citizen's *Lebenswelt* by administrative duties and military service, was uncontested. It was common sense. In the Greater Rhineland, the discourse of natural peoples, natural frontiers, natural rights, and natural legitimations shattered political and economic space by interjecting political frontiers to mark the site of "natural" antagonisms. The state, as embodiment of the nation, had, in the words of Etienne Balibar, "appropriated the sacred," not only in the cultural representation of political space, but in the daily legitimation of power – in the oversight of births and deaths as signifiers of the nation's health, in the control over the transmission of the national language through education, in the certification of individual qualifications as they relate to the construction and maintenance of the "one body" that the nation claimed to be.[148]

---

[147] Beate Jahn, in *The Cultural Construction of International Relations* (Houndmills and New York: Palgrave, 2000), shows how modern international relations theoretical debate, at least in the English-speaking world, occurs within a universe of discourse that posits a state of nature which reprises (using the terminology of the present book) Ossianic myth. That universe is itself a cultural construction whose roots are, Jahn argues, in Europe's early modern discovery of and engagement with non-European peoples.

[148] See Etienne Balibar, *Nous, citoyens d'Europe?* (Paris: La Découverte, 2001), p. 43.

Today, the proposition that nations emerged only in a recent past, as a representational component of modernity, is not widely disputed. In Ernest Gellner's famous phrase, "nationalism is not the awakening of nations to self-consicousness: it *invents* nations where they do not exist."[149] This kind of claim, as explanation of nationhood, has come under critical scrutiny by sociologist Anthony Smith, who, while eschewing the romantic claim that nations have deep roots, observes nevertheless that many of the discursive and representational components of nationhood effectively descend to us from antiquity. That antiquity makes plausible the claim that modern nations have roots in ontologically real human groupings, which Smith calls *ethnies*.[150] Without delving deeply into Smith's objection, suffice it to note how difficult it is to sort out the *ethnies* of the Greater Rhineland, where so much imagery of the "cultural self" is shared, from Charlemagne to the great architectural canons (Romanesque, Gothic, Renaissance, Baroque), to religion and the great books. The virtuous warrior – the noble savage of Tacitus – strides (with angel's wings) beside *Germania* in Rüdesheim and (without wings) beside Charlemagne, "king of France," before the cathedral of Notre Dame in Paris. Only in the nineteenth century did scholars bother to expend energy trying to sort out cultures according to "national genius." Even nationhood's most elementary claims – *mono*lingualism and the mythical claim of linguistic integrity from antiquity – are the product of modernity. The only historical legacy that brings the *ethnie* unambiguously "to light" is its *name*. "It is the *name* symbolically attached to national existence, to a territory ... that often makes (*contribue à faire en sorte*) the nation identify itself by itself (*s'identifie elle-même*) with the help of a collection of 'national'

---

149 Quoted in Anderson, *Imagined Communities*, p. 6. See Smith, *Myths and Memories of the Nation*, ch. 6. For the "modernist" claim, see Ernest Gellner, *Nations and Nationalism* (Oxford: Basil Blackwell, 1983); Gellner, *Nationalism* (London: Weidenfeld and Nicolson, 1997); Eric Hobsbawm, *Nations and Nationalism since 1780* (Cambridge: Cambridge University Press, 1990).

150 Anthony Smith, *The Ethnic Origins of Nations* (Oxford: Blackwell, 1986); Smith, *Nationalism and Modernism* (London: Routledge, 1998). See discussion in Graham Day and Andrew Thompson, *Theorizing Nationalism* (Houndmills: Palgrave, 2004), ch. 4. For a recent overview of the debate, see Len Scales and Oliver Zimmer, eds., *Power and the Nation in European History* (Cambridge: Cambridge University Press, 2005). Modernists have an easy time documenting the post hoc appropriation of the archeological and textual signifiers of nationhood. Smith would have those signifiers constrain ante hoc, through generations, the construction of a discourse of self and other. It is a difficult demonstration to make.

tales (*récits*) in which it plays an important imaginary role."[151] The existence of the name, the signifier, *invites* (but does not determine) efforts to provide it with a "signified," by inventing, by "reconstructing," by placing emphasis on things that "distinguish nations" bearing different names, and by wilfully neglecting things that efface that distinction. The "national name," offspring of the *coup de force*, emerges, recedes, and reemerges in history as a justificatory and mobilizing myth.

The *coups de force* of Ossian and the French *département* inspired the grand experiment in "ethnic reconstruction" that fractured Greater Rhineland space. The *re-presentation* of Greater Rhineland space by eighteenth-century *coups de force* is the great hiatus in the region's cultural and political history. Unmaking that fracture is what European Union is about. European Union assumes meaning against the backdrop of the invention and fancy that inaugurated the frontiers that European Union seeks to deconstruct. European Union is about pacifying a site of mythical antagonisms through the deconstruction of the frontiers that situate and legitimate them. But deconstructing the frontiers with the sole tool of common economic policy leaves the mythical foundations of the frontiers untouched. The realization of European Union's possibilities demands deconstruction of the myth, the culture, of difference and separation.

---

[151] Balibar, *Nous, citoyens d'Europe?*, p. 46.

7

Wacht am Rhein: the Ossianic fracture
of Rhineland space

Discursive *coups de force* "re-presented" European space by ascribing "reality" (in the common sense of the term) to something "imaginary" (in the common sense of the term). The epics of Ossian inaugurated a new ontopology by locating "the nation" archeologically, by signifying a "people," rooted from the dawn of history in a place, speaking the "language of the place," and marking the place culturally. The French *département* "brought to light" the new ontopology by locating it spatially, by effacing rival customary names, by "clearing a space" for the *peuple* as *nation*. Modern scholarship generally supports the claim that the nation is an eighteenth-century invention. Forgeries, fashion, and militant historiography helped to establish nationhood in the social imaginary. States were enticed or obliged to engage nationhood's (de)legitimating power. They recast themselves as defenders of the nation, and helped assure the authority of the new discourse not only through oratory, but through cultural investment (museums, monuments), compulsory schooling, and military service. Ernest Gellner emphasizes the importance of state-instituted education. The "monopoly of legitimate education," he argues, was more crucial to nationhood's success than the monopoly of legitimate violence. Benedict Anderson stresses the importance of literary production, as a capitalist industry. "Print capitalism" halted and rolled back linguistic entropy – the tendency of spoken, unwritten languages to divide and diverge infinitely – and thus provided the linguistic conditions for "a new form of imagined community, which in its basic morphology set the stage for the modern nation." "The novel and the newspaper ... provided the technical means for '*re-presenting*' the *kind* of imagined community that is the nation."[1] Education and culture "naturalized" the

---

[1] Ernest Gellner, *Nations and Nationalism* (Oxford: Basil Blackwell, 1983); Benedict Anderson, *Imagined Communities: Reflections on the Origin and Spread of Nationalism* (rev. and extended 2nd edn, London: Verso, 1991), p. 46.

discourse of nationhood. "National identity" became common sense. In the words of Bernhard Giesen, "that identity itself is socially constructed is precisely the circumstance that collective identity is designed to hide."[2]

But Gellner and others also maintain that nationhood, as invention, responded to a "need." There was a functional logic to its emergence. Gellner argues that the social dislocations that accompanied industrialization and sapped confidence in the certitudes of agrarian life produced a *need* for a new communicative code, for cultural homogeneity. Nationhood satisfied that need by providing a *common* language and *shared* symbols. I interrogate here the claim that nationhood emerged in response to some functional requirement. The purpose of this interrogation is not to advance a rival explanation of the emergence of nationhood, but to subvert contemporary scholarship's *new legitimation* of nationhood by "function," or "need." I interrogate specifically Gellner's claim that industrialization generated a functional need for nationhood and national identification. Industrialization in the Greater Rhineland was a broadly regional, "transnational" phenomenon. It occurred within the geographic framework of the Greater Rhineland region as a whole, and responded to the geophysical endowments of Greater Rhineland space. Industrialization did not "call forth," or "demand" nationhood in the Greater Rhineland. Its epicenter was "Belgium," the most problematic of the region's "nation-states." The migrations unleashed by industrialization did, as per Gellner, condition adoption of widely used idioms – "national languages." But, as shown by the resistance and survival of multilingualism where it was not repressed, nothing compelled monolingualism, the conceptual foundation, indeed the necessary condition of nationhood, the social practice that makes language "sacred" and worthy of defense, as discussed later in this chapter. Nothing compelled Gellner's "single code" to be a "national code," expressed in a "national language" rather than, say, a "cosmopolitan code" expressed in a lingua franca unattached to nationalist myths of foundation (much like "Wall Street English" or "globish" in much of the world today). Finally, industrialization failed to foster a *common* language and *shared* symbols in the Greater Rhineland. On the contrary, industrialization accompanied if it did not cause the emergence of exclusive – sacred – *official*

---

[2] Bernhard Giesen, *Intellectuals and the German Nation: Collective Identity in an Axial Age*, trans. Nicholas Levis and Amos Weisz (Cambridge: Cambridge University Press, 1998), p. 12.

languages and symbols of difference, each claiming "territorial" roots. The discourse of nationhood, far from promoting social cohesion, inscribed frontiers in Greater Rhineland space that interfered with and even distorted the industrial development of the region by diverting industrial production to the task of building the nation, as political creation, as, one might say, a socially *dysfunctional* work of art.

The myth of nationhood cracked the Greater Rhineland into parts, "national" spaces legitimated by literary myths of territorial rootedness and linguistic/cultural identity. Frontiers bred, rather than tempered, social dislocations and anxieties, and proved arguably less supportive of the new capitalist order than other conceivable *re-presentations* of Rhineland space, as, for example, a space in which multilingualism is cultivated by political authority (as in modern-day Luxemburg), or as a space governed by a network of more or less autonomous towns that are culturally unattached to the nation's definitional landscape. In a word, it makes little sense to associate nationhood with social cohesion under new socioeconomic circumstances when the nation itself conditioned the most destructive outbreak of collective violence in human history, within the bounds of one of the world's most highly industrialized regional economies.

Industrialization in Greater Rhineland space

Industrialization in the Greater Rhineland responded to the threefold invitation of fluvial geography, mineral wealth, and urban network. It obeyed a regional, not a national logic. The exploitation of the region's resources, made easier and profitable by the region's network of communications, was a "transnational" enterprise. But industrialization provided states with new resources with which to assert control over territory, and so "bring to light" the "nation" as well-spring of state legitimacy. Nationhood fractured Greater Rhineland space just as industrialization was reviving the region's economic fortunes and coherence.

The industrial revolution entered the Greater Rhineland through Wallonia in the first decades of the nineteenth century. Coal deposits, ease of transport and communication, Napoleon's destruction of guild privileges, the region's commercial culture, a centuries-old tradition of metal working on the Meuse and Sambre rivers, and England's proximity all conditioned a process of industrialization that was as precocious as it was rapid. "Belgium was ... the one country in Europe which kept pace industrially with England in the first half of the nineteenth century."[3] William Cockerill, an English engineer and textile manufacturer, settled in Napoleonic "Belgium" in 1799. Over the next half century, his factories initially produced mechanical looms, and later specialized in locomotives and the steel needed to manufacture them. He installed one of the continent's first steam engines at Seraing, near Liège, in 1813. By mid-century, Seraing's iron mill, with its "four coal pits, two blast furnaces, rolling mills, forges and shops for making locomotives, engines and machinery of any description" employed thousands of workers.[4] European demand for Belgian machine-tools and railway components exceeded supply. In the first decades of the nineteenth century, Belgium's coal production outpaced that of France, but Belgian factories had to import coal from England to meet industrial demand.

By 1835, the newly founded Belgian state was intervening in the economy to carry out an ambitious plan of state-led railway construction. The plan sought to exploit the complexities of river Rhine politics and Belgium's lowland geography to increase traffic in Belgian ports. Representatives to the Congress of Vienna tried to free shipping on the Rhine from taxes and duties, but were blocked by Prussia and, later, the Dutch.[5] The Rhine Shipping Act of 1831 eliminated tolls along the river and established a commission to oversee Rhine navigation – an early instance of "international organization" in the Greater Rhineland – but did not affect fees and duties imposed by Dutch ports.[6] Belgian independence in 1830 freed the port of Antwerp from Dutch control. Belgian leaders saw railway development as a way to provide Antwerp with business. "Belgium meant to exploit the advantages of her position as a land of passage."[7] The first trunk line between Brussels and Antwerp opened in 1836. By 1844, railways linked the Rhine and the iron and coal regions of Wallonia with Antwerp and cities along the French and Dutch borders (see figure 7.1). Belgian exports doubled between 1836 and 1845. Exports of cast iron grew by a factor of eight.

---

[3] J. H. Clapham, *The Economic Development of France and Germany, 1815–1914* (4th edn, Cambridge: Cambridge University Press, 1961), p. 57.

[4] Clapham, *The Economic Development of France and Germany*, p. 58, quoting from a "Report of the Assistant Commissioner to the Handloom Weavers' Commission."

[5] See, however, Albert Demangeon and Lucien Febvre, *Le Rhin* (Paris: Armand Colin, 1935), p. 138.

[6] Hermann Kellenbenz, "Wirtschafts- und Sozialentwicklung der nördlichen Rheinlanden seit 1815," in Franz Petri and Georg Droege, eds., *Rheinische Geschichte*, vol. III, *Wirtschaft und Kultur im 19. und 20. Jahrhundert* (Düsseldorf: Schwann, 1979), p. 56.

[7] Clapham, *The Economic Development of France and Germany*, p. 141.

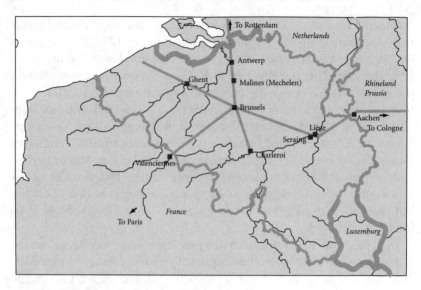

Figure 7.1 Belgian railway development

Industrialization was a more gradual process in the German Rhineland, where the urban economy was still marked by the destructions of the Thirty Years War and the unfavorable economic effects of political marginalization.[8] The entire urban population of Germany was only half again as great as that of Paris. The French had dismantled the guilds on the left bank, but the right bank retained the most rigid manufacturing regulations in Europe. German industry was composed primarily of traditional handicrafts: weaving in Silesia, and cutlery in Solingen in the valley of the Wupper, an affluent of the Rhine. The German Rhineland's extensive coal reserves lay largely untapped. Prussian annexation stimulated economic activity by absorbing the region into a market unified by Prussia's 1818 abolition of internal tariffs.[9] In that same year the Prussian Rhineland already boasted twenty-two steam engines, most of which were used to pump water from mines, and seven of which were used by the textile industry, particularly in and around the city of Aachen. James Cockerill, son of the Anglo-Belgian industrialist, settled there in 1825, and another Englishman, Samuel Dobbs, introduced steam to the region.[10]

[8] Demangeon and Febvre, *Le Rhin*, pp. 120–3.
[9] Kellenbenz, "Wirtschafts- und Sozialentwicklung der nördlichen Rheinlanden," p. 35.
[10] Kellenbenz, "Wirtschafts- und Sozialentwicklung der nördlichen Rheinlanden," p. 42.

Despite the stimulus of Prussian policy, the industrialization of the Prussian Rhineland, as in Belgium, occurred not within a national framework, but within that of the Greater Rhineland regional economy. Coal was abundant in the valley of the Saar and near Aachen. Iron had long been mined in the valley of the Wupper. South of the river Ruhr, coal deposits rose to the earth's surface. Napoleonic France had already dispatched engineers and administrators to assess the region's potential. In the 1830s, French and Belgian capitalists began investing in Rhenish mines. The first steel factories in the Ruhr employed French and Belgian workers.[11] English innovations in metallurgy stirred demand for the Ruhr valley's important coking coal reserves, while steam pumps made it possible to exploit deep-lying veins. Supply and demand encouraged railroad and river port construction to bring Ruhr coke to market. Cologne financiers invested heavily in the region in the 1840s. Financiers outside "Germany" also invested heavily in the new mines. The Société Anglo-Belge des Charbonnages du Rhin was founded in Düsseldorf in 1847, as were the Belgisch-Rheinische Bergwerks-AG in 1849, the Belgian-funded Belgisch-Rheinische Ruhr-Bergbau-AG in 1851, and the Mühlheimer Steinkohlenbergbau-Commandit-Deutsch-Holländischen Aktieverein für Bergbau und Hüttenbetrieb in Duisburg. Between 1834 and 1846, two important companies, Eschweiler and Steinkohlengruben Berghaupten, grew out of French mining concessions near Aachen. In the late 1830s, French capitalists established the mining company of Hardenberg in the Ruhr, and participated in the capital of the Ruhrort Coal Company, Herne-Bochum, the Mengede Company, and the Coal Company of the Rhine. The Frenchman Charles Detillieux organized and directed the Gelsenkirchener Bergwerks, the largest coal mining firm in Germany at that time (see figure 7.2).[12]

Just as steam navigation spurred the growth of the German Rhineland coal industry (see previous chapter), the railway stimulated the growth of its iron and steel industry. Railway construction required rails, which in the period 1835–45 were imported from England and Belgium. The left bank of the Rhine was "inundated with Belgian iron."[13] It was about this time that Friedrich Krupp applied lessons he had learned in England to a steelmaking firm he established in Essen.

---

[11] Maurice Niveau, *Histoire des faits économiques contemporains* (Paris: Presses Universitaires de France, 1970), pp. 92–3.

[12] Raymond Poidevin and Jacques Bariéty, *Les relations franco-allemandes, 1815–1975* (Paris: Armand Colin, 1977), p. 36.

[13] Kellenbenz, "Wirtschafts- und Sozialentwicklung der nördlichen Rheinlanden," p. 41.

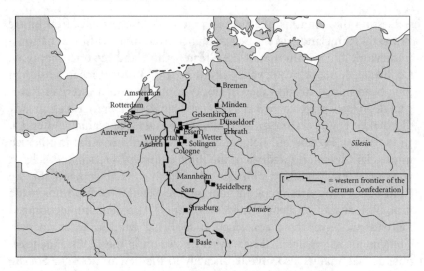

Figure 7.2 Industry and railways in the German Confederation

The firm employed ten workers in 1832, but 340 in 1852, and 12,000 in 1873.[14]

In 1826, Friedrich Harkort, manufacturer of steam engines and gas lighting equipment in the Ruhr town of Wetter, urged construction of a railway line between Cologne and Minden, on the Weser, as the first leg of a line that would extend to the port city of Bremen, which he hoped would break the Dutch stranglehold on Rhine commerce with the North Sea. In 1828 he created the first joint stock company for financing German railways to build a line from Hinsbeck, on the Ruhr, to coal fields at Elberfeld. The line, christened the Prince William Railway, opened in 1831. In 1838, the first rails laid along the banks of the Rhine joined Erkrath with Düsseldorf. In 1840, rails linked Frankfurt and the Rhine at Wiesbaden. The Rhenish Railway Company, connecting Cologne, Aachen, and the Belgian network at Liège opened in 1841. Cologne had railway service to Antwerp by 1843. Speakers at the inaugural ceremonies praised the community of interest and culture between Belgium and the German Rhineland.[15] Rails linked

---

[14] The figure climbed to 167,000 by the end of World War I. See Clapham, *The Economic Development of France and Germany*, p. 322. See also Kellenbenz, "Wirtschafts- und Sozialentwicklung der nördlichen Rheinlanden," p. 41.

[15] Abigail Green, *Fatherlands: State-Building and Nationhood in Nineteenth-Century Germany* (Cambridge: Cambridge University Press, 2001), p. 263.

Amsterdam with Rhenish cities as far upstream as Mannheim and Heidelberg by 1843. Harkort's dream of a Minden–Cologne line was realized in 1847.

Railway construction in Germany, however, was complicated by the political ambitions and fears of the *Mittelstaaten*. The Treaty of Vienna juxtaposed a sprawling but geographically incoherent Prussia with a number of Belgium- or Luxemburg-sized *Mittelstaaten*, kingdoms and duchies. Cologne, the Rhineland metropolis of the middle ages, became a provincial Prussian city. The Catholic cathedral town of Mainz was incorporated into the Protestant duchy of Hesse-Darmstadt. A "German Confederation" brought representatives from the kingdoms, duchies, and free cities (Bremen, Hamburg, and Frankfurt) together irregularly to coordinate political repression. But in practice the kingdoms were sovereign in all areas of domestic policy, including education. Industrialization, however, concentrated investment and growth in the Greater Rhineland (and, to a lesser extent, Silesia). The *Mittelstaat* governments sought to resist that trend by building railways.[16] The Württemberg Board of Trade and Industry claimed that "it cannot be a matter for indifference to the country if individual districts are diverted from their habitual traffic with its heartlands, and if their economic interests become increasingly entangled with those of a neighboring state." A commission in Saxony argued that "our fatherland is threatened from all sides with the loss of international trade through the construction of directly competing railways."[17] French plans to lay rails between Basle and Strasburg on the left bank prompted Baden to construct a line between Basle and Mannheim on the right bank. Prussia inaugurated the important but politically motivated line between the Rhineland and Berlin in 1847.[18] Political resistance to industrial concentration helps explain why railway construction in Germany was precocious. Most of the trunk lines were in operation by 1850, a decade earlier than in France. But the "territorial fragmentation and the importance of state railways in Germany created not so much a single German railway network as a conglomeration of state networks," making for a highly decentralized system.[19]

---

[16] Green, *Fatherlands*, p. 243.
[17] Green, *Fatherlands*, pp. 247, 250 (quoting an administrative report).
[18] Kellenbenz, "Wirtschafts- und Sozialentwicklung der nördlichen Rheinlanden," p. 54; Green, *Fatherlands*, p. 241.
[19] Green, *Fatherlands*, p. 242. Gertrud Milkereit, "Sozial- und Wirtschaftsentwicklung der südlichen Rheinlande seit 1815," in Petri and Droege, *Rheinische Geschichte*, vol. III, pp. 242–6.

However much German railway construction was diverted by the political ambitions of the *Mittelstaaten*, it nevertheless benefited Rhineland steel and manufacturing. Railways attracted between 14 and 20 percent of industrial investment in the period 1850–71. By 1873, they accounted for 55 percent of German industrial capital. Between 1850, when railways employed 26,000 workers, and 1870, when they employed more than 200,000, rail freight increased by more than 16 percent annually.[20] Railway construction prompted bridge-building on the Rhine. At mid-century, the old floating bridges that spanned the Rhine at Koblenz and Mannheim, and the wooden pile-bridge at Strasburg, were joined by the massive and modern Hohenzollernbrücke in Cologne in 1859 (see plate 8.1) and other rail bridges in Koblenz (1864), Mainz (1862), Gernsheim (near Worms, 1877), and Worms (1898). A second bridge was erected in Koblenz in 1878, and two more were erected in Mainz in 1885 and 1902. The effort continued into the twentieth century with bridges at Rüdesheim (1915, subsequently destroyed) and Speyer (1936).[21]

Industrial growth stimulated shipping on the Rhine. The Dutch energetically promoted the use of their steamboat fleets in the 1820s.[22] New ports at Duisburg and Ruhrort and a new channel cut through the Bingerloch rapids in 1832 contributed to a fivefold increase in Rhine shipping between 1836 and 1866. In 1846, the Bavarian government made good on an effort to link the Rhine by canal to the Danube, first attempted by Charlemagne in 793.[23] Cologne reigned supreme over Rhine shipping, despite the loss of its staple market in 1831.[24] The 1868 Mannheim Acts cleared fiscal obstacles to shipping and spurred construction of major ports at Mannheim and Ludwigshafen, which, at the confluence of the Neckar, was the crossroads for traffic circulating between southern Germany and the ports of France, Belgium, and the Netherlands.[25] By the first decades of the twentieth century the Rhine and the Ruhr were linked by canal with the Weser and the North Sea.[26] The construction of dikes and a channel above Mainz turned Strasburg into a modern port by 1892.[27] Further improvements made it possible for Basle

---

[20] Green, *Fatherlands*, p. 230.
[21] Milkereit, "Sozial- und Wirtschaftsentwicklung der südlichen Rheinlande," pp. 234–7.
[22] Milkereit, "Sozial- und Wirtschaftsentwicklung der südlichen Rheinlande," pp. 240–2.
[23] Milkereit, "Sozial- und Wirtschaftsentwicklung der südlichen Rheinlande," p. 240.
[24] Kellenbenz, "Wirtschafts- und Sozialentwicklung der nördlichen Rheinlanden," p. 53.
[25] Milkereit, "Sozial- und Wirtschaftsentwicklung der südlichen Rheinlande," p. 204.
[26] Kellenbenz, *Wirtschafts- und Sozialentwicklung der nördlichen Rheinlanden*, pp. 102–6.
[27] Milkereit, *Sozial- und Wirtschaftsentwicklung der südlichen Rheinlande*, pp. 233 and 267–8.

to receive large-tonnage shipping by 1936. Though competition from the railway caused the volume of river traffic through Cologne to decline after 1830, industrial growth in the Saarland, Aachen, and the Ruhr caused it to climb again after 1880. By the end of the century, the volume of traffic flowing through the old Roman port was three times the 1830 figure.

By 1880 the Rhine had long ceased to look like either a "natural frontier" or a mysterious, brooding, romantic site of a nation's roots. It was an intensely navigated international waterway. The Franco-German-Belgian "borderland" was the most industrialized region of continental Europe, and the site of vigorous development, much of it financed internationally. Abraham Oppenheim, a Cologne banker and director of Crédit Mobilier, an industrial lending bank chartered by Napoleon III to speed railway investment in France in the 1850s, established the Bank für Handel und Industrie in Darmstadt on the Crédit Mobilier model. The Crédit Mobilier was also the inspiration for the Berliner Handelsgesellschaft, in which the Paris Rothschilds were important shareholders.[28] In 1850, the ubiquitous Charles Detillieux created the Mining and Foundry Company of the Rhine, with which André Koechlin, an Alsatian industrialist, merged his Phoenix Mining and Metallurgy Company in 1855. The new entity's twelve blast furnaces employed 6,000 workers, produced more than 15 percent of Prussia's cast iron, and was the largest employer in Germany.[29] By 1860, Germany, with Luxemburg, was producing over 12 million metric tons of coal, in addition to Belgium's 10 million and France's 8 million. By 1860, 120,000 miners were working Germany's coalfields. That number would surpass half a million by the end of the century.[30] German pig iron production, at 214,560 tons in 1850, reached 988,200 tons in 1865 and 1,390,490 tons in 1870. Mining and metallurgy spurred the development of a chemical industry, fed by lead mined in the Eifel, sulphuric pyrites from the Eifel and the Ardennes, and potash from Alsace. Potash propelled the industrial development of the newly created Rhine port of Ludwigshafen.[31]

Industrialization in France was also inscribed within the broad framework of the Greater Rhineland regional economy. In France, as in

---

[28] Poidevin and Bariéty, *Les relations franco-allemandes*, pp. 45–6.
[29] Poidevin and Bariéty, *Les relations franco-allemandes*, p. 47.
[30] Clapham, *The Economic Development of France and Germany*, pp. 280–3.
[31] Kellenbenz, *Wirtschafts- und Sozialentwicklung der nördlichen Rheinlanden*, pp. 45–6.
   Milkereit, "Sozial- und Wirtschaftsentwicklung der südlichen Rheinlande," p. 254.

Germany, industrialization polarized economic space by shifting capital, resources, and labor northeast, to the "French Rhineland." France south and west of a line from Lille to Marseilles remained generally traditional and agricultural. The polarization remains visible in France's economic geography today. In 1801, a Lille spinning mill already employed ninety workers. Alsace was home to a dynamic cotton textile industry, established by immigrant industrialists from Switzerland and southern Germany who were attracted by France's vast, unified market space. Alsace's water-driven spinning machines were the first in France, as was its steam-driven mill, built in 1812. The first city in France to experience a veritable "industrial revolution" was Mulhouse, which, following the Napoleonic wars, adopted the power loom with the same enthusiasm as the mill towns of Lancashire. Steam power was adopted more slowly in the north, though new technologies in the manufacture of woolens turned Roubaix, near Lille, into one of the first industrial "mushroom towns" of France.

Although the modern factory was still a rarity in France at mid-century, modern iron works were operating by 1830 near iron ore and coal fields at Le Creusot near Dijon, Fourchambault on the Loire, Denain near the Belgian border, and Decazeville in the south.[32] Rhineland geography governed the pace as well as the location of French industrialization. Coal fields were few, difficult to exploit, and often peripheral to national space (however central to Greater Rhineland space). Fields along the Belgian border near Valenciennes, and – at a depth of more than a thousand feet – between Lille and St. Omer, were producing one million metric tons annually by 1852, compared with 1.6 million from the Loire basin near St. Etienne and 0.4 million from Le Creusot (see figure 7.3). By 1869, production in the northern fields surpassed that of the Loire, with 4.3 million tons against the latter's 3.1 million, but at a cost of exploitation that made French coal half again more expensive than British coal. French production grew to 16 million tons in 1872 and 41 million in 1913, but paled in comparison with Britain's 292 and Germany's 279 million tons. French coal mines never sufficed to meet French demand.[33]

Rhineland geography nevertheless enabled France to become one of Europe's principal steel producers. At mid-century, 60 percent of France's pig iron was still being produced by small charcoal furnaces scattered across the country. France was producing a mere fourteen

[32] Clapham, *The Economic Development of France and Germany*, pp. 59–60.
[33] Clapham, *The Economic Development of France and Germany*, p. 234.

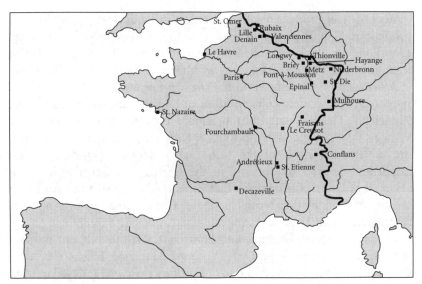

Legend: The continuous line indicates the northern and eastern frontier in 1870.

Figure 7.3 Industry in France

tons of steel, primarily for weapons and cutlery. But in the mid-1860s, industrial-scale iron works at Le Creusot in Burgundy and Hayange in German-speaking Lorraine adopted Bessemer converters and Siemens furnaces which, by 1869, were producing 110,000 tons of steel yearly. When war broke out in 1870, French industry was producing more than one million tons of iron and steel a year, a figure surpassed in Europe only by Great Britain. Most of France's major steel mills were located in the Rhine basin. Others were disseminated along the Saône–Rhône corridor. Besides the mills at St. Etienne near Lyons, major producers were the Schneiders of Le Creusot, De Wendel of Hayange, Moyeuvre and Sieringen-Wendel of Lorraine, and Dietrich of Niederbronn, in Alsace. Other firms existed in Fourchambault on the Loire (downstream from St. Etienne), Fraisans in Franche-Comté, Longwy in Lorraine, and Anzin and Denain in the lowlands near the Belgian frontier.

France's steel industry expanded rapidly following the discovery of ways to use Lorraine's iron deposits, rich in phosphorus and not easily transformed. Thomas Gilchrist, an amateur chemist of London, developed a method to remove the phosphorus in 1878. Half of Lorraine had been annexed by the German Empire in 1871, but Conflans, Briey, and Longwy remained French and, thanks to the new technology, became centers of steel production. In the 1890s, the industry's expansion was prodigious. France produced 3 million tons of cast iron in 1905, but 13 million in 1913. In that same year, French mills were producing 5 million tons of steel, compared with Great Britain's 7.5 million tons and Germany's 17 million tons. The development of Lorraine steel reinforced the regional concentration of French industry in the Greater Rhineland. The German Ruhr produced coke in quantity but lacked France's iron reserves. Transportation costs favored exporting Lorraine ore to the coal fields of the Ruhr valley, making France the most important exporter of iron ore in the world, with Germany its chief client. It is a fact of geography that explains the massive investment in the city of Metz by the German military. It was also a fact of geography that would loom large in European unification.[34]

Industrial growth in Rhineland France attracted investment in other sectors. The Schlumbergers of Mulhouse launched France's premier textile machine industry, and one of Europe's principal industrial firms. A number of Alsatian textile manufacturers crossed the Vosges, following German annexation, to settle in towns like St. Dié and Epinal, preserving the importance of the eastern provinces to France's textile industry after 1880. The Vosges and Moselle valleys surpassed more established textile regions, such as Lille and Normandy, despite the fact that cotton had to be transported from ports at Antwerp and Le Havre. Rhineland geography also explains French industrial failures. Despite its long coast line, its colonial empire, and its importance as a steel producer, France did not develop a strong shipbuilding industry. The rivers that linked the Greater Rhineland industrial region to shipbuilding seaports flowed north, to Antwerp, Rotterdam, and Bremen, rather than to Le Havre and St. Nazaire, the sites of French shipbuilding.[35]

In France, as in Germany and Belgium, the geography of coal determined the first sites of railway construction. An ordinance of 1823 authorized the construction of France's first (horse-powered) railway between the coal fields of St. Etienne and the Loire river port of Andrézieux. In 1832, the first locomotive linked St. Etienne to Lyons, on the Rhône. But France's centralized state did not delay in asserting its rights. In 1835 a line was authorized between Paris and the posh suburb of St. Germain, with plans to continue down the Seine to Rouen and Le Havre. In 1837, new proposals were advanced for a network of

[34] Clapham, *The Economic Development of France and Germany*, pp. 235–8.
[35] Clapham, *The Economic Development of France and Germany*, pp. 243–4.

lines between Paris and Le Havre, Valenciennes in the north, Tours in the west, and Marseilles. The state chartered companies, lent money, and guaranteed private loans. Significantly, it financed the Valenciennes line directly "when it became obvious that Valenciennes must be linked to the new Belgian system."[36] In 1842 France cobbled the various proposals together to form a national railway program. But financing was difficult, and the project was not completed until 1860. By then railways employed 86,000 workers, a figure that climbed to 223,000 in 1881. The Freycinet Plan of 1878, an ambitious scheme of railway, canal, harbor, and road construction, linked backwater villages to the broader, national network of roads and railways.[37]

Peasants into Frenchmen

The industrialization of the Greater Rhineland, as a regional, "transnational" phenomenon, could not per se have evoked or provoked the emergence of nationhood. It did, however, provide states with resources with which to bring nationhood to light, to make it real. It provided states with the means to force the intrusion of nationhood as discourse in the *Lebenswelt* of its citizens or subjects, to press *departmentalization* – the subversion of traditional ontopologies – as administrative fact in France and, as imperative of power, *Realpolitik* in Germany. It provided states with the means to educate its citizens or subjects in the language and discourse of nationhood, to reward its most assiduous students with attractive careers, and to intervene in economic life to forge a political economy of national power and assertion.

Eugen Weber, in his classic history of social change in France, describes the coercive practices the state deployed in order to make the nation true. Far from preserving autochthonous idioms from extinction (its averred purpose), the myth of nationhood informed a process of linguistic and cultural cleansing that imposed the idiom and world-view of a literate elite on the general population. Although Ossianic mythology, in the eighteenth century, expressed resistance to the cultural and linguistic marginalization of subordinated cultures, in the nineteenth century it was legitimating the imposition of the language of power on populations with all the coercive resources of the modern

---

[36] Clapham, *The Economic Development of France and Germany*, p. 145.
[37] See Eugen Weber, *Peasants into Frenchmen: The Modernization of Rural France, 1870–1914* (Stanford: Stanford University Press, 1976), pp. 209–20.

state. States turned political frontiers into linguistic and cultural – national – frontiers.[38]

From the first days of the Revolution, delegates to the Constituent Assembly expressed fear of linguistic diversity and regional particularism. Regional diversity was real. Weber reports that inhabitants of Marseilles in the mid-nineteenth century "still spoke of 'the Frenchman' and 'the French' as if they were a race apart." In the central province of Velay in 1884, the word *patrie* "signifies nothing and stirs nothing."[39] He quotes a teacher near St. Etienne, writing in 1864: "in the villages, anyone who tried to speak French wouldn't escape the jeers of his neighbors. He would be turned to ridicule."[40] In 1863, according to official figures, 8,381 of France's 37,510 communes, representing about a quarter of the country's population, spoke little or no French. More than 10 percent of school children aged 13 and younger spoke no French at all; another 30 percent spoke or understood it but could not write it. In the southern *département* of the Hérault, more than one fourth of the children did not speak French, while to the west, in Dordogne, a third did not.

In 1833, in the reign of Louis Philippe, every commune was ordered to establish and maintain an elementary school that would teach reading from French rather than Latin texts. The number of such schools doubled over the next fifteen years. In 1882, Jules Ferry, minister of education, established the system of free but compulsory education that exists today by requiring every hamlet of twenty or more school-age children to provide and maintain a school, which the state supplied with trained personnel. The growing availability of state employment began to fuel demand for French fluency. "The recognition of new possibilities, and of the school as a key to their exploitation, was in full evidence by the 1890s. By 1894 practically every child in a village of lower Provence that had been almost totally illiterate a generation earlier was attending school, even those who lived one and a half hours' walk away."[41] But opportunity does not explain how France became uniformly French-speaking and essentially monolingual. State schools actively repressed local idioms through punishment and ridicule. Students, for example, were made to pass a "token" from one

---

[38]   Elie Kedourie, in *Nationalism* (London: Hutchinson, 1960). See also Michael Mann, *States, War, and Capitalism* (Oxford: Blackwell, 1988); Anthony Giddens, *The Consequences of Modernity* (Cambridge: Polity Press, 1990) and discussion in Graham Day and Andrew Thompson, *Theorizing Nationalism* (Houndmills: Palgrave, 2004), pp. 54–9.

[39]   Weber, *Peasants into Frenchmen*, pp. 98, 100.

[40]   Weber, *Peasants into Frenchmen*, p. 312.   [41]   Weber, *Peasants into Frenchmen*, p. 328.

to another as they were "caught" speaking the local dialect. The student left holding the token at the end of the day received a punishment. State repression as well as state employment fed the expansion of French. By 1890, all the young people of the mountainous Cévennes spoke French. By the turn of the century, literacy among conscripts in Brittany was not far below the national average. *Patois* "was increasingly rejected after the 1890s by the young, especially by girls and women, attracted by a language that was considered a badge of refinement and emancipation." The language to which the girls and women were attracted was the language of political and cultural power. Regional dialects, restricted to casual conversation, became increasingly localized. "Many erstwhile languages had been let loose from all the disciplines that maintain a language, to become what the revolutionaries called *jargons*."[42]

Language education imparted more than communicative sounds and symbols. It introduced provincials to the cultural style of Parisian administration. It offered "a pedagogy of reason."[43] "The music of discourse, once spare or lyrical, became coldly didactic, swollen with the terminology of administrative French."[44] Language instruction imparted an alien worldview. Weber relates that the river Aude, in the *patois* of its riverside population, was not a thing, but a person. The article was not employed: one "went to Aude," or observed that "Aude was high, that Aude growls." "A whole mentality had to be bent for a small article to be added."[45] The "national" language became the vector of a certain representation of the nation. The classroom teacher *embodied* that representation. Carefully trained, formally dressed, eloquent, licensed and inspected by the state,

> the schoolteachers, in their worn, dark suits, appear[ed] as the militia of a new age, harbingers of enlightenment and the republican message that reconciled the benighted masses with a new world, superior in wellbeing and democracy ... In a department like Bas Rhin where a third of the mayors were completely ignorant of the French language and five sixths of the *fonctionnaires* could not write it, the teacher was indispensable. By the 1890s, they not only ran the administration in almost all the communes, but also in some instances worked as correspondents for the local newspapers.[46]

---

[42] Weber, *Peasants into Frenchmen*, p. 89. See also pp. 311, 78.

[43] François Furet, *Revolutionary France*, trans. A. Nevill (Oxford: Blackwell, 1992), p. 474.

[44] Weber, *Peasants into Frenchmen*, p. 91.   [45] Weber, *Peasants into Frenchmen*, p. 93.

[46] Weber, *Peasants into Frenchmen*, pp. 303, 317–18.

The French word for teacher, *instituteur*, coined during the Revolution, made explicit the teacher's duty to "*institute* the nation." Pierre Bourdieu writes:

> In the process which leads to the construction, legitimation and impo-sition of an official language, the educational system plays a decisive role: 'fashioning the similarities from which that community of consciousness which is the cement of the nation stems.' ... the schoolmaster, a *maître à parler* (teacher [expert or master] of speaking) ... is thereby also a *maître à penser* (teacher [expert or master] of thinking): by virtue of his func-tion, [he] works daily on the faculty of expression of every idea and every emotion: on language. In teaching the same clear, fixed language to children who know it only very vaguely or who even speak various dialects or *patois*, he is already inclining them quite naturally to see and feel things in the same way; and he works to build the common con-sciousness of the nation.[47]

Cultural change opened up a generation gap. A 1911 survey shows peasants speaking French to their children, but *patois* to priest and teacher, whom children, in turn, addressed only in French. It was not simply a gap of idiom. For a contemporary observer in Brittany: "children and parents form two worlds apart, so separated in spirit, so estranged by speech, that there is no more community of ideas and feelings, hence no intimacy."[48]

State schooling naturally taught children to revere the nation. "Patriotic songs, readings recalling the lost provinces [Alsace and Lorraine; see below] or exalting the heroism of warriors, filled the young Frenchmen."[49] In France, as in Germany, physical exertion, such as hiking and mountain climbing, fostered military preparedness and love of the land. Historiography nurtured a sense of national belonging. "Historians," Eric Hobsbawm writes, "are to nationalism what poppy-growers ... are to heroin addicts: [they] supply the essential raw material for the market ... What makes a nation is the past, and historians are the

---

[47] Pierre Bourdieu, *Language and Symbolic Power* (Cambridge, MA: Harvard University Press, 1999), pp. 48–9. Bourdieu cites Georges Davy, *Eléments de sociologie* (Paris: Vrin, 1950), p. 233. Many dialects disappeared within two generations. The schools dispensed training in what Weber does not hesitate to call an "artificial" language, and in so doing propagated a dominant discursive style. "Just as legislation can create crime by fiat, so education created stupidity by setting up standards of communication that many found difficult to attain." Weber, *Peasants into Frenchmen*, p. 336.

[48] Weber, *Peasants into Frenchmen*, p. 338.

[49] Poidevin and Bariéty, *Les relations franco-allemandes*, p. 111.

people who produce it."[50] Ernest Lavisse (1842–1922), whose career began, not insignificantly, with works on the Holy Roman Empire and the Prussian monarchy, published the classic history curriculum, the *Cours d'histoire de France*, in 1884. The narrative was one of teleological progress toward unity and national self-awareness. Lavisse invited school teachers to emphasize France's essential *douceur* and cultural achievement. He asserted that it was the duty of every Frenchman not to forget Alsace-Lorraine and recommended that a flag draped in the symbols of mourning be attached to the lost provinces on the classroom map. To advance the cause of patriotism, Jean Macé created the Ligue Française de l'Enseignement, which encouraged teachers to form armed student battalions. Public education sustained a market for patriotic children's literature. *Le tour de France par deux enfants* appeared in 1877 and sold over 8 million copies. Charles Bigot published *Le petit Français*, which exalted France's superior conception of law, civilization, and the republic, and stressed the need to arm against the German threat.

Military service was a second, but surprisingly hesitant instrument of nation-building. Anthony Smith and others who critique the mainstream explanation of nation-formation attach much importance to the revolutionary *levée en masse* and the reaction it produced in nations subjected to the Napoleonic yoke. "Prolonged, increasingly savage and comprehensive wars ... began to fuel and shape the ethnic revival directly."[51] But the causal arrow should probably be reversed. Ethnic "revival" engendered militarization, which engendered savage wars. The Greater Rhineland, as discussed in the previous chapter, was slow to embrace the nationalist enthusiasm stirred further east by Napoleon's advance. Mass conscription in France was even slower in fostering a sentiment of national belonging. Before the Revolution, warfare in Europe was a mercenary affair. In the eighteenth century, the proportion of foreign mercenaries in the armies of the major European powers ranged from 20 to 70 percent.[52] Mass conscription in France, the first country to decree the *levée en masse* (in 1793), was introduced in the nineteenth century. In the beginning, however,

---

[50] Quoted in Cris Shore, *Building Europe: The Cultural Politics of European Integration* (London: Routledge, 2000), p. 41.

[51] Anthony D. Smith, *The Antiquity of Nations* (Cambridge: Polity Press, 2004), p. 167.

[52] See Christer Jönsson, Sven Tägil, and Gunnar Törnqvist, *Organizing European Space* (London: Sage, 2000), p. 74, citing Janice Thomson, *Mercenaries, Pirates, and Sovereigns: State-Building and Extraterritorial Violence in Early Modern Europe* (Princeton: Princeton University Press, 1994), pp. 29–30.

military service was neither universal nor conceived as an exercise in nation-building. Military ranks in France were filled by lottery. The sons of wealthy families filled their obligations, if drafted, by hiring replacements. As the poor substituted for wealthy conscripts, military service became a mark of low birth, not patriotic sacrifice. As for the poor who were drafted directly, conscription intervened in their lives as capriciously as disease. "Conscription was seen not as a duty owed to some larger community or nation, but as a heavy tribute exacted by an oppressive, alien state."[53] Weber cites the case of a village in the Allier where, as late as the 1870s, most boys, at birth, were registered as girls to evade the draft.[54] Villagers and townspeople feared the soldiers, not only in the towns in which troops were billeted, but in the villages in which soldiers had grown up and to which they returned with alien ways. Military archives record numerous cases of soldiers being attacked or stoned. In the Hérault, "even in cities garrisons are sometimes exposed to the provocations of inhabitants of all classes who show a decided malevolence for the military."[55] The army, moreover, made no claim to embody the nation. It did not join forces with the republican school to forge a monolingual nation. As a conservative institution more like the Church than the republican school, it used whatever linguistic practice happened to work. Weber cites the case of Breton conscripts in 1849 who refused to obey orders given in French. Breton was still heard in the military in the late nineteenth century. Bilingualism was tolerated into the twentieth century.[56]

The Third Republic abolished the practice of substitution and other dispensations in 1873. Military service became truly universal. Service was reduced from five to three years in 1889, and to two years in 1905. School-inculcated patriotism, moreover, began to show its effects. By the 1890s, "there is persuasive evidence that the army was no longer 'theirs' but 'ours.' "[57] The terms *nationaux* and *nationalité* had entered the vocabulary by mid-century.[58] Thanks to public education, universal military service became an introduction to a nation – a fatherland – that young provincials had only read about. Perhaps for the first time, recruits made practical use of the French language their school teachers had inflicted on them. Above all, military service, like state service

---

[53] Weber, *Peasants into Frenchmen*, p. 294.   [54] Weber, *Peasants into Frenchmen*, p. 296.
[55] Weber, *Peasants into Frenchmen*, p. 297.   [56] Weber, *Peasants into Frenchmen*, p. 299.
[57] Weber, *Peasants into Frenchmen*, p. 298.
[58] Rogers Brubaker, *Citizenship and Nationhood in France and Germany* (Cambridge, MA: Harvard University Press, 1992), p. 99.

generally, was experienced by many recruits as a kind of emancipation from life in the countryside. They encountered an "unfamiliar abundance" during their years of service that fostered new attitudes. "Wine, coffee, and meat at every meal taught the survivors habits they would not easily unlearn."[59] By 1914, the French nation had a national army.

Civil servants into Germans

The *départementalisation* of German political space, that is, the suppression of customary ontopologies that controvert national unity, was not the fact of a revolutionary government legitimated by the mythical restoration of a nation – a *peuple* – to power, as in France. Revolution was repressed in Germany, and political space rearticulated around conservative, monarchical *Mittelstaaten*. The *Mittelstaaten*, however, lent authority to the representation of German nationhood by justifying their rule as representatives of ancient, Ossianic *Stämme* or tribes – Saxon, Swabian, Bavarian, etc. The *Mittelstaaten re-presented* themselves as "rooted" (*angestammt*) components of the German nation. The ideal of German national unity legitimated the tribes, or *Stämme*, as the embodiment of ancient German ways and liberties. Inversely, the *Mittelstaaten* legitimated German unity as the necessary condition of their own security and cultural identity. As Friedrich von Beust, foreign minister of Saxony, proclaimed before a gymnastics festival in 1863: "Germany's princes and their governments do more than recognize and appreciate the gradual rise in general German consciousness, they positively welcome it because they see this growth of German feeling as the best support for their own efforts."[60] Though the discursive revolution did not unfold with the ruthlessness of French-style departmentalization, Ossianic discourse and its *re-presentation* of German nationhood successfully took hold as common sense.

As in France, the *Mittelstaaten* looked to the schools to legitimate rule by teaching language and patriotism. Unlike France, however, the monarchies intervened in and through education to repress radical, nationalist thought, particularly influential among instructors. In 1827, King Ludwig of Bavaria announced that "the animation of the national [Bavarian] spirit, the study of the history of the [Bavarian] Fatherland,

---

[59] Weber, *Peasants into Frenchmen*, p. 477.
[60] Green, *Fatherlands*, p. 137; see also pp. 98, 104, 134–9.

and the spread of the discipline" of history would be official state policy.[61] The *Württemberger Jahrbuch* complained in 1822, "We have old and new Württembergers, Hohenlohers, Ellwangers, Upper Austrians, imperial city dwellers, and all the rest, but as yet we have no Württemberger *Volk*."[62] In the midst of a revolutionary crisis, Frederick William IV scolded a conference of seminary directors in 1849: "All the misery that has erupted throughout Prussia during this last year is your fault and only your fault, the fault of your bad instruction (*Afterbildung*), of the vulgar, irreligious mass education (*Massenweisheit*) that you disseminate as authentic education, with which you have uprooted faith and loyalty from the spirit (*Gemüte*) of my subjects and turned their hearts away from me."[63] The states made school attendance compulsory, and grappled with ways to modernize and standardize an education system composed of Reformation-era catechism schools and turn that system into a legitimizer of rule. Saxony reformed its educational system in 1835, Württemberg in 1836, Hanover in 1845, and Prussia in 1854. By 1848, most German governments had established a ministry for religion and education, the *Kultusministerium*. Governments established or reformed seminaries with the intention, according to the text of Saxon reform legislation, of producing "a knowledgeable, moral, devoutly Christian and religiously minded ... teaching class."[64]

The discursive tension between *Stamm* and nation was difficult to sustain. The growing authority of Ossianic discourse interrogated the purpose and authenticity of the *Mittelstaat* monarchies. The 1840 war alert and the 1848 Jacobin revolution challenged their legitimacy. George V of Hanover complained that the imperial constitution proposed in 1849 by national revolutionaries in Frankfurt would reduce the monarchs "to the situation of becoming *préfets* [the French state's representatives in the *départements*], or governors of provinces, to which I for one would never submit."[65] Prussia, after some confusion, intervened decisively to suppress the revolution. But it was a close call

---

[61] Celia Applegate, *A Nation of Provincials: The German Idea of Heimat* (Berkeley and Los Angeles: University of California Press, 1990), p. 39.

[62] Green, *Fatherlands*, p. 97.

[63] Kurt Düwell, "Das Schul- und Hochschulwesen der Rheinlande: Wissenschaft und Bildung seit 1815," in Petri and Droege, *Rheinische Geschichte*, vol. III, p. 477.

[64] Green, *Fatherlands*, p. 203; Düwell, "Das Schul- und Hochschulwesen der Rheinlande," pp. 477–8.

[65] Green, *Fatherlands*, p. 76.

that spurred the *Mittelstaat* monarchs to look more energetically for ways to legitimate their rule. They raised monuments, built museums, organized folk festivals, and disseminated propaganda.[66] They modernized economic legislation and used railway construction to consolidate their territories. Italian unification in 1861, however, again inspired demonstrations of nationalist enthusiasm. Nationalists looked increasingly to Prussia to imitate the Italian Piedmont and assume leadership in the national cause. *Mittelstaat* policy responded once again by reforming education, emphasizing the importance of history, and using French educational methods, which familiarized "every schoolchild [with the] map of his country," as a model.[67]

Austria, not Prussia, assumed the role of Germany's Piedmont. It summoned a congress, in 1863, to provide the Confederation with greater institutional and political unity. Prussia, under the leadership of Minister President Otto von Bismarck since 1862, refused to participate. Bismarck, like George V of Hanover, feared *départementalisation*. More specifically, like William I, he feared that Austria's initiative jeopardized Prussian autonomy and the aristocratic privileges of the *Junkers*, the landed gentry. To curtail Austria's influence, Bismarck leveraged an altercation over Schleswig-Holstein into a diplomatic crisis and war. His brazen gambit was not widely applauded, even in Prussia. When war broke out, Berliners demonstrated against it and Rhineland reservists refused to serve. But the Prussian army nevertheless won a stunning victory at Königgrätz in July 1866. That victory gutted Austrian influence in Germany and caused the German Confederation to dissolve. Prussia annexed Hanover, Nassau, Hesse-Cassel, Frankfurt, and part of Hesse-Darmstadt, uniting the Prussian core with the Prussian Rhineland, and making Prussia one of the most extensive realms of western Europe. "For more than three hundred years the powers of the circumference – France on the one side, Sweden and later Russia on the other – had laid down the law to central Europe. In the two years 1864 to 1866 the situation was reversed."[68]

Louis Napoleon III, as emperor of France, did little to oppose Prussian policy. Because national uprisings in Germany, Spain, Italy, and Russia had ravaged his uncle's imperial ambitions, Napoleon III

---

[66] Green, *Fatherlands*, pp. 111–17. See Anne-Marie Thiesse, *La création des identités nationales: Europe XVIIIe–XXe siècle* (Paris: Seuil, 1999).

[67] Green, *Fatherlands*, p. 212.

[68] A. J. P. Taylor, *The Course of German History* (New York: Capricorn Books, 1962), pp. 106–7.

sought to make nationalism an ally, entertaining the additional hope that Prussia's victory would force the revision of the Vienna settlement and win territorial compensation in the Greater Rhineland, in Saarbrücken, Luxemburg, or Mainz.[69] But Napoleon's territorial machinations served only to fan the flames of German nationalism. Bismarck felt compelled to quench that fire by uniting the German *Mittelstaaten* in war against France. Exploiting a contested succession to the throne of Spain, Bismarck maneuvered Napoleon into a declaration of war on July 19, 1870. German armies, intoning the *Wacht am Rhein*, marched into France.[70] Their victory at Sedan forced Bonaparte from power. Bismarck gathered the kings and princes of Germany into Versailles' Hall of Mirrors on January 18, 1871, to proclaim the creation of a new German empire, with William of Prussia as its emperor.

German unification was forged by the powers that had opposed unification in the past. It was a unification that expressly forbade administrative, institutional *départementalisation*. Victory at Sedan excited nationalists, but unification at Versailles disappointed them.[71] The new empire's powers were limited to monetary, commercial, diplomatic, and military matters. Unification placed Germany, without Austria, under the rule of a Prussian king as emperor. It created a democratically elected *Reichstag* that had the power to approve or reject the imperial budget, notably the defense budget, but which had little say in diplomatic and military affairs. Simultaneously, it invested power – notably the power to veto Prussian proposals – in the *Bundesrat*, or federal chamber, where the German *Mittelstaat* monarchies held sway. The monarchs retained their thrones. Both Bismarck and William I showed deference toward them. Imperial unity, in a word, was a "triumph [for] the most successful of German particularisms."[72]

Education remained the responsibility of the various state governments. Although historians have underscored the importance of public education in fostering German national identity, Abigail Green has shown that this appreciation is based on Prussian textbooks. Bavarian and Württemberger textbooks paid less attention to German unity, and less still to Prussia's importance in forging that unity. They emphasized instead the origins and character of the regional "fatherland," its history,

---

[69] Taylor, *The Course of German History*, p. 97.
[70] Horst-Johannes Tümmers, *Der Rhein: ein europäischer Fluss une seine Geschichte* (Munich: Verlag C. H. Beck, 1994), p. 225.
[71] Green, *Fatherlands*, p. 334.
[72] Geoffrey Barraclough, *The Origins of Modern Germany* (New York: Norton, 1984), p. 423.

and its ruling dynasty.[73] The Ossianic *re-presentation* of space as parceled out among cohesive, totalizing nations acquired salience in the social imaginary, but not without making room for the *Stämme*. For the *Leipziger Zeitung*, each *Stamm* had a right to its "own language, customs and 'tribal characteristics.'"[74] According to the *Neue Hannoversche Zeitung*, German nationhood differed from French-style centralization and territorial homogenization because the German "wants to observe his own morals at home, his own customs in his towns and his own law in his country." Even the gymnastic, singing, hiking, and sharp-shooting associations, which organized festivals to celebrate the nation that attracted tens of thousands of participants, were *local* organizations. Their core constituencies were typically middle-class elites involved in regional state administration or education.

The *Heimat* (homeland) movement formed in the mid nineteenth century in order to preserve "the characteristics and traditions of a particular locality, state, or region, as a unique expression of the wider national culture." By the 1890s it was producing a "flood of *Heimat* publications," founding museums, preserving folklore, and protecting sites of historical significance.[75] In the Palatinate (Pfalz), "the invented traditions of the *Heimat* bridged the gap between national aspiration and provincial reality ... The Pfälzers of the *Heimat* movement set out to reclaim the nature of their region with the zeal and high-mindedness of their contemporaries the Arctic explorers."[76] As Green observes, it is impossible to ignore the anti-centralizing and anti-Prussian aspects of *Heimat* ideology. But it is equally impossible to ignore that the agonistic encounter of kinds of representations of a distinctly *German* nationhood forged a vocabulary and a common sense that identified nationhood with a *shared* language, a *shared* culture, and a *shared* territory. Alon Confino, in his history of Württemberg in the first decades of German unification, observes that national identity was not exclusive of regional identities, but was constructed between the "intimate, immediate, and real local place and the distant, abstract, and not-less-real national world."[77]

---

[73] Green, *Fatherlands*, pp. 320–3. See Applegate, *A Nation of Provincials*, p. 87.

[74] Green, *Fatherlands*, p. 272.   [75] Green, *Fatherlands*, p. 330.

[76] Applegate, *A Nation of Provincials*, pp. 13 and 63. Note the apposition of "invented traditions" and "provincial reality." See p. 19: "*Heimat* has never been a word about real social forces or real political situations. Instead it has been a myth about the possibility of a community in the face of fragmentation and alienation." The construction of the myth can involve discovery of "natural frontiers." See p. 32.

[77] Alon Confino, *The Nation as Local Metaphor: Württemberg, Imperial Germany, and National Memory, 1871–1918* (Chapel Hill: University of North Carolina Press, 1997), p. 213.

The "distant nation" conditioned and enabled "local" specificity. The Württemberg *Volksschule* reader taught that, because Germany had no firm geographical borders, security required unity among the various German peoples.[78] Only in Bavaria was education used to forge a distinctly Bavarian nationalism.

Départementalisation in Germany did not assume the form of a constitutional *diktat* that erased customary named places from the map, as it did in France. Rather, it assumed the dramatic attire of a *telos*, a shared fate that informed efforts to bring the German nation "to light." Though the revolution of 1848 did not succeed in unifying the nation, it engendered a new way to *imagine* the nation by inspiring the historiography of the "Prussian school," as represented by Friedrich Christian Dahlmann, Johann Gustav Droysen, Heinrich von Sybel, and Maximilian Duncker. All had served as delegates to the Frankfurt assembly. Dahlmann, indeed, was an important revolutionary figure. The failure of that revolution informed their historiography. *Contra* Jacobin or Hegelian optimism, they contended, the events of 1848 demonstrated the impotence of progressive idealism and the importance of political power. For Ludwig August von Rochau, author of *Grundrisse der Realpolitik*, the "law of the stronger" in political life is like the "law of gravity on the world of bodies," a sentiment echoed by Droysen in his *Grundriss der Historik*.[79] *Realpolitik* as political vision made little reference to the prior existence of a legitimizing people, from whom rights and political powers derived. Rather, it assigned centrality to the political will, which fashioned the raw material of cultural and linguistic similarity into a nation in order to tap its mobilizing energies. The nation was not only the source of the state's legitimacy, but the means of the state's becoming.[80] The nation, thus conceived, effectively erased, as necessary sacrificial victims of creative struggle, the individual, customary, and particularistic characteristics that intervened between nation and state. The foundation of the German *Reich* by Prussia, like the forging of Italy by Piedmont, was proof and vindication of this theoretical vision. Prussia embraced the mission to create the German nation, to bring it to light through the medium of state unity, from the raw material of cultural and linguistic similarity. If that mission excluded parts of the German-speaking world, notably the Habsburg lands, "*realpolitik* cunning" in a matter that concerned the exercise of

---

[78] Green, *Fatherlands*, p. 270.
[79] Giesen, *Intellectuals and the German Nation*, p. 133. For Droysen, see pp. 131–2.
[80] Giesen, *Intellectuals and the German Nation*, p. 135.

state power demanded that sacrifice.[81] Politics is an art, nationhood its medium, and power its hammer and chisel.

Realpolitik informed and legitimated a discursive representation of German nationhood that was no less unitary and cohesive to the imagination than that which emerged in France through cultural and linguistic cleansing. The erasure of customary cultural boundaries within national space was the result not of institutional revolution, but of a discursive, conceptual revolution that delivered custom as hostage to statecraft, to manipulate or to efface as political expediency dictated. The Ossianic *re-presentation* of political space not only legitimated rule, but served as an instrument of power, as motivating and mobilizing myth, in a world in which creative action is constrained and inspired by the law of the stronger. *Realpolitik*, as philosophical history, tamed the particularisms that the *Heimat* movement discovered or invented, and lent authority to the representation of national space not merely as "natural" anthropological fact, but as political creation and, in a world governed by the law of the stronger, as political imperative.

The disruption of Greater Rhineland economic space

The exploitation of the Greater Rhineland's natural resources, facilitated by new technologies and old facilities of communication, restored the region to a central position in the European, indeed the world economy. Capital, capitalists, workers, technology, and resources ignored boundaries to bring the machine age to the region as a whole, ahead of the rest of continental Europe. But the insertion of national frontiers in Greater Rhineland space disrupted the regional economy, not so much with tariffs, taxes, and regulatory policies – it will be shown below that the regional, "transnational" logic of the Greater Rhineland economy remained compelling up to the outbreak of World War I – but because it mobilized the region's creative assets to forge the nation, as work of art, as acclaimed by *Realpolitik*. That aesthetic project conditioned war on a scale not yet known and brought ruin to the region on a scale not seen since the Thirty Years War and the great invasions.

---

[81] Giesen, *Intellectuals and the German Nation*, p. 139. As matter for speculation, it is a both fascinating and significant feature of international relations scholarship that the most creative adepts of *Realpolitik* today are found in the United States. See Raymond Aron, *Paix et guerre entre nations* (Paris: Calmann-Levy, 1984), pp. 578–87.

The Vienna settlement awarded the German Rhineland, from Bingen to the Dutch border, to Prussia. Because German waterways flow north to the Baltic and the North Sea, Prussia's command of the Rhine gave it power to mold German economic space. Prussia initially showed little interest in this power, but began to adopt aggressive trade policies in the late 1820s when Bavaria, Württemberg, Baden, and Nassau, in response to refusals by France – in 1819–20, 1822, 1824, and 1828 – to open its market to their exports, turned to Austria as a potential trade partner. Prussia feared that free trade in southern Germany would move the German states toward some form of political union, inimical to Prussian particularism. Prussia therefore proposed in 1828 to form a first, experimental tariff union with Hesse-Darmstadt as a device, observes A. J. P. Taylor, "for making the unification of Germany less necessary."[82] In 1829, Prussia invited other German states to join the Prussia–Darmstadt union. The initiative alarmed French diplomats in Berlin, who warned that trade liberalization would make Germany a "more homogeneous and compact national body (*corps de nation*)," immune to the kind of influence and power that France had enjoyed there since the mid-seventeenth century.[83] But when Paris proposed a countervailing tariff union with Saxony, Hesse-Cassel, Frankfurt, and Hanover, French business representatives scuttled the project. (The French government, in any case, was pinning hopes on the Polignac plan, discussed in the previous chapter.) Saxony and Hanover subsequently signed a trade union without the French.

The revolutions of 1830 spurred interest among the French and Belgians in forming a customs union, but business opposition in France again blocked the idea. Nevertheless, that effort, along with the 1831 collapse of the Saxony–Hanover union, strengthened Prussia's resolve to use trade policy to assert influence in Germany. New negotiations culminated in the 1833 establishment of a *Zollverein* uniting Prussia, Hesse-Darmstadt, and the southern states of Bavaria and Württemberg (see figure 7.4).[84] Concerned by the political ramifications of the agreement, France entered negotiations with the *Zollverein*. Business interests again rebuffed the initiative even though the *Zollverein*, per se, had few adverse economic effects on France. Indeed, it facilitated exports to Germany and helped assure France's supply of coal. The

[82] Taylor, *The Course of German History*, p. 62. Taylor observes that the members of the *Zollverein* all fought with Austria against Prussia in 1866.

[83] Poidevin and Bariéty, *Les relations franco-allemandes*, p. 40.

[84] See Milkereit, *Sozial- und Wirtschaftsentwicklung der südlichen Rheinlande*, pp. 200–2.

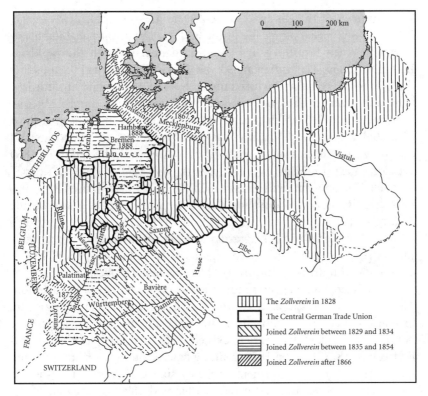

Figure 7.4 The *Zollverein*

Source: Raymond Poidevin and Jacques Bariéty, *Les relations franco-allemandes* (Paris: Armand Colin, 1977), p. 41.

Zollverein would soon become France's fourth-ranked trading partner, accounting for 7 percent of its foreign trade. Nevertheless, the war alert of 1840 spurred the French to raise tariffs yet again in 1841 and 1842.

When the 1848 revolutions prompted the Habsburg court to exploit nationalist sentiment to win influence in the German-speaking world, Prussia used the *Zollverein* to oppose it. Prussia's industrial power in the Rhineland and Silesia enabled it to drive tariffs below levels that made Austrian participation possible. Saxony and Hanover, acquiescing in the *Zollverein*'s economic and political strength, joined in 1851–4. Württemberg's mistrust of Prussia was such that it contemplated withdrawing in 1852, but "the Württemberg Board of Trade and Industry argued that leaving the *Zollverein* would be very disruptive for Württemberg's northbound trade flows, because Prussia controlled long stretches of the Rhine."[85] To cultivate its geographical advantage, Prussia raised levees along the Rhine and cut canals that enabled heavy barges to reach Strasburg. It blasted a channel through the rapids at Bingen in 1839–41, and financed the St. Gothard tunnel, connecting the Rhineland to the Mediterranean by rail. Following unification, Germany, under Prussian leadership, financed Holland's *Nieuwe Waterweg* in 1872, which positioned Rotterdam to become a seaport of global dimensions. Prussia's growing awareness of the Rhineland economy's potential as a tool of political power was reflected in its 1860 decision to expel French investors from the direction of Prussian firms.[86]

When Europe entered recession in 1873, Bismarck used the new protectionist mood to consolidate Rhineland support for Prussian rule by forging the political coalition of "iron and rye" between the region's industrialists and Prussia's agrarian aristocracy. By protecting agriculture, the 1879 tariff increased the cost of industrial labor, but it compensated industry with protection and higher prices. In 1887–9, as recession deepened, German industrialists pressed for more protection. The government responded, not with tariffs, but by encouraging cartel formation and vertical concentration, especially in steel.[87] Cartels were not new to Germany. Six were in existence at the time of unification, and fourteen in 1877. But the 1879 tariff, by fencing out foreign competition, greatly favored cartel agreements. Seventy-six cartels were established in the period 1879–85 and 120 between 1885 and 1890. By the end of the century, Germany numbered about 275 cartels. The cartels stabilized prices, protected industries against the business cycle, and helped German industrialists compete on foreign markets (through dumping, compensated by price fixing at home).[88] The first large-scale experiment with cartels occurred among Rhineland-Westphalian coal-mining firms, which agreed in 1877 to reduce output by 10 percent to maintain price levels. The coal cartel's effort to organize the market culminated in the establishment in 1893 of the Rheinisch-Westfälisches Kohlensyndikat (Rhineland-Westphalian Coal Syndicate), which controlled about 80 percent of the coal production of the Ruhr and half the production of Germany.[89]

[85] Green, *Fatherlands*, p. 238.
[86] Poidevin and Bariéty, *Les relations franco-allemandes*, p. 47.
[87] Jacques Valette, *Vie économique et sociale des grands pays de l'Europe occidentale et des États-Unis: début du XXe siècle – 1939* (Paris: SEDES, 1976), pp. 41–4. Kellenbenz, *Wirtschafts- und Sozialentwicklung der nördlichen Rheinlanden*, pp. 72–4.
[88] Clapham, *The Economic Development of France and Germany*, pp. 310–14.
[89] See Kellenbenz, *Wirtschafts- und Sozialentwicklung der nördlichen Rheinlanden*, pp. 88–95.

Tariffs and cartels distorted economic activity in the Greater Rhineland. They caused German steel production to double in the 1880s, when across the border in France and Belgium it remained flat.[90] They also stimulated the development of the chemical, and especially the electrical industry, "the greatest single industrial achievement of modern Germany."[91] No other nation approached Germany's superiority in this sector, and, in general, only the United States kept pace with Germany's rise as an industrial power. But protectionist policy stimulated a level of production that required the state to intervene with massive purchases. "The power of the industrialists ... was built on unstable foundations; for German heavy industry ... was a top-heavy structure, extremely sensitive to economic trends and unable to maintain itself without lavish government support."[92] Bismarck's politics had set in motion a chain of mutually reinforcing policy and investment decisions that culminated in this "top-heavy" and fragile economic structure. Bismarck sought to preserve social order in his native Prussia, to preserve regional ambitions against the *départementalisation* of German national space. Trade policy served a political purpose, "the continued predominance of a landed squirearchy in a nation whose wealth and population had shifted to the cities."[93] But in pursuing this purpose, Bismarck bequeathed to his successors a political economy admirably structured to "bring to light" the nation of *Realpolitik* discourse, that is, the nation "departmentalized" – cleansed of its particularisms – as ardent political project if not as administrative fact. As the state turned to military procurement to sustain industrial activity, it sought legitimation of its policies in the language of power politics and assertion of nationhood. Industrialists responded by supporting military spending and the expansionist politics it enabled. They supported and financed societies – the Pan-German League, the Colonial Society, the Navy League – that justified armaments programs and stimulated state purchases, and in so doing enhanced the authority of national, military, power political discourse. The exalted nature of the nation's mission consigned regionalist *Heimat* discourse to folklore.

---

[90] Clapham, *The Economic Development of France and Germany*, p. 284, but economic historians hesitate to attribute expansion to protectionist policy. See Kellenbenz, *Wirtschafts- und Sozialentwicklung der nördlichen Rheinlanden*, pp. 97–9.

[91] Clapham, *The Economic Development of France and Germany*, p. 308.

[92] Barraclough, *The Origins of Modern Germany*, p. 431.

[93] Kenneth D. Barkin, *The Controversy over German Industrialization, 1890–1902* (Chicago: University of Chicago Press, 1970), p. 274.

Industrialists conceptualized business interest within the discursive frame of *Realpolitik* and gave support to the expansionist ambitions of William II, who succeeded to the imperial throne in 1888. William abandoned Bismarckian diplomacy in order to cultivate closer relations with Britain in the hope of winning its support for his maritime and colonial *Weltpolitik*. Bismarck, a *Junker* of the old school, defended long-standing relations with Russia, Britain's rival in central Asia. Those relations, he argued, were needed to assure stability in Poland and the eastern Baltic – *Prussia*'s periphery – as well as maintain France in a state of diplomatic isolation. William II forced Bismarck's resignation and named General Georg Leo von Caprivi, a military man and *apparatchik* with little political experience, to replace him. Caprivi placed industry at the center of his policy. He negotiated commercial treaties with Austria, Italy, Switzerland, Spain, Serbia, Romania, Belgium, and Russia, reducing tariffs on food imports and winning new export markets for German industry.[94] But industrial production continued to outpace demand, and the treaties alienated agriculture. The Agrarian League (*Bund der Landwirte*) opposed Caprivi. Conservative economists justified their criticism in the same Ossianic discursive frame that enabled militarism, by arguing that industrial growth and urban living were destroying the culture of the German people.[95] "Therein lies the great danger, not only from the standpoint of our military strength, for the land delivers, all in all, better soldiers than the cities, but for our whole social structure."[96] The discourse of nationhood, from Macpherson and Herder forward, *always* located the nation, the *peuple*, the *Volk*, in the countryside, not the city. But the assertion of nationhood in Germany depended on the economic power of its cities.

Trade policy became a burning issue in 1900 following the accession of Count Bernhard von Bülow to the chancellorship. Von Bülow was an accomplished diplomat, a former foreign minister, and advisor to the emperor since 1897. Like Caprivi, he looked west rather than east for his political inspiration. "His pride was aroused by the sight of Hamburg docks rather than Pomeranian estates."[97] But Von Bülow as politician nevertheless sought Prussian, agrarian support for his policies by

[94] Barkin, *The Controversy over German Industrialization*, p. 105; see also p. 29. Food prices placed pressure on wages and fueled German emigration to the United States: "the number deserting Germany, mainly for the United States, had risen to startling proportions."
[95] Barkin, *The Controversy over German Industrialization*, pp. 146–62.
[96] Barkin, *The Controversy over German Industrialization*, p. 220.
[97] Barkin, *The Controversy over German Industrialization*, p. 215.

proposing a significant increase in agricultural tariffs. He explained his position to the emperor in words that again reflect the marginalization of the town – the *industrial* town – in Ossianic/national discourse: "I hold increased protection for agriculture absolutely necessary out of economic, and still more out of social, political, and national grounds ... the cities are swelling into a hypertrophied state, the land is being depopulated." To win industrial support for higher agricultural duties, which meant higher food prices and pressure on salaries, Von Bülow divided and ruled by protecting heavy industry, whether threatened by foreign competition or not, at the expense of small manufactures. Some new duties virtually excluded foreign competition from the German market. Export-dependent industries often shifted production abroad, particularly to Bohemia. Hjalmar Schacht (the artisan of currency stabilization in the interwar period) castigated the legislation: "By no logic did the chemical industry require duties, since it had evolved to its worldwide dominance in a free trade economy." Schacht cited industries that received tariff protection despite export–import ratios of 15 to 1, and voiced suspicion that the purpose of such legislation was to promote cartel expansion in iron and steel.[98] The incentive to form cartels had already become overwhelming as industrial growth responded increasingly to naval procurement rather than world markets. In 1898 Admiral Alfred von Tirpitz, minister of the navy, won approval for a vast expansion of Germany's war fleet. In 1902, just months before the passage of the new protectionist trade legislation, the Imperial Diet approved an even more ambitious program that would, over a seventeen-year period, create a navy strong enough to deter even the greatest rival and affirm the power of the German nation throughout the world.

The militarized political economy brought the nation "to light" not in its "essential identity," the putative "sameness" that reduced regional particularisms to details of folklore, but in the claim to find in that putative identity both the ardent imperative and the strength of will to defend identity – *ipséité*, to borrow Levinas's suggestive term – against decline and collapse. Ossianic discourse, in its first romantic emergence, expressed a "joy of sorrow." Ossianic discourse, in its construction as *Realpolitik*, expressed spiritual exaltation, "pride," for example in the contemplation of Hamburg's docks. Ossian mourned a golden age. But *Realpolitik* aspired to immortality. Benedict Anderson attributes the

---

[98] Barkin, *The Controversy over German Industrialization*, p. 236.

success of nationhood discourse to its power to tame the spiritual anxiety engendered by pre-industrial society's decomposition and the rejection of its myths and dogmas:

> Disintegration of paradise: nothing makes fatality more arbitrary. Absurdity of salvation: nothing makes another style of continuity more necessary ... Nations ... always loom out of an immemorial past, and, still more important, glide into a limitless future. It is the magic of nationalism to turn chance into destiny.[99]

Whether the spiritual construction of nationhood corresponded to an actual need is debatable. "Spiritual need" was, and is, diversely met. But the *language* of nationhood, of survival, destiny, expansion, and immortality, undeniably opened new worlds of political possibility that enabled industrialists, politicians, military leaders, and intellectuals to discern new horizons, new ambitions. The emergence, within the onto-pological world of Ossian, of a discourse of immortality that *re-presented* the world as a (forever potential) menace, and all nations as a (forever potential) threat, legitimated the militarization of the German Rhineland economy. (One encounters this language today, largely fossilized, in the odd but foundational focus on "national survival" that characterizes "realist theory" in American international relations scholarship.) An accumulation of military power through industrial growth occurred within what philosopher Marc Crépon has characterized as a "struggle to the death for immortality." The language of that struggle articulated the wish "to impose a given identity (a language, a 'spirit', a culture) as chosen (*élu*), and in this respect, eternal."[100] The chosen people was, of necessity, one. It was *départementalisé*. It affirmed its oneness and its election in the "expansion" of its national, collective "self" through power politics and colonization. Economic militarization was justified by, and assumed meaningfulness with reference to, the nation's willing reception of the burden of election. Within this universe of discourse, free trade could only be seen as "a reactionary philosophy unworthy of men with a modern outlook."[101]

By 1913, German industry was producing 24 percent of the world's chemical goods, compared with Great Britain's 11 percent and the United States' 34 percent. "Made in Germany" resounded in British

---

[99] Anderson, *Imagined Communities*, p. 11.
[100] Marc Crépon, *Altérités de l'Europe* (Paris: Galilée, 2006), pp. 99–103.
[101] Barkin, *The Controversy over German Industrialization*, p. 229.

ears like "made in Japan" in 1980s America. Critics in France railed against a commercial *invasion germanique*, and experienced German prosperity as a threat to their own "national" security. Not only were Germany's war industries powerful, but its population, in an age of mass military conscription, was growing rapidly, from 25 million in 1816 to 36 million in 1871 to 56 million in 1911. The population of Germany's Rhineland provinces grew from 2 to 9 million. France, the most populous country of western Europe at the time of the Revolution, saw its population grow by a mere 2.5 percent between 1871 and 1911. Though it occupied fourth place among the world's commercial powers, its foreign trade grew by only 16 percent between 1895 and 1905, while that of Germany grew by 66 percent.[102] By 1910 Germany's naval yards were turning out nearly 400,000 tons of merchant shipping a year, raising the tonnage of its fleet from 1.3 million in 1900 to 2.4 million in 1910. Though Britain's ship builders were turning out about 2 million tons and its merchant fleet in 1910 boasted a capacity of 11.4 million tons, Germany's efforts to become a naval and colonial power alarmed the British. Britain signed agreements with France, with whom it had almost gone to war in 1891 following a clash in Africa, and with Russia, its perennial rival for power in central Asia, especially Afghanistan. German efforts to break the "unnatural" alliance by provoking the Morocco crises of 1905 and 1911 not only failed, but put Germany's adversaries on a war footing.

The enduring cross-border cohesion of the Rhineland economy

The militarization of the German political economy, though formidable, never completely stifled the Greater Rhineland region's integrative pull. The exploitation of the iron mines of Lorraine and France's industrial growth in the 1890s conditioned a revival of cross-border collaboration. The German steel industry's demand for imported iron caused its purchases of French ore to climb prodigiously. In 1901, the steel giant Thyssen acquired mines in Jouanville and Batilly. Between 1906 and 1910, German firms – Thyssen, Krupp, Phoenix, Hasper, Hoesch – invested heavily in French mines, not only in Lorraine but in Normandy where Thyssen acquired the Société des Hauts Fourneaux de

---

[102] Great Britain's foreign trade grew by 34 percent, and that of the United States by 80 percent. For more figures, see Demangeon and Febvre, *Le Rhin*, p. 146.

Caen. Inversely, French steel's demand for imported coke goaded Schneider, Les Forges d'Alais, and Saint-Gobain to create, with German participation, the Internationale Kohlen Bergwerks-Gesellschaft, with thirty-seven mines in German Alsace-Lorraine. When rising German demand for Ruhr coke threatened France's supply, the French firms Micheville, Pont-à-Mousson, and Marine-Homécourt acquired mines near Aachen. French firms proposed mergers with German firms. In 1907, the Aciéries de Longwy swapped shares with the German firm Röchling, which agreed to provide Longwy with half its coal production, while Longwy agreed to provide Röchling with half its iron ore production.[103] That agreement presaged efforts to pacify the Rhineland frontier in 1923 and 1948 by regionalizing the coal and steel industries (see next chapter).

Regional, cross-border economic ties were not limited to steel. The chemical giant Bayer constructed a factory in Flers-en-Breuc, near Lille. Chemische Elektron established a French subdivision at La Motte-Breuil in central France. Continental, a Hanover tire manufacturer, created a French division in 1904. The electrical giant AEG bought shares in France's Thomson-Houston. Another German electrical firm, Schuckert, assumed control of the French Compagnie Générale d'Electricité in Creil, near Paris. Parisian banks invested in Germany's capital-starved but profitable industries. Financial agreements totaling 2.5 billion francs were signed between French and German firms in the period 1898–1905.[104] German banks – the Deutsche Bank and the Dresdner Bank among others – sought to attract short-term investment from French lenders. Jacques de Gunzbourg, an influential Parisian financier and friend of the minister of foreign affairs, proposed that German stocks be quoted on the Paris exchange. By 1900, the flow of French capital into German assets was averaging about a billion francs yearly.

The ideal of free trade, however incompatible with economic manipulation in pursuit of national power, was never entirely forsaken. Paul de Leusse published a pamphlet entitled "Peace through Franco-German Tariff Union" in 1888. The 1890 McKinley Tariff in America spurred German interest in Franco-German economic cooperation (foreshadowing economic diplomacy in the twentieth century). As economic ties grew thicker at century's end,

---

[103] Poidevin and Bariéty, *Les relations franco-allemandes*, p. 179.
[104] Poidevin and Bariéty, *Les relations franco-allemandes*, p. 160.

diplomats looked for ways to normalize relations. The French fleet participated in the opening celebrations of the Kiel Canal in 1895. Germany, which refused to participate in the Exposition Universelle de Paris of 1889, took part in the Exposition of 1900. For the first time since the Franco-Prussian War, large crowds of German tourists, the most numerous foreign contingent at the fair, could be seen strolling along Paris' boulevards. But the Morocco crisis of 1911 brought such initiatives to an end. French bankers withdrew funds from Germany (though long-term investment by French and German industrialists was unaffected). Trade between the two countries, which had grown by about 35 percent in the four years before the war, fell victim to a tariff war unleashed by diplomatic crisis.

Parenthesis: Alsace-Lorraine

Alsace-Lorraine was the mythical flashpoint of pre-World War I Franco-German relations. Ossianic discourse fractured Greater Rhineland space, generating bitter tensions between the French and German nations. But it did not trump the integrative logic of Greater Rhineland geography. There was tension, not rupture. That tension culminated in war in the first half of the century, but in European Union in the second half.

In 1871, the German empire placed the annexed territories of Alsace and the German-speaking regions of Lorraine under an imperial governor. Nearly 130,000 inhabitants fled the provinces, especially Metz and Mulhouse, for France. About 50,000 of these were fleeing conscription into the Prussian army. Among those who stayed, some resisted the annexation, while others, disposed toward accommodation, fought for regional autonomy and equality with other German states. The Ligue d'Alsace, supported by the Catholic clergy, encouraged resistance against Protestant and anticlerical Prussia. Inversely, newspapers like the *Courrier du Bas Rhin* and the *Elsässer Volksblatt*, supported by the business class, pressed for equality of rights with the *Mittelstaaten*. Germany established an elected but consultative council in 1874, empowered to legislate on provincial issues subject to approval by the German *Reichstag*. Resistance candidates prevailed in the 1874 elections, but accommodationists won in 1878 and 1881. In France, the republican left, the traditional champion of the Rhine frontier and ideological opponent of monarchical, "reactionary" rule, clamored for a war of *revanche* or reprisal. Appealing shamelessly to Ossianic mythology, it called for an alliance of "Latins" in the west and "Slavs" in the east to defeat the "Germanic" empire. Numerous publications, poems, and patriotic songs bewailed the loss of Alsace-Lorraine. But Germany also had many influential admirers in France. Michelet, in *La France devant l'Europe*, denounced Prussian rule but applauded the principle of German nationhood. Quinet, though alarmed by the rise of Prussian power, advanced a similar argument. Ernest Renan attributed France's defeat to the loss of its military spirit. It had adopted the calculating, utilitarian mind-set of the Anglo-Saxons, and had become "a second America, but lacking in everything which made the United States an exceptional case, that is to say, a second-class America, mean and mediocre."[105] Germany retained its military spirit, a lesson for the French.

After a decade, the clamor for *revanche* subsided. The electoral victory of the *opportunistes* (conservative republicans) in 1879 was welcomed by the manipulative Bismarck, who anticipated that the government's anticlericalism would ratify his own campaign against Rome while making it more difficult for France to find allies among Germany's monarchical and Catholic neighbors. In diplomatic affairs Bismarck supported France's occupation of Tunis and, more generally, French imperialism in Morocco, Egypt, Madagascar, and Indochina, if only because it kept their military occupied and generated tensions with Great Britain. Following Jules Ferry's election as President of the Council in 1883, Bismarck called for a *rapprochement* between France and Germany, declaring before the *Reichstag* in 1884 that "between us and the French government there reigns a perfect confidence in the honesty and the sincerity of our reciprocal relations."[106] Bismarck asked to meet Ferry, and made it known that Germany was prepared to support France's colonial and African policy "without reserve."[107] But opposition in France, particularly in the press, prevented Ferry from following up on Bismarck's invitation. Ferry's leftist critics, notably Georges Clemenceau, reviled him as "Bismarck's protégé," and greeted him in the Assembly with cries of "A bas le Prussien!" Ferry fell in 1885. Georges Boulanger, rhetorically committed to a war of *revanche*, became minister of war in the new Freycinet government. His actions triggered a crisis in 1887 that mobilized the reserves, and sent stock markets crashing and suspected spies to prison. Historians speculate

---

[105] Furet, *Revolutionary France*, p. 507.
[106] Poidevin and Bariéty, *Les relations franco-allemandes*, p. 139.
[107] Poidevin and Bariéty, *Les relations franco-allemandes*, p. 140.

that Bismarck exaggerated the crisis in order to manipulate the *Reichstag* into approving his military budget and to frighten Russians and Austrians who might be contemplating a French alliance. In Alsace-Lorraine the crisis brought victory to resistance forces and prompted the German government to introduce an administrative novelty, the passport, into Greater Rhineland space so as to control passage back and forth across the French frontier. The passport was abolished in 1900, but was reintroduced after the war, when it would become emblematic of international relations in the twentieth century.

Following the crisis, Alsace-Lorraine faded as a political issue. With the exceptions of *Les Oberlé* by novelist René Bazin, and *L'âme alsacienne* and *Une nouvelle position du problème alsacien-lorrain* by Maurice Barrès, a Lorraine native, novelist, and theorist of nationalism, the lost provinces ceased to sell books. The socialist Jean Jaurès, writing in 1890, had called Germany's annexation of Alsace-Lorraine a criminal act. But in 1901 he exhorted the French to abandon all ideas of military revenge. French internationalists proposed that Alsace-Lorraine be reorganized as a neutral state within a European framework. In Alsace-Lorraine itself, attitudes toward Germany changed. Lorraine's iron fields brought prosperity. Output increased by a factor of five between 1871 and 1891, and thirteen between 1871 and 1902. Lorraine's regional economy became closely intertwined with those of the Saarland and the *Ruhrgebiet*. German "immigrants" living and working in Alsace-Lorraine accounted for about 16 percent of the population – 40 percent in Strasburg, and 50 percent in Metz. Directors, engineers, and miners of Lorraine's iron mines were generally of German origin. A new generation of Alsatians, educated in German schools and drafted into German military service, assigned greater importance to political equality than to further resistance to annexation. They constructed a German identity and deliberated within the representational space of German particularism. Alsatian authors began to employ the Alamannic dialect in drama and literature, whether in resistance to the Prussian-dominated empire, or in compliance with *Heimat* ideals.[108]

Tensions between France and Germany abated further following Bismarck's removal from power and Germany's embrace of *Weltpolitik*. Russia, France, and Germany joined forces to colonize China in 1895. Both Gabriel Hanotaux, foreign minister in 1896, and his successor,

---

[108] Poidevin and Bariéty, *Les relations franco-allemandes*, pp. 152–4. Cf. Applegate, *A Nation of Provincials*, p. 81.

Théophile Delcassé, worked to improve relations with Germany. Delcassé confided to the German ambassador that "France was saturated, oversaturated [with the idea of *revanche*] and [was] ready to support Germany's colonial aspirations everywhere, particularly in China."[109] But William II insisted that the two countries agree first to guarantee their mutual frontier. This was not yet politically feasible in France.

Ossianic autoimmunities

State efforts to bring Ossianic myth to light, to make it "real," fractured Greater Rhineland space. Nationhood became common sense, such that when Trier native Karl Marx sought to foster working-class solidarities across frontiers, he could only conceptualize that solidarity within the Ossianic category of a workers' Inter-*national*. As recently as 1750, the map of Europe delineated only sites of legitimate (or "legitimately contested") dynastic rule, the frontiers of which fluctuated as did the marriages and military fortunes of the dynasts. It did not indicate lines of separation – by language or culture – between the peoples that lived there. The ruling aristocracy shared social norms, courtly language, and high culture across political frontiers. Townspeople expressed themselves in one or more local dialects and a business lingua franca. Courts imposed administrative idioms, but they did not impose cultural, liturgical, or commercial linguae francae, or repress autochthonous dialects. The peasants employed a motley of *patois* unrelated to the tracing of political frontiers. Not that it mattered, for the peasant, per se, had no dwelling place on the map of 1750 Europe. He was invisible, or, if remarked, was a figure of disdain, of melancholy, and even repulsion, as recalled by the English jibe "peasant!" or the French "vilain!"[110] The life of the peasant was as unaffected by frontiers as the life of the aristocrat.

The map of 1900 reveals dramatic change. Court, town, and countryside all expressed themselves in the national idiom. *Patois* were widespread, but narrowly circumscribed by class, and, in France, actively repressed by the state. The peasant was no longer reviled, but extolled as the cultivator of the national style, as expressed in dress, habitat, landscape,

---

[109] Poidevin and Bariéty, *Les relations franco-allemandes*, p. 167.
[110] *Vilain* in French, meaning "ugly," is a common word of reproach for misbehaving children.

and cuisine. Peasant dress, given canonical definition in the first decades of the nineteenth century, became emblematic of the nation. "*Tracht* – the meaning of which depended to a large degree on the existence of its opposite, modern fashion – became the plaything of the big-city bourgeoisie, available in mail order catalogues and advertised in local magazines."[111] Peasant dwellings and other components of the "typical" national landscape were carefully catalogued and reconstructed in the glazed-in hollows of museum dioramas, first introduced at the universal exposition of 1878. Composers of "classical" music, emulating James Macpherson, scoured the countryside to discover and draw inspiration from the "national sound." Nations adopted mascots, "national animals": the German eagle, the Russian bear, the French cock (from the Latin *gallus*, meaning both rooster and Gaul). The monarch became the "national monarch," the nation's ambassador to the world.[112] Monuments in stone, dedicated to the heroism of fallen warriors, reminded citizens of the debt they owed their forebears, and taught them that the survival and transmission of the national heritage was a privilege won by arms. Within this discursive universe, the city was an object of suspicion, the site of a motley, often foreign working class, and of political loyalties that jeopardized *national* solidarity. It was the site of a business and financial class distrusted because of its inter-*national* interests and contacts, its cosmopolitanism, and its Jews, "always already" foreign.

The representation of nationhood had its source in poetic imagery, but political coercion, in the form of military conquest, state administration, economic intervention, and compulsory education, made the imagery "real," brought it "to light" in the *Lebenswelt*. Citizens took part in new rituals and ceremonies that were national in meaning and scope. "Within less than a century [of the Revolution], all civic ceremonies in France had a national, not a local, character."[113] Bastille day was a national holiday. Conscription was cause for festivity as young men joked and paraded their way to the induction center, in playful approximation of military formation. The daily press apportioned the front page to news of the nation. France, for Eugen Weber, had become a colonial empire, "a complex of territories conquered, annexed, and integrated in a political and administrative whole, many

---

[111] Applegate, *A Nation of Provincials*, p. 83.
[112] See Thiesse, *La création des identités nationales*, Pt II, ch. 2.
[113] Weber, *Peasants into Frenchmen*, p. 474.

of them with strongly developed national or regional personalities ...
A lot of Frenchmen did not know that they belonged together until the
long didactic campaigns of the later nineteenth century told them they
did, and their own experience as conditions changed told them that
this made sense."[114] In Germany nationhood emerged as common
sense not through administrative erasure of customary categories, but
as ardent obligation, made tangible through the militarization of the
political economy and claims to a "place in the sun," as demanded by
Emperor William II (after stealing the sound bite from Von Bülow) in
a 1901 speech before the North German Regatta Association.

This representation of populations as peoples – nations – confined and
protected by state frontiers occurred *after* the cultural *re-presentation* of
the entities that the frontiers were "intended" to separate. First came the
named space. Then came the named peoples who filled the space. Filling
the new map with peoples demanded decades of state labor. That labor
consumed most of Europe. In the Greater Rhineland, it partitioned a
space that historically, though nameless, had shown integrity as a
regional economy and cultural sphere. The fracturing of Greater
Rhineland space was most dramatic along the middle Rhine, where
castle ruins echoed with a "call to hatred, to revenge, and to battle to the
bitter end." In the 1920s, following the "war of nations," the *Völkerkrieg*,
Pfälzer *Heimat* literature celebrated the Palatinate's front-line heroism.
"As in 1689, when the French general Mélac had lain waste to the Pfalz, so
in 1791, in 1919, and in 1923."[115] In an ultimate discursive act of German
national unification, the National-Socialists, who assumed power in 1933,
departmentalized Rhineland space. Departmentalization in Nazi Germany
was not as radically inventive as in revolutionary France. Administrative
boundaries and names often reprised those of provinces now extracted
from *Mittelstaat* rule. But departmentalization nevertheless challenged
customary spatial representation. The National-Socialists split Bavaria, a
rival "nation," into four *Reichsgaue*: Bayreuth, Franken, Schwaben, and
Oberbayern. Formerly hegemonic Prussia was divided into nine: Berlin,
Mark Brandenburg, Pommern, Wartheland, Danzig, West Preussen,
Ost Preussen, Ober- and Niederschlesien. They freely employed names
of urban administrative centers, especially in the Rhineland: Köln-
Aachen, Essen, Düsseldorf. The *Reichsgau* of Weser-Ems, like so many
of its French counterparts, was named for rivers. Significantly the

---

[114] Weber, *Peasants into Frenchmen*, p. 485.
[115] Applegate, *A Nation of Provincials*, pp. 115, 117, 147, 201.

National-Socialists chose to ignore Pfälzer patriotic sacrifices and simply merged it with the recently recovered Saarland in order to form the *Reichsgau* of Saar-Pfalz. In 1940 they attached formerly French Lorraine to Saar-Pfalz to form the *Reichsgau* of Westmark. The Ossianic fracture of Greater Rhineland space now consigned Europe's industrial core to the defensive edge, the nominal Mark or march, of German national space.

The incision of "national" frontiers was not a smooth process, however. The frontiers often remained political, not linguistic or cultural. In the lower Rhineland, the dialect of the eastern Netherlands extended without a break into Germany. As late as the mid-twentieth century, German laborers, crossing the frontier in significant numbers to work in Dutch factories, conversed unproblematically with their Dutch colleagues in the shared idiom (see figure 6.1).[116] In Flanders, where the use of French had caused the Flemish idiom to atomize into a multiplicity of dialects, the Flemish looked north, to the Netherlands, for the language that would unite and define them as a people. That "union" was accomplished by adopting a "foreign" dialect, standard Dutch or the *algemeen beschaafd*, with only minor adjustments of spelling and pronunciation as the official speech of education, culture, and administration.[117] Just as national frontiers failed to signify linguistic and cultural boundaries, linguistic and cultural variety within political borders also problematized Ossianic mythology. In Germany, the difference between literary and spoken German is still appreciable in many parts of the country in our day. Urbanization, education, and migration helped promote the success of a lingua franca, an *Umgangsprache* that united Germans in a standard speech. But within the bounds of that idiom, differences are still great enough to require a concentrated effort on the part of, say, a Hamburg native to "avoid unfamiliar expressions" when conversing with a visitor from Munich.[118] Differences of accent are great in the British Isles, but speech differences in Germany cross the line to become differences of idiom.

Not only was there tension between myth and *Lebenswelt*. By the mid nineteenth century the foundational image of Ossianic myth, that of anthropological *authenticity* as revealed and sustained by monolingualism, began to generate subversive "auto-immunities." The term is borrowed from Derrida, who used it to refer to the "illogical logic" that

[116] W. B. Lockwood, *An Informal History of the German Language* (London: André Deutsch, 1976), pp. 188–9.
[117] Lockwood, *An Informal History of the German Language*, pp. 187–8.
[118] Lockwood, *An Informal History of the German Language*, pp. 119, 133–9.

turns something against itself in self-defense (like democracy in its defense against terrorism).[119] In like manner, one can observe how the criteria of exclusion that preserve a mythological authenticity turned inward to attack the body of the nation itself. In 1854, Frédéric Mistral, poet and son of wealthy landowners, founded the Félibirge in France to promote the use of Provençal and the preservation of regional customs. Mistral's Provençal was a literary language based on the poetry of troubadours, and not easily understood by speakers of the regional *patois*. But that fact did not discourage Mistral from compiling a Provençal dictionary and writing an epic, *Mirèio*, that Charles-François Gounod turned into a popular opera. His *Lou pouèmo dóu Rose* relates, against the geographical backdrop of the Rhine–Rhône corridor, the romantic encounter of a Dutch prince and a Provençal ferryman's daughter, whose idyll is cut short by the particularism-effacing appearance of the still-experimental steamboat. Boats collide, uniting lovers in death who, in life, were separated by frontiers of place, language, culture, and social caste. Despite Mistral's Nobel Prize for literature in 1904, which enabled him to found – the mark of modernity – an ethnographic museum in Arles, Provençal had no chance of asserting its rights against the *départemental* state, and remained a museum curiosity. But a more successful effort to resurrect a linguistic victim of nation-building occurred in Frisia, at the far end of the Rhine–Rhône corridor. When the Habsburg court sent Dutch-speaking officials north of the Zuiderzee in 1524, Frisian ceased to be a language of government and suffered the fate of all discarded idioms. It splintered into local dialects and was "polluted" by "official" Dutch vocabulary. Nineteenth-century "Frisian" intellectuals, moved by the spirit of the times, took a patriotic interest in the dialect. Unlike Provençal, it was allowed to return to the corridors of administration and law, and so was kept alive as a spoken language.[120] It remains today the mother tongue of several hundred thousand Netherlanders.

Nationhood's autoimmunity interrogates national unity by "bringing to light" regional identities that *départementalisation* – administrative or discursive – sought to suppress. But there emerged in the middle of the nineteenth century a second autoimmunity, more menacing and destructive, that interrogated the "scientific" meaningfulness of national

---

[119] See Jacques Derrida, *Voyous* (Paris: Galilée, 2003), ch. 1; and Michael Naas, "One Nation ... Indivisible: Jacques Derrida on the Autoimmunity of Democracy and the Sovereignty of God," unpublished paper.

[120] Lockwood, *An Informal History of the German Language*, pp. 221–3.

separations by introducing a new construction of "authenticity" grounded in race.[121] Tea merchants in eighteenth-century India noticed Sanskrit's likeness to Greek and Latin. In 1789, the London barrister William Jones observed similarities between these languages and others: Celtic, Gothic, and Old Persian. Jones hypothesized a common origin. Friedrich Schlegel in 1808 and the Berlin linguist Franz Bopp in 1816 defended Jones' hypothesis. The German philologist and Oxford professor Friedrich Max Müller (son of the Heidelberg author of Schubert's *Die Schöne Müllerin*) theorized in the 1850s that the folklore that flowed so abundantly from the pens of philologists and poets had a common "Indo-European" origin.[122] Müller translated the *Rig Veda*, which he theorized was the common source of the primitive religions of the "Aryan races." The Veda's impact on philologists was tremendous, as was its implications for discursive, mythical representations of "Europe."[123] The idea that the peoples of Europe shared common Indo-European or "Aryan" roots nourished, within the supportive ecology of Ossianic common sense, the development of "scientific racism," first adumbrated by Joseph Arthur de Gobineau in his 1853 *Essai sur l'inégalité des races humaines*. To demonstrate the superiority of the Aryan (*arya*: noble) race, Gobineau resurrected the two-peoples myth of political France. In a departure from Republican orthodoxy, however, he defended the claims of the Germanic aristocrat (of which he himself was a specimen) to a privileged political role. His work influenced Houston Stuart Chamberlain, the Englishman who emigrated to Germany under the spell of Richard Wagner. (He married Wagner's daughter, Eva, in 1908.) In 1899, Chamberlain published *Die Grundlagen des Neunzehnten Jahrhunderts* (The Foundations of the Nineteenth Century) in which he portrayed all human history as racial struggle. The Aryan race, superior by its culture and creativity, whose purest, most unsullied offshoot was the German, was the bulwark of Christian culture against the corrosive influence of Judaism (Jesus, Chamberlain explains, was not a Jew but a Galilean). The contest was in doubt, however, as the Aryan race languished under the debilitating effect of racial mixing. Adolf Hitler, who met Chamberlain in 1924, placed his theory at the center of his political project. Whereas Ossianic discourse imagined "natural" nations that, though separated by linguistic and cultural boundaries, were equal

---

[121] See Day and Thompson, *Theorizing Nationalism*, ch. 7.
[122] Thiesse, *La création des identités nationales*, p. 172.
[123] Thiesse, *La création des identités nationales*, pp. 174–6.

in honor, "scientific racism" *re-presented* the nation as the agent of race in a historic racial struggle. That struggle denied equality in honor, and subverted the frontiers of Ossianic Europe.

European Union "is about" deconstructing the Greater Rhineland frontiers as the *enabling site* of this (new, in historical perspective) auto-immune discourse of imagined authenticity. But the fact that European Union leaves intact the foundational discursive categories of "nation" and "people" preserves the autoimmunity and obscures worlds of political possibility that frontier deconstruction might open up.

8

Carolingian discourse and Rhineland pacification

The Roman roads that once led south from *Colonia Claudia Ara Agrippinensium* to *Moguntiacum*, and west to *Augusta Treverorum*, still meet at the intersection of Höhe Strasse and Schildergasse, in Cologne's "Old Town." Trains rumble across the nearby Hohenzollern Bridge, above which rise the magnificent cathedral and the striking Römisch-Germanisches Museum, a testament to Roman Cologne's brilliance. German troops marched across this bridge in 1936 to occupy the left bank in defiance of the Versailles settlement.[1] Six years later, in 1942, the Royal Air Force launched the first of more than thirty bombing raids that utterly devastated this most emblematic of Greater Rhineland cities (see plate 8.1). The bridge was rebuilt. The cathedral and the city's dozen or so Romanesque churches were painstakingly restored.[2] But many of the Old Town's historic buildings survived only as bits and pieces of masonry embedded, as a testament to Cologne's precarious geopolitics, in the metal and glass surfaces of industrial-age offspring.

Cologne's ruin culminated the disruption of western Europe's core regional economy by frontier geopolitics and the collision of mythical nations. As argued in previous chapters, that collision was the fact of an aesthetic project, conceived by poets in the eighteenth century and imposed on populations by state action in the nineteenth. That aesthetic project did not bring to light "authentic peoples," as it claimed. It simply exalted named places, ontopologies – Gallia, Germania – by molding people so as to bring to light the place, as linguistic and cultural entity, that would legitimate the political powers that were doing the molding. But ontopology located western Europe's economic core at the "edge" of named space. The core straddled the frontier. European Union in the twentieth century sought to pacify that "edge" by deconstructing the

---

[1] Hermann Kellenbenz, "Wirtschafts- und Sozialentwicklung der nördlichen Rheinlanden seit 1815," in Franz Petri and Georg Droege, eds., *Rheinische Geschichte*, vol. III, *Wirtschaft und Kultur im 19. und 20. Jahrhundert* (Düsseldorf: Schwann, 1979), p. 11.

[2] Kellenbenz, "Wirtschafts- und Sozialentwicklung der nördlichen Rheinlanden," p. 154.

Plate 8.1a Cologne, 1945 (with permission of Edition Wünnenberg)

Plate 8.1b Cologne, 2005

Greater Rhineland frontiers and, in so doing, "shifting" the economic core from the "edge" to the "center" of the place called "Europe," imagined once again, within the discursive frame of a resurrected Carolingian ontopology, as the site of a progressive political, even spiritual enterprise.

Carolingian discourse, however, failed to inspire, failed to "carry" the European project with the force and vigor with which Ossianic discourse, in the previous century, inspired the extraordinary investments in schools, monuments, museums, and citizen armies that succeeded in making "nations" "real." Carolingian discourse is not a mobilizing discourse. It was arguably never meant to be a mobilizing discourse. Rather, its role has been to facilitate diplomatic normalization, rooted not in aesthetic vision but in geopolitical urgency. Carolingian discourse, as such, has complicated the progressive project that it situates by exacerbating discursive pathologies, and by obfuscating worlds of political possibility as it points away from, rather than at, the geopolitical problem that European Union "is about."

This chapter reviews the history of European Union. It does not propose a new narrative, but highlights the importance of geopolitical urgency in the formation of the EU, and traces the reemergence of Carolingian discourse to that urgency. Nor does it propose to demonstrate the putative "role of ideas" in generating European Union. On the contrary, the purpose of this book is to interrogate the language in which European Union is discussed and crafted, and to destabilize that language as the source of pathologies that threaten the EU with delegitimation. By revealing the way in which Carolingian ontopology in the twentieth century dignified geopolitical haggling with the language of progressive purpose, by probing the tensions between Carolingian discourse and the geopolitical urgency it was enjoined to resolve, one places in question that discourse's capacity to sustain the project it frames and legitimates.

Versailles

The geopolitical urgency that governed EU construction after World War II was already driving statecraft in the interwar period. The destructions of the Great War – the *Völkerkrieg*, the *der' des der'* – made imperative the political reorganization of Greater Rhineland space. Steel, railways, chemicals, and human fertility rates, all generously supplied by the regional economy, had become the stuff of national military power. Post-war governments therefore worked to deny, control, parcel out access to the region's economic potential. Following the armistice of November 11, 1918, the French demanded the return of

Alsace-Lorraine, the demilitarization and deindustrialization of the German Rhineland, the annexation of the Saarland, and indemnification for the costs and destructions of the war. French premier Georges Clemenceau also advanced a more radical demand: the restoration of a kind of *status quo ante*, a kind of pre-unification Germany. Specifically, he called for the creation of a new state, a Rhineland Republic, forbidden by treaty from adhering to a revived German federation, but exonerated from war reparations. In spirit, Clemenceau's proposal recalled the 1815 Vienna settlement, whose purpose, in an age when Ossianic discourse had not yet become common sense, was not to secure homes for nations, but to secure a "balance" of power among states. At Vienna that discursive practice gave birth to Belgium, the Netherlands, and Luxemburg. In like fashion, Clemenceau proposed the creation of a new Belgium-like state, the Rhineland Republic, the statehood of which was legitimated not by myths of nationhood but by the functional requirement of preserving stability in the region. Viewed within the frame of Ossianic discourse, however, Clemenceau's proposal was punitive. It unmade "Germany." It denied its right to national self-determination. One can only speculate how the creation of a Rhineland Republic might have altered the *discursive* representation, and therefore the geopolitics, of Greater Rhineland space in the twentieth century.

In 1815 Vienna, Clemenceau's approach to settlement was common sense. But in 1919 Versailles it was rebuffed, ironically, by the most radically reformist government at the negotiating table, that of the United States of America. The United States entered the war in 1917 not as an ally but as an "associate" of the Triple Entente, intent on using victory not to punish the vanquished, but to reform the very nature of international relations. The Great War was, in American President Woodrow Wilson's memorable (or borrowed) phrase, the war to end all wars. But Wilson's reformism assumed unproblematically the existence of nations in the full-blown Ossianic sense of the term. For Wilson, that assumption was common sense. But common sense cramped negotiations. It dulled suspicion that the affirmation, indeed the coercive *imposition*, of the nation in the preceding generation – between 1880 and 1914 – conditioned the outbreak of war. On the contrary, Wilson claimed that war was the consequence of the denial of the *nation's* right to statehood. It was the consequence of imperial expansion and competition, frustrated nationalism and irredentism. The denial of the "right to national self-determination," an eminently deconstructible trope, bred unrest, wars of liberation, and Machiavellian maneuvering to advance imperial interests at the expense of natural but subjugated nations. Wilson's thought evinced a law-like supposition that nations, living in security behind linguistic and cultural frontiers, exercising their legitimate freedoms, would naturally coexist in peace. The nation legitimized the state, and made possible republican government, that is, government by the *peuple*, the *nation*, and participation in collective self-policing through the League of Nations. That conviction induced Wilson to claim sovereignty for the subjugated *nations* of eastern Europe: Poles, "Czecho-Slovaks," and "Yugoslavs." It also spurred Wilson to defend Germany's right to territorial integrity, while denying that of "Germans" living in Czechoslovakia, a territory "reserved" – by nature? by history? – for the "Czecho-Slovak" people.[3]

Wilson's reformist agenda reveals the extent to which the Ossianic representation of a world parceled out among autochthonous, linguistically and culturally monotonous nations had become naturalized in diplomatic discourse. Such proposals would have been incomprehensible in 1815 Vienna, not because the idea of collective security was a novel one, but because the idea of nationhood at that time held court only among poets and revolutionaries. The commonsense understanding of "nation" at the time, translating the Latin *gens*, did not dissociate "people" from the polity that gave it political organization. Nor did it legitimize political organization with reference to its emanation from a "pre-existing" people. Collective security, in the proposal of the abbé de Saint-Pierre, as revisited by Jean-Jacques Rousseau, assumed the form of an alliance among potentates, *Puissances*.[4] Kant, in his famous treatise, adumbrates the Wilsonian representation of a federation of peoples, but its members are *civitates*, not (necessarily) Ossianic nations represented as ontologically prior to the states – *civitates* or *poleis* – that organize them. The terms *international relations* and *international law* both appear *after* the Vienna

---

[3] See Sanjay Seth, "Nationalism in/and Modernity," in Joseph A. Camilleri, Anthony P. Jarvis, and Albert J. Paolini, eds., *The State in Transition* (Boulder, CO: Lynne Rienner, 1995), p. 51. See also the contemporary reaction by a German scholar, in Georg Künzel, "Deutschland und Frankreich im Spiegel der Jahrhunderte," in Rudolf Kautzsch, Walter Platzhoff, Fedor Schneider, Franz Schulz, and Georg Wolfram, eds., *Frankreich und der Rhein: Beiträge zur Geschichte und geistigen Kultur des Rheinlandes* (Frankfurt: Englert und Schloffer, 1925), pp. 85–6.

[4] Charles Irénée Castel de Saint-Pierre, "A project of perpetual peace, and rewritten later, with abbreviations, additions and modifications, by Jean-Jacques Rousseau." See Derek Heater, *The Idea of European Unity* (New York: St. Martin's Press, 1992), ch. 4. See also ch. 5 on Bentham and Saint-Simon. Rousseau portrayed the *Puissances* as the principal source of discord and violence among peoples – plural – whom geography and history naturally united, despite their diversity.

settlement, as the invention of a philosopher, Jeremy Bentham.[5] But by century's end the concepts of "nation" and "inter-national" were common sense. When Pierre de Coubertin, like Woodrow Wilson, sought to foster peace among *nations* by resurrecting the Olympic festival, he found it normal to "internationalize" the practice of the German *Turnverein*, the nineteenth-century gymnastic club that cultivated *national* solidarity.

Ossianic discourse had assumed such authority by the early twentieth century that it was informing new, revolutionary interpretations of international law. Nathaniel Berman draws striking parallels between, on the one hand, a new international legal "primitivism," the source of which was the assumption that the earth was populated by autochthonous peoples endowed with pre-customary, pre-rational claims on world political society, and, on the other hand, the fascination with folk (*Volk*) art that characterized the revolutionary work of such artists as Picasso, Kandinsky, and Stravinsky. The parallels suggest "an overlapping series of cultural desires pervasive in early-twentieth-century culture." Both art and legal scholarship evince a similar "critique of representation," which, for international lawyers, "took the form of a rejection of so-called 'international legal positivism' – that is, the notion that established sovereign states were the sole source of international legal authority and that the relationships between sovereigns constituted that law's sole subject matter."[6] The Ossianic celebration of "roots" affected international legal thought as it did artistic innovation.

Ossianic ontopology survived its trial at Versailles. Great Britain supported Wilson on the German question. Though skeptical of his idealism, the British opposed the creation of a Rhineland Republic for reasons of Vienna-like geopolitical balance. Britain's policy toward the Greater Rhineland, since 1815, had been one of balancing the principal military powers against each other. The French, facing American and British resistance, tried to strengthen their hand by stationing troops at key bridgeheads on the Rhine. But the need for American financial aid negated their military advantage. Bolshevik revolutions in Russia, Germany, and Hungary, and social unrest at home, further weakened

---

[5] The *jus gentium* of the Romans made no claims regarding the foundational status of "nations." *Gens* can mean clan, family, class, status. See Marc Crépon, Barbara Cassin, and Claudia Moatti, "Peuple," in Barbara Cassin, ed., *Vocabulaire européen des philosophies* (Paris: Seuil, Dictionnaires Le Robert, 2004), pp. 918–31.

[6] Nathaniel Berman, "Modernism, Nationalism, and the Rhetoric of Reconstruction," in Cecelia Lynch and Michael Loriaux, eds., *Law and Moral Action in World Politics* (Minneapolis: University of Minnesota Press, 2000). Passages quoted on pp. 109, 111, 117.

their position. Clemenceau therefore accepted Britain's proposal to abandon the Rhineland Republic in exchange for a British–American security guarantee, a thirty-year military occupation of the left bank of the Rhine, the creation of a demilitarized zone extending 50 kilometers into the right bank, and on-site inspections to assure German compliance. The proposal gave France control of the Rhine, which was essential in the eyes of the French military: "If you are master of the Rhine you are master of the whole country. But if you are not on the Rhine, you have lost everything."[7]

Although American reformism had the ironic effect of ratifying Ossianic discourse, American isolationism, a nationalist posture, had the ironic effect of problematizing it. Isolationism pushed the French toward more radical designs that *deconstructed* national frontiers. When, in April 1920, German troops intervened in the Ruhr – in the demilitarized zone – to quell a revolutionary uprising, the French cried foul and crossed the Rhine. Both Great Britain and the United States protested. But the United States relinquished much of its influence over France when, in November 1920, the Republican Party's victory at the polls signaled a dramatic shift in American policy. An isolationist Senate rejected both the Versailles treaty and the tripartite security agreement. The new administration refused requests for supplementary aid from its allies and rejected proposals to alter international trade and financial arrangements so as to speed economic reconstruction in Europe. Change in US policy also caused the British to withdraw from the tripartite alliance.

Without the alliance the French looked more than ever to their presence on the Rhine and to the material constraints that reparations placed on Germany's recovery to assure their security. In March 1921, the French accused the Germans of defaulting on reparations and, with Belgian support, crossed the Rhine again, occupying Düsseldorf, Duisburg, and Ruhrort. Raymond Poincaré, named prime minister in 1922, reinforced the power-political thrust of French policy. As a Lorraine native and former general counsel of the French steel trust,

---

[7] Henry Blumenthal, *Illusion and Reality in Franco-American Diplomacy, 1914–1918* (Baton Rouge: Louisiana State University Press, 1986), p. 78. The author of the citation is French military commander Ferdinand Foch. See *passim* pp. 74–86. The final agreement retained the demilitarized zone but reduced the term of occupation to fifteen years. It also united the Saarland to France through a customs union, but placed it under the protection of the League of Nations and stipulated that inhabitants would determine their final status by referendum.

the Comité des Forges, Poincaré was keenly aware of the geopolitical importance of the Rhineland. Despite US objections, France and Belgium sent military "control missions" into the Ruhr in January 1923, which they justified by Germany's failure to make good on reparations payments ... of wood and telephone poles. Germans called a general strike. The occupation forces expelled tens of thousands of workers, imported French and Belgian miners, commandeered railways, and drowned demonstrations in blood. They entered into informal contact with German Rhineland separatists to explore anew the possibility of a break-away Rhineland Republic. After meeting with French and Belgian occupation officials and members of the French government, Hans Dorten, a separatist leader, proclaimed the creation of a Rhineland Republic in Aachen in October 1923. The Poincaré government did not formally endorse the initiative, but it did enter into negotiations with the mayor of Cologne, Konrad Adenauer, to develop a regionally specific and therefore separatist solution to the monetary crisis provoked by the occupation and strike. Although Adenauer was Dorten's rival, his good relations with the British raised French hopes that the move might win British approval. But the stabilization of the German mark and uncompromising British opposition to the separatist republic caused the French to withdraw their support in December, and the movement was repressed.[8]

The occupation of the Ruhr, however, did stir the Americans to forsake their isolationism, not because of its military implications but because of its potential impact on American business. French coal and steel moguls, having enjoyed a cordial relationship with their German counterparts for decades (see chapter 7), were suggesting that the answer to France's security challenges lay not in French militarism, but in Franco-German economic cooperation. Representatives of the French Comité des Forges had already approached the Verein Deutscher Eisen- und Stahlindustrieller before the occupation in order to explore solutions to both the specific problem of reparations and the more general challenge of Rhineland geopolitics. Jacques Seydoux of the French Ministry of Foreign Affairs supported the initiative. The Comité des Forges proposed that the reparations debt be paid by transferring Ruhr coal mines to French steel firms. When the Germans protested, the Comité des Forges followed with a second, more acceptable plan that called for the transfer of a smaller number of mines and

---

[8] See Celia Applegate, *A Nation of Provincials: The German Idea of Heimat* (Berkeley and Los Angeles: University of California Press, 1990), pp. 140–8.

long-term contracts between French and German firms to supply French mills with German coke in exchange for German purchases of French semi-finished goods. The plan would also have created a Franco-German-British-Belgian cartel for steel rails.[9] The proposal, in substance, foreshadowed the 1951 Treaty of Paris which created the European Coal and Steel Community. More generally it adumbrated the deconstruction of the Rhineland frontiers through the unification of economic space. National steel industries, nationally managed and integrated economically and strategically in national space, would become regional steel industries, regionally managed and integrated economically and strategically in Greater Rhineland regional space.

The proposal alarmed American industrialists. The French occupation of the *Ruhrgebiet* compounded that alarm. To counter the French initiative, Charles Schwab, president of the Bethlehem Steel Corporation, proposed purchasing German steel firms outright. American business concerns goaded the administration to set aside its isolationism and counter the threat with a workable reparations plan. Henry Blumenthal writes:

> Disturbing as [the immediate economic] consequences of the occupation were, they paled by comparison with the potential problems growing out of the gigantic struggle for control of the steel industry. As long as neither France nor Germany singly controlled the coal, iron, and steel plants of the Rhine, Ruhr, and Saar regions, their industrial, military, and political power remained limited. As matters now stood, full control of all these resources by France, or by a combination of France and Germany with France in the driver's seat, promised to assure the French the "security" they coveted. For whoever was absolute master of this region was in a geopolitical position to guide the destiny of Europe. Indeed, by seizing the Ruhr, France threatened not only the interests of Germany, but those of England and the United States as well. France would be able to compete with their steel industries and act in the world-political arena with greater independence from them than in the past. Henceforth, the policies of Britain and the United States, and those of the American steel industry, would strive to block the emergence of such a colossal competitor.[10]

In a February 27, 1923, letter to Secretary of State Charles Hughes, the US ambassador to Germany, Alanson B. Houghton, criticized isolationism

---

[9] Stephen A. Schuker, *The End of French Predominance in Europe* (Chapel Hill: University of North Carolina Press, 1976), pp. 222–9.

[10] Blumenthal, *Illusion and Reality in Franco-American Diplomacy*, p. 120.

and advocated active American involvement in Greater Rhineland politics.

> Having destroyed any balance of power in Europe and left France for the moment all powerful, we have simply let loose a *great elemental force* which inevitably seeks to satisfy itself. France must be met by force. One might as well attempt to reason with *the law of gravitation*. I believe sincerely if it is to America's interest to save what is left of German capital and German industry some positive action is required without too much delay.[11]

The language of the American ambassador to Germany, with its allusions to "balance" and "gravitation," reprised the imagery of German *Realpolitik*, a discourse that emerged to make "real" and "present" the mythical ontologies of Ossianic discourse (see chapter 7). The ambassador was exhorting the government to intervene to preserve commonsense ontopology by opposing the peril of reform in the organization of Rhineland space by the "realist" physics of Ossianic atavism.

Despite the fact that the recommendation's purpose was to put an end to the French initiative, Poincaré welcomed it. The occupation was straining French finances, and the franc was faltering on currency markets. For their part, the Germans had been working to enlist American involvement since 1921. German Chancellor Gustav Stresemann recognized that the surest means of regaining sovereignty over the Rhineland was to cling to US and British diplomacy. Stresemann therefore welcomed an international loan, floated by the United States, as "the only means of alleviating the situation" in the Ruhr.[12] Early in 1924, the German Foreign Ministry speculated that "if the United States could somehow be persuaded to invest large sums of idle and unproductive money in German industry, not only would Germany's capitalistic system benefit, but its economic recovery and the revision of the Versailles treaty would almost certainly be accelerated."[13]

American banker Charles Dawes, chairman of the board of directors of the Chicago Central Union Trust Company, and Owen D. Young, chairman of the board of General Electric, worked to develop a reparations payment scheme that would banish the plan of the Comité des Forges from polite conversation. Their scheme, characterized as "business, not politics," provided temporary relief pending a definitive reparation payments

---

[11] Blumenthal, *Illusion and Reality in Franco-American Diplomacy*, p. 118. Emphasis added.
[12] Blumenthal, *Illusion and Reality in Franco-American Diplomacy*, p. 119.
[13] Blumenthal, *Illusion and Reality in Franco-American Diplomacy*, pp. 130–1.

schedule, the reorganization of German finances, and the French evacuation of the Ruhr. It instructed the German government to proceed with a 5 billion mark bond issue, the principal purchasers of which would be American financiers. German manufacturing plant would provide the collateral for the loan, and the interest would be paid with revenues from the German railways. Germany agreed, and the plan was endorsed by the London conference in July 1924. Edouard Herriot, who succeeded Raymond Poincaré as prime minister, made one last effort to parlay military advantage on the ground into a bilateral agreement with Germany that shortened the occupation in exchange for arms controls and a bilateral trade treaty. But German negotiators refused, knowing that America's involvement could secure the withdrawal of French troops without German concessions. The House of Morgan and the governor of the Bank of England in effect made clear to the French that they "could not advance sizable loans to Germany [to facilitate reparations payments] unless unilateral sanctions were banned in the future."[14] The French, financially strapped and hounded by speculators, withdrew from the Ruhr in 1925, and agreed to withdraw from the left bank by 1929, five years ahead of the schedule established at Versailles. The 1929 (Owen D.) Young Plan ratified and refined the Dawes Plan by scheduling annuities over a period of fifty-nine years and creating the Bank for International Settlements (BIS) to facilitate and supervise the operation. Dean of contemporary "international" organizations, set significantly in Basle on the banks of the Rhine, the BIS materialized the link between Rhineland geopolitics and Wilson-style "inter-national" organization. Not unlike German unification under Bismarck, its unstated purpose was not to promote integration through frontier deconstruction, but to make frontier deconstruction unnecessary – to preserve the common sense that Ossianic discourse had become.

The reemergence of Carolingian discourse

The Dawes Plan transformed the diplomatic landscape. For Stephen Schuker, it signaled "the end of French predominance in Europe."[15] For the French, America's reengagement in Greater Rhineland geopolitics did not alleviate, but aggravated geopolitical urgency. They now explored ways to pacify the frontier that were compatible with the new discursive

---

[14] Blumenthal, *Illusion and Reality in Franco-American Diplomacy*, p. 135.
[15] Schuker, *The End of French Predominance*. Dawes and Austen Chamberlain were awarded the Nobel Peace Prize in 1925.

universe of "inter-national" organization, and within the new power-political environment created by American economic and political involvement. At Locarno in the autumn of 1925, France, Germany, and Belgium agreed to establish a demilitarized zone along the Rhine while acknowledging Germany's right to national self-determination by admitting it to the League of Nations. Aristide Briand, French foreign minister, sought to "show France's good will in order to favor 'moral disarmament' in Germany; to incite the German government to abandon any idea of an agreement with Soviet Russia and to admit to collaboration with the western powers; and finally to pave the way toward some '*European organization in economic affairs.*'"[16] In 1926, at an informal meeting with Briand in the French town of Thoiry, Stresemann offered to speed reparations payments in exchange for an accelerated evacuation of the Rhineland. In June 1927, Briand sought to infuse the spirit of Locarno in relations with the United States by proposing that both countries solemnly renounce war as an instrument of policy in their mutual relations. The Kellogg–Briand pact is perhaps the most notorious expression of interwar inter-nationalism, but for Briand it was a means to a more concrete end: that of improving relations with America following the conflict of 1924, and winning greater understanding of France's geopolitical anxieties.[17]

Such efforts in time made discernible and/or abetted and sanctioned the reemergence of Carolingian discourse, which helps frame frontier deconstruction in present-day Europe. In 1929, Briand proposed, with Stresemann's approval, a more radical reorganization of Greater Rhineland political space modeled on the Swiss confederation. For Briand, the League of Nations was "too vast and weak. The treaties of Locarno too limited and too directly linked to the bad treaties of 1919."[18]

> The more Briand contemplated the League, for all his deep commitment to it, the more he was conscious of its weaknesses. At the same time, the amelioration of Franco-German relations was proceeding apace with agreements on reparations and the evacuation of the Rhineland. By 1929 he had therefore come to the conclusions that the need to strengthen the League was urgent while the atmosphere of amity in Europe rendered further collaboration possible. The two considerations converged in his

---

[16] Pierre Renouvin, *Les crises du XXe siècle*, vol. I, *De 1914 à 1929* (Paris: Hachette, 1969), p. 259.

[17] Blumenthal, *Illusion and Reality in Franco-American Diplomacy*, pp. 164–5.

[18] Henri Brugmans, *L'idée européenne, 1920–1970* (Bruges: De Tempel, 1966), p. 54.

proposal for a European regional union within the framework of the League of Nations.[19]

Briand used the signifier "Europe" to refer to a discursive site that enabled imaginative thinking about ways to pacify the Greater Rhineland. In 1931, when Germany and Austria raised the possibility of entering into a bilateral tariff union, France, rather than ignore the geopolitical significance of the proposal, as it had done in a similar situation a century earlier, suggested that the initiative apply to all "Europe," whereby "the further pursuit of the Austro-German plan would become super-fluous."[20] "Europe" as signifier framed France's objection.

Briand's European confederation gestured toward an ontopological site that, by its history, was called upon to *transcend* the nation and assert its *common* political and cultural identity. The war had brought new life to Carolingian ontopology. After falling from use in the thirteenth century, Europe as signifier was resurrected in the sixteenth century by William of Orange, who commanded that it be used in propaganda pamphlets instead of *Christianitas* in order to deny legitimacy to the myth of imperial unity.[21] Dissociated from its Carolingian significance, "Europe" entered modernist discourse as the named place within which to imagine state sovereignty and the various ways to institutionalize and pacify that sovereignty, a meaning the term retains today, and which endows it with a distinctive polysemy.[22] But between 1920 and 1950 the term began to evoke once again a "Carolingian" connotation as site of a salvationist project, as the abominable losses of war stung literati, businessmen, and public figures to interrogate "Europe"'s future. There is "salvationism" in Kant, but there is no European specificity – no election of "place" for humanity's growth in reason. By contrast, the signifier "Europe" in the twentieth century began to connote just such an "election," as ontopology designated by its legacy of accomplishment and

---

[19] Heater, *The Idea of European Unity*, p. 132. The actual text was written by Briand's *chef de cabinet*, Alexis Saint-Léger, who would become the poet-diplomat and Nobel laureate Saint-John Perse.

[20] Blumenthal, *Illusion and Reality in Franco-American Diplomacy*, p. 140. Blumenthal argues that this was a theme in a long-range plan to contain and diminish "Anglo-Saxon" penetration in Europe. That may well be, but concern with Anglo-Saxon penetration was linked to anxieties over Greater Rhineland geopolitics, and to the inability of the "Anglo-Saxons" to grasp those anxieties or take them seriously.

[21] Etienne Balibar, *Nous, citoyens de l'Europe?* (Paris: Découverte, 2001), p. 22.

[22] See Heater, *The Idea of European Unity*, for a history of Europe as site of an organized, pacified, sovereignty system.

tragedy to become the ground of a new political experiment in moral betterment.[23]

Groups such as Neues Vaterland, founded in Berlin in 1914, and De Europeesche Staatenbond, founded the same year in the Netherlands, challenged the "inevitable fact" of war and called for Europe's "supra-national unification." After the war, Walther Rathenau, industrialist, consultant to Ludendorff and Hindenburg, and, following Germany's defeat, a founder of the left-leaning German Democratic Party, appealed to Europe's youth to "replace international anarchy by a voluntarily accepted higher authority" that he located in a united Europe.[24] Literary figures such as Jules Romain, novelist and popular playwright of the interwar period, and Ortega y Gasset, philosopher and essayist whose widely translated *Revolt of the Masses* advanced an elitist critique of European mass society, deplored the "civil war" that had ripped the fabric of Europe's "homogeneous civilization." Derek Heater describes the "veritable torrent of publications advocating European political union [that] poured from the presses at this time, both journal articles and books." He cites Gaston Riou, active in the European Economic and Customs Union, who authored *Europe, ma patrie* (1928) and *S'unir ou mourir* (1929), the diplomat Carlo Count Sforza, author of *Les Etats-Unis d'Europe* (1930), and Edouard Herriot, author of *Europe* (1930).[25] Paul Valéry, poet and member of the League of Nations' Committee of Letters and Arts, lamented the decline of Europe and the rise to prominence of peripheral powers, America and Russia. Albert Demangeon published the widely read *Le déclin de l'Europe*. With historian Lucien Febvre, a founder of the *Annales* school of historiography, which abandoned the grand narratives of nationhood in favor of regionally circumscribed or transnational social history, Demangeon wrote one of the classic historical geographies of the Rhine.[26] François Delaisi, an economist whose *Les contradictions du monde* enjoyed great success, argued that national frontiers and national policies impeded economic development. In the business world, Emile Mayrisch, a Luxemburger leader of the Greater Rhineland steel industry, actively

---

[23] Or, more precisely, Europe became the site of a collective experiment in "self"-betterment. The sense of election turned inward, rather than outward toward Europe's colonial, "civilizing" mission.

[24] Walter Lipgens, *A History of European Integration*, trans. P. S. Falla and A. J. Ryder (Oxford: Clarendon Press, 1982), p. 37. Rathenau, Jewish and internationalist, was assassinated in 1922.

[25] Heater, *The Idea of European Unity*, p. 124.

[26] Albert Demangeon and Lucien Febvre, *Le Rhin: problèmes d'histoire et d'économie* (Paris: Armand Colin, 1935). See Heater, *The Idea of European Unity*, ch. 6, on Coudenhove.

supported the cause of European integration. The international reformist Norman Angell argued that a European Federation of States was necessary to the success of the League of Nations. Leading political figures such as Léon Blum in France and Luigi Einaudi in Italy advocated European integration, like Aristide Briand, as a response to the League's lack of political authority and power.

The principal voice of European federalism during the interwar period was that of Count Richard Coudenhove-Kalergi, organizer of the Paneuropean Union in 1923. Coudenhove-Kalergi feared Europe's diminishing role in world affairs and deplored the economic costs of nationalism. The Union was an elitist organization that assembled an impressive number of statesmen, politicians, scientists, and businessmen. Aristide Briand presided (his 1931 proposal before the League was not, therefore, a fortuitous inspiration). The Federal Chancellor and Vice-Chancellor of Austria served on its executive committee. Paul Löbe, president of the *Reichstag*, Erich Koch-Weser, president of the German Democratic Party, and Joseph Koeth, minister of agriculture, directed the German section. The executive board of the French section included Louis Loucheur, minister of finance and commerce, Léon Blum, Socialist leader and future prime minister, and Joseph Barthélemy, minister of justice.

Within weeks of Stresemann's death in 1929, the crash on Wall Street brought new urgency to Greater Rhineland geopolitics. Repatriation of capital by American financiers provoked bank failures in Austria and Germany, prompting President Herbert Hoover to propose a one-year moratorium on intergovernmental debts and reparations. The French demanded that the moratorium not jeopardize the principle of reparations, and adamantly opposed any suggestion that they be abolished. To do so, claimed Pierre Laval, a Socialist colleague of Briand, "would put German industry in such a favorable position compared with France, England, or America that we would all regret it."[27] France, moreover, refused to join an international effort to redress the financial position of Austria because of its opposition to the proposed German–Austrian customs union. That diplomatic crisis forced Briand from office in January 1932. At the Lausanne conference of June 1932, a new reparations scheme based on a Franco-American compromise was approved, but rejected by the American Congress.

---

[27] Blumenthal, *Illusion and Reality in Franco-American Diplomacy*, p. 158. Laval would become a Nazi collaborator in 1940 in response to his conviction that Germany would ultimately be victorious.

The realization of Carolingian ontopology

Renewed crisis and war lent new authority to Carolingian ontopology. When war broke out, French leaders Edouard Daladier, prime minister and signatory of the Munich Accords, and Paul Reynaud, Daladier's successor and opponent of Munich (who, as prime minister in 1940, would name Charles de Gaulle as minister of war), both proposed, once again, the creation of new, specifically European organizations within the League of Nations. Clement Attlee, Labour leader and a member of Winston Churchill's wartime coalition cabinet, argued that Europe must federate or perish. Edward Hallett Carr, formerly of the British Foreign Ministry and author of *The Twenty Years Crisis*, advanced that the reconstruction of post-war Europe would require a pan-European framework, and proposed the creation of a European Planning Authority.[28] Even in the United States, an advisory committee in the US State Department argued in May 1940 that "there must be in Europe such derogation to the sovereignty of states that quick and decisive action" by a supranational European authority would be possible. The Catholic Association for International Peace advanced a similar proposal in 1941, as did the New York Council on Foreign Relations in 1942.[29] The theme of European federation was "taken up by [non-communist] Resistance groups in country after country with an astonishing degree of unanimity."[30] The Lyons resistance proposed a program that could be reasonably compared with the 1992 Maastricht Treaty on European Union. It called upon national states

> to federate and transfer to the common federal state the right to manage the economic and commercial life of Europe, the sole authority over its armed forces and the right to take measures against any attempt to reestablish a fascist regime. The federation must also have the right to manage foreign relations and to administer colonial territories not ripe for independence, and the right to create a European citizenship in addition to national citizenship. The government of the federal state is to be chosen not by the nation-states but by democratic and direct elections by the peoples.[31]

[28] Carr's interest in some transnational organization in Europe problematizes his reputation in the US as a realist. The proposal is advanced in his work *Conditions of Peace* (New York: Macmillan, 1942).

[29] Lipgens, *A History of European Integration*, p. 66.

[30] Lipgens, *A History of European Integration*, p. 56.

[31] Document quoted in Lipgens, *A History of European Integration*, p. 52.

Following the war, Paul-Henri Spaak, Belgian minister of foreign affairs, spearheaded the first successful effort to deconstruct frontiers in the Greater Rhineland by establishing an economic union between Belgium, the Netherlands, and Luxemburg. But formal proposals for "European" unification advanced by Spaak and the Italian political leader Alcide de Gasperi in 1945 met with British and French (that is, Gaullist) skepticism. Roman Catholic intellectuals and statesmen like de Gasperi had become strong advocates of European federalism. Roman Catholicism, which emerged as spatial entity with the *coup de force* that begat Carolingian ontopology, had never entirely reconciled itself to the nation-state order. Moreover, the development of Catholic social thought in the late nineteenth and early twentieth centuries was causing many Catholic intellectuals to rethink their politics. Alexandre Marc, an influential literary figure, student of Charles Péguy, and member of the editorial staffs of *Temps Présent* and *Témoignage Chrétien,* was one of the leading figures of the interwar *renouveau catholique* in France.[32] With Henri Daniel-Rops, novelist, religious historian, and author of a best-selling *Jésus et son temps,* he advanced the cause of European federalism in the progressive Dominican journal *Sept.* In the resistance, Marc distributed *La Voix du Vatican* and worked with Albert Camus' clandestine journal *Combat,* as well as with the banned *Cahiers du Témoignage Chrétien.*[33] Catholic intellectuals like Marc grounded their federalism in a moral and political doctrine called *personnalisme communautaire,* or simply *personnalisme,* which inveighed against both the atomizing individualism of modern capitalist society and the annihilation of the individual by totalitarian regimes, and held both responsible for war in the twentieth century. The movement located the legitimate sources of political authority not in the abstract entity of "humanity in a state of nature," but in the "living communities" of society – the parish, the municipality, the region – and warned against the destructive effects of liberal ideology. Federalists admonished Europeans to resist the expansionism of the two world powers, the United States and the Soviet Union, and the materialist ideologies they championed, which threatened to undermine "Europe's" spiritual inheritance.[34]

---

[32] Marc and other Catholic reformers had flirted with more corporatist or fascist interpretations of the "third way" during the interwar period. The foundation of the left-leaning review *Esprit* was a watershed event that saw many Catholic reformists, such as Emmanuel Mounier, move to the left, while others, such as Marc, remain within the more corporatist ideological frame of *Ordre Nouveau.*

[33] Lipgens, *A History of European Integration,* p. 316.

[34] Lipgens, *A History of European Integration,* p. 349.

[Individualism] is a metaphysics of integral solitude, the only solitude that remains for us when we have lost truth, the world, and the community of men ... Can I use the word *I* in the case of this abstract individual, noble savage and solitary wanderer, without a past, without a future, without attachment, without flesh, on whom blows the fire of a Pentecost that does not unite, that of "sovereign liberty"? ... The average western man was constructed by a resurgent individualism, around a metaphysics, a moral philosophy, and a practice of *making claims*. The person is no longer a service in a society, a center of growth and of giving, but a cauldron of envy ... The human universe has disintegrated into a dust of closed worlds: professions, classes, nations, economic interests. There are not even frontiers that enable contact between them. All their force is focused inward, infinities separate them ... A *person* is not a bundle of claims turned inward within the bounds of an arbitrary frontier and some anxious desire for affirmation ... It is a nervous creative force within the framework of a human communion where all creation glorifies, where all mastery serves. It is liberty to begin anew, a hearth of beginnings, a first step toward the world, a promise of many friendships, an offer of oneself. One only finds oneself in losing oneself. One only owns that which one loves. Neither claim nor abandon: we reject the evil of the East and the evil of the West. But a criss-cross movement of appropriation and gift.[35]

Emmanuel Mounier, author of these lines and director of the influential review *Esprit* until his death in 1948, was the movement's principal philosophical inspiration. Jacques Maritain, the celebrated Thomist philosopher, lent support. But *personnalisme* transcended the world of Catholic social thought and embraced such figures as the Swiss Protestant theologian Karl Barth; the essayist, historian, and leading figure in the Jewish–Christian dialogue Robert Aron; the Swiss Protestant Denis de Rougemont; and the Russian Orthodox philosopher Nicolas Berdiaeff.[36] The phenomenologist Emmanuel Levinas, having introduced the work of Edmund Husserl and Martin Heidegger to a French audience, developed his Talmud-informed ethical philosophy in the pages of this same journal. Catholic and non-Catholic advocates of *personnalisme* organized the European Federalist Movement in France under the presidency of the Catholic industrialist Jacques Bassot. Its journal, *Fédération*, appeared in November 1944. Alexandre Marc,

---

[35] Emmanuel Mounier, *Refaire la Renaissance* (Paris: Seuil, 1961), pp. 62–6 *passim*.
[36] Lipgens, *A History of European Integration*, p. 350. Mounier, however, wrote little on international topics.

Daniel-Rops, the Catholic existentialist philosopher Gabriel Marcel, and the liberal economist and political theorist Bertrand de Jouvenel, all contributed to the journal's first issue.

Although the European Federalist Movement gave clear expression to a resurrected Carolingian discourse, other less philosophically oriented organizations also lent salience and authority to a reemergent Carolingian ontopology, to Europe as a community of fate, of *telos*. Winston Churchill called for the construction of "a kind of United States of Europe" in a 1946 speech in Zurich, and praised Richard Coudenhove-Kalergi's Paneuropean Union and Aristide Briand's vision of a European confederation. He urged that Europeans consent to "an act of faith in the European family," and called upon France and Germany, tied by their shared history of enmity, to assume leadership in unifying the continent. Churchill created a United Europe Committee (UEC) and assigned to his son-in-law Duncan Sandys the task of animating it. Paul van Zeeland, former prime minister and former minister of foreign affairs of Belgium, created the Independent League of European Cooperation, composed primarily of industrialists and bankers. Coudenhove-Kalergi formed the European Parliamentary Union (EPU) in 1947, which attracted an impressive collection of political leaders, including Vincent Auriol, president of the French National Assembly (and soon president of the Republic), Luigi Einaudi, who would become president of the Italian Republic in 1948, and former French prime minister Paul Reynaud.[37] Meanwhile, Social Democrats founded the Democratic and Socialist Movement for the United States of Europe, and Christian Democrats created the Nouvelles Equipes Internationales. Federalist movements met in September at Hertenstein, near Lucerne, to create the Union of European Federalists (UEF). The Hertenstein program called for the creation of a European Community whose members would transfer "a part of their sovereign, economic, political, and military rights" to the federation. It called for systematic social and constitutional reforms, informed by personalist philosophy.[38] Toward the end of 1947, the various federalist groups established a coordinating committee to prepare a European Congress in the Hague, scheduled for May 1948, and placed under the honorary chairmanship of Winston Churchill.

---

[37] Lipgens, *A History of European Integration*, p. 439.
[38] Lipgens, *A History of European Integration*, p. 595.

Despite widespread enthusiasm for some form of European federation, the diplomatic context of the immediate post-war period was not supportive. The Roosevelt administration opposed European federalism in order to keep the Soviet alliance alive. "As a result of the sudden change in American post-war planning decided on by Roosevelt in 1943, in October of that year the leaders of the two new world powers were united in the intention ... not to allow Europe any weight of its own in the future peace organization."[39] Some federalist parties, like the Dutch People's Movement (NVB), collapsed. Others, like France's Christian Democratic Mouvement Républicain Populaire, compromised their ideals in the exercise of state power. Post-war diplomacy focused on dismantling Germany, not constructing "Europe." But geopolitical urgency, provoked by incompatible demands regarding the political reorganization of the German nation, would soon lend new authority to Carolingian discourse as a site of deliberation and consensus.

In contrast to the Versailles negotiations, discussions of post-World War II Germany were all predicated on the denial of the German people's right to self-determination. In October 1945, Charles de Gaulle, leader of the French Provisional Government, demanded, as had Georges Clemenceau in 1919, that the Rhineland be organized as a separate state which, though independent, would be supervised by an international authority made up of French, British, and Benelux representatives. The new state would have its own currency and trade policy, but its foreign supervisors were to assure that its mineral wealth went to pay reparations and help reconstruct the allied economies. De Gaulle's stance was shared by other governments. Stalin demanded the break-up of Germany into three smaller states: the Rhineland, Bavaria, and North Germany. Churchill proposed the creation of a south German "Danubian Federation" that would have included Bavaria, Baden-Württemberg, and the Palatinate. The Americans, in stark contrast with their position at Versailles, now advanced the most radical of all proposals, the Morgenthau Plan, which would have divided Germany into two independent states, northern and southern, and awarded France the territory bounded by the Rhine and Moselle rivers: Mainz, the Palatinate, and Saarland. The plan would have internationalized the *Ruhrgebiet* and all lands north of the Moselle and the Main, and west of the Weser, in order to shut Germany's mines

---

[39] Lipgens, *A History of European Integration*, p. 75.

Figure 8.1 The Morgenthau Plan

Source: Henry Morgenthau, Jr., *Germany is Our Problem* (New York: Harper, 1945).

and remove its industrial plant to allied countries (see figure 8.1). The Ruhr, "the heart of German industrial power ... should not only be stripped of all presently existing industries but so weakened and controlled that it cannot in the foreseeable future become an industrial area."[40]

---

[40] Henry Morgenthau, Jr., *Germany Is Our Problem* (New York: Harper, 1945). The memorandum, unpaginated, figures as preface to this book.

But the United States' deteriorating relations with the Soviet Union soon moved the Americans to view Germany in a more sympathetic light, as the territorial anchor of their effort to "contain" Soviet power. American success depended on economic recovery in the German Rhineland. In May 1946 the Allied Control Council limited German industrial production to half its 1938 level. But the United States stopped dismantling factories, and in December merged its occupation zone economically with that of the British. The French refused to comply and, as an occupying power, blocked further moves toward German reunification. It had already rejected specific proposals to coordinate economic reconstruction in the three western occupation zones in 1945, insisting that the Rhineland and the Ruhr be placed under separate administration. "The French veto was perhaps the first postwar example of France's capacity for surprising its allies by bold use of such power as it possessed to promote its distinctive policies."[41]

In opposing reunification the French sought not only to deny German military access to Rhineland resources, but to use German resources to modernize their own economy. Their defeat in May 1940 was, they reasoned, the consequence of general economic and social stagnation. They now planned to use victory to infuse economic life with new dynamism, with the help of American money, German coke, and access to Germany's former markets. Jean Monnet, who within a few years would become the most energetic and compelling advocate of European integration, authored the government's Modernization and Reequipment Plan of March 1946. As Alan Milward explains, the Plan was predicated on the maintenance of restrictions on German economic activity.

> If the Monnet Plan was to be fully realizable, [it required] permanently maintaining the German economy at so low a level of industrial output as to guarantee the availability for the future, not just of the 3 million tonnes of coke and 1.8 million tonnes of coking coal on which the French steel industry had depended before the war, but of at least twice those quantities. Far from being based on a liberal internationalism, the Monnet Plan was based on the crudest possible expression of mercantilist principles. It was aimed at seizing German resources in order to capture German markets.[42]

---

[41] A. W. DePorte, *Europe between the Superpowers: The Enduring Balance* (New Haven: Yale University Press, 1979), p. 146.

[42] Alan Milward, *The Reconstruction of Western Europe, 1945–51* (Berkeley: University of California Press, 1985), p. 137.

In this context, German economic unification meant German demand for coal and coke sorely wanted in France, and the prospect of German dominance in markets that France wanted to enter.

When civil war in Greece spurred the United States to press harder for German unification as a bulwark against Soviet expansion, George Marshall, in a context of growing political and economic anxiety in Europe, proposed financial support for European reconstruction. Marshall hoped not only to stave off impending monetary crisis but to make German unification palatable to the French by subjecting it to multilateral supervision by a Committee for European Economic Cooperation (CEEC), created for the purpose of allocating the money. The proposal, however, did not put French fears to rest, particularly as German production allowances were again revised upward in August.

It is in this context that the idea of Europe, as a "project" of progressive politics, left the conference halls of the federalists and became a central part of diplomatic negotiations. March 1948 was a month of high international tension. The Soviets were denying western access to Berlin. France, Great Britain, and the Benelux had just signed a treaty of defensive alliance, the Brussels Pact. The inaugural meeting of the CEEC, scheduled for April, was compromised by enduring disputes over the "German question," despite the fact that the Soviet Union's exit from the Allied Control Council gutted any power the French might still have had to halt German recovery and unification. The Congress of Europe was scheduled for May. At this dramatic moment, Jean Monnet advanced a bold proposal that pointed to a sea-change in French thinking. Though the signifier "Europe" scarcely appeared in early iterations of his modernization plan, he appealed publicly, in April 1948, for the creation of a "federation of the west" as a moral and political mission.[43] For Alan Milward, "the suddenness, boldness, and timing of [the] declaration strongly suggest that the ideas had come from America. The Marshall Aid legislation had just passed through Congress and the Economic Cooperation Agency was optimistically preparing the way for the OEEC [successor to the CEEC] to become the first step towards a Western European federation."[44] Monnet was close to American leaders, having "carefully cultivated" friends on Wall Street and in Washington during the war years.[45] These included Dean

---

[43] Alan Milward, *The European Rescue of the Nation-State* (Berkeley and Los Angeles: University of California Press, 1992), p. 335.

[44] Milward, *The European Rescue of the Nation-State*, p. 335.

[45] Milward, *The European Rescue of the Nation-State*, p. 333.

Acheson, Foster Dulles, George Ball, and John J. McCloy. He was also close to Konrad Adenauer. Nevertheless, however reasonable Milward's suspicions, Monnet's experience as Adjunct General Secretary of the League of Nations and, during the war, as director of allied economic planning, suggests he did not need (though he may well have received) American encouragement to think outside the frame of a narrowly conceived national interest. The proposal did not initially receive much attention. But within months it became the point at which geopolitical urgency and renascent Carolingian ontopology met to indicate a way out of the crisis.

The Marshall Plan gave the European project new authority. Alexandre Marc wrote in reaction to Marshall's proposal: "Our cause, after being dismissed as a utopia by so-called realists, is now suddenly the focus of political attention. The federal cause is in the very forefront of political actuality."[46] The Congress of Europe in April drew eight hundred participants representing most of the countries of western Europe. Konrad Adenauer led a large German delegation. Debate was heated, but the Congress agreed to press for the "exercise in common" of state sovereignty. In June 1948, the United States approved in principle the creation of a six-power International Authority of the Ruhr (US, Britain, France, and Benelux) that would oversee *Ruhrgebiet* steel. Although the plan complicated America's goal of West German unification and sovereignty, it mollified French fears. A new allied military security board that was designed to examine regional security concerns also addressed French concerns. For the French, however, the International Authority was a new line of resistance against American aspirations in Germany. In August, representatives of the European Congress asked the five Brussels Pact states to call a constitutive meeting of a Council of Europe. They responded by creating a study commission under the chairmanship of Edouard Herriot, president of the French National Assembly, which proposed the establishment of a Council that would juxtapose an executive committee of ministers, demanded by Churchill's less federalist UEC, with a consultative assembly as required by the UEF.

Despite movement, no way out of the geopolitical urgency was yet in sight in March 1949, at the height of the Berlin airlift. Legal experts and political representatives were drafting a constitution for a Federal German Republic. European foreign ministers were preparing to meet

---

[46] Lipgens, *A History of European Integration*, p. 570.

in Washington to lay the groundwork for the North Atlantic Treaty Organization. But American efforts to use Marshall Aid to win French consent to German unification were in tatters. Secretary of State Dean Acheson found the *impasse* so vexing that he appealed to Robert Schuman, the French foreign minister: "I believe that our policy in Germany, and the development of a German Government which can take its place in Western Europe, depends on the assumption by your country of leadership in Europe on these problems."[47] Jean Monnet now approached Robert Schuman with a proposal to construct a European coal and steel community, as a first step toward European federation. Schuman seized on Acheson's offer and embraced Monnet's plan enthusiastically. Schuman later recalled:

> We were making very broad, important concessions, well-intentioned, but always strenuously bargained, concessions that the victors, reticent, distrustful, allowed to be won by a nation that had been defeated, and which was humiliated by the fact that it had to beg for concessions, but which, moreover, was increasingly conscious of its returning strength ... France was always hesitant, measuring, timidly, the risks of each new renunciation, renunciation to a right or a guarantee.

Hendrik Brugmans, Dutch co-founder of the UEF who quotes these lines, continues in his own voice:

> In these conditions, it became shocking, impossible to impose the control of an interallied commission on German heavy industry, which was proving itself to be increasingly ineffective. Guarantees were needed, but of what kind? It was time to adopt new methods, not *intergovernmental* this time, but *community*-wide. For this reason it's not surprising that the word "supranationality," which up to that point had been the reserve of the federalist movements, *introduced itself into day-to-day political vocabulary.*[48]

Brugman's text, with its striking reference to the "introduction" of community discourse into "day-to-day political vocabulary" and to a "community" that transcends national frontiers, dates the *instrumental* embrace of Carolingian discourse as a site of "day-to-day" diplomatic exchange. That discursive site enabled Monnet and Schuman to produce a detailed blueprint for a transnational organization for steel policy that won Acheson's approval on May 7, 1950. On the morning of May 9, Schuman

---

[47] Milward, *The Reconstruction of Western Europe*, p. 392.
[48] Brugmans, *L'idée européenne*, pp. 126–7, emphasis added.

sent a confidential copy of the proposal to Konrad Adenauer, chancellor of the new Federal Republic since September, in which he declared:

> The coming together of the nations of Europe requires the elimination of the age-old opposition of France and Germany. Any action which must be taken in the first place must concern these two countries. The French government proposes that action be taken immediately on *one limited but decisive* point. It proposes that Franco-German production of coal and steel as a whole be placed under a common High Authority, within a framework open to the participation of the other countries of Europe. The pooling of coal and steel production should immediately provide for the setting up of common foundations for economic development as a first step in the *federation of Europe*, and will *change the destinies of those regions which have long been devoted to the manufacture of munitions of war*, of which they have been the most constant victims ... The solidarity in production thus established will make it plain that any war between France and Germany becomes not merely unthinkable, but *materially* impossible.[49]

The declaration makes explicit the link between Rhineland geopolitics, Carolingian ontopology, and the proposal to deconstruct the Rhine frontier as separator of national steel policies. Where there were two policies, there would, henceforward, be one. In the words of Cris Shore, "removing [the] sinews of war from national governments and relocating them under the control of a 'higher' European authority was more than simply a measure of symbolic importance." Shore quotes Schuman, speaking on August 10, 1950: "[the participating governments] are convinced that ... the moment has come for us to attempt for the first time the experiment of a supranational authority which shall *not be simply a combination or conciliation of national powers*."[50] Shore quotes Adenauer: "I was in full agreement with the French government that the significance of the Schuman proposal was first and foremost political, not economic. This plan was to be the beginning of a federal structure of Europe."[51] Adenauer approved Schuman's proposal the day he received it. Negotiations between Germany, Italy, and four of the five Brussels Pact countries (Great Britain chose not to participate) began in June

---

[49] Quoted in Ben Rosamond, *Theories of European Integration* (New York: St. Martin's Press, 2000), pp. 52–3.

[50] Cris Shore, *Building Europe: The Cultural Politics of European Integration* (London: Routledge, 2000), p. 136. Emphasis by author.

[51] Quoted in Shore, *Building Europe*, p. 16.

1950. The final agreement placed coal and steel policy under a European High Authority modeled on the French Commissariat Général du Plan, created a common market for coal and steel products, and directed the Authority to manage the market in an interventionist manner.[52] It deconstructed frontiers by creating a unified coal and steel policy space.

In the eyes of the Americans, the ECSC marked the reconciliation between France and a reunified West German republic. For France, it assured access to Rhineland coal and markets for French steel, thus assuring the success of the Monnet Plan. Milward writes:

> The market would be regulated more in the French than in the German interest, because the Federal Republic would have to make economic sacrifices in return for so dramatic an acknowledgement of its equal political status. And in those sacrifices France would achieve a better guarantee of access to German resources than by any other policy now conceivable. The Schuman Plan was called into existence to save the Monnet Plan.[53]

But it would be inaccurate to characterize the Schuman Plan as national interest disguised as supranational idealism. The "salvation" of the Monnet Plan occurred within a new ontopological site. It had the effect of making the new ontopology, henceforward, the habitual site of diplomatic thought and speech among Greater Rhineland governments.

The question of cultural predilection

Scholars have speculated that negotiations succeeded because of shared cultural proclivities among the principal actors, Schuman, Adenauer, and Italy's de Gasperi. They were all devout Catholics. They were all "frontiersmen." Adenauer, as mayor of Cologne, had advocated placing the coal, iron, and steel industries of Germany, eastern France, Belgium, and Luxemburg under some form of joint management decades earlier, during the French occupation of 1923–4. He had also considered the Rhineland's possible break with Weimar (see above). De Gasperi had represented his native Alto Adige in the Austrian *Reichsrat* before the war. Schuman, a native of Lorraine, had been educated in imperial Germany and served the German war effort. All adhered to (some variant of) the new social teaching of the Roman Catholic Church, and all adopted the salvationist rhetoric inherent in Carolingian discourse.

---

[52] See Rosamond, *Theories of European Integration*, p. 61.
[53] Milward, *The Reconstruction of Western Europe*, p. 395.

For Schuman Europe was a redemptive project.[54] Adenauer argued that "the *salvation* of Europe and Germany" lay in federation. Adenauer was consumed by the destructive power of nationalism and the need to fill the void left by Nazi ideology with new political convictions. He looked to European federalism to inspire those convictions: "One has to give the people an ideology," Adenauer told his cabinet, "and that can only be a European one."[55] De Gasperi portrayed the struggle for Europe as a struggle for "the souls of men." It was about securing the "spiritual reattachment of the population to democratic government, which for [de Gasperi] meant also Christian government."[56] He valued the federalist ideal for its mobilizing power: " 'Someone', he told the Italian senate, 'has said that European federation is a myth. It is true, it is a myth in the Sorelian sense.' "[57] Adenauer and de Gasperi were both active in the federalist movement, though Schuman was not.

But caution reminds us that Charles de Gaulle, whose Ossianic nationalism once prompted him to call the European Community "Volapük," was also a practicing Catholic who hailed from Lorraine and spoke fluent German.[58] The Belgian statesman Paul van Zeeland, founder of the Independent League of European Cooperation, shared the Catholic, "frontiersman" perspective of Adenauer, de Gasperi, and Schuman, and wrote eloquently of the need to preserve Europe's "spiritual roots" from the Marxist left and the fascist right by imbuing European capitalism with a sense of spiritual renewal and by revising "our superannuated conception of sovereignty."[59] But Van Zeeland's enthusiasm for the European project stopped short of federalism. Nevertheless,

---

[54] Milward, *The European Rescue of the Nation-State*, p. 327.

[55] Milward, *The European Rescue of the Nation-State*, p. 330. Adenauer's unquestioned acceptance of "the racial prejudice of mainstream German conservative thought, that Russia was a barbaric non-European country" (Milward, *The European Rescue of the Nation-State*, p. 329) revealed a dark, exclusivist side to his representation of Europe as the site of a project of moral and political redemption. See Thomas Risse and Daniela Engelmann-Martin, "Identity Politics and European Integration: The Case of Germany," in Anthony Pagden, ed., *The Idea of Europe* (Cambridge and New York: Cambridge University Press and Woodrow Wilson Center, 2002).

[56] Milward, *The European Rescue of the Nation-State*, p. 333.

[57] Milward, *The European Rescue of the Nation-State*, p. 333. For Georges Sorel, 1847–1922, the idea that a general strike by labor could overthrow government and give rise to a workers' state was a myth, but a "mobilizing myth" that brought strength and focus to the worker movement. See Georges Sorel, *Reflections on Violence*, trans. T. E. Hulme and J. Roth (Glencoe, IL: Free Press, 1950).

[58] *Volapük* was an invented, "international language" of the late nineteenth century.

[59] Milward, *The European Rescue of the Nation-State*, p. 342.

it is not unreasonable to imagine that national interest was reconceived, "recalculated" within the new ontopology by statesmen who were "culturally predisposed" to work effectively within it. The "causal" link between religious faith, "frontier socialization," and innovative diplomacy was a discursive one. Faith and socialization in the form of memories, for example, of nation-state campaigns against Catholic schooling in France and Germany, or historical, architectural, and liturgical awareness of "Europe's" ontopology as spatial manifestation of Latin Christendom, facilitated the *re-presentation* of European space in a way that resisted the common sense of nationhood as the *natural* site of political action. Federalist discourse made available imagery and speech that enabled actors to challenge the legitimacy of nationalist rhetoric and resurrect the myth of European cultural identity. Alan Milward, vigorously skeptical of the importance of federalist idealism as ideology, writes: "It was for the *security of the nation-states* that the new [European] edifice was to be built, so that they in their turn could provide security to their citizens."[60] But he adds:

> the German threat to French national security simply would not go away and, because it was always there, forced French policy-formulation to consider a more distant horizon ... [But] European integration was not ... merely a device to make the Franco-West German tie possible. It genuinely embodied wider and greater aspirations which elevate the Franco-German tie beyond a mere traditional diplomatic alliance. And this in turn gave the alliance a deeper meaning and a nobler purpose for many in the population of both countries, no matter how frequently these beliefs were traduced at government level.[61]

European Union has lost none of its "deeper meaning" and "nobler purpose." But it remains true that European ontopology, with its palpable "trace" of salvationist teleology, entered diplomatic discourse *instrumentally* as a site that facilitated state-to-state negotiations. It is also apparent that "Europe," as the discursive site of diplomatic negotiations regarding the spatial reorganization of the Greater Rhineland, did not "bring to light" the geography of the diplomatic urgency that necessitated the negotiations but, on the contrary, obfuscated that geography. Carolingian ontopology does not name the nameless place referred to in this book as the Greater Rhineland, but leaves it nameless.

---

[60] Milward, *The European Rescue of the Nation-State*, p. 329. Emphasis added by author.
[61] Milward, *The Reconstruction of Western Europe*, pp. 501, 500. The order of the passages is reversed.

Indeed, if the Greater Rhineland had been named as the geographic site of a bold experiment in policy unification, it might have revived the fears of power and monopoly that so exercised the Americans in the 1920s. The site of diplomatic negotiation had to be a Camelot, an Erewhon, the mythical place called "Europe."

Ratification of Carolingian ontopology

The Treaty of Paris did not dispel the sense of geopolitical urgency. Even as ECSC negotiations were moving forward, American pressures to rearm Germany, fueled by war in Korea, grew intense and threatened to capsize the negotiations. To save the project, Jean Monnet proposed to create a European Defense Community on the ECSC model to oversee German rearmament. The EDC never won favor among allied governments, however, and the French Assemblée rejected Monnet's initiative in 1954. Within a month of that rejection, America intervened to address the tenacious geopolitical anxieties: West Germany was admitted into the North Atlantic Treaty Organization (NATO), thus subordinating German rearmament to NATO control; the United States and Great Britain agreed to maintain troops on the continent; and West Germany recognized France's protectorate in the Saarland.[62] But geopolitical urgency, rather than subside, now pressed France and Germany to address their relationship outside the framework of American-brokered treaty negotiations, through joint trade agreements, joint investment projects, and new protocols regarding Moselle shipping. Those efforts, in turn, affected the economic and security interests of the Greater Rhineland "buffer states," Belgium, the Netherlands, and Luxemburg. In response, the Benelux countries took up the defense of the federalist cause, endangered by the rejection of the EDC. Benelux initiatives culminated in the Messina Conference in 1955 and the Treaty

[62] See Peter Katzenstein, "Taming of Power: German Unification, 1989–90," in Meredith Woo-Cumings and Michael Loriaux, eds., *Past as Prelude: History in the Making of a New World Order* (Boulder, CO: Westview Press, 1993). Peter J. Katzenstein, ed., *Tamed Power: Germany in Europe* (Ithaca, NY: Cornell University Press, 1997). Great Britain renounced its commitment to maintain troops on the continent and invested in nuclear deterrence. In October 1955, a referendum held in the Saarland in application of a Franco-German agreement, signed the previous year, resulted in the rejection by two-thirds of the voters of a proposal to grant the province a special European statute. France agreed in October 1956 to return the Saarland to the Federal Republic on condition that it retain control over the production of the coal mines and receive 3 billion francs in compensation.

of Rome in 1957. The treaties established the European Economic Community, a "common market" that, like the ECSC, deconstructed frontiers by creating a trade policy space characterized by common tariffs vis-à-vis third countries and the commitment to eliminate all barriers to trade inside the common market. In effect it established a Greater Rhineland *Zollverein.*

The *Zollverein* still did not put French fears to rest. It seemed unreasonable to many Frenchmen to confide the crucial task of frontier pacification and stabilization to a project that gestured toward some kind of future federation of the space called "Europe" while depending in fact on the military presence of a power, the United States, that had already proved its inconstancy in the interwar period. Adenauer, inversely, like Stresemann before him, discerned in America's involvement in Greater Rhineland geopolitics the guarantee of German unification and sovereignty. The US-brokered multilateralism of 1955–7 had brought the Federal Republic to full diplomatic standing, while the Franco-German bilateral initiatives of 1955 had provoked fears and remonstrations among Germany's partners. Charles de Gaulle acceded to power in this context. In speech, de Gaulle freely indulged in nationalist hyperbole, grounded in an "unreconstructed" Ossianic representation of human tribalism in general, and of French and German nationhood in particular. But that representation coexisted with a visceral sense of the bond that history had woven between the French and German "peoples." On assuming power, he pledged to respect the Treaty of Rome.[63] He met with German chancellor Konrad Adenauer on September 14, 1958, at his home in Lorraine. Devout Catholics, the two leaders gave moving symbolic expression to the goal of Franco-German reconciliation at a *Te Deum* in Reims Cathedral, near the killing fields of World War I. De Gaulle traveled to Germany, where his ability to address the crowds in German assured a triumph. The two leaders met more than a dozen times before Adenauer's fall in 1963.

De Gaulle worked to secure a close bilateral partnership with Germany that would place limits on the sovereign exercise of its powers, while protecting the specific geopolitical challenges and requirements of that partnership by containing American power in the Greater Rhineland through "some sort of continental front against the Anglo-American

---

[63] De Gaulle accelerated France's integration in the EEC by freeing up protected sectors of the economy ahead of schedule, occasionally by shifting quotas to Great Britain and other non-EC countries.

domination of the Alliance."[64] To address Adenauer's concerns de Gaulle proposed the Fouchet Plan to form a more political, more conventional European organization. The plan proposed periodic meetings between heads of state and ministers of foreign, cultural, economic, and military affairs of EEC states; established a permanent secretariat that prepared consultations and implemented decisions; and created an assembly of members of national parliaments. Neither the secretariat nor the assembly had supranational authority. It created no unified policy space. Rather, it proposed a more classic concert of powers, bound by institutions that resembled those of NATO more than those of the EEC.[65] Adenauer supported the Plan, but other governments, as well as Adenauer's own ministers, rejected it as a threat to the EEC. Diplomatic forcing by de Gaulle brought crisis. Adenauer was soon alone among France's EEC partners in supporting the plan. In 1963 the two leaders signed a bilateral version of the Fouchet Plan, the Elysée Treaty, which institutionalized a kind of privileged relationship between the two principal Rhineland powers. The bilateral treaty did not spell diplomatic failure. On the contrary, a Franco-German treaty, writes Andrew Moravcsik, "had long been a Gaullist goal."[66]

The 1963 treaty laid the institutional foundations for Franco-German initiatives in the 1970s and 1980s that would culminate in the 1992 Maastricht Treaty of European Union. At the time of its signature, however, it only seemed to deepen the crisis first touched off by the storm over the Fouchet Plan. The German *Bundestag* attached a preamble to the treaty that professed commitment to "the common defense within the framework of NATO and the integration of the forces of countries belonging to this alliance, the unification of

---

[64] Michael M. Harrison, *The Reluctant Ally: France and Atlantic Security* (Baltimore: Johns Hopkins University Press, 1981), p. 44.

[65] Andrew Moravcsik, *The Choice for Europe: Social Purpose and State Power from Messina to Maastricht* (Ithaca: Cornell University Press, 1998), p. 177.

[66] Moravcsik, *The Choice for Europe*, p. 227. Moravcsik suspects that the true goal of the Fouchet Plan was to serve as leverage in agricultural negotiations. He cites (p. 186) as documentary evidence the advice of de Gaulle's chief strategist on Europe, Alain Peyrefitte, who argued that France must disguise its true goals and "never appear to be negative." Such evidence, however, does not adjudicate between Moravcsik's economistic interpretation and the one I advance here, which emphasizes the importance of Greater Rhineland geopolitics. Moravcsik dismisses the Plan as "an elaborate and deliberate deception" (p. 177) the purpose of which was to provide de Gaulle with integrationist credentials just "long enough to lock in agricultural integration." The Plan, however, was eminently supportive of de Gaulle's high politics, and too expressive of French geopolitical anxieties to serve as a mere front.

Europe in following the path defined by the creation of the European Communities and including England." In de Gaulle's mind, the "unilateral preamble changed the entire meaning" of the treaty.[67] When Adenauer retired and was replaced by the more staunchly liberal and pro-American Ludwig Erhart, Gaullist diplomacy again turned aggressive. France provoked a crisis in the EEC to block new federalist initiatives that threatened the principle of the nation-state veto in the Council of Ministers. De Gaulle "in [his own] words ... sought to 'profit from the crisis' in order to get 'rid of false conceptions ... that expose us to the dictates of others ...'"[68] Ironically, the crisis found its resolution in Carolingian ontopology. De Gaulle won a minor "constitutional" victory in the form of EEC ratification of nation-state veto power. But the major vehicle of crisis resolution was agreement on a Common Agricultural Policy (CAP), a French priority. The CAP was an important federalist-style advance in European construction. It created a third unified policy space, and was for many years the EEC's most ambitious integrationist project. The fact that food prices were henceforth European prices, and that agricultural policy was European policy, lent saliency to "Europe" as political space and project.

The salience of "Europe" and the authority of Carolingian discourse was sustained, in the twentieth century as in the ninth, by industry and commerce on the Rhine. The creation of a West German republic dissolved the ties that bound the Rhineland economy to a kind of messianic nationalism, as discussed in the previous chapter, and in so doing reordered and stimulated economic activity.[69] Monetary arrangements in Europe facilitated regional commerce and "provided a vigorous export market ... for all West Germany's neighbors."[70] Commercial ties to regions across the sea – America and the Persian Gulf – revitalized economic life. Etienne Juillard estimates that about half of all American direct investment in continental Europe occurred in the Greater Rhineland. Large firms like Standard Oil, General Motors, and Ford were present in the region before the war, but European integration and currency convertibility attracted new investment by

---

[67] Quoted in Alfred Grosser, *Affaires extérieures: la politique de la France, 1944–1984* (Paris: Flammarion, 1984), p. 185.

[68] Moravcsik, *The Choice for Europe*, p. 194.

[69] Kellenbenz, "Wirtschafts- und Sozialentwicklung der nördlichen Rheinlanden," pp. 156, 162.

[70] Milward, *The Reconstruction of Western Europe*, p. 471.

Table 8.1 *American direct investment in Europe (millions of dollars)*

	1950	1958	1963
France	217	546	1235
Germany	204	666	1772
Netherlands	84	207	445
Belgium/Lux.	69	208	351
Italy	63	280	668
Total EEC	637	1907	4471
Great Britain	847	2147	4426

Source: Etienne Juillard, *L'Europe rhénane* (Paris: Armand Colin, 1968), p. 201.

American firms, especially in the chemical and mechanical industries. Alcoa established its first European factory at Rotterdam in 1966. General Motors built plants at Bochum, Strasburg, and Antwerp (see Table 8.1). American firms purchased or added to the capital of existing firms: General Motors bought Opel, Texaco bought Erdöl. Figure 8.2 captures the Rhine basin's industrial preeminence.

The infusion of new resources is reflected in the evolution of Rhine river traffic, as seen by comparing figure 8.3, which represents river traffic in 1929, with figure 8.4, which represents traffic in 1965. Post-World War II traffic on the Rhine, at about 80 million metric tonnes, dwarfed that of other rivers, and embraced a greater part of the regional economy than did interwar traffic. Interwar commerce was dominated by the movement of coal between the river port of Duisburg and the sea port of Rotterdam, whereas post-war traffic was dominated by "other goods" – manufactured goods imported from and exported to world markets – moving between Stuttgart on the Neckar and Mainz and Frankfurt on the Main. Traffic in the 1960s was diversified and less tributary to the coal and steel heartland. Among the "other goods" working their way upstream were petroleum and petroleum products, unloaded and refined at Rotterdam, then disseminated throughout the Greater Rhineland region. Coal, accounting for 44 percent of commerce across the Dutch–German border in 1937, was the "Abbasid silver" of the interwar period. But petroleum, the signature fuel of American hegemony, was the "Abbasid silver" of the post-war era, when coal (in 1966) accounted for only 10 percent of Rhine traffic.

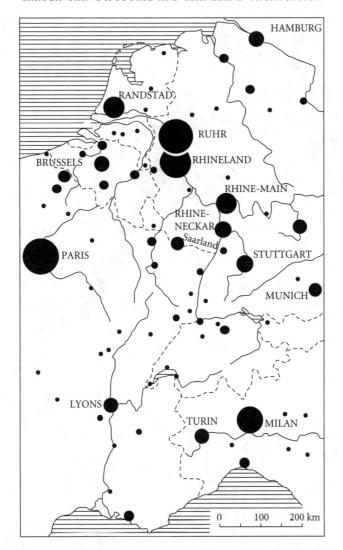

Figure 8.2 Principal industrial sites of continental western Europe (mid-1960s)
Source: Etienne Juillard, *L'Europe rhénane* (Paris: Armand Colin, 1968), p. 205.

Greater Rhineland geopolitics and Maastricht

Geopolitical urgency in the Greater Rhineland governed the two main phases of European construction, which coincided with the beginning and the end of the Cold War. In both phases Carolingian ontopology, the imaginary of Europe as a site of political and even moral *telos*, lent

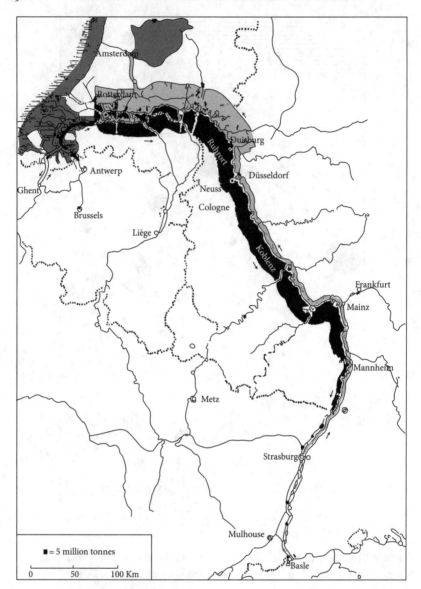

Figure 8.3 Rhine shipping traffic, 1929

Source: Albert Demangeon and Lucien Febvre, *Le Rhin: problèmes d'histoire et d'économie* (Paris: Armand Colin, 1935), p. 203.

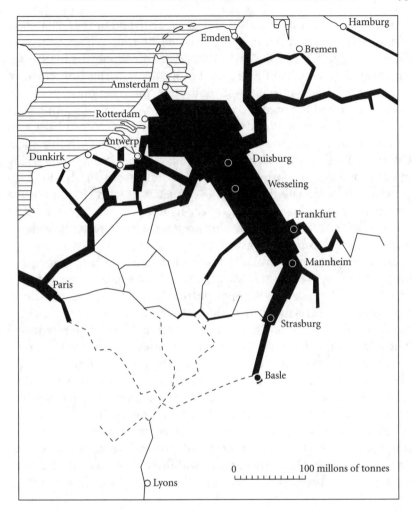

Figure 8.4 Rhine shipping traffic, 1965
Source: Etienne Juillard, *L'Europe Rhénane* (Paris: Armand Colin, 1968) p. 182.

itself as the discursive site for diplomatic negotiation. Monetary union in the 1980s, like common trade and agricultural policy in the first decades of European union, arose from the self-same encounter between geopolitical push and discursive facility.

Geopolitical urgency occasioned by the United States' disengagement from the Greater Rhineland prompted the creation of the European Monetary System in 1978. The exercise of hegemonic power by the

United States taxed America's financial capacity and unleashed a series of monetary crises that brought down the Bretton Woods system of fixed exchange rates in the early 1970s. Bretton Woods had anchored American hegemonic influence in Europe by squaring the circle of international trade liberalization and state interventionist policy in Europe, designed to speed recovery.[71] The non-system of floating rates that replaced Bretton Woods complicated trade interdependence and monetary policy-making in the EEC, prompting French president Giscard-d'Estaing and German chancellor Helmut Schmidt, working initially outside the formal institutional framework of the EEC, to conceive and negotiate the European Monetary System (EMS). For the next two decades, Franco-German leadership, prodded by the need to substitute for America's diminishing presence in the Greater Rhineland, would drive "European" construction.[72]

Soviet retrenchment in the 1980s was the source of new geopolitical urgency, setting the stage for Maastricht and the single currency. Soviet withdrawal from eastern Europe spurred German chancellor Helmut Kohl to push aggressively to unify East and West Germany. NATO's ratification of Germany's right to "national self-determination" precluded legal objections, yet evoked memories of Germany's interwar unification in a similar context of international legalism. François Mitterrand joined British prime minister Margaret Thatcher in calling Kohl's timetable for unification precipitous, and in inviting intervention by the Conference on Security and Cooperation in Europe (CSCE).[73] When Germany acted unilaterally to extend the Schengen agreement (on free passage of goods and peoples between France, Germany, and Benelux) to East Germany, France withdrew from the arrangement to signal its displeasure.[74] At the European Council summit of

---

[71] See Michael Loriaux, *France after Hegemony: International Change and Financial Reform* (Ithaca, NY: Cornell University Press, 1991); and Michael Loriaux, "Capital, the State, and Uneven Growth in the International Political Economy," in Michael Loriaux, Meredith Woo-Cumings, Kent Calder, Sylvia Maxfield, and Sofia Perez, *Capital Ungoverned: Liberalizing Finance in Interventionist States* (Ithaca, NY: Cornell University Press, 1996).

[72] See Pierre Gerbet, *La construction de l'Europe* (Paris: Imprimerie Nationale, 1994), pp. 299–308, 342–50.

[73] See the commentary on the 1996 conversation between George Bush, François Mitterrand, Mikhail Gorbachev, and Margaret Thatcher, in *Die Zeit*, March 15, 1996. See Julius W. Friend, *Unequal Partners: French–German Relations, 1989–2000* (Westport, CT: Praeger, 2001), pp. 23–6.

[74] See Friend, *Unequal Partners*, pp. 26–34. For a realist critique of Mitterrand's *Realpolitik*, see Pierre Béhar, *Une géopolitique pour l'Europe* (Paris: Editions Desjonquières, 1992), pp. 87–95.

December 8–9, 1989, Mitterrand and Thatcher held private conversations during which, according to Thatcher, Mitterrand observed that "at moments of great danger in the past France had always established special relations with Britain and he felt that such a time had come again." Thatcher "pulled maps of the Greater Germany of 1937 and 1937–45 from her fabled handbag to demonstrate the danger, which Thatcher seems to have seen as both political and economic."[75] She records in her memoirs, "If there was any hope now of stopping or slowing reunification it would only come from an Anglo-French initiative."[76]

Mitterrand, however, whether in response to his European convictions or to pressure to support unification, dropped the idea of such an initiative and proposed that France and the newly enlarged Germany work closely together to press the cause of European union. He argued for the reconstruction of a "civilizational Europe," and declared in 1989 that European Union's goal is "one currency, one culture, one social area, one environment."[77] Thatcher writes: "Essentially, he had a choice between moving ahead faster towards a federal Europe in order to tie down the German giant or to [defend] French sovereignty and the striking up of alliances to secure French interests." In Thatcher's mind, "he made the wrong decision."[78] But Mitterrand's policy adhered to the path that French diplomacy had so often followed since the mid-1920s: address the anxieties of Greater Rhineland geopolitics within the ontopological framework of the place called "Europe." "Only the full participation of Germany in this [European] construction makes it possible to look with serenity on the inevitable reunification of the two Germanies."[79]

Helmut Kohl, in turn, followed the diplomatic path charted by Stresemann and Adenauer: "Germany's house – our common house – can only be constructed under a European roof. This must be the objective of our policy."[80] Kohl and Mitterrand issued a joint communiqué on

---

[75] Friend, *Unequal Partners*, p. 24.

[76] Margaret Thatcher, *The Downing Street Years* (New York: HarperCollins, 1993), p. 796.

[77] Shore, *Building Europe*, p. 90. Shore cites Alan Clark, "François Mitterrand and the Idea of Europe," in Brian Nelson, David Roberts, and Walter Veit, eds., *The Idea of Europe* (New York and Oxford: Berg, 1992), p. 155. See François Mitterrand, *Réflexions sur la politique extérieure de la France* (Paris: Fayard, 1986), pp. 253–5.

[78] Thatcher, *The Downing Street Years*, p. 798.

[79] Passages quoted are taken from an interview with François Mitterrand by Jean Daniel, published in *Le Nouvel Observateur*, January 18–24, 1996. See Risse and Engelmann-Martin, "Identity Politics and European Integration."

[80] Quoted in Gerbet, *La construction de l'Europe*, p. 450.

March 13 publicizing their intention to advance European *political* union, and confirmed the "fundamental role of the Franco-German relationship in the context of the current evolution in Europe" and the need to intensify contacts at all levels. Franco-German initiatives, as in the days of EMS construction, were again setting the agenda of the European Council. In a joint letter of April 18, Mitterrand and Kohl placed the discussion of German reunification, political union, and monetary union on the agenda of the Council meeting of April 28. On April 19, 1990, Mitterrand and Kohl called for an intergovernmental conference to examine qualified majority rule in ministerial councils (opposed by de Gaulle in the 1960s) and a common European foreign and security policy.[81] The European Council debated the joint proposal nine days later and again in June, and agreed to convene a conference to discuss the prospects for political union.[82]

On May 18, the two CDU governments of West and East Germany signed a treaty of economic, monetary, and social union, a prelude to reunification. Soviet president Mikhail Gorbachev accepted the unified Germany's membership in NATO in exchange for limits on the size of its military, its renunciation of nuclear, chemical, and biological weapons, and the payment by Germany of a substantial indemnity. Kohl and Mitterrand, in a joint letter to the European heads of state dated December 6, 1990, laid out in detail their shared conception of political union. They called for the adoption of qualified majority rule in community affairs, and "a veritable common security policy that would lead in the future to a common defense policy."[83] Kohl's and Mitterrand's commitment to European Union was ably assisted by Jacques Delors, European Commissioner since 1985. An adept of Mounier's personalist philosophy, Delors had cut his political teeth in the Catholic labor union, the Confédération Française des Travailleurs Chrétiens. As Commissioner, Delors reprised the moral and political ideals of Carolingian discourse.

Geopolitical anxiety drove diplomacy toward the common currency. Arguments for and against monetary union were equipollent. France and other countries complained of the "interest rate penalty" they had to

---

[81] Qualified majority rule requires that the majority be larger, by some agreed factor, than half the representatives plus one. Various formulas have been adopted. The constitutional treaty, for example, advances that legislation is adopted in the Council of Ministers if approved by 60 percent of the member states representing at least 60 percent of the population.

[82] The Council, composed of heads of government, meets regularly in June and December.

[83] Quoted in Gerbet, *La construction de l'Europe*, p. 453.

endure to maintain parity with a Deutschmark bid high by the sale of government debt to finance reunification. Monetary union eliminated that "penalty." Inversely, the interest rate differential diminished in the 1990s and all but disappeared by the time the single currency was launched. Adversaries insisted on the high cost of abandoning an instrument so central to economic management. Pierre Chevènement, an influential leftist critic of Maastricht, complained that Europe was becoming a "financial Holy Roman Empire." Germany, "with its demographic, industrial, and financial power, 'geocentric' within the continent and primary beneficiary of the enlargement of the European Community," was using European integration to "extend itself" through the creation of "a second mark."[84] In German financial circles, however, the proposal met with skepticism and even hostility.[85] German monetary authorities insisted that economic criteria be imposed on weaker-currency countries as a condition for membership. As the jeremiads grew louder, the German and French governments advanced political rather than economic arguments in support of the single currency. Kohl and influential pro-Europeans like Helmut Schmidt countered the bank's technical objections by characterizing the single currency as a *geopolitical* imperative. Schmidt, in response to the project's German critics, argued that "progress toward European integration ... corresponds to Germany's vital, long-term, strategic interest in peace – if it were to be rejected, then we would face a third anti-German coalition ... Compared with this goal of vital importance, technical fault-finding with the currency union and self-righteous criticism of the bureaucracy in Brussels are at best a secondary concern."[86] Schmidt admonished his Social Democratic colleagues to "look after our friendship with France; it is the most precious good that has come to us in the twentieth century."[87]

Some scholars have, despite evidence to the contrary, disputed the importance of geopolitics to the construction of Europe. Neofunctionalist literature, in particular, portrays the EU as the product of prudent experimentation with functionally circumscribed international

---

[84] Pierre Chevènement, "Lettre à un ami allemand," *Le Nouvel Observateur*, May 19–25, 1994.

[85] Moravcsik, in *The Choice for Europe*, ch. 6, suspects that the Germans committed themselves to the project because they were convinced that it would abort.

[86] Helmut Schmidt, "Deutsches Störfeuer gegen Europa," *Die Zeit*, October 6, 1995.

[87] Helmut Schmidt, in a speech prepared for but not delivered at the Mannheim Congress of the Social Democratic Party. Published in *Die Zeit*, December 1, 1995.

organizations.[88] Geography is absent from neofunctionalist analysis. But neofunctionalism misconstrues the EU's origins. European Union sprang from bold, radically innovative initiatives that, as early as the 1920s, sought expressly to demilitarize the political economy of a specific region, the Greater Rhineland. The EU's geopolitical origins explain why there is no international organization that approaches it in scope and depth. The EU is the only tariff union, the only monetary union, the only agricultural policy union, the only commercial regulatory union, setting aside its ambitions in foreign policy. But neofunctionalism's critics, while they stress state interest, have also underestimated the importance of geopolitics. Andrew Moravcsik's important study, though attentive to historical contingency, concludes that state economic interest generally trumped geopolitics. Moravcsik arrives at this conclusion by noting that economic concerns surface frequently in the documentary record, while geopolitical anxieties do not. Moravcsik, however, considers only *crises* that, wherever located, coincided with negotiations, and asserts hypothetically that they should have mattered. The chronic *anxieties* arising from Greater Rhineland geopolitics make no appearance. He also assumes that important factors, whatever their nature and origin, will always figure in the record of negotiations. Why this is so is unclear. There is no reason to assume that negotiations about economic cooperation should address anything besides issues of economic cooperation. Indeed, one can imagine that negotiators would not feel compelled to refer to geopolitical urgency in negotiations that seek to dispel that urgency by diverting the gaze toward the bright prospect of a reemergent Carolingian Europe. Archives are not foundational. The hermeneutic circle is inescapable.[89]

What is European Union about?

European Union, I have tried to show in this brief survey, is not about making a federalist Europe, but about the instrumental exploitation of a resuscitated Carolingian discourse to situate diplomatic efforts to pacify

---

[88] See the excellent discussion of neofunctionalist theory by Ben Rosamond, *Theories of European Integration*, ch. 3.

[89] Married couples, by analogy, debate furniture, vacations, and household finances far more frequently than they debate marriage's foundational principle (and anxiety) of lifetime commitment. But one cannot conclude from that fact that the foundational principle (and anxiety) of lifetime commitment is unimportant to marriage.

the Greater Rhineland frontiers. I have sought to lay bare the geopolitical logic of the EU's development in order to justify suspicion regarding the discursive universe in which European Union is debated. Carolingian discourse "introduced itself into day-to-day political vocabulary" because it lent itself to the task of pacifying the Rhineland frontier by *re-presenting* Europe as the place of a teleological union, wherein frontiers dissolve and energies are directed toward political and moral improvement. "Europe" as ontopology legitimates agreements that generate not merely international cooperation, a commonplace in post-war politics, but that *deconstruct* frontiers by creating a *common* policy space. Common policies – in trade, agriculture, money, and market regulation – distinguish the European Union from other "inter-national" organizations. By this understanding, European Union is, in fact, not an "inter-national" organization at all.

Carolingian discourse, however, in its twentieth-century atavism, has not been the site of political mobilization on a scale comparable with Ossianic discourse in the nineteenth century. The energy deployed toward its realization, toward its being made "present" to the social imaginary, pales in comparison with the labor imposed on populations to make real their identity as "nations." It is easy to see why this is so. Carolingian ontopology responds, at its source, to the need to *unmake* the Ossianic ontopology of nationhood, as an ontopology that arose, and that endured, in tension with the geographic region that it claimed to partition. But in unmaking the frontiers, it subverted the lines of separation that brought to light the nations that legitimated the states that were deconstructing the frontiers. There was a flaw in the basic logic of the project, which had its source in the instrumental exploitation of the myth of Europe to resurrect Germany as a *national* state. That exploitation had the ironic effect of ratifying the principle, and legitimating the discourse, of national self-determination, that is, the discourse of the nation as the "atom" of world politics. The European project makes the national state the agent of its own transcendence.

For all its ambiguities, frontier deconstruction, within the discursive frame of Carolingian ontopology, has effectively pacified the Rhineland frontiers. But it has left as its legacy an EU discourse that is fraught with abnormality and autoimmunities, as analyzed in the final chapter. The question facing Europe in the post-Cold War era is that of its capacity to conceptualize European construction within this problematic discursive universe, now that Europe is, in all likelihood, bereft of the geopolitical urgency that conditioned the reemergence of that discursive universe.

9

Spatial representation and the political imagination

In 1988, Jacques Delors, in a speech before the European Parliament, urged member states to "wake up" to the fact that much of their policy-making powers had been transferred to the European Union. In 1990 he declared it his objective

> that before the end of the Millennium [Europe] should have a true federation. [The Commission should become] a political executive which can define essential common interest ... responsible before the European Parliament and before the nation-states represented how you will, by the European Council or by a second chamber of national parliaments.[1]

The goal was unmet, but not quixotic. Craig Parsons has shown how the "accumulation of community initiatives" recasts the institutional and discursive framework of European politics such that ideas that were once subject to heated debate now locate normal political deliberation.[2] Because so many aspects of national policy have become the province of Brussels, the Union already looks and acts more like a kind of federal entity than it does an "international organization."[3] Not only do (most) EU countries share a single policy in trade, agriculture, money, and market regulation, but institutionally the Single European Act and the

---

[1] Quoted in Cris Shore, *Building Europe: The Cultural Politics of European Integration* (London: Routledge, 2000), p. 29.

[2] Craig Parsons, *A Certain Idea of Europe* (Ithaca: Cornell University Press, 2003), p. 2.

[3] Denis Lacorne, "European Citizenship: The Relevance of the American Model," in Kalypso Nicolaïdis and Robert Howse, eds., *The Federal Vision: Legitimacy and Levels of Governance in the United States and the European Union* (Oxford: Oxford University Press, 2001), p. 436: "A specifically European democratic identity is being built before our eyes, and it is quite remarkably political." Lacorne cites the collective resignation of the Commission in 1999 following European Parliamentary accusations of impropriety, and the decision in 2000 to isolate Austria following its acceptance of Jörg Haider's xenophobic, right-wing Freedom Party in the governing coalition.

treaties of Maastricht and Amsterdam deprive member states of much of their power to oppose policies supported by a majority of members, and deny the Council, where state interests are represented, the power to pass (certain kinds of) legislation without the explicit approval of the European Parliament.[4]

The vision of a federal Europe to come is "embedded and implicit in the deep structures of the EU's organization."[5] It is "common sense" among the EU's 20,000 civil servants, of whom a large number hail from the Greater Rhineland core (in the mid-1990s, one third were Belgian, and nearly half, among the highest ranks, were supplied by the six founding states). Unlike the United Nations or NATO, the EU Commission does not solicit recommendations for staff positions from member governments, but recruits directly. New employees swear "'a solemn undertaking' before the Court of Justice to perform their duties in complete independence, in the general interest of the Communities, and neither to seek nor to take instructions from any Government or body."[6] Anthropologist Cris Shore quotes a personnel director in the 1990s: "if you're not Catholic, Socialist, or from the right class it is difficult to make your way here. By 'class' I mean the system of networks. You either have to belong to the Catholic Left, the Socialist Party, come from the Ecole Nationale d'Administration, or be from the Ecole d'Agronomie."[7] In the words of an employee: "I suppose it's a corporate identity of sorts. We feel a sense of solidarity whenever the Commission – our employer – is criticized. But remember, people have *chosen* to work here. Most people here do identify with the aims of the Commission. They wouldn't work for it if they didn't."[8]

For Marc Abélès, "the specificity of the Commission is less its bureaucratic character than the fact that it functions to a large extent with reference to an ideal (*à une idéel*). The existence of an ideational (*idéel*) framework articulated around the representation of a Europe to come (*à venir*) is a fundamental given: this framework is an integral part (*totalement imbriquée*) of the universe of the commission."[9]

---

[4] Much legislation now requires only a qualified majority, that is, some agreed upon majority, greater than 50 percent of electors plus one.

[5] Shore, *Building Europe*, p. 142.

[6] Shore, *Building Europe*, p. 139, quoting from Staff Regulations.

[7] Shore, *Building Europe*, p. 198.

[8] Shore, *Building Europe*, pp. 140–1. The interviewee admits to "less Euro-idealism in the new generation than in the past."

[9] Quoted in Shore, *Building Europe*, p. 178.

The EU elite is characterized by a sense of mission. The "ideational framework" within which it works resurrects a kind of "principality of priests." Like Charlemagne's army of monks, the "priests" of the EU have their own language, "a new language: a Euro-pidgin language," a kind of "Commission Eurospeak" composed of anagrams and made-to-order legal terms such as *acquis communautaire* and subsidiarity.[10] And like the monks, who were simultaneously priests, scholars, teachers, ideologues, state functionaries, diplomats, agricultural pioneers, and defenders of the frontier march, the EU officials' duties are also extensive. They include, according to Jacques Delors, policy innovation, law making, law enforcement, managing community policies, diplomacy, and political brokering. Cris Shore observes: "rarely have civil servants been given such complex roles or explicit political power and influence over the decision-making process." Berlaymont, in the words of a denizen, houses a "civil service *with attitude.*"[11]

The energy and commitment of the "priests" of the principality are impressive. The European Union's achievements are striking. Yet Europeans, surveys show, still have little sense of being "European." They remain loyal – often exclusively – to the national state.[12] Their representation of European space remains one that is parceled out among "nations," conceived as *indivisible* political-spatial "atoms," as opposed to simple "tracts of land," as in the past divisible and freely transferable from monarch to monarch. And yet the mythical emergence of the nation as "atom" from the Ossianic *coup de force* is relatively recent – the mid eighteenth century. The EU, by contrast, arose in the mid twentieth century. The "age difference" is not overwhelming. Enduring loyalty to the national state, of course, is fostered by the national state's enduring importance in education and socialization. But it is also fostered by ambiguities inherent in EU discourse. European Union, in its first decades, was not "about" itself. It was about using the myth of a "Europe to come" as discursive site of pacification of the Rhineland frontier. That pacification deconstructed frontiers to enable the realization of "Germany's" right to "national" self-determination. It dismantled the frontier in order to ratify the "nation" that the frontier brings to light ontologically. Carolingian discourse emerged as Derridean *supplément*

---

[10] Shore, *Building Europe*, p. 181; see also p. 134.

[11] Shore, *Building Europe*, p. 143. The "Berlaymont" housed the Commission from 1967 until 1991 when it was evacuated to remove asbestos.

[12] Juan M. Delgado-Moreira, *Multicultural Citizenship of the European Union* (Aldershot: Ashgate, 2000), p. 151. See also Shore, *Building Europe*, p. 224.

rather than as logical antithesis to the still-foundational language of Ossian.[13] Such ambiguities were temporarily put to rest by the press of geopolitical urgency, but as the EU's success dispels that urgency, they are left to fester to the point that they jeopardize Europe's "teleological" progress. It is the contradictions inherent in EU discourse that invite, indeed demand, new reflection on the European Union's inaugural geopolitics – the geopolitics of frontier deconstruction in the Greater Rhineland – in order to imagine new worlds of political possibility, to "visualize" a representation of European space that invites and excites political creativity.

Discursive pathologies

Carolingian discourse gestures toward the good *to come*, that *shall* emerge from the practical task of frontier deconstruction. Graham Leicester explains: "instead of an inherited myth about a nation forged in past battles, the Community is based on a 'myth of the future.' It is only in contemplating the eventual goal of federation, or 'ever closer union' as it became in the Treaty of Rome, that the peoples of Europe might discern a vision of their participation in a wider polity."[14] In the words of Timothy Garton Ash,

> Europe is obsessed with its own meaning and direction. Idealistic and teleological visions of Europe at once inform, legitimate, and are themselves informed and legitimated by the political development of something now called the European Union. The name "European Union" is itself a product of this approach, for a union is what the EU is meant to be, *not what it is.*[15]

The initiatives of the 1990s confirmed Carolingian ontopology as the site of deliberation about EU construction. They not only added new and important areas of state activity to unified policy space – monetary policy and market and industrial regulation (through the Single European Act) – but made the place called Europe more economically

---

[13] Jacques Derrida, *Of Grammatology*, trans. G. Spivak (Baltimore: Johns Hopkins University Press, 1997), Part II, section 2. The *supplément*, in French, is supplement or substitute. Derrida uses this polysemy to deconstruct a passage of Rousseau, exploiting the ambiguity between the reference to the other that is "added to," and/or to the self or same, *le même*, that "takes the place of."

[14] Graham Leicester quoted in Shore, *Building Europe*, p. 206.

[15] Quoted in Shore, *Building Europe*, p. 125, emphasis added by author.

and diplomatically visible. In monetary affairs demand for the euro and its growing importance in international transactions gave Europe greater leverage in international negotiations.[16] In trade relations, Europe as a trading bloc is sheltered by its low trade dependence – about 7 or 8 percent, as opposed to 25–35 percent for the individual EU countries, and 12–14 percent for the United States – from American reprisals, enabling greater assertiveness at the bargaining table.[17] The EU in the 1990s became a second "superpower" in international economic affairs.

But Ossianic habit endured even as Carolingian ontopology assumed new authority. It was, in fact, never expunged by Carolingian vision. EU discourse is abnormal discourse, characterized by incompatible constructions, Ossianic and Carolingian, of a shared vocabulary: nation, Europe, "ever close union" . . . Ossianic constructions of this vocabulary were ratified in the 1950s by the use of European Union to enable German national self-determination, and in the 1960s by Gaullist nationalism. It was ratified by the perverse effects of a fundamental auto-immunity in Carolingian discourse, that is, a self-debilitating defense and affirmation, which locates the site of the experiment in policy integration in the place, the Erewhon, called "Europe." That location invited participation by states that never experienced the urgency of Greater Rhineland geopolitics, and therefore never sought their resolution in frontier deconstruction. The EC admitted Greece, Portugal, and Spain following the collapse of their dictatorial regimes in the mid-1970s. The implementation of the Single European Act incited other "peripheral" countries, concerned by investor preference for EC assets, to seek membership. Sweden, Finland, and Austria became members in 1995, and many of the former peoples' republics of eastern Europe were admitted in 2004. Today the governments of the "periphery" tend to show skepticism regarding the more progressive and teleological aspects of European integration, and tend to be the more outspoken guardians of national sovereignty. Like Great Britain, they often look on the goal of "ever closer union," as set forth in the Treaty of Rome, with suspicion. Sweden and Denmark, like Great Britain, rejected the common currency.

Great Britain, though closely implicated throughout history in Greater Rhineland politics, has traditionally looked on regional geopolitics as an issue of power balancing, and so has preferred, going back to the days

---

[16] As evidenced by the rise of the euro in the early 2000s, in a context of significant fiscal imbalance in France and Germany.

[17] Inversely, financial interdependence remains a source of vulnerability, given massive European investment in the US economy.

of the UEC, a less constraining, Wilsonian style of "inter-national" organization. In 1950, as France, Germany, Italy, and the Benelux were negotiating the Treaty of Paris, Winston Churchill declared before Parliament: "[If I were asked], 'Would you agree to a supranational authority which has the power to tell Great Britain not to cut any more coal or make any more steel but to grow tomatoes instead?' I should say, without hesitation, the answer is 'no.'"[18] Churchill's proposed "United States of Europe" was a continental affair. Britain, while supporting it, would have acknowledged France's and Germany's "ownership" of the project. When in the early 1960s the British began to fear the costs of non-membership in a politically integrated Greater Rhineland economic space, they applied to join. But the Conservative party in power gave only measured support to the initiative. De Gaulle's defeat at the polls in 1969 and France's need to mend fences with its European partners enabled Great Britain to enter the EC (with Ireland, Denmark, and Norway) in 1973.[19] Once admitted, however, Britain soon objected that the Common Agricultural Policy tax on imports from Commonwealth countries made it one of the largest net contributors to the EC budget. Margaret Thatcher, Britain's prime minister from 1979 to 1990, placed those objections at the center of Britain's EC policy. In a ten-hour deadlock of the European Council, Thatcher insisted on a "rebate," and backed up that demand by blocking agreement on agricultural prices and by refusing to adopt the Social Charter, the keystone of Mitterrand's and Kohl's vision of a morally and politically progressive Carolingian Europe, which she dismissed as "Marxist." The authority of Ossianic discourse in Britain was such that federalists tried "to steer the European debate away from dangerous – or theological – constitutional issues." Cris Shore continues, "There is, and has long been, a politics of denial about the EU's federal intent. For reasons of political expediency, [Britons] who share the Europeanist vision, or have a vested interest in its promotion, have tried to de-politicize the European question on the grounds that the electorate are not yet ready to accept the EU goal of ever closer union."[20]

The Commission's response to the enduring authority of Ossianic ontopology was to stake "European" claims to Ossianic legacy and obligation. That response had the effect of aggravating "abnormality" in EU discourse. As early as the 1960s, in reaction to Gaullist nationalism,

---

[18] Shore, *Building Europe*, p. 136.
[19] Norway withdrew its candidacy following a referendum.
[20] Shore, *Building Europe*, p. 211.

the Commission began to introduce into EU discourse "concepts such as 'culture,' 'identity,' 'social cohesion,' and 'collective consciousness' as mobilizing metaphors for building 'European culture,' 'European identity,' and 'European consciousness.'"[21] The 1973 Declaration on European Identity acknowledged Europe's cultural diversity, but placed that diversity within the framework of a "common European civilization" based on a "common heritage" and "converging" attitudes and ways of life. It exhorted the European Community to make identity a criterion for admission, and to affirm EU identity in relations with the rest of the world.[22] The 1976 Tindemans report, prepared for the European Council, recommended that the EC become more visible in the social imaginary through signifiers like a common passport, European accreditation of university courses and degrees, and the elimination of border controls on travelers.[23] The 1983 Solemn Declaration on European Union, which reiterated the members' commitment to "progress toward an ever closer union," emphasized the need to promote greater awareness of the European Community by undertaking action in the cultural sphere.[24] In the 1980s, even as the tide of geopolitical change was lending new authority to federalist discourse, the Commission undertook to fashion cultural policies that would strengthen the "citizens' feeling of belonging to one and the same Community." "Cultural policy forms part of the European enterprise and, in this respect, is an integration factor within an ever closer union between the peoples of Europe."[25] The Commission declared in 1988 that "the world of culture clearly cannot remain outside the process of completion of the big European internal market: that process demands the formation of a true European culture area."[26] Commission, Council, and Council of Ministers all acknowledged the need to foster a European identity to avoid, in the words of Commissioner Jacques Santer, "fragmentation, chaos, and conflict." In 1984, the

---

[21] Shore, quoting Soledad Garcia and William Wallace, *Building Europe*, p. 25.

[22] See Gerard Delanty, "Models of European Identity: Reconciling Universalism and Particularism," Paper Presented to the 13th International Conference of Europeanists "Europe in the New Millennium: Enlarging, Experimenting, Evolving," Chicago, March 14–16, 2002; more generally, see Gerard Delanty, *Inventing Europe: Idea, Identity, Reality* (London: Macmillan, 1995).

[23] "European Union." Report by Mr. Leo Tindemans, prime minister of Belgium, to the European Council, *Bulletin of the European Communities*, Supplement 1/76.

[24] Solemn Declaration on European Union. European Council, Stuttgart, June 19, 1983, *Bulletin of the European Communities*, No. 6/1983. Quoted in Shore, *Building Europe*, p. 45.

[25] First Report on the Consideration of Cultural Aspects in European Community Action, 1988, quoted in Delgado-Moreira, *Multicultural Citizenship of the European Union*, p. 162.

[26] Quoted in Shore, *Building Europe*, p. 15.

Commission issued the Television Without Frontiers Directive to enhance EU coverage in the media.[27] In 1985, the European Council established a Committee for a People's Europe that recommended the creation of a European Academy of Science, a European lottery, school exchange programs, and the "Europeanization" of school textbooks. It proposed symbols: an emblem, a flag, an anthem, a passport, and automobile license plates. It recommended EU sporting events and awards, a European Youth Orchestra, an opera center, the restoration of the Parthenon, a European literary prize, a European Woman of the Year award, European weeks, culture months, and the establishment of Jean Monnet chairs in universities. Many of the proposals were adopted. The flag, a circle of gold stars against a blue field, was raised above Berlaymont for the first time in 1986. Beethoven's Ode to Joy became the EU anthem.[28]

In 1992 the Maastricht Treaty declared that a "European identity," along with democratic institutions and respect for human rights, was a "basic condition" for admission to the EU. The treaty also named culture an area for greater attention, notably as regards "the knowledge and dissemination of the culture and history of the European peoples," the "conservation and safeguarding of cultural heritage of European significance," "non-commercial exchanges," and "artistic and literary creation."[29] In 1993 the Commission named a *comité des sages* to explore ways to heighten EU awareness, chaired by Willy de Clercq, representative to the EU Parliament. The report acknowledged that there was "little feeling of belonging to Europe," and made the bold and ultimately controversial proposal that Europe be treated like a "brand product." The committee reasoned that the weak sense of European identity was the effect of bad marketing, and catalogued venues that might be used to trumpet the EU brand: birth certificates, a European library and museum, school textbooks, a new European Order of Merit, an EU motto – *in uno plures* – and direct sales pitches by the Commission President to the women and the youth of Europe. When the report was unveiled, journalists rebelled at their "priority target group" designation. The president of the Brussels International Press Association accused

---

[27] Shore, *Building Europe*, p. 45.

[28] See Shore, *Building Europe*, pp. 47–8. The flag was originally adopted by the Council of Europe. The idea of an "official" EU anthem was rejected by the proposed "Reform Treaty" of 2007.

[29] Delgado-Moreira, *Multicultural Citizenship of the European Union*, p. 145; Shore, *Building Europe*, p. 53.

the Commission of "behaving like a military junta."[30] In 2000, the EU launched its Framework in Support of Culture, in application of the Maastricht Treaty, whose aim was "to develop a common cultural area by promoting cultural dialogue, knowledge of the history, creation and dissemination of culture, the mobility of artists and their works, European cultural heritage, new forms of cultural expression and the socio-economic role of culture." The framework was also supposed to help meet challenges "such as the acceleration of European integration, globalization, the information society, employment and social cohesion." The project sought to "involve European citizens to a greater extent," and stressed culture's role both "as an economic factor and as a factor in social integration and citizenship."[31]

In Anthony Smith's words, the EU has been seeking to "territorialize memory."[32] For Delgado-Moreira, "the way in which the European Union is launching European identity is a form of nationalism, striving to create an imagined community. In following the chosen procedure to do so, the creation of European identity resembles the style of nationalism and imperialism that flourished in Europe after the 1850s."[33] Cris Shore evokes similarities with nineteenth-century nation-building by "a strategic cadre of intellectuals and administrators: a new elite composed of the professional and above all educated middle classes who were to become the pioneers of national consciousness." Jürgen Habermas, in reaction to such atavisms, argued for an EU citizenship that is detached from its moorings in the language of nationhood. Our postnational age, he claimed, requires a "constitutional patriotism" that would enable and invite the emergence of a "postnational identity," articulated around principles of universality, autonomy, and responsibility

---

[30] Shore, *Building Europe*, p. 55. The motto, "Many in One," recalls the US motto, "Ex pluribus unum," One (in the accusative) out of many. The EU motto subverts Carolingian discourse by legitimating the "many" as substantive, by abandoning reference to the progressive process that leads to One, *unum*, in the accusative, and perhaps by suggesting some kind of conceptual kinship with "globalizing" America. In 2000, the EU adopted the motto "In varietate concordia," or peace in diversity.

[31] Decision No. 508/2000/EC of the European Parliament and of the Council of February 14, 2000 establishing the Culture 2000 programme, cited in Delgado-Moreira, *Multicultural Citizenship of the European Union*, p. 155.

[32] Mabel Berezin, "Introduction: Territory, Emotion, and Identity: Spatial Recalibration in a New Europe," in Mabel Berezin and Martin Schain, eds., *Europe without Borders: Remapping Territory, Citizenship, and Identity in a Transnational Age* (Baltimore: Johns Hopkins University Press, 2003), pp. 8–10, quoting Anthony Smith. See Anthony Smith, *Myths and Memories of the Nation* (Oxford: Oxford University Press, 1999), pp. 243–4.

[33] Delgado-Moreira, *Multicultural Citizenship of the European Union*, p. 151.

under the law.[34] But Habermas' assumption that citizenship can be divorced from a sense of ethnic and cultural belonging has come under fire "from those who doubt that the bond of social unity created by the ... conception of citizenship [based on allegiance to principles and institutions] is sufficiently strong for a liberal political community to achieve some of its central goals."[35] Below, I suggest that frontier deconstruction problematizes the concept of identity. It points to a "possible Europe," freed from the obsession with identity as Ossianic legacy.

Frontier deconstruction

Abnormality in EU discourse manifests itself not only in the tense coexistence between claims to transcend territorial divisions and efforts to "territorialize memory," but in the coexistence of such efforts and initiatives to deconstruct frontiers, as political artifacts, by those whose *Lebenswelt* is most immediately imprinted by them. The Greater Rhineland's frontiers have little justification as a phenomenon of nature or culture. One might compare the Dutch–German frontier, discussed in chapter 7, with the borders of Belgium, another of the Greater Rhineland's "buffer states." Catholicism and the same "Flemish" accent-cum-dialect are prevalent on both sides of Belgium's border with the Netherlands, drawn at Westphalia in 1648 and reprised in 1839, whose trace, entirely geopolitical in inspiration, sought primarily to assure Belgium's control of the Scheldt and the Netherlands' control of fortifications at Maastricht. At Baarle-Hertog, near Eindhoven, diplomatic horse-trading erected an extraordinary enclave of thirty-three Belgian territories "inside" the

---

[34] Jürgen Habermas, *L'intégration républicaine*, trans. Rainer Rochlitz (Paris: Fayard Press, 1999); *Après l'état-nation: une nouvelle constellation politique*, trans. Rainer Rochlitz (Paris: Fayard Press, 2000). See Rainer Rochlitz, ed., *Habermas: l'usage public de la raison* (Paris: Presses Universitaires de France, 2002). Cf. Etienne Balibar, *Nous, citoyens d'Europe? Les frontières, l'état, le peuple* (Paris: La Découverte, 2001), p. 245: "les débats actuels, obscurément conscients de la nécessité de réexaminer chacune des implications, chacune des justifications de l'équation *citoyenneté* = *nationalité*, naguère considérée comme sacro-sainte, et toujours opérante à la base de l'organisation contemporaine des droits civiques."

[35] Sujit Choudhry, "Citizenship and Federations: Some Preliminary Reflections," in Kalypso Nicolaïdis and Robert Howse, eds., *The Federal Vision: Legitimacy and Levels of Governance in the United States and the European Union* (Oxford: Oxford University Press, 2001), p. 384; see 390ff. See, in the same volume, Denis Lacorne, "European Citizenship: The Relevance of the American Model," p. 432: "A mere, abstract, 'postnational citizenship' will not do," and *passim*.

Netherlands, "distinguished only by the color of the numbers on the houses, black on white in Belgium, white on black in the Netherlands. Each commune has its own town hall, post office, school and church." The border with France, elaborated in the seventeenth and eighteenth centuries and ratified at Vienna in 1815, runs capriciously through village and town. The Belgian–German frontier, drawn in 1919 with reference to the boundaries of the Napoleonic *département* of Ourthe, includes German-speaking populations in Eupen, Malmédy, and St. Vith. The frictions engendered by this trace were not addressed by treaty until 1956. The border between Belgium and Luxemburg also corresponds to no previously existing administrative or ecclesiastic division, nor to any linguistic or geophysical division.[36]

To the east, along the French–German border, the province of "Lorraine" was marked by the complex interpenetration of Romance and Germanic dialects. Annexations by Louis XIV and Napoleon stimulated the adoption of courtly French as a language of business and culture by the urban classes, giving rise to a bilingual French–*Hochdeutsch* town elite that evoked present-day Luxemburg. But the incision of a national frontier provoked the absorption of this regional civilization by two rival, monolingual national cultures. The installation of Prussia on the left bank of the Rhine in 1815 and the industrialization of the Saar valley in the nineteenth century spurred migrations that made the Prussian side more uniformly German-speaking. Free trade between France and the Saarland in the 1860s preserved a degree of unity in the trans-border regional economy, but the German annexation of eastern Lorraine in 1871 stimulated the development of Saarland-Lothringen as an industrial heartland comparable to the *Ruhrgebiet*, and increased the number of German-speaking migrants.[37] When eastern Lorraine reverted to France after World War I, regional economic integration endured because of the Saarland's attachment to French economic space. Simultaneously, coal and steel turned French Lorraine into France's most industrialized region, stimulating day migrations by Saarland laborers to jobs in Lorraine.

The reattachment of the Saarland to German space complicated economic development and the political response to decline in the steel

[36] Paul Guichonnet and Claude Raffestin, *Géographie des frontières* (Paris: Presses Universitaires de France, 1974), pp. 101–2.

[37] Gertrud Milkereit, "Sozial- und Wirtschaftsentwicklung der südlichen Rheinlande seit 1815," in Franz Petri and Georg Droege, eds., *Rheinische Geschichte*, vol. III, *Wirtschaft und Kultur im 19. und 20. Jahrhundert* (Düsseldorf: Schwann, 1979), pp. 260–4.

industry in the 1960s. Decentralized government on the German side facilitated efforts to lure new investment and diversify the economy. Manufacturing, electronics, and especially automobile construction became the new economic motors. Centralized policy-making on the French side, however, was less efficient. The pattern of daily cross-border migrations reversed. Workers, predominantly young, working-class French women who spoke the Saarland dialect as mother tongue, now began to cross the border from the French to the German side, followed later in the day by French shoppers flocking to Saarbrücken's department stores (a third of the inhabitants of the *département* of Moselle frequent Saarbrücken's shops and stores, more conveniently located than those of Metz). In the 1970s and 1980s, Luxemburg's shift from steel to banking produced yet new patterns of cross-border day migrations.

The border per se complicated both day migrations and efforts to lure new, diversifying investment. Decisions regarding infrastructure, transportation, production, and marketing were all framed by the presence of the frontier. Policies ignored needs and opportunities that might have been addressed by cross-border coordination. In the last decades of the twentieth century, encouraged by European unification but generally acting independently of EU institutions, local governments and business leaders moved to *restore* regional coherence by deconstructing the intrusive political artifact that was the national state frontier. Their action led to the establishment in 1971 of a Regional Commission, composed (today) of representatives of the local and regional governments of Saarland, Rhineland-Palatinate, Luxemburg, Wallonia, the French Community of Belgium, the German Community of Belgium, the regional government of Lorraine, and the *départements* of Lorraine. The commission sought to foster cross-border cooperation in the areas of regional planning, transportation, education, and tourism. It consulted with and lobbied national governments and the EU, but owed its existence to neither.[38]

That same year, three other Greater Rhineland cross-border associations joined forces to create an Association for European Border Regions. These were *Regio Rhein-Waal*, which grappled with issues of shipping and transportation across the German–Netherlands divide, *Euregio*, which dealt with economic and cultural exchange more broadly along

---

[38] See Guichonnet and Raffestin, *Géographie des frontières*, pp. 206–18. See also passages on Geneva and Basle, pp. 179–206. See also Milkereit, "Sozial- und Wirtschaftsentwicklung der südlichen Rheinlande", pp. 310–11.

the German–Netherlands frontier, and the *Regio Basiliensis*, which operated at the intersection of France, Germany, and Switzerland where multiple borders (and Switzerland's non-membership in the EU) distort relations in a region unified culturally by the survival of Alamannic dialects. In 1972 these three associations sponsored the creation of a European Conference on Border Regions (ECBR) within the institutional framework not of the EC, but of the Council of Europe, where Switzerland was represented. The ECBR subsequently worked with the European Parliament to develop legal instruments to facilitate cross-border cooperation. In the 1980s, the ECBR collaborated with the European Commission to develop cross-border programs for regional planning, transportation, and environmental policy, and helped launch the EU initiative INTERREG to promote interregional cooperation.[39] By the turn of the century, about one hundred cross-border organizations had been established, of which the greatest number, and the most influential, were located in the Greater Rhineland. These associations, observes Roland Axtmann, have "detached" cross-border affairs "from [national] territory." Axtmann continues,

> The phenomenon of state *downscaling* – the devolution of decentralization of regulatory tasks to subnational administrative tiers, coupled with a restructuring of subnational institutional spaces through various national, regional, and local policy initiatives – is arguably as fundamental to the contemporary remaking of European political space as the processes of state *upscaling* [to Brussels].[40]

Frontier reinscription

Discursive abnormality, however, is such that frontier deconstruction, through the creation of single policy space and the transformation of trans-border space, must coexist with a kind of frontier reinscription conditioned and legitimated by the EU's Ossianic effort to "territorialize memory." The Maastricht Treaty of European Union

---

[39] See Christer Jönsson, Sven Tägil, and Gunnar Törnqvist, *Organizing European Space* (London: Sage, 2000), pp. 147–50. The ECBR also sought to integrate the various bodies that report to the Council of Europe – the Congress of Local and Regional Authorities, the Council of European Municipalities and Regions, the Assembly of European Regions, and the Association for European Border Regions. Roland Axtmann, "State Formation and Supranationalism in Europe: The Case of the Holy Roman Empire of the German Nation," pp. 121–3, in Berezin and Schain, *Europe without Borders*.

[40] Axtmann, "State Formation and Supranationalism in Europe," p. 141.

(Title I Article F) asserts that "the Union shall respect the national identities of its member states." Article 128 asserts, more radically, that "The Community shall contribute to the flowering of the cultures of the Member States while respecting their national and *regional diversity* and at the same time bringing the common cultural heritage to the fore." By preserving the language of Ossian, the EU has preserved that language's autoimmunities (see chapter 7). As member governments prepared to sign the treaty, the Council of Europe adopted a *Charte de langues régionales ou minoritaires* that sought to assure the survival of subnational languages not only through education but through legal and administrative use. France did not sign the charter, deemed contrary to the French constitution, until 1999.[41] The EU endorsed the charter's subnational regionalism in a 1996 EU Commission report that declared that "culture is linked to regional development . . . Indeed, culture in its complexity expresses regional or local identity and the region's endogenous potential."[42]

In 1997, the Amsterdam treaty established a "Committee of Regions" (CoR), conceptualized discursively as subnational but monolingual (perhaps linguistically repressed or marginalized) territories.[43] Although the CoR's "subversive" impact is blunted by the fact that many of the participating regions are legally recognized and constituted federal states or other constitutionally recognized regional entities, the treaty nevertheless requires the Commission and Council to consult the CoR on legislation that might have an impact on regional cultural or economic identity. The CoR's *raison d'être* subverts Carolingian ontopology. Commission discourse still reflects its federalist/transnational/ Carolingian origins in its ambition to bring to light a *common* cultural legacy. The CoR, however, champions diversity. It insinuates that not only Europe but the national state are forms of empire, and reserves criticism for EU efforts to foster cultural cohesion at the European level. The CoR's regionalism "does not contradict any specific Commission policies, [but] it represents a different emphasis from the focus on economic benefits, transnationalism and liberal, unitary citizenship that are so characteristic of the Commission." CoR "ideology" situates substantial regional claims to national state power as a site of authentic Ossianic nationhood. For Cris Shore, EU cultural initiatives reify "an

---

[41] Berezin and Schain, *Europe without Borders*, pp. 18, 83.

[42] COM 96/512. Quoted in Delgado-Moreira, *Multicultural Citizenship of the European Union*, p. 162.

[43] Delgado-Moreira, *Multicultural Citizenship of the European Union*, p. 163.

outdated idea of cultures as fixed, unitary and bounded wholes that is both sociologically naïve and politically dangerous."[44] "So long as their interests coincide on regional development and multilevel Europe, the CoR will 'welcome' Commission initiatives on linking culture with almost anything else. But clearly their paths are set to diverge over culture and citizenship."[45]

Abnormality in EU discourse consists in *re-presenting* European space as the site of a civilization and a politics that both *transcend* and *embrace* territorially rooted cultural diversity.[46] For Sujit Choudhry, the survival of a nation-centered representation of political space in a federating Europe is a source of "normative dissonance."[47] Concern for "identity," European, national, or regional, assumes Ossianic mythology. It is debatable whether the term "identity" is even meaningful outside the Ossianic universe of discourse. Ossianic mythology constructs identity as a *reception* of meaningfulness, of language and culture, as located in a *place*. It portrays identity as an obligation to place construed as congealed past, as the "territorialization of memory," as the crypt of ancestors who bequeathed meaning, and as obligation to assure the transmission of meaning and meaningfulness to future generations. It is a commitment that is *received* by the present generation with obligatory gratitude.

It is significant that the most successful claim to nationhood by a "national minority" has been advanced in the heart of the Greater Rhineland core, where EU integration has overseen and facilitated the inscription of a new Rhineland frontier separating "French-" and "Flemish-"speaking Belgians. The Flemish demand for autonomy, it is true, antedates European Union. But it achieved its greatest success in the last decades of the twentieth century, in the context of European integration and interrogation of the European state system. At the time of Belgium's independence in 1830 the country's urban elite employed French as a language of law and administration. French coexisted with a number of "Flemish" dialects in the north and "Walloon" dialects in the south. The Ossianic *Zeitgeist* nurtured interest in Flemish language and culture as victims of French hegemony, just as German language and culture were in the eighteenth century. But that interest did not initially

---

[44] Shore, *Building Europe*, p. 58.
[45] Delgado-Moreira, *Multicultural Citizenship of the European Union*, p. 159.
[46] Delgado-Moreira, *Multicultural Citizenship of the European Union*, p. 151. See Berezin, "Territory, Emotion, and Identity," p. 42; Etienne Balibar, *Nous, citoyens d'Europe?*, pp. 248–53.
[47] Choudhry, "Citizenship and Federations," p. 389.

challenge the principle of Belgian unity. As was the case elsewhere, the fascination with cultural and linguistic "roots" accompanied a kind of republican faith in the brotherhood of peoples. In 1856, however, a report by a governmental *Commission Flamande* complained of unequal access to schools, courts, and administration by Flemings who were "non-native" French speakers, in apparent ignorance of the fact that French was a foreign language for much of the Walloon population as well. Whereas Ossianic discourse dignified Flemish dialects with admission to the category of repressed nationhood, that dignity was refused to Walloon dialects, which were simply derided as untutored French. An 1873 law authorized legal proceedings in an individual's language of choice. An 1878 law authorized the use of Flemish in elementary schools according to parental preference. In 1898, "Flemish" was declared Belgium's second official language.

Linguistic reform eroded the habit of bilingualism and fostered the emergence of a monolingual Flemish population. Resistance to change by the francophone elite and the polarizing effects of industrialization envenomed Belgian politics – the French-speaking south prospered; the Dutch-speaking north stagnated. Industrialization, moreover, fostered class politics and modernist discourse in the south, while the north remained Catholic and traditionalist. *Flamingants*, advocates of some form of Flemish nationhood, began to frame their demands in terms of territorial right, rather than individual preference, and pressed for autonomy for "Flanders." The term which once designated a specific "bilingual" duchy now applied to all of "Dutch"-speaking Belgium. The language of state administration was territorialized in 1921, and the language of primary education in 1931, despite the existence of large francophone populations in Antwerp, Ghent, and other northern cities. The political parties themselves split along linguistic lines in the 1960s. Linguistically sensitive ministries (culture, education) split in the late 1960s and early 1970s. By then, economic change of a different sort was feeding linguistic tensions. The steel industry of Wallonia was in decline. One tenth of the population was poverty stricken, of whom the majority lived in Wallonia's rust belt. Inversely, Atlantic trade brought growth to the north. But Flemish perceptions of steel belt privilege fueled resentment and regionalism. The state, in 1970 and again in 1980, devolved power to its various "national" communities and regions to quell tensions. As EU Brussels amassed policy-making powers, Belgian Brussels surrendered policy-making powers to subnational administrations: educational and cultural affairs to linguistic "communities,"

Flemish, French, and German; and regional economic and development responsibilities to "regions," Flanders, Wallonia, and Brussels (the latter officially bilingual). Justice, defense, and social policy remain the province of a federal government that has, inversely, surrendered monetary, trade, and agricultural policy to the EU.

Today the regional governments recycle about half the former unitary state's fiscal income. Voices in Flanders call for complete independence, and some political forces in Wallonia advocate attachment to France. The Nieuwe Vlaamse Alliantie, a small separatist party founded in 2001, advances the claim to independence in a polished Wilsonian idiom, defending

> the *right of self-determination of peoples* as a *fundamental principle of international law,* described in Article One of the charter of the United Nations. According to international law, *Flanders meets all requirements to become a state*: a permanent population; a territory with distinct external borders; a directly elected parliament with a thereby appointed government; an international recognition as state through treaties already concluded with other countries.[48]

Inversely, Wallonia's dim prospects roused a francophone novelist to predict that Belgium's days as a unitary state, the most "European" of EU member states, were numbered.

> The rupture will occur between 2002 and 2018. The introduction of the European single currency, the diminution of the debt, the progressive unification of social policies across Europe will supply the explosives, but, symbols being stronger than laws, I believe that Flanders' intention to maintain a strong presence in Brussels will hasten the event. Born Belgian, I hope not to die with this nationality, for Belgium is the cause of decline in my region, once an extraordinary laboratory for industrial, social, political, and cultural (*humaines*) experimentation, and which today is no more than a ruin – although still remarkable, here and there. A few years of fair treatment would suffice to change everything, but for that to happen one must free Wallonia from Belgian control.[49]

As one grapples with the question "what is European Union about?" one might imagine a counterfactual Belgium in which Walloons acquired fluency in Dutch and the Flemish retained fluency in French. That vision,

---

[48] See website at www.n-va.be/default.asp.
[49] René Swennen, *Belgique, requiem, suite et fin?* (Brussels: Editions Complexe, 1999), pp. 106–7.

not of a multilingual Belgium but of plurilingual Belgians, is neither utopian nor "unnatural."[50] A significant fraction of the world's population is bi- or plurilingual, as was, not so long ago, most of the population of the Greater Rhineland's towns and cities. That act of imagination reveals, by its presumed but counterfactual novelty, how deeply Ossianic imagery has embedded itself in the social imaginary. That imagery, which enables claims of linguistic and "cultural" or "ethnic" "authenticity" within a territory, derives new legitimation from the EU's discourse of cultural pluralism and regional identity. As Mabel Berezin observes, political aggregation upward has yielded social disaggregation downward.[51] The coexistence of this imagery of national and subnational coalescence with that of European federalism makes plain the abnormality of a discourse that ratifies the imagery, language, and legitimacy of nationhood as, simultaneously, it claims or promises to transcend that discourse. It invites definitions of what it means to be "European" that appeal to myths of "national" authenticity. Those myths have conditioned the reinscription of frontiers not only in the core geopolitical site of frontier deconstruction, but between the "European" and his imagined Other. Just as the "Indo-European," the Aryan, followed in the footsteps of Ossian, so has racism become the most characteristic feature of Flanders' principal nationalist movement, the Vlaams Belang.

The nameless enabler

European Union has become mired in a "social and symbolic world riven with contradictions."[52] The salience and authority of EU discourse is subverted by the autoimmunity provoked by designating the formless place called "Europe" as the site of pacification of the Greater Rhineland frontiers, and by the abnormality that arises from the instrumental use of "Europe" as site of transcendence of national separations through the recognition of the nation's (or even subnation's) right to self-determination. Autoimmunity has conditioned EU expansion to include nation-states far removed from the geopolitics that motivated its construction. Abnormality has spawned a Europe that invites its citizens *both* to look back to the territorially grounded

---

[50] In the rest of this chapter I use the term "plurilingual" to convey individual mastery of two or more languages. Belgium as a nation may be multilingual, but Belgians, outside of Brussels, are decreasingly "plurilingual."

[51] Berezin, "Territory, Emotion, and Identity," p. 19.

[52] Quoting Shore, Building Europe, p. 207.

Table 9.1 *The ten largest urban agglomerations of France and Germany*

FRANCE (1999)		GERMANY (1990)	
Agglomeration	Population (1000s)	Agglomeration	Population (1000s)
Paris	9644	*Rhine-Center Ruhr*	4598
Marseilles	1350	Berlin	3624
Lyons	1349	*Rhine-Ruhr-Wupper*	2461
Lille	1001	*Rhine-Ruhr-Cologne*	2147
Nice	889	Hamburg	2051
Bordeaux	754	Munich	1594
Toulouse	650	*Frankfurt*	1355
Nantes	545	*Stuttgart*	1138
Toulon	520	Dresden	768
Grenoble	410	Bremen	736

Agglomerations of the Rhine–Rhône–Alpine corridor in *italics*.
Source: Jacques Guillaume, *La France dans l'Union européenne* (Paris: Belin, 2003), p. 107.

source of cultural meaningfulness, *and* to look forward to the day when EU construction will transcend territorial boundaries. EU discourse, meanwhile, fails to foreground the nameless site of the Union's origins in a way that could, potentially, account for its existence and its purpose in a manner that is potentially more legitimating and mobilizing. That nameless region is not only the reason for the EU's construction, but the economic foundation of its success. If the EU has expanded to include most of "Europe" it is because "peripheral" states fear exclusion from Rhineland markets.

The Greater Rhineland owes its prosperity, in the present as in the past, to its preeminence as a land of passage, inviting human settlement, urbanization, investment, and industry. Table 9.1 shows that five of Germany's ten largest (and three of its four largest) urban agglomerations are situated in the Greater Rhineland, and six of France's largest agglomerations are situated in the Rhine–Rhône–Alpine corridor, in direct relation with the Greater Rhineland and its northern Italian extension.[53] Nice and Strasburg, peripheral in French national space, are central relative to the Rhine–Alps–Rhône economic corridor. "Many of Europe's old conflict areas and risk zones have today been

---

[53] See Jönsson *et al.*, *Organizing European Space*, pp. 160–3.

transformed into areas of cooperation and development."[54] Traffic on the Rhine, at about 110 million tonnes in 1983, continued to grow despite the steel industry's difficulties (see figure 8.4). The state of North Rhine-Westphalia, with the *Ruhrgebiet*, produces one-fifth of Germany's GNP, one-fifth of its exports, and attracts one-third of foreign investment. The Saarland has replaced coal and steel with successful technology research institutions (the Max-Planck-Institut für Informatik) and IT start-ups. Luxemburg became, like Switzerland, a land of banks, and, per capita, the wealthiest member of the EU. Lorraine, where 25 percent of the workforce was once employed in steel, coal, or textile manufacturing, has shown signs of new vitality. Only 3 percent of its workforce is still employed in these industries. Inversely, employment in the automobile industry grew by a factor of four. The chemical industry, particularly plastics, made significant gains. Lorraine today is one of France's more diversified, though still one of its most industrialized, regional economies. Wallonia saw the beginnings of economic diversification in the 1990s, but lags behind other regions. The trauma provoked by steel's fall is still painfully visible in cities like Liège and Charleroi.

Outside the steel belt, Rhineland-Palatinate is home to global firms like BASF, Boehringer Ingelheim, and Nestlé Waters. Baden-Württemberg's economy is highly diversified: mechanical, automotive, and electrical engineering, IT, and metal working. It is home to Porsche, Daimler Chrysler, Hewlett-Packard, SAP, and many small and medium-sized companies that are a driving force in the *Land*'s economy. Hesse, with Frankfurt's banks and trade fairs, is one of the strongest economic regions in Europe, attracting about a quarter of Germany's foreign direct investment. West of the Rhine, Alsace, per capita, is France's most affluent region after Paris. Its economy is highly industrialized, but diversified. It is the Greater Rhineland's most productive agricultural region. Further south, Basle, with its world-class pharmaceutical industry, anchors Switzerland's most dynamic regional economy. Beyond the Alps, Milan remains the economic hub of the Italian economy. Across the Channel, London remains the hub of the British economy, and, indeed, a global economic center.

Throughout the Greater Rhineland, the city, the human social concomitant of Rhineland geomorphology, occupies a social and economic space that nation-state frontiers no longer delimit.[55] Neil Brenner laments

---

[54] Jönsson et al., *Organizing European Space*, p. 147.

[55] Neil Brenner, "Rescaling State Space in Western Europe: Urban Governance and the Rise of Glocalizing Competition State Regimes," in Berezin and Schain, *Europe without Borders*, p. 154. See also Jönsson et al., *Organizing European Space*, pp. 154–6.

the "self-reinforcing polarization of high-level activities in well-resourced and well-connected nodes"[56] that concentrate economic activity within a "vital axis," an economic heartland extending "from the industrial triangle of northern Italy through the German Ruhr district to northern France and the English Midlands." He recounts efforts in the post-World War II period to subject this heartland to national policies that would correct for industrialization's polarizing effects.[57] But economic integration – the deconstruction of the Rhineland frontiers – pressed national states to abandon the goal of regional equality in order to attract investment to their most competitive regions. The "new regionalism," he concludes, benefits "a select number of powerful, globally competitive urban regions" that are no longer separated by the frontiers that frame state-specific regional development policy.[58] One may well lament the national state's incapacity to restrain or otherwise govern the growth of the Greater Rhineland's cities. But that growth also generates political possibilities, which Ossianic discourse, as habit, obscures, notably the possibility for a kind of urban-based, non-hierarchical, "hanseatic" governance. The EU Commission occupies the hub of a broad system of expertise networks that it sets up deliberately through a kind of "reverse lobbying." The EU, "rather than an ethnic and cultural region, associated with identity, [is] best thought of as a functional region, demarcated in terms of travel, transportation, contacts and other dependency relations."[59] Christer Jönsson and his collaborators characterize Europe as an "archipelago of scattered regions, connected *via* networks of different kinds." "The European Union is the primary example of a multilevel political organization based on networks that include representatives of states as well as subnational and supranational entitites."[60]

But deliberation regarding both the perils and the opportunities that arise with the emergence of new forms of "post-national" governance is rendered difficult by the fact that the Greater Rhineland, as the EU's economic and urban core, is not brought to light by EU discourse. The

---

[56] Brenner, "Rescaling State Space in Western Europe," p. 153.
[57] Brenner, "Rescaling State Space in Western Europe," p. 143.
[58] Brenner, "Rescaling State Space in Western Europe," pp. 154–61.
[59] Jönsson et al., *Organizing European Space*, p. 175.
[60] Jönsson et al., *Organizing European Space*, pp. 187–8. See Ariane Chebel d'Appollonia, "European Nationalism and European Union," in Anthony Pagden, ed., *The Idea of Europe* (Cambridge and New York: Cambridge University Press and Woodrow Wilson Center, 2002); Jönsson et al., *Organizing European Space*, p. 99.

urban core's importance, Jönsson observes, has "yet to find [its] political expression."[61] European space as network, more or less detached from national space, plurilingual, and oriented toward cultural encounter, makes no appearance in the commonsense representation of EU space. The nation endures as common sense. The state retains the coercive power to socialize children into the culture of nationhood and monolingualism. Although surveys show that younger Europeans are acquiring greater fluency in a foreign language (especially English), it remains an exceptional achievement.[62] Meanwhile, linguistically circumscribed space continues to sustain the "belief in group affinity."[63] "The nation-state," observes Krishan Kumar, "remains the principal focus of popular identity and the main basis of legitimacy."[64] Nor has linguistically circumscribed space been breached by migration. "There is less transnational mobility of labor in Europe [in the 1990s] than there was two or even three decades ago."[65] In 1995, only 1.5 percent of the EU's inhabitants were living in a member state other than their own.[66] With the exception of an educated elite, the people of Europe remain a people of nations.[67] "There is no such thing as a European people."[68] Europe is a distant abstraction, the site of a vaguely perceived and vaguely attractive political project. As Anthony Smith observes, "if 'nationalism is love' ... a passion that demands overwhelming commitment, the abstraction of 'Europe' competes on unequal terms with the tangibility and 'rootedness' of each nation."[69]

European Union confronts difficult decisions – about its institutional "nature" and development, about its place in the world of high

---

[61] Jönsson et al., Organizing European Space, p. 188.

[62] Shore, Building Europe, p. 229.

[63] Berezin, "Territory, Emotion, and Identity," p. 8. See Luisa Passerini, "From the Ironies of Identity," in Pagden, The Idea of Europe.

[64] Krishan Kumar, "The Idea of Europe: Cultural Legacies, Transnational Imaginings, and the Nation-State," in Berezin and Schain, Europe without Borders, p. 45.

[65] Shore, Building Europe, p. 78.

[66] Delgado-Moreira, Multicultural Citizenship of the European Union, p. 156. Significantly, the Greater Rhineland states, with Austria, boasted the highest proportions of non-nationals, EU and non-EU. In general, the percentage of immigrants from outside the EU was almost three times as great, at 4 percent.

[67] Shore, Building Europe, p. 226.   [68] Quoted in Shore, Building Europe, p. 20.

[69] Anthony Smith, Nations and Nationalism in a Global Era (Cambridge: Polity Press, 1995), p. 131. Berezin and Schain, Europe without Borders, p. 261. See Thomas Risse and Daniela Engelmann-Martin, "Identity Politics and European Integration: The Case of Germany," in Pagden, The Idea of Europe.

international politics, about its place in a globalizing political economy, about its adaptation to growth in Asia, about its expansion and limits. The "image" – the "visualization" of Europe – conditions, guides, constrains, inspires those decisions. A "Europe" represented in the social imaginary as home to a cultural legacy that provides "meaning" to life and implores its defense will frame deliberation about "Europe's place in the world" in a different way from a "Europe" represented as a missionary site of political and moral improvement, and in a different way from a "Europe" represented as a site of plurilingual cities responsive to but not bound by legacies emerging from the "soil," engaged in transactions with world cities around the globe. Unfortunately, debate about Europe's future occurs within an abnormal discursive framework in which it is true *both* that *only* past legacy can legitimate, *and* that *only* the *transcendence* of past legacy can legitimate. The two poles of this abnormal discourse are articulated around two representations – mental images – of space. The first, Ossianic, posits as "natural" the partitions that European Union has sought to deconstruct. The second, Carolingian, posits as "ardent obligation" a space "discursively cleansed" of such partitions. The incongruence between these two images, coexistent within the universe of discourse in which Europe is discussed and debated, jeopardizes the EU's future and obfuscates worlds of political possibility that European Union makes available.

Bringing to light the Greater Rhineland as ontopology

European Union is about deconstructing the Rhineland frontier. But the discursive universe in which deconstruction occurs obfuscates that fact. Bringing to light the EU's "hidden mission" would dissolve the entangling abnormality of EU discourse and open new worlds of political possibility. Bringing to light the fact of Rhineland frontier deconstruction would make it possible to *re-present* "Europe" *otherwise*, to *imagine* – to *visualize* – Europe in a way that is undistorted by the habitual discursive frames of Europe as patchwork of nations, or of Europe as missionary project. That *re-presentation* would foreground the *fact* of geopolitical compulsion, the *fact* of the geography, physical and human, that sustained or capsized the region's geopolitical construction, the *fact* of the Greater Rhineland as a land of passage, of cities, of encounters-in-cities, of economic and cultural transaction, and the *fact* of the disturbance of that human geographical fact by the intrusion of frontiers, whose purpose was to invoke ontological entities, ontopologies, nations, that emerged as fictions from the minds of poets, and which did so, when viewed in historical perspective, *only yesterday*.

Deconstruction thus conceived goes beyond the dismantling of institutional frontiers that delimit policy space. It invites deconstruction of the mythological ontopologies that justify and are brought to light by, that owe their existence to, those frontiers. It invites the deconstruction of the common sense – the cultural prejudice – of those frontiers in order to lay bare the geographical fact of Greater Rhineland space, as suggestive of a "vision" of Europe, an "image" and representation of Europe that affords new inspiration to efforts to reflect on institutions, policies, and constitutions, a *re-presentation* that is more meaningful, mobilizing, and legitimating. A Greater Rhineland cleared of Ossianic frontiers, as *re-presentation*, becomes a new site of deliberation and debate. It makes available discursive frame within which to work to "bring to light" the geographic fact that both called forth and enabled Europe's ambitious project. As such it is an agonistic site, an enabling image. It does not "spawn" policy in the manner of ideology, but makes available a shared signified, a new ontopology, with reference to which one might envision ways to make that ontopology "real," just as Ossianic myth provided a shared signified with reference to which one could envision ways to make the nation "real."

The frontiers of nationhood were first brought to light through educational reform and the imposition of monolingualism as indispensable link between "national" culture and "national" territory. Deconstructing the frontier means deconstructing that mythical link. That link can be deconstructed by *restoring* plurilingualism to the regional *Lebenswelt*. One might envision the emergence of a plurilingual space, extending from Lyons to Amsterdam and Dunkirk to Frankfurt, characterized by widespread fluency in two of the three national languages that dominate the region, German, French, and Dutch, and in which regional dialects, where they survive, are ratified and sustained by educational policy. One imagines a kind of "Greater Luxemburg," as a linguistic and cultural, if not political, entity. The restoration of such a space would subvert the common sense of frontiers as separators of peoples, of languages as purveyors of cultural legacy and political obligation, of territory as possession of peoples and condition of their existence as "people." The effort to restore plurilingualism in the Greater Rhineland would bring to light the region's specificity as the causal and enabling site of transformation of a "dysfunctional" geopolitics. It would bring to light the region's geographic attributes as land of passage, of encounter as political and enabling condition of the European project's inception, and in so doing bring to light the realities and unexplored possibilities of non-hierarchical governance that the region's urban network makes available.[70]

Such speculations lend interest to the 2005 Commission decision to foster trilingualism throughout the EU: "The long term objective of the Commission is to increase individual multilingualism until every citizen shall have acquired practical competence in at least two languages other than his or her native language."[71] The proposal follows upon a series of initiatives, going back to 1990, to promote "linguistic diversity" through language instruction. But the terms in which the Commission justifies the initiative reflect the frustrating tangle of abnormal discourse. Multilingualism, according to the proposal, "encourages us toward greater openness toward others, their cultures and values, improves cognitive abilities and strengthens the learner's competence in his or her maternal language; it makes it possible to take advantage of the freedom to work or study in another member state."[72] In other words, cosmopolitan "openness" toward the other assumes the – Ossianic – assignment of "culture and values" to that other. Political and moral progress through "openness" is made to coexist with defensiveness and obligation: "Language is the most direct expression of culture; it is [language] that ... gives us a sense of identity."[73] "Europe," in this formulation, is imagined as the site of a "set" of geographically juxtaposed languages, cultures, and identities. Life within that "set" defines an occasion to show openness, understood as the obligation to acknowledge the culture, identity, and territorial rootedness of the Other, and as the opportunity to affirm culture, identity, and territorial rootedness of Self. The banality of that image – banality, that is, within an Ossianic discourse that is not contested – leads directly to the "default" appeal to personal benefit, contained in the phrase, "makes it possible to take advantage of."

If European Union is about frontier deconstruction, plurilingualism should not aim merely at expressing or, therefore, at apprehending

---

[70] Fluency in English as a second language, as a global lingua franca, would leave the frontier intact.

[71] Commission des Communautés Européennes, Communication de la Commission au Conseil, au Parlement Européen, au Comité Economique et Social Européen et au Comité des Régions, "Un nouveau cadre stratégique pour le multilinguisme" (Brussels: COM(2005) 596 final, 22.11.2005), pp. 4–5.

[72] "Un nouveau cadre stratégique pour le multilinguisme," p. 4. The report, ten pages later, alludes to the instrumental value of multilingual conversation, "essential to the smooth functioning (*bon fonctionnement*) of the union, and important to the pursuit of 'European strategic objectives.'"

[73] "Un nouveau cadre stratégique pour le multilinguisme," p. 3.

culture as a gesture of "openness" toward the Other of an alien (though proximate) culture. It should aim at problematizing Ossianic discourse regarding identity – identity of self, of other, identity as expression of culture, as conveyed by language, and as nourished by territory. Frontier deconstruction raises – forcefully – the question, is identity real? Is it a good? Philosopher Marc Crépon states emphatically that identity is "impossible." Either it must confront the fact of its foundation in myth, or it must negotiate the fact that cultures do not exist as timeless singularities, but rather exchange, import, translate, and interpenetrate in a way that subverts the reference to soil, "blood," or character. Refusal to acknowledge identity's foundation in myth can condition a kind of paranoia, a gnawing suspicion that the object of one's "love" – to borrow Anthony Smith's charged term – is scorned and imperiled. Paranoia itself can be cherished as a measure of fidelity, as patriotism. The European project assumes meaning in the agonistic encounter with that paranoia. "The imminence of Europe is inseparable ... from the ever-present risk of seeing all the tensions of some particularist identity making its bed in a European identity that is *impossible* reinvested, renewed, and fantasized."[74] Crépon contends that identities can only assume meaning, "possibly" rather than "impossibly," as they refer to and/or recall (*rapporter*) the "alterities that they have reworked (*travaillées*)."[75] He enlists Herder, the cantor of nationhood, in support of this claim. Herder, he argues, was insistent that culture is not essence, but a conceptual construction in which alterity is of necessity incorporated.[76] Crépon writes,

> In order for something to come (*arriver*) to "us" with or through (*par*) Europe, the spiritual (or yet again cultural) identity that was accorded it *must* cease to be held as evident. The Europe to come is of necessity a Europe which no longer allows what is proper to it to be circumscribed, appropriated, redirected (*reconduit*) to some kind of belonging (*une quelconque appartenance*), any more than to a determinate origin, tradition, or heritage. What one *can no longer* expect [or hope: *espérer*] from Europe is some answer to the question "who are we?" which would construct, as fiction or fantasy, some or other monogenealogy.[77]

[74] Marc Crépon, *Altérités de l'Europe* (Paris: Galilée, 2006), p. 189. Cf. Balibar, *Nous, citoyens d'Europe?*, p. 112: "le couplage d'une conscience de soi identitaire et de pratiques d'exclusion et de discrimination relève à la fois de la persistance, de l'exacerbation des héritages nationaux ('francité,' 'germanité,' etc.) et des tentatives pour transférer au niveau européen les marques de souveraineté, d'appartenance et d'adhésion à des 'valeurs' communes."

[75] Crépon, *Altérités de l'Europe*, pp. 57–8.   [76] Crépon, *Altérités de l'Europe*, pp. 81ff.

[77] Crépon, *Altérités de l'Europe*, p. 189.

If European Union is about deconstructing the Rhineland frontier, then plurilingualism is a possible means to that end. Conceived within the discursive space of Rhineland frontier deconstruction, plurilingualism discloses the illusion of identity as Ossianic "authenticity." It loosens the obligation to identity as legacy. Crépon cites Theodor Adorno's characterization of plurilingualism as interference "in the conformist moment of language."[78] Language is the site of innumerable "idioms" – a term that Derrida uses to convey his childhood efforts to appropriate, to make his own, the language imposed on him by others – the construction of which is a kind of resistance against the totalizing pretension of language to assign identity.[79] "The diversity of European languages," argues Crépon, "multiplies infinitely ... the number of idioms that it is possible to invent." Crépon considers this possibility of invention the great opportunity of European life, "the very exercise of liberty."[80] It loosens "one's attachment to *one* language from all political expectations," so that language "refers to no historically and politically predetermined 'us.'"[81] Plurilingualism makes possible the *translation-encounter* that "enables the *idiomatic* invention of new forms and styles of existence." Language and culture are *received* not as legacy and obligation, but as canvas for the deployment of creativity, of construction and reconstruction of "self" as singularity within a space that invites freedom of invention.[82]

> Each European, negotiating his own way (*inventant son propre parcours*), between several languages, between several places, attracted by (*partagé*) several memories, in free-circulation space, would have to invent (*inventer*) a new form of belonging – to love his language(s) otherwise, to cultivate otherwise the memory, the complex heritage of Europe as *a* memory and *a* heritage that Europeans share, and whose culture invokes (*appelle*) an invention that is at each iteration singular (*chaque fois singulière*).[83]

Crépon's analysis unfolds – meaningfully if not intentionally – before a backdrop, a *mise en scène*, that is recognizably Rhenish. His point of

---

[78] Crépon, *Altérités de l'Europe*, p. 44.

[79] Jacques Derrida, *Le monolinguisme de l'autre* (Paris: Galilée, 1996), pp. 79, 99, 104, 116–17.

[80] Crépon, *Altérités de l'Europe*, pp. 40–1.

[81] Crépon, *Altérités de l'Europe*, pp. 48, 49 *passim*.

[82] In this regard, multilingualism cannot be equated with instruction in English as a second, "universal" language, which, as vehicle of economic and cultural hegemony, suggests reception, compulsion, and contempt for the specificity of local space and the capacity of local space to make and create, not merely to receive.

[83] Crépon, *Altérités de l'Europe*, pp. 199–200.

departure is a text of Valéry that compares Europe to a stock exchange, a *bourse* (from the Flemish *beurs*; see chapter 4), where doctrines, ideas, discoveries and the most varied dogmas are listed, "*mobilized* ... go up, go down, are subjected to the most pitiless criticism and the blindest crazes." Europe, Valéry continues, "becomes ... a huge factory; factory in the literal sense, a *transformative machine*, but more than that, an incomparable intellectual machine."[84] Crépon's point of arrival is Derrida's *L'autre cap*, an essay that, like his own, also begins with a text of Valéry, in which the poet bemoans the *deminutio capitis*, the declining influence or authority of Europe (see chapter 8). Derrida evokes the mutual resonances, the constellation of signifieds, as traces or "scars," that enmesh the utterance *cap*: as cape or headland, *caput* as site of deliberation and intelligence, *capitale* as political "headland," and *capital* as creative "headland." Europe, in its history, has been the political and economic "head" of much of the world.[85] Although Europe today is bereft of its imperial preeminence, an alternative realization of *cap* is available to it, *l'autre cap*, conceived with reference to its geography as a *cap* or headland that gestures in an exemplary way "toward that which is not it," toward alterity, " toward the other *cap* or the cape [headland] of the other," perhaps "the other of the *cap*." It is a representation of a Europe that exceeds its confines, that gathers on the margins of the European "cape" to transact with the other on the far shore. Europe, Derrida writes,

> can neither be dispersed in a puff (*poussière*) of provinces, in a multiplicity of hived-off idioms or small, jealous, and untranslatable nationalisms. It should not, it must not renounce sites of grand circulation, the widest avenues of translation and communication, thus of mediatization. But, *inversely*, it cannot and must not accept the *cap*ital of a centralizing authority that, through transeuropean cultural administrations (*appareils*), through editorial, journalistic, academic concentrations ... control and make uniform, subjecting artistic discourse and practice to a grid of intelligibility (*grille d'intelligibilité*), to philosophical or esthetic norms, to effective and immediate communication channels, to the quest for audience ratings or commercial profitability.[86]

---

[84] Quoted in Crépon, *Altérités de l'Europe*, p. 14.

[85] Jacques Derrida, *L'autre cap* (Paris: Editions de Minuit, 1991). Derrida offers the word *cicatrices*, scars, as synonym of traces in *Monolinguisme*, p. 118. Cf. Pierre Béhar, *Une géopolitique pour l'Europe* (Paris: Editions Desjonquières, 1992), p. 32: "L'Europe se définit d'abord comme le cap de l'Asie, ou, si l'on préfère, comme son promontoire."

[86] Derrida, *L'autre cap*: first passage at p. 33; second passage at p. 41. Translation by author.

The realization of Europe as *l'autre cap* involves Europe in an *épreuve de l'aporie*, in a trial by *aporia*.[87] For Crépon, the Europe that exceeds its frontiers is a Europe that "might be," a Europe "maybe," *Europe, peut-être*, which stands as alternative to the *Europe impossible* of identity.

Representing the European project as one of frontier deconstruction in the nameless place that is its enabling and generative core helps us imagine, visualize, a Europe that responds to Derrida's and Crépon's kindred calls to engage this trial by *aporia*, the necessary trial beyond which lies the possibility of "Europe, maybe." The term *aporia* itself is a geographical metaphor. It affixes the privative prefix *a-* to *poros* – a passage, ford, ferry, narrow sea, or strait. The Rhine, within this image, is the *poros* that from earliest times served as passage, as site of encounter, of cultural as well as economic transaction. It is the *poros* that engages agonistically with the obstructive potential of *aporia*.[88] It is the *poros* that ties the edge of the *cap* to the heart of the continent, the *poros* from which emerges the core regional economy of the European Union. By bringing its generative geopolitics to light, the European project frees the imagination from totalizing discourses of identity, whether national or European, Ossianic or Carolingian, and makes "visible" to the mind the Rhenish *poros* as discursive site of concrete, meaningful, political deliberation, as political space in which frontiers are *in fact* being deconstructed. By its accessibility, its suggestive history of non-hierarchical urban networks, Rhineland geography enables the "disidentification" and disappropriation that is the mark of the Europe that might be, the *Europe peut-être*.[89] It is the enabler of creativity and inventiveness that makes it possible to ask what the region might "look like" if the frontiers were *effectively* deconstructed. It is the invitation to try to bring to light a region in which the totalizing, Ossianic discourse of one-territory/one-culture/one-language has lost its grip on the social imaginary. The *re-presentation* of the Greater Rhineland as a site of pervasive plurilingualism, embraced purposefully as a means to deconstruct frontiers that impose identity and language, gives new meaning to

---

[87] Derrida, *L'autre cap*, p. 43. Etienne Balibar, in *Nous, citoyens d'Europe?*, p. 9, writes of an *impossible nécessaire*. And p. 25: "Le cœur de l'aporie me paraît être justement là, dans la nécessité où nous sommes, et l'impossibilité contre laquelle nous butons, d'inventer collectivement une nouvelle figure du peuple."

[88] *Caput* can mean estuary, as in Caesar's description of the mouth of the Rhine: *multis capitibus in Oceanum influit*. The estuary is the encounter of the *cap*, the headland, and the *poros* defined by the Rhine.

[89] Crépon, *Altérités de l'Europe*, pp. 198–9.

the European project as the "exercise of liberty," by transforming a cultural geography characterized by the obligation to "love" (Smith's term once again) a mythical fatherland and its language, into a cultural geography characterized by the *invitation* to "love otherwise" (Crépon's term) one's language by loving "in it the experience of the foreign and foreignness to which it becomes available in each idiom."[90]

One might object that foregrounding the Greater Rhineland in the EU imaginary, bringing to light the Greater Rhineland as site of geopolitical compulsion, political possibility, and cultural invention, casts a shadow on the states of the "periphery" that are not immediately implicated in the geopolitics of this nameless place. Inversely, however, such a representation has the great advantage of not *conscripting* the periphery in the pursuit of a contested teleology. On the contrary, the periphery is freed to participate in the construction of a linguistic space that invites encounter and inventiveness to the extent that it finds such participation attractive, as, for example, a rival possibility to the reception of a "globalizing" cultural hegemony conveyed by business English. When one foregrounds Rhineland geopolitics in the EU imaginary, and when one acknowledges that the place called "Europe" emerged in a moment of messianic fantasy and even forgery, the desire of peripheral states to limit their participation in the European project to, for example, market access no longer appears to be so uncooperative.

I offer this vision of a *plurilingual* Greater Rhineland for purposes of illustration, as an exercise in stimulating the political imagination by foregrounding the geopolitics that gave rise to European Union. The intention is not to make policy recommendations, but to clear away discursive obfuscations that mask the geopolitical purpose of European Union and the political, civilizational possibilities that that purpose makes available to us through its call to deconstruct frontiers. It is that geopolitical purpose, more than the reference to the more or less fictional place called "Europe," that makes meaningful Crépon's portrayal of linguistic encounter as a site of cultural invention. Greater Rhineland geopolitics, when placed at the center of our representation of what the EU "is about," becomes a site of imaginative political debate and deliberation, a site that nurtures the imagination by its history and geography as a place of encounter, of urban civilization, of cultural invention, of informal, networked governance. It becomes meaningful as a site that mobilizes and legitimates, not merely by recalling the pathologies

[90] Crépon, *Altérités de l'Europe*, p. 47.

of territorial closure in the past, but by recalling civilizational possibilities that one might *re*construct as suggestive, inspirational legacy, and as a site that by its physical and human geography is suggestive of a kind of cosmopolitanism that takes root in geographical fact, a cosmopolitanism that is not "uprooted," not imported. European Union is about deconstructing the Rhineland frontier. But in every deconstruction there is discovery, invention, creation, and reconstruction.

INDEX

Aachen (Aix-la-Chapelle) 57, 67, 69–71, 74, 76, 78, 80, 83, 84, 108, 115, 128, 139, 145, 183, 185, 191, 216, 217, 218, 221, 246, 264
Abélès, Marc 301
abnormal discourse 20, 303, 312, 314, 317, 322, 324
Académie Celtique 162, 191, 198, 199
Acheson, Dean 279, 281
Adenauer, Konrad 264, 280, 282, 287, 288, 295
Agri Decumates 41, 46, 50
Alamanni, Alemannic 45–7, 48, 49–51, 56, 59, 63, 65, 84, 114, 117, 163, 166, 167, 249, 312
Alsace 40, 59, 63, 74, 79, 80, 106, 107, 115, 133–5, 137, 139, 141, 144, 145, 163, 176, 181, 187, 222, 223, 224, 228, 319
Alsace-Lorraine 229, 246, 247–50, 261
Amsterdam 5, 104, 130, 143, 219, 323
  Treaty of 301, 313
Anderson, Benedict 243
André, Louis 179
Angell, Norman 271
Antwerp 5, 7, 62, 89, 104, 105, 120, 121, 130, 131, 171, 200, 202, 205, 215, 218, 224, 315
Ariovistus 31, 34, 35, 36
Arminius (Hermann) 39, 156, 207
Arndt, Ernst Moritz 190, 206
Arnim, Ludwig Achim von 17, 190, 191
Aryan 192, 255
Ash, Timothy Garton 303
Augustus (Octavian) 38, 55, 68, 71, 80
aura 98, 119, 141

Ausonius 54–5
Austrasia 62, 63, 64, 70, 84, 114, 135
autoimmunity 20, 313, 317
Axtmann, Roland 312

Baghdad 75–6
Balibar, Etienne 209
Baltic Sea 5, 7, 8, 9, 25, 34, 57, 71, 72, 75–6, 79, 82, 88, 98, 99, 100, 101, 103, 104, 105, 138, 142, 238, 242
Bank of International Settlements 267
Barraclough, Geoffrey 93
Bavaria 73, 167, 186, 206, 220, 231, 234, 236, 238, 276
Belgium, Belgae (*see also* Benelux) 32, 33, 35, 45, 48, 57, 59, 135, 137, 146, 185, 186, 187, 200–3, 204–7, 213, 214–15, 217, 218, 219, 220, 221, 222, 223, 224, 238, 241, 242, 260, 263, 268, 273, 275, 283, 286, 301, 309, 311, 314–16
Benelux 276, 279, 280, 286, 305
Benjamin, Walter 107
Bentham, Jeremy 262
Berezin, Mabel 317
Berlin 7, 167, 188, 199, 219, 221, 233, 238, 270, 279, 280
Berman, Nathaniel 262
Bertram, Ernst 208
Bismarck, Otto von 233, 234, 240–2, 248, 249, 267
Blum, Léon 271
Blumenthal, Henry 265
Bourdieu, Pierre 228
Brenner, Neil 20, 319
Brentano, Clemens 17, 190, 191, 192
Briand, Aristide 268–9, 271, 275